George Mackay Brown

George Mackay Brown

The Life

MAGGIE FERGUSSON

JOHN MURRAY

© Maggie Fergusson 2006

First published in Great Britain in 2006 by John Murray (Publishers)
A division of Hodder Headline

The right of Maggie Fergusson to be identified as the Author of the Work has been asserted by her in accordance with the Copyright, Designs and Patents Act 1988.

4

A CIP catalogue record for this title is available from the British Library

ISBN 0 7195 5659 7

Typeset in 11.5/14 Monotype Bembo by Servis Filmsetting Ltd, Manchester

Printed and bound by Clays Ltd, St Ives plc

Hodder Headline policy is to use papers that are natural, renewable and recyclable products and made from wood grown in sustainable forests. The logging and manufacturing processes are expected to conform to the environmental regulations of the country of origin.

John Murray (Publishers)
338 Euston Road
London NW1 3BH

For Jamie

Contents

Illustrations   viii
Preface   ix
Map   xv

1. A Place of Vision   1
2. The Green Coat   9
3. The Prison on the Hill   24
4. Bloody Orkney   43
5. What the Blood Dictates   55
6. Tir-nan-Og   67
7. Late but in Earnest   87
8. One Foot in Eden   101
9. A Pocketful of Hope   119
10. The Muse in Rose Street   138
11. Grief at Every Milestone   163
12. Heaven and Hell Play Poker   180
13. Involved with Mankind   191
14. Words of Resurrection   213
15. A Place of Burnings and Ice   224
16. A Rack of Flowers   237
17. A New Star   258
18. Content with Silence   275

Notes   290
Acknowledgements   328
Index   335

Illustrations

1. John Brown with fellow Stromness tailors
2. A view of Stromness and Hoy
3. The infant class at Stromness Academy, 1926–7
4. George with his mother, c.1930
5. George with his father, c.1926
6. George in a pushchair, surrounded by his siblings
7. George with fellow students at Newbattle Abbey College
8. *Poets' Pub* by Alexander Moffat
9. George, c.1968
10. George in Rackwick, c.1960
11. Edwin and Willa Muir at Newbattle, 1951
12. Norah Smallwood
13. Ernest Marwick
14. Stella Cartwright
15. Nora Kennedy
16. Kenna Crawford
17. George with Peter Maxwell Davies
18. Gunnie Moberg with George

Photographic credits: 1, 3, 4, 5, 6, 14 and 18, Erlend Brown; 2 and 13, the Orkney Library; 7, Flora and Ian MacArthur; 8, Alexander (Sandy) Moffat, Scottish National Portrait Gallery; 9 and 10, Paddy Hughes; 11, *The Herald*; 12, Ann Hobden; 15, Nora Kennedy; 16, Kenna Crawford and Graham McGirk; 17, Archie Bevan.

Preface

IN THE AUTUMN of 1991, I started working for one of the strangest and most beguiling organizations in London. The Royal Society of Literature, in those days, occupied gracious, dilapidated premises north of Hyde Park in what had once been the home of General Sir Ian Hamilton, leader of the Gallipoli expedition. The general as a young man, in full fencing fig, gazed down from two life-size portraits on the stairs over the ballroom where he and his wife had held parties between the wars – parties, Compton Mackenzie wrote, where 'decade met decade as gracefully as dancers meet in a quadrille'; where 'the present and the past were always in urbane accord'.

The Royal Society of Literature held its lectures in this ballroom, and in the Hamiltons' panelled dining-room John Mortimer presided over monthly meetings of the Society's Council. From here, french doors led on to a terrace garden, overgrown with roses, where there were parties and book launches in the summer. The first floor, however, was used only by the staff. There was an office roughly the size and shape of a tennis court, and a library of similar dimensions. Off this was an archive room – 'the arcades', Frank, the cleaner, called it – filled with shelves labelled PAST FELLOWS, on which sat lever arch files stuffed with yellowing correspondence. The files were alphabetically arranged, and their spines read like a register of literary ghosts: Barrie, Beckett, Beerbohm, Blunden, Brooke . . .

Not all the Fellows were 'past', of course, and it was in the lists of the Society's existing Fellows that I first came across the name George Mackay Brown. A friend pointed it out to me: this man's work, he said, had meant more to him than that of any other living writer, and he gave me some of his poetry. It was not quite like anything I had read before. The imagery was dazzling: fresh and spontaneous, and yet so natural as to seem almost inevitable. Lovers at harvest-time lay under the 'buttered bannock of the moon'; sunset drove 'a butcher blade in the day's throat'; in April, a lark splurged through 'galilees of sky', and, as a man drowned, the sea 'turned a salt key in his last door of light'. Behind these images was a poet both absent and present: absent in so far as he practically never used the word 'I', yet at the same time passionately present in every word he wrote. One of Brown's closest friends once commented on his gift for writing with 'involved detachment'. She put it perfectly.

In the odd way of these things, once I had become aware of George Mackay Brown, his name cropped up again and again. At a party following one of the Society's lectures, I overheard two writers discussing his work. One of them, John Heath-Stubbs, argued that Brown would have made the perfect Poet Laureate after the death of Betjeman in 1984; and, as I later discovered, Betjeman's actual successor, Ted Hughes, agreed with him. 'It has to be said, George – how marvellously you would produce exactly the right poems for this job,' Hughes wrote just after his appointment. 'Roll up the whole historic pageant into a beautiful, dignified, private moment.'

Among his fellow poets, it seemed, George Mackay Brown's standing could hardly have been higher. Seamus Heaney had first come across his work in 1965, in *The Year of the Whale*, and his colleagues at Queen's University in Belfast remembered him bursting into the common room with a copy, waving it, shouting with excitement. 'The encounter with that stuff gave me what the good stuff always gives,' Heaney says, looking back, 'a feeling of being newly wakened, of the lens widening – you have been brought beyond the usual and found the *terra* still *firma* as it were.' Every succeeding collection of Brown's work 'sweetened and deepened' that first experience for Heaney. 'George strikes me as one who followed his true course,' he reflects. 'He didn't fail himself.'

Following his true course was often painful for George Mackay Brown. It meant being regarded by some in the south, and in the 'literary world', as eccentric or, worse, quaint. It meant, in Heaney's words, 'martyring himself to modernity'. He had been born to poor parents in Orkney in 1921, and had barely left the islands. He had never taken part in a book signing, or a public performance of his work; he had only once been to London. In his late thirties, he had studied English as a mature student at Edinburgh University, and here he had got to know the extraordinary generation of Scottish poets who followed Hugh MacDiarmid: Norman MacCaig, Sorley MacLean, Iain Crichton Smith, Sydney Goodsir Smith. In Alexander Moffat's painting *Poets' Pub*, in the Scottish National Portrait Gallery, he sits among them, central and lantern-jawed. But, if these poets were a group, Brown was not really a part of it. He found himself unable to write in Edinburgh and, after six years, he returned to Orkney. And there he remained, a poet as rooted in his landscape as Barnes or Clare, Herrick or Herbert, in an age of Intercity trains and Concorde travel.

There were practical reasons for his staying put. He suffered from agoraphobia; leaving home was an ordeal for him. But his stability had its roots in something more profound than a dislike of travel. By drawing his boundaries closely about him, he believed, he had freed his imagination to travel through space and time. He had reached an understanding of the Orkney islands, and of the generations who had inhabited them for over five thousand years, that hurtling about in the modern world would have denied him.

It intrigued me, this idea of a trade-off between travel and depth of understanding. Just down the road from the RSL headquarters in Hyde Park Gardens, hard on Marble Arch, is a community of enclosed Benedictine nuns. Their convent stands by what once was the site of Tyburn Tree, a gallows where, in the sixteenth and seventeenth centuries, men and women were hanged for their Catholic faith. One afternoon, an elderly nun showed me the relics in the convent basement, and told me the stories of some of the martyrs – Blessed Philip Powel, Blessed Thomas Maxfield, Saint Edmund Campion. She had lived in the convent for more than forty years, she explained, and, because she never ventured into the wider world, these characters had become quite as real to her as her sisters in the community. Past and present had fused. Was this what had happened for George Mackay Brown? In the summer of 1992, his novel *Vinland* was published, and *The Times* agreed to let me travel north to interview him.

I arrived in Orkney in mid-June, and the islands were bright with wild flowers and young crops, and spilling over with light. It was 10 p.m. by the time I reached the harbour town of Stromness and, although colours were becoming less distinct and shapes more blurred, it was not dark. At midnight, birds were still wide awake and singing outside the windows of my B&B. I was wide awake too, turning the pages of Brown's *An Orkney Tapestry*, gripped. We had arranged to meet the following afternoon. I could hardly wait.

But that first meeting was a disaster. 'I instinctively shrink from journalists,' George Mackay Brown once wrote to a friend. Lilting and generous in his writing, he was so sparing in response to my questions as to be almost monosyllabic. Within minutes, I had run out of things to ask. Brown sat back in his rocking-chair, folded his legs, rested his chin on long, tapering hands, gazed into the middle distance and hummed.

Fortunately, I did not have to fly straight home, and the next day I bumped into Brown in Stromness. He had some friends dropping by in the late afternoon, he said: would I join them? In familiar company, he was transformed — witty, vivacious, a brilliant raconteur and an attentive host. He offered to boil each of us an egg for tea, and, before we left, showed us something that had arrived in the post that morning. A friend had sent him a copy of the letter written by Mary Queen of Scots to her cousin the King of France the night before her execution. Mary Queen of Scots had been a childhood heroine of Brown's, and he drew our attention to the firmness of her script in the face of death.

I returned to London enthralled by George Mackay Brown, by his work, and by the islands that had inspired it. Orkney was such a different world as to seem almost unreal in the hard light of a Battersea day, and for most of that first morning back I kept my curtains tightly drawn in an attempt to seal in the memories. A week or so later, an envelope arrived with a Stromness postmark, addressed in Brown's neat, deliberate hand. Tucked in among comments about the weather, and the progress of the annual St Magnus Festival, were two sentences that pleased me very much: 'I hope you'll come back often, Maggie, and enjoy a walk to the kirkyard and Warbeth. I feel you belong here in Orkney.'

I did go back, as often as I could, not only to visit George, and to explore 'mainland' Orkney, but also to get to know some of the smaller islands. On Papa Westray I interviewed Christine Hopkins, voted Scottish Teacher of the Year for 1996, in charge of just three pupils in a large, bright schoolroom overlooking the sea. On this island are the oldest standing houses in Europe, and the seventy islanders dance a reel — the Queen Victoria — unknown in any other part of Scotland.

Eynhallow, 'the holy island', is surrounded by ferocious tides – or 'roosts'. It has been uninhabited for nearly a hundred years, but in the centre of the island are what some believe to be the remains of a twelfth-century monastery. Fishermen dropped me there with a friend late one summer afternoon and, as we walked around the shore, we came upon an expanse of warm, shelving rocks carpeted with seals. They flopped into the sea as we approached, and bobbed about staring back at us, a congregation of several hundred. In Orkney legend, seals are the key to the inextricable unity of sea and land. 'Selkies' swim ashore at night, throw off their pelts, and dance like humans on the sand. One wet August evening, on skerries off the island of Hoy, I heard for the first time the sound of seals singing – a high, plangent moan like a musical *memento mori*.

Two or three times, friends and I rented a house on one of the small tidal islands in Stromness harbour, and in the mornings we made our way across the water to the town in a flimsy fibreglass dinghy. 'It was so pleasant those few autumn days, knowing that you and your friends were nearby, over on the Inner Holm,' George wrote on 12 October 1994. Pleasant for us, too, picking out his rooftop as we rowed towards Stromness, knowing that he was sitting at the Formica surface in his kitchen, with a block of Basildon Bond paper and a Bic pen, working his magic.

It was Hugo Brunner, George's editor at John Murray, who suggested I write this biography, and it was he, one morning, who put the idea to George. So long as nothing was published in his lifetime, the answer came back, George would help in any way he could. I was staying on the Holms at the time, and in the afternoon George and I went for a walk. Sitting on a bench looking out over Scapa Flow, he spoke about his childhood, without prompting or interruption, for more than an hour. He then sent me back to London with a draft copy of an autobiography, written in 1985 and awaiting posthumous publication.

For the Islands I Sing, as it was to be titled, is a book that yields more on every reading, but it is written within a tight constraint. In one early passage, George expresses his unease at the modern tendency to exaggerate the importance and interest of writers' lives: 'In fact,' he states, 'the lives of writers are not greatly different from the lives of plumbers.' It is almost as if, to prove his point, he then feels obliged to downplay the interest of his own life, skating over whole decades, and inserting occasional baffling statements. 'One of the great experiences of most lives never happened to me,' he writes. 'I never fell in love with anybody, and no woman ever fell in love with me.' It is possible, given the context in which it appears, that this claim should be understood to apply only to George's youth; but it is a claim he repeated well into middle age. 'I have never been in love in my life,' he wrote to a friend in 1975, when he was fifty-four. This, as I was to discover, was not true.

Early in 1996, we arranged that I should spend the month of May in Stromness, visiting George to talk to him in the evenings. On 13 April, quite suddenly, he died. As a result, I spent most of May not in Stromness but in Edinburgh, looking through the George Mackay Brown archives in the National Library of Scotland and in Edinburgh University Library. In the latter, in a reading room overlooking the Pentland Hills, the librarian presented me with a large package, as yet unsealed, containing hundreds of letters from George Mackay Brown to Stella Cartwright, the woman known in Edinburgh in the sixties as the 'Rose Street Muse'. The letters spanned more than twenty years and, together with Stella's to George in the National Library, they told an extraordinary love story.

It was a strange feeling reading those letters, and not altogether a comfortable one. I felt sure that, had George lived, he would never have spoken to me about Stella Cartwright. Yet the anxiety that I was trespassing was eased, as I read on, by occasional hints that George had wanted his feelings for Stella one day to come to light. 'Some day we must print all Stella's Birthday poems in a little book and launch it upon the world,' he writes on 7 June 1984. 'Everyone will say, "They Liked Each Other More Than a Little" . . . They sure did.'

I believe that this sentiment can be applied more generally, to the rest of George's life: that, in a part of himself at least, he was content that some of his secrets should eventually be known. 'We move from silence into silence,' he once wrote, 'and there is a brief stir between, every person's attempt to make a meaning of life and time.' His own attempt was so unusual and brave and fruitful that his story deserves to be set down, before the silence subsumes it.

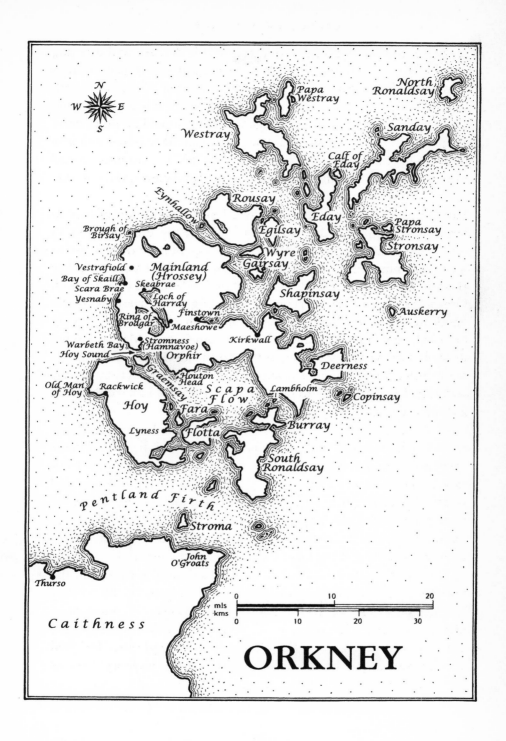

ORKNEY

I

A Place of Vision

Orkney – 'orcs' – the school of sleeping whales,
To those who glimpsed it first,
Hills half-sunk in the sea.
                    GMB, 'Haiku: for The Holy Places'

A POET IS born, not made – that was George Mackay Brown's
belief; and his gifts might either flourish or wither, depending on
circumstance. In his own case, he suspected that, had he grown up in
a city, he might never have written a word. As it was, he spent his
childhood in Orkney, and the islands became for him 'a place of order,
a place of remembrance, a place of vision' which sustained him in his
writing for the rest of his life.

But if it was Orkney that nurtured George's talents, he thought that
the talents themselves probably had their roots in his Celtic, Highland
ancestry – a maternal inheritance, not Orcadian at all. His mother,
Mhairi Sheena Mackay, was sixteen when she boarded the mail-boat
St Ola on the north coast of Scotland, and sailed further north still to
make a life for herself in the Orkney seaport of Stromness. Born in
1891, Mhairi had spent her childhood on a croft in Strathy, on the
Sutherland coast, with her parents and eight siblings. She had not left
home before. Yet she had reason to hope that her new surroundings
would not be entirely unfamiliar. The man for whom she was to work
was a distant cousin, John Mackay, who had done well for himself and
built a hotel in Stromness; and, although she had never set foot in
Orkney, she had, in a sense, known it all her life. From Strathy Point,
on a fine day, the Orkney islands are clearly visible across the water:

the mountainous form of Hoy and, beyond it, an archipelago of low, bluish humps on the horizon.

But that 25-mile journey across the Pentland Firth carries the traveller into a new world. It is the vividness of Orkney that surprises one first. On the Sutherland coast, where Mhairi Mackay had grown up, the soil is thin and stony; there are expanses of brown moorland, pitted with peat-bogs, where only sheep thrive; much of the land is unenclosed. 'Mainland' Orkney, by contrast, looks like a Hopkins landscape – 'plotted and pieced – fold, fallow, and plough'. The soil is fertile, and the island neatly patchworked with fields, often running right down to the sea. In April and May, in the ditches and along the roadsides, there is a profusion of daffodils. In June and July, brown beef cattle and milking cows graze knee-deep in clover and buttercups, and the rocks are speckled with sea-pinks.

'Hrossey' – 'island of the horse' – was what the Norsemen called the largest of the seventy-odd Orkney islands and, when Mhairi Mackay arrived, Hrossey would have seemed still an apt name. Further south, farmers were beginning to work their land with tractors, but in Orkney the crofters remained entirely reliant on their horses, yoked in tandem for ploughing in the spring, and, in the autumn, for harvesting crops of oats, bere,* turnips, kale. These crofters worked their small, stone-dyked fields against a backdrop of overwhelming space. Apart from Hoy – the 'high island' – the Orkney islands are low and undulating, and, because of the wind, they are almost treeless. Without trees or mountains to interrupt the view, your eyes are carried constantly to the curve of the horizon: you can see that you are on a globe. At midsummer, when the sun barely sets, and there is a superabundance of light, you feel you are standing on top of the world.

The vastness of space is matched by an awareness of a great sweep of time, stretching back well beyond the scope of history, and even of legend. Little is known about the first men and women who lived in Orkney over five thousand years ago, yet, if they were to return today, they would find the islands still strewn with their creations – their cairns, standing stones and burial mounds, even their domestic possessions. In a field by the road that runs between Stromness and the

---

*A kind of barley, used in Orkney for making bannocks.

Orkney capital, Kirkwall, is Maeshowe, a grassy hillock that seems to swell like a breast out of the earth. Sheep graze on its surface, but inside it is a chambered tomb where Orcadians laid their dead long before the first pyramid was built in Egypt. Crude in appearance, it is sophisticated in construction. As darkness falls on the shortest day of the year, the setting sun points a finger of light into the centre of the tomb: a promise of renewal after death. A few fields away, on a neck of land between two lochs, is the Ring of Brodgar, a circle of twenty-seven massive slabs of stone, quarried at Vestrafiold, pointing sunwards and enclosing a grassy disc. A place of worship? Of sacrifice? Nobody knows. In Orkney lore, the stones are darkness-loving giants who came down one night to the lochs to drink and dance, lingered too long, and were petrified by the rising sun.

Archaeologists have picked and combed over these sites; but the most spectacular discoveries are yielded up by the islands themselves, in their own time. One night in the winter of 1850, Orkney was swept by a wild storm. The wind ripped the grass from a high dune by the Bay of Skaill on the west coast, revealing an almost perfectly preserved Neolithic village. The interiors of the small, round houses of Skara Brae were immediately familiar to the Orkney crofters: there were stone box-beds, stone dressers, stone cupboards let into the walls. Laid out across a stone surface was jewellery made of bone; but of the owner of the jewellery, and of the other villagers, there was not a trace. It was like a scene from a Stone Age *Mary Celeste*.

It is not known quite when the Vikings made their first raids on Orkney, but by the end of the ninth century the islands were ruled by Norse earls. In theory, these earls were vassals of the Norwegian kings; in practice, the strongest of them were independent rulers, as powerful at least as the kings of Scotland. From the Brough of Birsay, a tidal promontory on the north-west Orkney mainland, an eleventh-century earl, Thorfinn the Mighty, ruled nine Scottish earldoms, the Hebrides, and great tracts of Ireland. Towards the end of a life of ruthlessness, Thorfinn is said to have ridden with his regicide cousin Macbeth over the Alps to Rome, where he was granted absolution by Pope Leo IX. He returned to Orkney and devoted the last fifteen years of his life to good and peaceful government. The islands prospered.

No wonder that after Orkney passed to Scottish rule in 1468, and the islanders became little better than serfs under Stuart earls, Orcadians looked back on their Norse days as a golden age, and clung to romantic notions of Viking descent. Well into the eighteenth century, Norn, a mixture of old Norse and Icelandic, was still spoken in the remoter parts of the islands; and even today Orcadians have a lilting, sing-song accent more Scandinavian than Scots in intonation.

Such were the voices that Mhairi Mackay heard around her as she stepped for the first time on to the quay at Stromness, and they were strange to her. Her own first language was Gaelic. When she had started school at the age of five she had known only two words of English, and to her dying day she would sing in Gaelic as she went about her housework. Her ancestors had come from the green glens of Strathnaver and Strathalladale, where the clan Mackay had lived for centuries in long, stone, sod-roofed huts, raising goats and black cattle, and growing potatoes and oats. When required, the clansmen had banded together and fought bravely for their chiefs; but most of the time they had lived insulated from the outside world by the lack of a single road.

In the early nineteenth century, however, their landlord, the Countess of Sutherland, with her husband, the Marquess of Stafford,* initiated ambitious 'improvements' that turned much of the vast Sutherland estate over to large sheep farms, and the indigenous crofters were 'cleared', with some brutality, out of the straths. Mhairi's grandfather, Angus Mackay, passed down his own grandfather's description of leaving his home in flames when his family were forced out of Strathnaver. Some of those who were cleared left on ships for North America. Most, like Mhairi's family, moved north and north-east to eke out a difficult and dangerous existence as crofter-fishermen on the coast. Hundreds of them had probably never seen the sea before, let alone built boats or fished, and many drowned; and the arable soil on the rocky headlands was so thin that, in a dispute over ownership, it was said that any man could have carried away his share in a lobster creel.

Mhairi Mackay's ancestors seem to have fared better than many of their fellow clansmen. At Braal, on a rocky headland above the sea,

*Created Duke of Sutherland in 1833.

stand the ruins of the small croft that her great-great-grandparents built after leaving Strathnaver. Mhairi was born in this croft, and as a child she visited it often from her parents' home two miles away in Strathy. Her niece, now an old lady living along the coast at Reay, remembers it as a place of warmth and celebration where Angus Mackay made wooden toys for his grandchildren, and where at any excuse the fiddle was taken down from the wall and used to accompany dancing and the Gaelic songs handed down from generation to generation. Mhairi inherited this spirit of celebration. She was a buoyant character, and no setback ever floored her for long.

Her cheerfulness stood her in good stead as she got to grips with her new life as a waitress-chambermaid in Mackay's Stromness Hotel. John Mackay and his wife were good to the girls who worked for them, but the work was quite new to Mhairi. She had been used to spending much of her time out of doors, helping on her father's croft; now she was immured in a monstrous modern edifice with forty bedrooms, waiting on southern tourists who had come to Orkney to explore the archaeological sites and to fish for trout. Her hours were long and, after her strict Free Presbyterian upbringing, she was so shocked to discover that she was required to work on the Sabbath that she considered heading straight back home. She was equally shocked by the behaviour of some of the hotel guests. Mhairi was an attractive girl, tall, blue-eyed, black-haired, with a slightly snub nose and a bright, open expression. One day, a visiting clergyman turned the key of his bedroom and began to make advances. She kept her nerve, ordered him to unlock the door, and refused to serve him again.

Outside the hotel, too, she found herself warding off unwelcome attention. On one of her rare free evenings, probably at a dance, she met a local postman, John Brown. He was stoutish and handsome, with a waxed moustache and a wry, witty expression, and at the end of the evening, after walking her home, he kissed her. Mhairi thought this unacceptably forward, and she made up her mind not to see him again. Somehow, however, he won her round; and she found herself falling in love with this man several inches shorter than herself, and fifteen years her senior.

John Brown could not claim Viking descent, but he was an Orkneyman through and through. His ancestors had almost certainly come over from Scotland as servants and retainers under the Stuart earls, and the Session Book of St Peter's Church in Stromness records Browns baptized, married, and ordered to repent for fornication and other mis-demeanours from the late seventeenth century onwards. They had large families, and they made their mark. On the outskirts of Stromness is a farm called Brownstown, and, when Mhairi Mackay arrived, a whole area south of the town was called Brownsquoy. John Brown himself had grown up in Brown's Close, where his father worked as a cobbler.

John Brown had no interest at all in his ancestry, and almost nothing is known even of his parents. It has come down by word of mouth, however, that his father, the cobbler, had a weakness for alcohol. He did not drink regularly, but periodically he would dress up in his best clothes and tour around the alehouses.* Often these sprees lasted several days, until his money ran out, and then he returned home to his cobbler's bench and broken boots. It seems probable that this drink-ing was brought on by melancholy; certainly, among the cobbler's eight children, there was a strain of depression and even mental insta-bility. One of his sons, Jimmy, was so unstable as to be unable to work or live normally. He believed in the existence of fairies – they often seemed more real to him than human beings – and he saw apparitions of ships' masts emerging from Stromness harbour. Then there was a daughter, Kitty, severely depressive and possibly schizophrenic. In late middle age she suffered a crippling breakdown, was certified, and was sent south to Edinburgh to live out the remaining thirteen years of her life in a Morningside asylum, Craighouse.

By the time Kitty Brown arrived in Edinburgh, Craighouse had such a large proportion of Orcadian patients that it had been chris-tened 'Little Orkney' by visiting relations, and chronic depression was so rife in the islands that it had come to be known as *Morbus orcaden-sis*. Just before the First World War, an Edinburgh professor, Sir

---

*In the Revd Peter Learmonth's Statistical Account of 1842, there is mention of over forty places in Stromness where alcohol could be bought. Most of these would not have been full-blown pubs, but private houses where ale was brewed on the premises. 'There would have been 40 different varieties of ale to choose from along the street,' George reflects in the *Orcadian*, 30 May 1974. 'Also there would have been a com-plete scale of quality of house from Login's Inn at the top to some unspeakable grog-shop up some filthy close.'

Thomas Clouston, had made a study of mental weakness in the Orkney parish of Harray in which he had been born and spent his childhood. Clouston concluded that though these were 'country people, decent folks for the most part, hard working, thrifty, few very poor, healthily money-loving' and strangers to 'vice in its grossest forms', excessive intermarriage over many generations was responsible for half the families in the parish betraying clear symptoms of idiocy, congenital imbecility, epilepsy, or what he termed 'ordinary unsoundness of mind'. George Mackay Brown would later offer a less categorical, but more haunting, description of the malaise in a short story, 'The Drowned Rose':

> There is a trouble in the islands that is called *Morbus orcadensis*. It is a darkening of the mind, a progressive flawing and thickening of the clear lens of the spirit. It is said to be induced in sensitive people by the long black overhang of winter; the howl and sob of the wind over the moors that goes on sometimes for days on end; the perpetual rain that makes of tilth and pasture one indiscriminate bog; the unending gnaw of the sea at the crags.

To his friends and neighbours, John Brown appeared mercifully free of the *morbus*. He had been apprenticed to a tailor in the last years of the nineteenth century, when Stromness tailors ran a thriving trade exporting moleskin trousers to Orcadians working in the Canadian outposts of the Hudson's Bay Company. In the early years of the twentieth century, however, ready-made clothes from the south had begun to make tailoring a lean trade, and he had been forced to take on two other part-time jobs. The Glaitness Laundry Company in Kirkwall employed him to collect and deliver the Stromness laundry, and he worked as a postman.

Stromness housewives looked forward to seeing John Brown on his rounds. There are still many in the town who remember him well, and they describe him as clever and quick-witted, with a gift for mimicry, and a dry, ironic sense of humour. He made people laugh as he passed down the street – 'Ah, Jack Broon, it does me good to hear thee' – and, in his spare time, he cut a dash in Stromness amateur dramatics.

Perhaps it was this wit and flair that won over Mhairi Mackay; perhaps she was drawn to something more complex beneath the larky exterior. The couple were married in June 1910, in Strathy, and a band of passing tinkers danced at their wedding. For their journey home to Stromness, the *St Ola* was dressed in flags. They settled down in a small house by the pier, and here, ten months after the wedding, Mhairi gave birth to a daughter, Ruby. Sons followed in quick succession: Hugh in 1913; John, known as Jackie, in 1915; Harold, who would die of measles in infancy, in 1917; Richard, known as Norrie, in 1919. When, in the spring of 1921, Mhairi found herself expecting her sixth, and last, child, she hoped very much for another girl, whom she planned to name after her mother, Georgina Mackay. On 17 October she gave birth to a boy, George Mackay Brown.

2

The Green Coat

I dreamed I was a child in Orkney, and I owned the whole world,
cow and buttercup and rockpool, and the men and women and
animals put looks of love on me and on each other.

GMB, 'Magi'

'EARLY YEARS ARE remembered in gleams only,' George writes in
his autobiography, 'and the gleams illumine what seem to be
quite unimportant incidents.' He remembered sitting on the blue
flagstones of the kitchen floor, a seagull standing in the doorway; and
looking, from his pram, at the silhouette of his father's postman's hat
against a window. Two fragments of memory, however, seem more
significant, and both involve the tinkers who came to Orkney from
Caithness in the summer, and lived in tents on the outskirts of
Stromness. Later, tinkers would move through George's work: clever,
anarchic, exotic characters, enviably free of the monotonous cycles
of conventional life, able to shift their ground like herring. But in
these infant memories they are figures of pure threat. As George was
sitting playing on the doorstep one morning, at the age of two or
three, a tinker wife approached carrying a pack of haberdashery. She
was large, with a face brown and wrinkled as a walnut, a tartan shawl
wound around her head, and a clay pipe sticking out of her mouth.
George was so terrified that he fainted. Then he had a dream – the
most vivid dream of his life – that the tinkers had stolen him from his
mother and were hurrying him away in a pony cart, further and
further from home.

A terror of being separated from what was familiar to him was to
remain with George for the rest of his days, and it had a profound

effect on the way that he lived and wrote. Yet, on the face of it, his early years were stable and secure, and few children could have had less reason than he to fear being uprooted or abandoned.

Some time after their marriage, his parents had moved to 80 Victoria Street, a small, rented house whose front door opened on to a fisherman's pier. Mhairi Brown had her hands full with five children, and often, after school and at weekends, Ruby was asked to take care of her youngest brother. Towards the end of her life, Ruby set down her memories of life in Victoria Street, and she described George as a lovely child with dark, curly hair, very bright blue eyes – 'a true Celt' – and an insatiable appetite for stories.

> The kitchen was also the living-room: a stove polished so that one's face shone in it, a rag rug, a large wooden dresser with its complement of dishes. Two basket easy chairs, six wooden kitchen chairs. A statue of Burns ploughing forever on the mantelpiece . . . And there on the rug sat George, begging forever for yet another story.

George, in turn, remembered Ruby's gift for story-telling, and her beautiful voice. She was ten years older than he, a flamboyant, dramatic character with a taste for tales of emotional entanglement, invariably ending in tragedy. Often, the girls in her stories were deserted by their lovers and died of broken hearts; in his mind's eye, George then saw the flat red symbol from a playing card fracturing painfully somewhere inside the heroine's body. 'Of course I had no conception of what this all-important state of mind called "love" was,' he reflected in middle age, 'but I accepted it as an essential mysterious part of every story. The breaking of the heart was a wistful beautiful satisfying way to die, I supposed.'

Of all Ruby's tales, the one he loved best was 'Willie Drowned in Yarrow', a ballad whose verses are loaded with mounting foreboding:

> Down in yon garden sweet and gay
>> Where bonnie grows the lily,
> I heard a fair maid sighing say,
>> 'My wish be wi' sweet Willie!'

Willie's fateful day begins happily enough: he goes to a fair to buy a gift – a 'fairing' – for his sweetheart. But, hurrying to the love tryst to give it to her, he is drowned.

> She sought him up, she sought him down,
>> She sought him braid and narrow.
> Syne in the cleaving of a craig
>> She found him drowned in Yarrow.

George could picture precisely the distraught girl standing on the bank, watching as her lover's ribboned boater eddied and swirled down the river, knowing that he was lost for ever: 'I was beginning to learn that there was a thing in the world called evil; but I learned a thing even more important, that all the bad things of life, that happen to everybody sooner or later, could be faced, and controlled, and even made beautiful, by poetry.'

While Ruby was at school, and his mother washed and cooked and cleaned, George sat for hours on the stone doorstep, absorbing scenes and characters that would fill his own stories years later. A few steps away from the house, on Clouston's pier, he watched old women rinsing headless haddock, or feeding the seagulls. The shriek of the gulls was said to sound like the cry of a drowning man, and there were old women who believed that every one of the birds was the embodied spirit of a drowned fisherman. 'That's Jock Seatter,' they would say. 'There's Andrew Isbister. And there's Mansie Mowat.' But to George the gulls – or 'whitemaas' – seemed terrible creatures, their throats bulging with the fish-guts the old women threw to them.

In the summer, boys swam from the pier, and sometimes, in the late afternoon, borrowed the fishermen's yawls to row out and ride in the wash of the *St Ola* as she arrived from the Scottish mainland. Two fishermen, Tammack Clouston and Bill Sinclair, worked on Clouston's pier, and George watched them as they baited their lines and mended their creels before setting out to fish for cod, haddock, lobster and ling beneath the Black Craig and the Old Man of Hoy. Bill Sinclair, in particular, fascinated him. He had a twist of red beard, shaved off once a week by the barber, and he was never seen, winter or summer, out of his long leather sea boots: 'He would never say more than about six words at a time, and then he would sum up a situation like a master of epigram or haiku. One day the crew of a certain boat were all drunk. "They must have pawned their ship," he said, nodding his head sagely.'

Looking the other way, to the road, most of the population of Stromness passed by in the course of a day. In the morning, retired skippers and sea captains came out for their constitutionals, and in the early afternoon fishermen sold haddock along the street from barrows, weighing them – sixpence a pound – from small brass hand-scales. Two tall policemen paced up and down the length of the town, back and forth, all day long; mothers pushed prams; the minister glided past – 'a drooping black column'; and, whenever there was a funeral, blinds were drawn along the street while the cortège made its way through the town and around the coast to the kirkyard at Warbeth. Very occasionally, a car – there were just three in Stromness when George was a boy – bumped over the flagstones.

There was a wealth of local eccentrics. Geordie Chalmers believed he was a ship and wandered about Stromness in a reefer jacket and cheese-cutter hat muttering 'Starboard' or 'Port' or 'A splash astern'. Titty Bell skipped through the town with a washing basket under one arm, dancing pirouettes, talking to nobody; and there was a one-eyed town crier, or 'bellman', Puffer, who had spent some time in Kirkwall jail, and who hid in closes and tripped up children with his stick as they ran past.

Stranger than any of these to George were the southern tourists who arrived to stay in the Stromness Hotel in the spring and summer – among them, when he was three, George Bernard Shaw and his wife, Charlotte.* Sometimes Englishwomen set up easels in the street and painted watercolours, and this puzzled George. 'What could there be in our familiar surroundings worth painting?' he wrote, reminiscing about his childhood in middle age. 'We and our town were the norm, they (the tourists) were creatures touched with poetry and romance, come from enchanted places in the south.' He was puzzled, too, by the way these southerners spoke, and their voices echo through his work in characters like the laird's spinster daughter in his novel *Greenvoe*:

> 'A simply lovely morning,' announced Miss Fortin-Bell. 'She's coming. That must be her now.' She spoke as if she were shouting into a gale. (The islanders could never understand why the gentry spoke in

---

*The weather was bad for Shaw's visit, and he spent most of his time in the Stromness Hotel, emerging in the evening to walk gravely down to the pier. But he was impressed by the Orkney people, who seemed to him 'neither servile nor rapacious', and he was deeply struck by the fury of the Pentland Firth. Properly harnessed, Shaw thought, its power could supply all of Europe with heat and light.

such heroic voices – their own speech was slow and wondering, like water lapping among stones.) Miss Fortin-Bell faced seawards. The ferry-boat *Skua* entered the bay in a wide curve and glided towards the pier with shut-off engine. Ivan Westray stood at the wheel. A young girl waved from the stern, a little white flutter of hand, and smiled, and stroked down her dark wind-blown hair. 'Welcome to the island, darling,' shouted Miss Fortin-Bell. 'Isn't this lovely, all the village has come out to welcome you . . .'

When his mother went shopping, or when his father took the children for rides in the wicker barrow he used to deliver laundry, George ventured further into Stromness. 'Hamnavoe' – 'haven inside the bay' – was what the Norsemen had called it, and, centuries on, it still seems a fitting name. Walk a mile out of the town to the south and the tides in Hoy Sound rip so ferociously that the sea seems to boil; but Stromness harbour itself is almost always calm, sheltered on one side by a great outcrop of granite, Brinkie's Brae, and on the other by two low green tidal islands, the Holms. Following the shoreline, a flagstoned street winds a mile from one end of the town to the other. To the seaward side, squat, thick-walled fishermen's houses are built into the rock, gable-ends to the road, standing out into the harbour like stone arks. Beside each is a cobbled pier, so that as one walks down the road the grey houses are separated by bright, bookmark-shaped glimpses of the sea. To the other side, merchants and shopkeepers built their houses and small plots of garden along steep, narrow closes twisting up Brinkie's Brae. At the top, commanding wide views over the harbour, and beyond to Scapa Flow, retired sea captains and shipping agents put up solid, double-fronted villas, and named them after their old ships, or the trading posts where they had spent their working lives: Hopedale, Arranmore, Manora, Pictu.

To men like these, who had travelled widely, life in Stromness must have seemed almost oppressively quiet. Contact with the outside world was limited, to say the least. Not a single private house had a telephone when George was born, and not one of the 1,900-odd inhabitants of the town owned a wireless set. Nor were there any pubs. During the First World War, hundreds of Irish navvies had been sent to Orkney to defend the naval base at Scapa Flow, and many had been billeted in Stromness. Rowdy and often drunk, they had not been

universally popular and after their departure the women of the town –
for it was the women, George maintained, who held the reins – voted
Stromness dry. Shutters went up in the inns and pubs and the distillery
was closed. For the next quarter of a century, the men of Stromness,
thirsty at the end of the day, were forced either to brew illicitly at
home or to make their way seven miles down the road to an inn at
Finstown.

In the absence of pubs, men who might have spent their evenings
propping up a bar gathered instead around the counters of the local
shops, most of which stayed open until nine o'clock. These shops were
places of delight to George. Each had a distinct atmosphere and smell;
each attracted its particular customers. John D. Johnston, the drapers,
was where the tinkers congregated, and bargained for pins and needles
and ribbons to sell from their packs on the outlying farms. In the
saddler's shop, there was an intoxicating smell of leather and resin, and,
while Bill Mathieson sat rhythmically pulling thread through bridles,
girths and satchels, a retired bellman, Soldier John, told tales of his
service under General Gordon in India. The chandler's shop smelt of
rope, tar and apples, and its owner, Geordie Linklater, kept old copies
of *Lloyd's List and Shipping Gazette*, pored over by retired seamen. The
grocer, Willie Duncan Shearer, had white whiskers and spectacles in
silver frames, and always slipped George a pandrop, a brandy-ball or a
yellow butternut after filling brown paper pokes with tea, sugar,
oatmeal and flour for his mother.

> Home we would go then, under the hissing gas lamps, among the other
> shopping lingering clucking women. Always the Salvation Army raised
> a glad brazen sound at the pierhead or at the foot of Kirk Road.
>   Then it was the wooden bath-tub, with a few drops of Lysol in the
> warm water to kill germs, and a clean shirt, and a warm bed . . .

Beyond the shops was the Stromness Museum, and on New Year's
Day, when John Brown took his children out to walk off their one
roast-beef dinner of the year, this was their destination. Housed on the
first floor, above the Town Hall, the museum was so crammed with
cabinets and display cases that it looked as if a huge wave had crashed
across it, leaving behind flotsam and jetsam from almost every century
and corner of the earth. Natural history had been the passion of the

Revd Charles Clouston, who had established the museum in 1837, and among the exhibits were a stuffed golden eagle, the head of a whale stranded one summer on Outer Holm, and the shells of Caribbean turtles which had followed the Gulf Stream and drifted ashore in Orkney. There were also domestic curiosities: an eighteenth-century clock, the first to have come to Stromness – 'the brass face beaten like a boxer's' – ships in bottles, gravity beads used by distillers of illicit whisky. But most thrilling to George were the treasures gathered by Orkneymen who had left their homes and adventured in other parts of the world.

During the eighteenth and nineteenth centuries, ships from the Hudson's Bay Company, journeying north from London, had regularly called at Stromness to recruit boys from the overcrowded crofts to work in their fur trade outposts in Canada. One corner of the museum was stuffed with the mementoes these men had brought home: moccasins decorated with Cree Indian beadwork; thick, white blankets with stripes woven through them to show the number of beaver pelts for which they had been exchanged; exquisite ivory carvings, like Inuit netsuke, of dogsleds and hunters. Among these were sepia photographs of Orkneymen who had never returned to the islands, but had chosen to make lives for themselves in Canada: swarthy, proud-looking characters, wearing embroidered moosehide jackets over their moleskin trousers, flanked by Cree Indian wives and flocks of children.

The most distinguished of all the Hudson's Bay Company's Orkney recruits was John Rae. Born in 1813 at Clestrain in Orphir, Rae trained as a doctor, and was appointed surgeon at the Company's Moose Factory trading post in Ontario. From here, he led three expeditions to map Canada's Arctic coastline, and discovered 'Rae's Strait', the final link in a navigable north-west passage. He also established the fate of the Franklin expedition which had set off from Stromness in 1845,* and made himself unpopular with the British navy by suggesting that in their desperate last moments Franklin's men had resorted

*Sir John Franklin was a naval officer and Arctic explorer. On a final expedition to northern Canada to explore the feasibility of a north-west passage linking the Atlantic and Pacific Oceans, his two ships, *Erebus* and *Terror*, called in at Stromness for supplies and water on their way north. It was their last port of call before the entire party disappeared.

to cannibalism. In Orkney, Rae was a hero. He had bargained with the Inuit for some of Franklin's men's possessions – an ivory powder horn, for example – and they sit in the Stromness Museum among Rae's own exploring tackle: his Inuit sun-goggles, his octant, the inflatable cloth boat with which he made his way across the Richardson River using two tin plates as paddles.

Not all of those who went to sea were so respectable. In the early eighteenth century, a boy called John Gow had grown up in Stromness. In 1724, in the Mediterranean, he led a mutiny on board the *George*, renamed her *Revenge*, and turned pirate. After robbing ships off Spain, Portugal and France, he made his way home to Orkney, and fell in love with the daughter of a Stromness merchant, James Gordon, who promised to marry him. Before they could be wed, however, Gow was captured, taken to London, and hanged at Admiralty Dock.

Daniel Defoe wrote an account of Gow's trial, and the museum displays an original edition: *An Account of the Conduct and Proceedings of the late John Gow, alias Smith, Captain of the late pirates, Executed for Murther and Piracy . . . with A Relation of all the horrid MURTHERS they committed in cold Blood*. As a boy, George was gripped by Gow's story, and in particular by one final twist in the tale. According to local legend, Miss Gordon had plighted her troth to Gow by shaking his hand through the hole in the Odin Stone that stood between the lochs of Harray and Stenness, and the only way she could free herself from her obligations to the pirate after his death was to travel south and touch the fingers of his corpse. In his short story 'The Pirate's Ghost' George imagines this final encounter:

> Thora found her way, somehow, to Wapping. The pirates were still there, creaking and clanking in their chains. They dangled so idly in the air, they were so clotted with tar, that they hardly looked like human bodies. She recognized Gow, among the others, by his shattered thumbs, by his strong teeth, even by the shape of his cheekbone under its flap of skin . . .
>
> Thora clasped the tarred and salted right hand. She said, 'The fires are out. There's nothing left for you here, Jack. Farewell. This is the last mingling of our flesh – a touch only – but it gives us both peace.' . . . A wind coming up the Thames took the body and set it

creaking like a stiff sack. The wind increased – the chain about the
pirate rang. The chains round all ten of the pirates rang.

The girl turned her face to the north.

Compared with the lives of these adventurers and vagabonds, George's
own life was quiet, almost monotonous; and this suited him well. If his
imagination was fired by the stories of men like Rae and Gow, what
he wanted for himself, from a very early age, was stability and order.
Even as a small boy, on the doorstep in Victoria Street, he enjoyed the
predictable rhythm of the days. The tides rose and fell, so that, if in the
morning the stones of Clouston's pier were underwater, in the afternoon they emerged ragged with barnacles and bright green weed.
Every morning at eight o'clock, the *St Ola* set sail for the Scottish
mainland; every evening, at six o'clock, she nosed back into the
harbour like 'a serene black swan' and announced her arrival with two
hoots. As darkness fell, the lamplighter, Ali Thomson, walked through
the town with a long, flickering pole and set the gas lamps alight with
a hiss (he was absent only on the evenings around the full moon, when
there were no street lights at all). And at about eight o'clock, whatever
the weather, John Brown set off on his postal rounds in a blue, red-
piped uniform, with a glass lantern pinned to his coat to help him read
addresses. One of George's earliest memories was of his father coming
into the kitchen one wild night, 'half blind with rain, his black oilskin
gleaming, drops spilling from the twin-peaked cap . . . He trimmed
the wick and re-lit the lamp before setting out again into the storm.'
At midnight, Ali Thomson moved down the street again, extinguished
the lamps and plunged Stromness into darkness.

Every day of the week, too, had its particular character. Monday
was Mhairi Brown's washing day, when the family's laundry simmered
in an enormous, oval, tin boiler on the kitchen range. On Tuesday,
she ironed, and the house filled with the smell of fire and hot, pressed
linen. Wednesday was market day, when farmers from the outlying
countryside brought their cattle into Stromness. On Friday evening,
the Brown children were each given a ha'penny as pocket money, and
on Saturday morning George spent this on sweets. Mhairi Brown had
craved sweet things when she was expecting George, and he had
inherited the craving. In Stromness, in the twenties, there were

endless small 'magical caves' where he could indulge his sweet tooth.
Most were kept by old ladies, many of them, like 'Ginger Beerie
Babbie', widows of the First World War. George's favourite was Ma
Cooper's, a little walk from home:

> You pushed the door open – the bell pinged brightly – you stood in
> darkness and fragrance. Presently Ma Cooper entered from sweeping
> her kitchen or feeding her cat; and among the jars of black-striped balls
> and Sharp's toffee (two pence a quarter) serious negotiations began.

On Sunday, John Brown led his family to the service in the United
Presbyterian Church. What religious beliefs he held is not clear. He
refused to have his children baptized, and he made his contempt for
some of the Stromness ministers and elders quite plain. 'Hurry on past
the Jews,' he would say to his sons as they approached the church porch,
where two elders held collection plates. Yet Jackie remembered – and
his memory is borne out in photographs – that his father often wore an
ivory crucifix suspended from his watch chain, and John Brown would
brook no argument from his children about Sunday worship.

For George, the weekly visits to church were a painful combination
of utter tedium and acute embarrassment. Not only did his father sing
the hymns very loudly, but he did so standing sideways on to the pew
with his foot resting on the seat and his trouser-leg hitched up so that
a length of his drawers showed. While the minister delivered a long and
fiery sermon – 'pacing to and fro', Jackie remembered, 'like a caged
lion' – Mhairi Brown tried to relieve her children's boredom by passing
a paper bag of sweets along the pew. George found this excruciating:
'the rustling of the bag sounded like a small electric storm in the pauses
of the minister's discourse . . . I was sure that all the congregation must
be listening to that paper bag and disapproving.'

Sunday afternoons, when John Brown took his children on long
walks, were altogether happier. Above all, George enjoyed his visits to
the kirkyard at Warbeth, a mile west of the town. From a distance, the
Warbeth headstones, huddled on the edge of a low cliff, are silhouet-
ted against the sky like a cluster of black, broken teeth. Close up, they
tell the story of the births, marriages, labours, epidemics and shipwrecks of an island community over four centuries. Bounded by a dry
stone wall, the kirkyard stands on the site of a medieval monastery

whose tumbled ruins remain in one corner, but its position has a significance reaching back even further. For the Vikings, the sea represented eternity, and the dead at Warbeth are close to the waves, their gravestones facing east to catch the rising sun.

One particular tombstone fascinated George. It was the memorial of a girl called Ellen Dunne who had died in 1858, aged seventeen, and the rhyme at the foot of it, overgrown with ivy, troubled him 'with its wistful ghostly melancholy':

> Stop for a moment, youthful passer-by,
> On this memento cast a serious eye.
> Though now the rose of health may flush your cheek,
> And youthful vigour, health and strength bespeak,
> Yet think how soon, like me, you may become,
> In youth's fair prime, the tenant of the tomb.

'There are more folk lying dead in this kirkyard than there are living nowadays in the whole of Orkney,' John Brown used to tell his children, and this impressed George deeply. In his late forties he set down his feelings about Warbeth in a poem much anthologized in succeeding years:

> A silent conquering army,
> The island dead,
> Column on column, each with a stone banner
> Raised over his head.
>
> A green wave full of fish
> Drifted far
> In wavering westering ebb-drawn shoals beyond
> Sinker or star.
>
> A labyrinth of celled
> And waxen pain.
> Yet I come to the honeycomb often, to sip the finished
> Fragrance of men.

Warbeth was about as far from Stromness as George could happily go without longing to be back at home; and, on the rare occasions that he travelled further afield, he was unsettled. One summer, when he was very small, his mother took him with his brother Norrie on the *St Ola* to the Scottish mainland to meet his Mackay grandparents. His memories of the visit were grim. His grandmother, Georgina, was sweet and kind enough, but his bearded, Gaelic-speaking grandfather, Hugh, struck him as stern and frightening, and the countryside around Strathy seemed unremittingly dour.

Remote in the Scottish Highlands [it was] lonelier and more desolate far than any moor you would find in Orkney. I have dim memories of a few desolate roads straggling over steep brown deserted hills where crofters' cottages were falling into ruin; of black peat bogs and shaggy sheep-dogs; of fishing boats and monster-haunted seas snarling under the cliffs; and soft, melancholy, gentle voices speaking in Gaelic.

Another summer, the Brown family spent a week in Birsay, on the north-west coast of mainland Orkney. They stayed in a cottage called 'Hell' (the neighbouring cottage was 'Purgatory') and the name, for George, was apt. He was terrified of the bulls in the fields nearby and, when his brothers saw his terror, they seized on it and teased him. During what was supposed to be the family's great treat of the year, George spent his time counting the days until he could return to Stromness, to the 'warm igloo' of home.

Yet life in 80 Victoria Street was not as seamlessly secure as George sometimes suggests. It seems likely, in fact, that his reluctance to face the wider world had its roots, at least in part, in the anxieties bred in him at home. Despite his three jobs, George's father found providing for a wife and five children a constant struggle, and there were relentless worries about money. The Post Office were generous with their allowance of uniforms – a new one every year – and, to clothe his sons, John Brown was able to use his tailoring skills to 'make down' his old uniforms; but for winter shoes (the children went barefoot in the summer) he was obliged to apply for handouts from Humphrey's Bequest, a charitable trust for the Stromness poor. George would later claim that he and his siblings were not troubled by the knowledge that they were poor. 'Our poverty never rankled or oppressed,' he wrote. 'It was the kind of poverty that makes people generous and free and open-handed.' But this is not the whole truth. Shortage of money caused friction between George's parents, and for a sensitive child, in a small house, this was painful.

Mhairi Brown had a tendency to extravagance – a symptom, George believed, of her natural generosity – and every so often bills would arrive from shoemakers or other tradesmen that her husband was unable to settle. These never resulted in full-blown rows but, perhaps worse, they led to 'turnings-away, seethings, stony silences'. For a few hours, the low Gaelic chant that Mhairi kept up as she went about her housework would cease, and to George this was terrifying. The protectiveness he felt towards his mother was exacerbated by concerns about her health. Mhairi Brown suffered from asthma, and there were times, particularly in the summer, when she could do nothing but lie back in a chair, or in bed, gasping for breath.

His father was also a source of anxiety. The humour and merriment that the people of Stromness loved in John Brown was loved by his children too. George particularly cherished the way he used his wit to puncture gossip and melodrama among the Stromness housewives: 'He would say something scathing to the lament on the threshold, and usually it was so funny that it kindled laughter. It was as if Falstaff had exchanged a few words with a chorus of Trojan women.' George admired his father's theatrical gifts, and had happy memories of him at New Year, after a glass or two of whisky, holding the floor singing Victorian and Edwardian music-hall songs with great style – 'standing behind his chair, gesturing with his small, beautifully-shaped hands as if he was sculpting the lyrics from the lamplight and the smoke'. He had, George believed, the makings of a really good actor. But, beneath this extrovert exterior, John Brown was a complicated, troubled character. As a young man, he had visited London and Glasgow, and he was haunted for the rest of his life by the wretchedness of the slums in both cities. He borrowed regularly from the Stromness public library, and the books that most absorbed him were those about the difficult lives of the poor: Patrick MacGill's *The Rat-Pit* and *Children of the Dead End*, and Jack London's *The People of the Abyss*. He was keen that his children should share these concerns, and determined that they should not get above themselves, and he would quote to them from *The Pilgrim's Progress*:

> He that is down needs fear no fall,
> He that is low, no pride;
> He that is humble, ever shall
> Have God to be his guide.

'Much better to remain poor and content than to become, out of lowly beginnings, a professional man or a businessman and then give oneself airs,' George wrote of his father's beliefs. 'That was insufferable, in his scale of values.'

But, at the same time as being preoccupied with those poorer than himself, John Brown was also dissatisfied with the treadmill of his own life, and this created a tension. He urged his children to 'get on' in the world, and to make sure they ended up in better jobs than he. Jackie remembered his father chiding Ruby when it looked as if she might fail her Highers, and warning her of the disappointment he would feel if she were to end up working in a shop. Mhairi Brown echoed these sentiments. 'Try and get on,' she used to say. 'Get out of the rut.' For George, the knowledge that his parents saw themselves as living in a rut cannot have been comfortable.

Moreover, although he kept it hidden from friends and neighbours, John Brown, like his brother Jimmy and his sister Kitty, was prone to depression. As a small boy, George often heard him in his bedroom, alone, walking back and forth, speaking to himself, arguing out his problems. George would eavesdrop outside the closed door, and what he heard frightened him. He could never quite catch his father's words, but he knew that they were 'loaded with pain and anxiety, either for himself and his family or for the terrible poor of the cities of the world'. It gave him a first glimpse of the complexity of human nature.

The strains of life in Victoria Street should not be exaggerated. John and Mhairi Brown's marriage was, by any standards, a happy one. George's brother Jackie could not remember his parents ever exchanging a harsh word, and he talked of his childhood home as a place of harmony. In Stromness, too, Mhairi was as popular as her husband. George wrote after her death of 'a special sweetness of disposition that was felt far beyond the bounds of the family', and Ruby remembered feeling twinges of jealousy at having to share her mother not only with her brothers, but with all their neighbours. Young girls came to talk to Mhairi Brown of their problems in love and, when a child was hurt or an old person dying, a cry went round: 'Send for Mother Brown!' 'She exhaled comfort and peace and humanity,' Ruby wrote. 'Everyone loved her.'

Everyone, that is, except her landlady. Number 80 Victoria Street was owned by a middle-aged spinster who had been saved from a bigamous marriage to a sailor during the First World War, and who had, ever since, been mentally unhinged. In 1928, when George was six, this woman turned suddenly against Mhairi Brown and ordered her to remove her family from the house. George remembered the anguish he felt at seeing his mother, for the first time, in tears – 'For she too was a stranger then'. From Victoria Street, the Brown family moved 200 yards down the road to Melvin Place, to a dark house with a drain running under the flagstone floor. For George, the move signified the closing of a chapter. 'This is true,' he wrote towards the end of his life: 'Not wisdom or wealth can redeem / The green coat, childhood.'

3

The Prison on the Hill

No more ballads in Eynhallow.
The schoolmaster
Opens a box of grammars.
GMB, 'Runes from a Holy Island'

TIME MEANS LITTLE to a small child. It sits on the wrist of each
day, in the words of the poet Edwin Muir, 'with its wings folded'.
Writing in the *Orcadian*, towards the end of his life, George recalled
a moment when he began to be aware of time. He was nine or ten
years old, and returning from a walk to Warbeth with a group of
friends, when a boy said, 'In three weeks we'll be back at the school.'
The words, uttered carelessly, sent a chill through George. 'That innocent summer afternoon,' he reflected, 'I must have passed from child-
time into man-time, where everything begins to be different.'

George had joined his brothers at Stromness Academy shortly
before his fifth birthday, and it had come as a shock. In a photograph
of his class at the beginning of their 'Infant' year, he sits on the edge
of a group of forty-nine children, fixing the camera with a steady,
untrusting gaze; and his mother later told him that, at the end of his
first school day, he came home, dumped his satchel in the corner of
the kitchen and announced that he was never going back. Gradually,
he was 'broken in', but he was never completely reconciled to life in
the 'huge gray unimaginative machine' that sat halfway up Brinkie's
Brae, at the back of the town.

Education had been compulsory for only fifty years when George
started school, and there was still a handful of older people who felt
that children might be better employed helping on crofts or fishing

boats than sitting behind desks. Leafing through back copies of the *Orkney Herald*, George later discovered that some time after the Education Act of 1872 his Brown grandfather had been taken to court and fined ten shillings for allowing his children to play truant: perhaps it was from him that George inherited a visceral resistance to rules and regulations, particularly those whose aim was to dragoon their subjects into uniformity. And subduing individuality, remoulding pupils to become more like children further south, was a high priority for the staff at the Academy. Orcadian accents were frowned upon: the children were urged, sometimes forcibly, to speak 'accepted English'; pupils were not encouraged to take an interest in Orkney's past. The prize days of all the schools in the islands were reported exhaustively in the *Orcadian* and *Orkney Herald*, and the addresses made to the children by local dignatories give a flavour of the kinds of values and ambitions these schools aimed to instill. In September 1930, pupils at the secondary school in Kirkwall were informed of the precise sum – £8,000 – spent on them by the Education Committee in the past year, and were asked to consider whether they had applied themselves sufficiently to their studies to justify 'that enormous expense'. Two years later, children at Stromness Academy were told that, just by being born in Orkney, they had started life at a disadvantage to their peers in mainland Scotland, and that they would have to work hard to overcome this.

What mattered, the children were told, was not what family they came from, but how hard they tried. Longfellow was repeatedly quoted:

> No endeavour is in vain;
> Its reward is in the doing,
> And the rapture of pursuing
> Is the prize the vanquished gain.

But, in practice, children like the Browns were left in no doubt about their lowly position in the social pecking order. The teachers' snobbery, Ruby Brown remembered, 'was transparent to an intelligent child. The child of a bank clerk, a teacher, a minister was in a different category altogether to the child of a humble postman.' Ian MacInnes, who started at Stromness Academy at the same time as George, and who was to remain one of his closest school friends throughout his life, had a similar experience. His father had been an officer on the *Pole Star*, the ship that serviced the Orkney lighthouses, but he had died when Ian was four, leaving his widow struggling to bring up nine children. Like the Browns, the MacInnes children were made to feel socially inferior by the teachers at the Academy.*

Built in 1875, three years after the Education Act, Stromness Academy was a source of pride to the establishment of the town. It was extended and modernized during George's time there: a report in the *Orcadian* in March 1934 boasts gas lighting throughout, and a 'commodious gymnasium' – a place of horror to George – equipped with 'wall bars, beating boards, climbing ropes manipulated by the latest devices'. The children were summoned from their homes in the morning by a bell salvaged from a British war vessel. 'Of all the dolorous noises I have heard on this earth,' George later reflected, 'that bell of Stromness Academy takes some beating.'

The school was ruled over with rigid, sometimes brutal discipline by its headmaster, John R. Learmonth, known to the children as Napoleon, or 'Nap'. His presence, Ian MacInnes remembered, 'cast a pall over the whole building'. Learmonth had served in Salonika during the First World War, and was unattractive, almost sinister, in appearance. 'He was baldish,' recalls Archie Bevan, another of George's close friends, 'and seemed to have a skull with skin on it rather than a face.' Years of chain-smoking had stained his hands yellow, and he spoke with elongated vowels, and wore heavy boots, so that from some distance the children could hear him crashing down the corridors. This sound was charged with menace: by his footfall, it was possible to judge his mood.

Learmonth instilled in his staff a firm belief in education through punishment, which George later recaptured in stories like 'Five Green Waves':

> 'You will go home at once to your father,' said Miss Ingsetter, rapping her desk with a ruler, 'and tell him I sent you, because you have not prepared the mathematics lesson I told you to prepare. Now go!'

---

*Ian MacInnes later became headmaster of Stromness Academy (1977–84). He used the position to support the underprivileged and to fight for the rights of children, no matter what their background.

A rustle went through the class-room. The pupils looked round at me, wide-eyed. A few made little sorrowing noises with their lips. For it was a terrible punishment. My father was a magnate, a pillar of authority in the island – Justice of the Peace, Kirk Elder, Registrar, Poor Inspector, a member of the Education Committee itself. He was, in addition, the only merchant in the place and kept the shop down by the pier; even before I was born he had decided that his boy would be a credit to him – he would go to the university and become a minister, or a lawyer, or a doctor.

Now, this summer afternoon, while blue-bottles like vibrant powered ink-blobs gloried in the windows and the sun came four-square through the burning panes, my stomach turned to water inside me.

'Please, Miss Ingsetter,' I said, 'I'm sorry I didn't learn the theorem. I promise it won't happen again. I would be glad if you punished me yourself.'

The bust of Shelley gazed at me with wild blank eyes.

Her spectacles glinted. Down came the ruler with a snap. 'You will go to your father, now, at once, and tell him of your conduct.'

Fiction, but not exaggeration. George recalls in his autobiography that children at Stromness Academy were routinely beaten with a leather strap for making mistakes in spelling, and Ian MacInnes remembered having his tongue scrubbed with soap as a punishment for swearing.

It was less the discipline that George resented, however, than the dullness of the teaching. 'My zeal for education,' he wrote to a friend in 1960, when he was himself unwillingly undergoing teachers' training, 'extends to teaching [children] how to read and write and count up to a thousand. A really able person requires no more. He will absorb what he needs thereafter, in his own good time. For the rest of the time, I would teach them to swim and sail a boat and climb hills; also how a farm is run, and the economics of fishing; and they would listen much to music and poetry, and take part in plays. Out of such a fruitful soil, an Einstein, a Plato, or a Keats would have a better chance of growing.'

By contrast, George looked back on his own schooldays as a dreary, repetitious slog of 'parsing, analysis, vulgar fractions', force-fed to the children of Stromness by men and women in whom teachers' training college had extinguished any spontaneity or imagination or sense of rhythm. 'Art' consisted of tedious hours spent trying to draw a jug draped about with a duster; the weekly music class was largely taken up with ear-tests; and, in a period called 'drill', held in the concrete-floored gymnasium, a young lady teacher took the children through a series of spasmodic exercises – 'as though children in our circumstances were not already perfectly fit and healthy with the wild sweet freedom that sea and hill gave us in our own free time'. In English, pupils were presented with chunks of text to break down and 'parse'. For many, George felt, 'that cutting up and examining of parts must have given to literature and language a charnel-house revulsion', and he felt uneasy, in later life, at the thought of Scottish schoolchildren being forced to study his own work for Highers.

Memories of the staff of Stromness Academy provided George with rich material for stories and novels. Teachers, in his work, fall broadly into two types: radical, progressive characters like Mr Smellie in 'The Laird's Story', bent on thrashing into the island children 'facts, information, numbers', and sad, bitter spinsters like Miss Inverary in *Greenvoe*, slowly withering into a pinched middle age. Hardly a single teacher is portrayed as attractive or sympathetic. Yet it would be wrong to think of George's school years as a time of unrelieved unhappiness. Not all those who taught him were blinkered and unimaginative – George considered his science master, John Shearer, one of the most patient, humorous and charitable people he ever met – and not all the lessons were dull. The stories from the Old Testament, read aloud to the children in religious education, enthralled George, and history, when the teacher departed from lists of dates to describe the victories of Wallace or Robert the Bruce, 'made the blood sing along my veins'. Ruby remembered George sitting often on winter evenings in Melvin Place drawing up elaborate family trees of the kings and queens of Scotland. (The kings of England struck him, by comparison, as nothing more than a 'succession of grey schemers, dolts and braggarts', and moved him not at all.)

And, if English lessons were uninspiring, they nevertheless helped to nourish in George the fascination with poetry that Ruby's ballads had sown in him as a very small child. In 'The Tarn and the Rosary', a short story that reads like a thinly veiled fragment of autobiography, he describes a boy, Colm, from an imaginary island called Norday, asked to learn Wordsworth's 'Fidelity' by heart for homework. Colm, like George, detests school. He glances at the poem at bedtime, expecting to be bored stiff. But to his amazement, as he reads, he is gripped by a mysterious conviction that he understands just what Wordsworth felt as he wrote the poem: a lonely elation, a confusion of sadness and delight.

His mouth moulded the words: *mists that spread the flying shroud*. He hoarded the lines, phrase by phrase.

It was the interior of Norday that was being bodied forth in a few words.

The lamp splashed the page with yellow light.

This poet must have seen Tumilshun too, or else some loch very like it. He had felt the same things as Colm. This was strange, that somebody else (and him a famous dead poet) felt the dread, for none of the other boys seemed to; at least, if they did, they never spoke about it. But this was even stranger: there was a joy at the heart of the desolation . . .

Colm stood at his desk next afternoon, when his turn to recite came. He uttered the magical words in a high nervous treble. He looked sideways at Phil Kerston. Phil Kerston had taken trout out of Tumilshun with his hands; his father's croft was thatched with heather from the flank of Brunafea; Phil was bound to like the poem, far more even than he did himself. But Phil sat knotting a piece of wire under his desk, idly, making a rabbit snare. Poetry to him was just another cell in the dark prison of school.

'De-dum-de-dum-de-dum,' said Miss Silver. 'No, Colm. You have learned the words, good, but you destroy the life of the poem the way you recite it. Listen now. This is the way it should be spoken: "There sometimes doth a *leaping* FISH . . ." '

Tennyson was about as close to contemporary as the poetry teaching got during George's primary education, and with Tennyson, George assumed, real poetry had died. Privately, however, he began to try his own hand at verse. At the age of eight or nine, sitting in a field on top of Brinkie's Brae on a summer's day, and looking out across the harbour, he wrote his first poem, a ballad in praise of Stromness.

At moments like this, George relished solitude. In a piece in the *Orcadian*, he later recalled the thrill he felt as a boy on the first morning of the summer holidays, and how, in order to savour it, he withdrew from his school friends and took himself off to spend time alone. Yet he seemed anything but a loner to his contemporaries. In 1929, Ruby Brown left home to train as a teacher in Aberdeen. She remained closely in touch with her family, and when, in her second year at college, she was asked to prepare a thesis on any chosen subject, she decided to write on 'My Brothers: Norrie and George'. The two boys, then aged eleven and nine, had always been very close, and they seemed to Ruby to offer an interesting study in opposites. Norrie, she felt, was bookish, shy, very much an introvert. George, on the other hand, was boisterous, gregarious, comic, quintessentially extrovert. His school friends describe him in much the same way. He was extremely popular and, like his father, he had a gift for making people laugh. Ian MacInnes remembered how, at the age of six, George had won the astonished admiration of all his peers for telling the headmaster to 'bugger off' in the middle of a dressing-down for having arrived late at school. And his wit, it seemed to MacInnes, went hand-in-hand with integrity and strength of character: George was 'a peacemaker with a great deal of moral courage'.

Ian MacInnes disliked Stromness Academy as heartily as George did, but the school day did not begin until 9 a.m., and it ended at 4 p.m., and in MacInnes's view 'our lives outside more than compensated for the prison on the hill'. In the early mornings, George had a job helping a local farmer, Tommy Firth, with his milk rounds. Together, they processed down the main street of Stromness on a pony-drawn milk-cart – a sort of chariot, Jackie Brown remembered, 'not unlike the Roman chariots of *Ben-Hur*' – mounted with a churn. George was responsible for pouring milk from the churn into a zinc can which he carried into kitchens, where jugs were waiting to be filled. The job gave him entry into most of the houses in the town, offering him glimpses of the quirks and secrets lying beneath the surface of a small community – glimpses he would later draw on in his fiction, particularly in *Greenvoe*.

In the late afternoon, George and Ian MacInnes regularly made their way to Peter Esson's tailor's shop where John Brown worked and where, sitting out of the way playing cards beneath the oak counter, MacInnes felt they had their real education. The tailoring tackle enthralled George – the bolts of cloth, the notebooks full of measurements, the flat triangular chalks, the hot, heavy iron known as a 'goose', the men cross-legged on their workbench. The images of looms and weaving, warp and weft, that run through so much of his work surely have their origins in that 'cloth-smelling cave'. But tailoring was only a secondary activity in Esson's shop: the main business was talk. Open until eight o'clock in the evening for the farmers, the shop was a sort of unofficial club where a particular group of Stromness men exchanged news and commentary, and tales about local folk reaching back as far as the early nineteenth century. Peter Esson – tailor, librarian, kirk elder and veteran of the First World War – had a kind of genius for giving gossip and stories shape and meaning. 'Because he had a flawless memory,' George wrote,

> he could relate story to story, person to person – he saw the complex intertwining drift of the generations through the history of Stromness until all was a unity. So in my dark corner of the tailor shop I got to know that I was a member of a living community, as the tales old and new and the names of folk living and dead shuttled back and fore, to and fro, perpetually woven and rewoven through the loom of Peter's mind. The legend of the town took shape for me. It was a precious heritage.

Peter Esson died suddenly in 1954, and George acknowledged his debt to him in a poem written a few days after his death:

> Peter at some immortal cloth, it seemed,
> Fashioned and stitched, for so long had he sat
> Heraldic on his bench. We never dreamed
> It was his shroud that he was busy at.
>
> Well Peter knew, his thousand books would pass
> Gray into dust, that still a tinker's tale
> As hard as granite and as sweet as grass,
> Told over reeking pipes, outlasts them all.
>
> The Free Kirk cleaves gray houses – Peter's ark
> Freighted for heaven, galeblown with psalm and prayer.
> The predestined needle quivered on the mark.
> The wheel spun true. The seventieth rock was near.
>
> Peter, I mourned. Early on Monday last
> There came a wave and stood above your mast.

Without Esson's early influence, George believed, he might never have begun to write stories.

If much of the material on which he was to draw came from outside school, however, it was at Stromness Academy that George's gifts were first recognized. When he and his peers were ten, a composition class was added to their weekly timetable. The subjects set were dreary: 'The Autobiography of a Penny', or 'A Day in the Life of a Tree'; but, to his amazement, George found that the words flowed fluently from his pen. Through the imaginary schoolboy, Colm, he describes the thrill that this gave him:

> Colm . . . discovered that he could remember things much better writing them down than speaking them. When he had time to assemble his material the past ceased to be a confused flux; it became a sequence of images, one image growing out of another and contrasting with it, and anticipating too the inevitable exciting image that must follow. He liked making sentences. He put commas in, and full stops; in that way he could make the word sequences (which were, of course, inseparable from the image sequences) flow fast or slow; whichever seemed more suitable. He even put a semi-colon in the part about the moon and the snow, and then the sentence seemed to hang balanced like a wind-slewed gull. Writing gave Colm a small comfortable sense of power.

Every week, when the compositions were handed back, Miss Garson, the English teacher, announced: 'George Brown has written the best essay again.' He wrote well, she insisted, because he read good books; but this was not the case. Such was George's resistance to force-feeding that for the rest of his life he could get little pleasure from the works of authors he had been made to read at school: Dickens, Robert Louis Stevenson, Jane Austen, Sir Walter Scott. (Scott, at least, might have been expected to interest him. In 1814, inspecting the lighthouses of Scotland in his capacity as Sheriff of Roxburgh, he had stopped off in Stromness and climbed the brae to visit an old lady called Bessie Millie, reputed to be a witch. Bessie Millie had girlhood memories of the notorious John Gow, and, inspired by her reminiscences, Scott wrote *The Pirate*. Despite a number of attempts, however, George could never really get to grips with the novel and, in general, he found reading Scott 'like chewing hunks of stone'.)

Books that he discovered for himself, outside school, were altogether different. At some point in his childhood, a copy of *Grimms' Fairy Tales* came into the Brown household, and George read the stories again and again, enraptured. He also found himself moved to tears by some of the late-nineteenth-century school stories: Dean Farrar's *St Winifred's, or The World of School*, and Talbot Baines Reed's *The Fifth Form at St Dominic's*. Otherwise, until he was about fifteen, the only publications George really enjoyed were the 'twopenny dreadfuls' – the boys' magazines *Gem, Magnet, Wizard, Adventure, Rover, Hotspur, Skipper*, produced weekly by D. C. Thomson in Dundee.

Gem and *Magnet* were devoted entirely to stories about English public schools and, reading them, George wished that his father was a rich man, able to send him south to Eton or Harrow, to a life of practical jokes and tuck-boxes, cricket and rugby. It was a bizarre desire in a boy who hated leaving home, and he later wondered whether it might have had its roots in a wariness of girls. 'It may,' he writes, 'have been an early instinctive revolt against the mysterious perilous feminine principle, without which life is barren and unfulfilled; and yet the growing boy dreads the intimations of that mystery. Most of the women I knew were gentle good people, except for a few schoolteachers and neighbours going with whispered gossip between the doors. Girls were strange creatures to be avoided as best one could.'

The 'twopenny dreadfuls' arrived on the *St Ola* every Tuesday evening, and were furiously exchanged between the boys. By the end of the weekend, George had read every one, cover to cover, several times, and, to help fill what felt like a great gulf of time between shipments, he began to produce a magazine of his own. He called it *The Celt*, after his favourite football team, and appointed himself sole contributor of stories, crossword puzzles, jokes and letters, painstakingly transcribed in his neat copperplate hand. He circulated copies among his classmates in exchange for sweets.

The Celt was popular, and gave George a feeling of confidence. It was dawning on him gradually that he wanted to make his living by the pen, and by his early teens, if asked what he was going to do with his life, he would answer without hesitation: he was going to be a football reporter. For football, more than reading or poetry, was George's passion. During the day, when school allowed, he and his classmates divided into teams and played game after game, in the playground, on the street, or in a high field near the summit of Brinkie's Brae. At night, in the bedroom George shared with his brothers, he invented imaginary teams and played them off against each other in his mind, throwing dice to decide the result of each game. In the early thirties, the first wireless sets had begun to arrive in Stromness. Very few families owned one and, for those who did, listening was plagued by what were called 'atmospherics': the volume rose and fell 'as though Henry Hall was playing from a raft somewhere in the mid-Atlantic'. For George, nevertheless, it seemed a magical experience to crouch over a neighbour's wireless on a Saturday afternoon listening to fragmentary murmurs from Hampden Park or Wembley. The Celtic footballers became, in his mind, figures invested with as much romance as the kings and queens of Scotland, and when, one day, he overheard a woman reading a newspaper to her father and learned that the great Celtic goalkeeper John Thomson had died after a collision in a match with Rangers, it seemed a tragedy as vivid as Fotheringhay or Flodden.

> He too died in the glory of the field
>   Young and beautiful
>   John Thomson, goalkeeper of Celtic.
> For the boys of Hamnavoe
> Football was war, was magic and chant.
> A star glittered and went out.

George himself was a formidable footballer. Jackie Brown remembered being amazed at his youngest brother's skill when he watched him playing in a match one weekend: 'He could swerve and run with the ball at his feet, making circles round his opponents and scoring goals.' And Ruby remembered the Boys' Brigade team carrying George shoulder-high off the field after one match, because he had scored all the four goals. In one report in the *Orkney Herald*, there are references to the thirteen-year-old George Brown as the star of a victorious team in a match between Stromness and Kirkwall: 'Once again Stromness brought the ball up to Craigie, who had a hard time keeping it out of the net, until Brown, who made no mistake, sent a rasping shot into the rigging.'

But this exuberance and energy masked the fact that, at home, life was difficult. The Browns' years in Melvin Place were not happy ones. John Brown's health began to fail – whether because of the drain beneath the house, or as a result of years of going out in the wind and snow to deliver letters, nobody knew. He developed rheumatic fever, from which he never fully recovered, and his limbs became twisted with arthritis. In 1934, when George was thirteen, the family moved to a house on a new council estate, Well Park, at the south end of Stromness. It was a modern house, their first with a bath, and fitted with gaslight, and Mhairi Brown was delighted with it. Here, at last, she hoped, her husband's health would stand some chance of recovery.

It was not to be. Hobbling, and in constant pain, John Brown did his best to keep up his postal rounds, but in December 1936 he was forced to retire. He had no pension, and money became extremely short. Occasionally, he still managed a small amount of tailoring for Peter Esson. Otherwise he sat at home, depressed and frustrated. His inability to provide properly for his family so tormented him that when somebody suggested that the root of his trouble might be his teeth, he took a desperate gamble and arranged to have them extracted, all in one go, without anaesthetic. He and Teddy Tait, the dentist, consumed half a bottle of whisky between them during the operation, and he was fitted with a set of false teeth. These he found it impossible to eat with, and so, at mealtimes, he was forced to remove them, fold them away in a brown envelope, and chew pathetically on his gums.

George did what he could to cheer his father along. He was regularly sent with a bucket to fetch freezing Atlantic water from Hoy Sound, into which John Brown plunged his sore feet; and in the evenings, under the gaslight, he read him poetry. 'He was not a poetry-reading man himself,' George wrote, 'but he seemed to like those raw recitals.' George remembered particularly his father's enjoyment of *The Ballad of Reading Gaol* and Ralph Hodgson's 'The Bull'. He also read out loud some of his own 'first crude verses', and was encouraged by his father's approval.

His siblings were in a position to offer more practical support. John and Mhairi Brown's hopes that their children would 'get on' had, on the whole, been fulfilled. Hughie had left school at fourteen to be apprenticed to a Stromness baker. Jackie, on leaving school, had secured a job at the Union Bank in Kirkwall, and he sent a generous proportion of his weekly salary home to his mother. Ruby, after completing her training, had taken a job teaching English at Stromness Academy, and had come home to live with her parents, paying 'digs' money, taking her turn at cooking and housework and occasionally buying her mother clothes and shoes. George was not as fond of Ruby as he had once been. For all her disapproval of the snobbery she had experienced as a child at Stromness Academy, she had herself returned from teachers' training college with singular and superior attitudes. 'What great victory did Nelson win in 1805?' Archie Bevan remembers her asking her pupils towards the end of one afternoon. 'Trafalgar, miss?' one ventured. 'Not Trafalgar,' she corrected him, 'Trafalgah!' 'Trafalgah! Trafalgah!' the children chanted as they spilled out into the playground.

In the wider family, too, there were problems. John Brown's younger brother, Jimmy – the one who saw fairies and apparitions of ships' masts rising out of the harbour – had left his wife. She was a strange and powerful woman and, after they parted, he remained so frightened of her that he paid his nephew Jackie a shilling a week to deliver her alimony. Living alone, Jimmy Brown became melancholy and doom-ridden. George dreaded his weekly visits for dinner. Then, one day in March 1935, Jimmy went missing. Three and a half weeks later his body was found floating in Stromness harbour, and it was assumed, though never proved, that he had killed himself.

Jimmy Brown's disappearance and death affected George deeply. Fifty years on, in 1985, the nephew of one of his close friends committed suicide at Bristol University. George revealed to her then that the discovery of his uncle's body had triggered in him feelings of despair that he had found hard to shake off. An elegy for the Bristol undergraduate reflects, at a distance of half a century, his morbid perplexity at the notion of a man's taking his own life, and the misery he felt at the prospect of passing into the 'iron-gray country of adulthood':

> That one should leave The Green Wood suddenly
>   In the good comrade-time of youth,
>   And clothed in the first coat of truth
> Set out alone on an uncharted sea:

Who'll ever know what star
 Summoned him, what mysterious shell
 Locked in his ear that music and that spell,
And what grave ship was waiting for him there?

The greenwood empties soon of leaf and song.
 Truth turns to pain. Our coats grow sere.
 Barren the comings and goings on this shore.
He anchors off The Island of the Young.

Sadness and anxiety took their toll on George's health. When he was fifteen, both he and his brother Norrie were struck down by a bout of measles. Norrie recovered quickly, but for six months George was left half-deaf, and his sight was permanently damaged. Psychologically, too, he was in a fragile state. 'Suddenly, in mid-teens,' he later wrote, 'the boy becomes the man. It can be a metamorphosis very dreadful and devastating.' Between the ages of fourteen and sixteen, George experienced 'intense loneliness and suffering'. He was overwhelmed by an irrational sense of shame and dread over which he seemed to have no control, and which centred on a terror of losing his mother. When Mhairi Brown left the house to go shopping, George became convinced that she would never return: 'I would shadow her along the street, and dodge into doorways if she chanced to look back.' He could confide these fears to no one, partly because his family were preoccupied with their own troubles, and partly because there was nothing real to tell or to describe.

These were the first inklings of the depressions that were to stalk George, on and off, right up until his death. 'The "black bird" has been with me all my life,' he wrote in a letter to a friend in Edinburgh shortly after his sixtieth birthday. 'When it comes and sits on my shoulder, and whets its beak it is unpleasant, to say the least.' His depressions could go on for months, years even, with hardly a break; and occasionally they became so intense that he feared for his sanity, and longed for oblivion. 'Sometimes such a mass of dark clouds pour through my skull,' he writes in January 1983, 'I wish I was dissolved into the 4 elements.'

As the years went by, George would develop ways of coping with depression, forcing himself to recognize that it always, eventually, subsided – 'There *is* delight, though it is withdrawn for a time' – and burying himself in his writing. 'A lovely day, but depression hanging round my skull like a cloud,' he writes on 11 December 1982. 'I *fight* depression by work; so I inflicted 2 bright wounds on the dragon by writing, in the early afternoon, 2 "stone poems": they seemed to come swiftly and joyously, as tho' they were waiting to be bidden!' But when that first depression hit during his schooldays, George had no idea what was happening to him, or how to combat it.

Woodbine cigarettes became his chief source of solace. He had started smoking them, on and off, at the age of twelve; by fifteen, he was addicted, inhaling deeply, and prepared to cheat and steal for the tuppence he needed for every packet of five. If tuppence could not be found, he would smoke the ends of black twist from his father's pipe, or watch where his older brothers threw their cigarette butts and, when the coast was clear, pick them out of the cinders and smoke them down to the point where they began to burn his lips. John Gilmour, whose family had come to live in Stromness in 1936 when his father was appointed lighthouse keeper at Sule Skerry,* remembered George arriving later and later for school – 'and, on more than one occasion, Mr Ritchie, our Latin teacher at the time, would assemble the class at the window to watch [him] stub out his Woodbine cigarette on the school steps'. Once inside, George sat through lessons with his head in his hands 'like a youth shunned and branded'. It had become an agony to speak in class.

Following the measles, and aggravated by the Woodbines, George had developed a hacking cough, which he seemed unable to shake off. Football was now out of the question; and anyway, his enthusiasm for boyish games and company was waning in favour of more solitary, cerebral pursuits. He was preoccupied, in particular, with religion. There had been little in George's upbringing to nurture loyalty to the Presbyterian Church. He shared his father's contempt for the elders and ministers, and added to this, as he grew older, he had begun to feel uneasy about the lack of unity among the Presbyterians of Stromness. There were no fewer than three Presbyterian churches in the town, each with a distinct congregation. That one small subsection of Christians should be so divided struck George as wrong. But as his

---

*A tiny, uninhabited island 40 miles west of Orkney mainland, home to thousands of puffins and seals, and the backdrop for much local legend.

disenchantment with the Presbyterian Church grew, so too did his belief in the fundamental tenets of Christianity. Certain psalms and passages both from the Old and from the New Testament, read out in church or at school, struck him as irresistibly compelling, and in the gospel accounts of the Passion he sensed a beauty which could only have its roots in truth.

At school, when he was about fifteen, George felt the first stirrings of interest in Catholicism. The English master at Stromness Academy one day read aloud to the class Francis Thompson's 'Hound of Heaven'. Later, George would think the poem seriously flawed, but at that stage he was overwhelmed by it, and read it again and again until he had it by heart: 'And I knew that the man reeling from delight to vain earthly delight was a Catholic – a very sad and weak and fallible one – and that the Hound in relentless pursuit of him was Christ, or the Church. And, for some reason, these facts gave to the poem an extra relish.' At about the same time, he came across a copy of Lytton Strachey's *Eminent Victorians*. Strachey's essay on Cardinal Manning gave George one of the greatest thrills he ever experienced from a piece of literature. His clear purpose in writing about Manning had been to pour scorn on the Catholic Church as a hotbed of arrogance, corruption, pretension and inconsistency, to which Pope Pius IX had added a final, ludicrous flourish with the declaration of Papal Infallibility in 1869. But, somehow, every weakness that Strachey demonstrated in Catholicism only strengthened George's inclination to believe that the vast claims of the Catholic Church might, in fact, be true:

> That such an institution as the Church of Rome – with all its human faults – had lasted for nearly two thousand years, while parties and factions and kingdoms had had their day and withered, seemed to me to be utterly wonderful. Some mysterious power seemed to be preserving it against the assaults and erosions of time.

George kept these feelings to himself. Along with most other children in Stromness, he had been brought up to regard the Catholic Church as suspect, and to consider the various strange items and practices that clustered about it – rosaries, popes, confession, relics, purgatory, monks, penances – vaguely sinister. If he had never specifically been instructed to be anti-Papist, he was aware nevertheless of a general feeling that 'Catholicism and its mysteries lay outside our pale, and it was better so'. There were just two Catholics living in Stromness: an Irish barber, Paddy Mee, and Giulio Fugaccia, an Italian ice-cream seller. There was no Catholic church in the town, and no priest. At sixteen, however, George took a decisive step away from Presbyterianism. He stopped going to church with his parents, and began instead to attend the local Episcopal church, where he was put in charge of lighting candles.

His family raised no objections, but the changes that had come over George did not go unnoticed. Ruby looked back perplexed on the college thesis she had written about her younger brothers a few years earlier. Norrie, who had been so shy and bookish as a boy, had become gregarious and handsome: tall, wavy-haired, popular with girls. George, meanwhile, was beginning to look gaunt and angular, especially in the face. Of the two, he was now decidedly the introvert. He was also becoming a voracious reader. Feeling that there was no one in whom he could safely confide his adolescent fears, he had turned instead to books; and in poetry, above all Romantic poetry, he found some consolation:

> As heroin addicts inject brief tastes of heaven into themselves, perhaps at that time I could not have lived without daily shots of 'Adonais', 'Ode to a Nightingale', 'Christabel', 'To a Skylark', 'The Garden of Proserpine', 'The Lady of Shalott', 'Lines Written Among the Eugenian Hills'. . . It was the words and sound and rhythms that made me drunk. I never stopped to ask what the poets meant; the music and the dance of words were the whole meaning. All this delight I absorbed in secret, like a drug-taker.

George was fortunate that his conversion to reading coincided with a revolution in the publishing industry. In July 1935, when he was thirteen, Allen Lane had brought out the first ten 'Penguins', reprints in paperback of novels by authors including Agatha Christie, Dorothy Sayers, Ernest Hemingway and the Orcadian writer Eric Linklater, priced at sixpence each. In the face of much doubt and dis-couragement, Lane persisted in the belief that there was a huge appetite for 'serious' books among people who could not possibly afford new hardbacks (generally about fifteen times the price of the early paperbacks) and he proceeded to bring out two or three new Penguins a month.

George was exactly the kind of person Lane was aiming at, and when the Stromness stationer, Rae's, began to stock Penguins, he responded immediately. 'The enormous pleasure we all got from those early "Penguins"!' he later wrote in the *Orcadian*. 'There's nothing like it at all now. I feel like Wordsworth watching the shepherd boy on a May morning – something has vanished from the earth . . . My hands trembled as I took down from the shelf Neil Gunn's "Morning Tide", or Maurice O'Sullivan's "Twenty Years A-Growing", or E. M. Forster's "A Passage to India" – and handed over my sixpence and silently stole away. A book in those early days was the most exquisite pleasure that life could give.' Gradually, he began to build up a small private library in Well Park. John Gilmour remembers being amazed at seeing George's bedroom at this time, piled with paperbacks – 'I wondered how on earth he could read so many.'

Alone in his book-lined bedroom George was also devoting himself to the business of writing poetry. It was, he claimed towards the end of his life, 'a hobby, a pastime, a foible', but almost certainly, even at this early stage, he took it more seriously than he dared admit – even, perhaps, to himself. 'I have cultivated this secret vice of poetry for 9 years, since I was 15 years old,' he wrote to a friend in 1946, 'and it is my ambition some day to leave one or two really good poems behind me.'

Very few of his poems from this time survive, and those that do are gloomy, mawkish, sub-Tennysonian pieces:

> The purple night is hushed and calm
> Save here, where crashing breakers roar,
> And sigh again with ceaseless moan
> On northern shore . . .

But perhaps, George reflected in middle age, 'those bad verses, like dim lanterns, helped me to endure the black winter that raged all around'; and at the time he was sufficiently proud of them to show them not only to his father, but also to his Classics master, John Cook. Cook was impressed. By the age of forty, he predicted, George would be a well-known writer. He typed out some of the poems and, at the sight of them in formal typescript, George felt 'a tremble of joy'. Emboldened, he showed his work to the editor of the *Orkney Herald*, and in June 1939, when George was seventeen, the *Herald* accepted a sonnet for publication.

'The Hills of Hoy at Sunset' reads like an Orcadian pastiche of 'Composed on Westminster Bridge':

> Blue swelling hills! O, never shall I see
> A picture more magnificent and still,
> An evening scene so peaceful and tranquil . . .

It was not a poem George liked to be reminded of later in life. Yet he freely admitted that its publication in the *Orkney Herald* in his penultimate summer term at school was more thrilling to him than the publication of anything else in his entire writing career. His audience had suddenly, if momentarily, swelled from two to several thousand, and it was an audience made up of just the kind of people he most wanted to reach: ordinary people living in a place for which he was coming to feel an extraordinary love. At the time the poem was published, however, life in Orkney was about to change for ever.

4

Bloody Orkney

I thought it was absolute hell, and it's the only place in the world I've never had the slightest desire to return to until I started reading the poems and prose of George Mackay Brown.
Charles Causley on the experience of being posted to Orkney with the Royal Navy during World War II

O N 14 JUNE 1939, the day that 'The Hills of Hoy at Sunset' appeared in the *Orkney Herald*, Winston Churchill was guest of honour at a dinner party given by Kenneth Clark, the young director of the National Gallery, in London. In March, Hitler had invaded Czechoslovakia, and in May Mussolini had signed the Pact of Steel, finally throwing in his lot with the Nazis. One of Clark's guests let slip that the American Ambassador, Joseph Kennedy, felt that war was now inevitable, and that Britain would be 'licked'. Incensed, Churchill gave an impromptu oration. 'It may be true,' he proclaimed, stubbing his cigar for emphasis, 'that steel and fire will rain down upon us day and night scattering death and destruction far and wide. It may be true that our sea-communications will be imperilled and our food-supplies placed in jeopardy.' Yet trials and disasters, he insisted, would only strengthen the resolution of the British people to defeat the Nazis, and he was confident that Britain would triumph over 'these most sinister men'. The country was bracing herself for battle, and Orkney, which had slipped out of the national consciousness since the end of the First World War, was about to re-emerge as an area of vital strategic importance.

Scapa Flow, the expanse of deep sea enclosed by mainland Orkney to the north, and by the islands of Lamb Holm, Burray, South

Ronaldsay, Flotta and Hoy to the east, south and west, has been used as a shelter by ships since before the arrival of the Vikings; but it was not until Kaiser Wilhelm's Germany began to engage in a race with Britain for naval supremacy, in the run-up to the First World War, that its defensive potential was exploited on a national scale. The Admiralty knew that it was vital that they should be able to stop the German navy from slipping out into the Atlantic and cutting off Britain's seaborne supplies, and Scapa Flow, because of its size and depth and good anchorage, was the obvious place to position a fleet. From Scapa, in May 1916, the British navy had sailed north to fight the Battle of Jutland; to Scapa, after the Armistice, seventy-four German ships had been ordered to sail and surrender. They lay at anchor in the flow for six months, manned by skeleton crews who became increasingly hungry and unruly.* Then one hot June afternoon in 1919, following the announcement by the League of Nations of draconian peace terms with Germany, the German commanding officer, Vice-Admiral Ludwig von Reuter, ordered the entire fleet to scuttle itself. That very afternoon, a party of pupils from Stromness Academy had been taken out in a small craft to look at the German ships. Eight-year-old Ruby Brown was among the children who watched in delighted terror as the battleships, cruisers and destroyers began to list and sink, and the sea filled with German sailors swimming for their lives.

Twenty years later, as the threat of war escalated, the defence of Scapa Flow became once again a national priority. During the summer and autumn of 1939, as one and a half million children were evacuated from British towns and cities, and the West End of London became a ghost town, cluttered with 'To Let' signs, Orkney underwent an invasion of troops. Shipload after shipload descended the gangplank of the tubby troopship the *Earl of Zetland*, until in the end 60,000 servicemen and women had arrived in the islands: three to every native Orcadian. Most took a pretty dim view of their new surroundings, to begin with, at any rate. Orkney was classed as a foreign posting, and it felt decidedly foreign to the troops as they arrived in Stromness – a town with few cars, no trains, no pubs, no electricity, no organized social life. Their

*Their food supplies were brought direct from Germany. The crews existed on a diet of black bread, potatoes and turnip jam.

duties were demanding: the anti-aircraft guns around Scapa Flow had to be manned day and night, in all weathers. Off-duty, they were housed first in tents, and then in Nissen huts ill designed to withstand the extremes of an Orkney winter – horizontal rain and sleet, gales lasting days on end. The servicemen's initial disdain for both the islands and the islanders is summed up in a lengthy piece of doggerel, 'Bloody Orkney', over whose authorship a number of them still squabble:

> This bloody town's a bloody cuss
> No bloody trains, no bloody bus
> And no one cares for bloody us
> In bloody Orkney.
>
> Everything's so bloody dear
> A bloody bob for bloody beer
> And is it good? – no bloody fear!
> In bloody Orkney.

And so on and so on, verse after gloomy verse. One young conscript, writing home after arriving in the islands in 1939, summed up the mood more succinctly: 'Dear Mum, I cannot tell you where I am. I don't know where I am. But where I am there is miles and miles of b–gg–r all. Love, Ted'.

The Orcadians felt equally disoriented. In *Greenvoe*, George describes what happens to a sleepy fishing village when, without warning, the lives of its inhabitants are turned upside down by the arrival of teams of workmen and bureaucrats engaged in a mysterious project, 'Operation Black Star':

Men with drawing-boards and theodolites and briefcases crossed over to the island; security officers with Alsatian dogs; clerks, cooks, cable-men, crane-drivers, pier-builders, more and still more labourers . . .

The labourers moved into huts adjacent to the work-site. A wooden town sprang up overnight, with cook-house, laboratory, laundry, canteens, sick bay, offices, a hall, a detention centre. The Irishmen began to beat out a hard black ribbon between the pier and the site. Work started on a perimeter fence.

The island began to be full of noises – a roar and a clangour from morning to night. A thin shifting veil of dust hung between the island and the sun. The sea birds made wider and wider circuits about the cliffs. Rabbits dug new warrens at the very edge of the crags.

Writing this in 1970, George was surely drawing on memories of the autumn of 1939. Nissen-hut villages sprang up like mushrooms around Scapa Flow. Road-blocks, pillboxes and anti-tank traps were set up on all the approach roads to Stromness, and between them snaked cordons of barbed-wire entanglements, so that the town was completely encircled against invasion. The harbour was jammed with freight. The war years brought record harvests of lobster, but in order to reach their creels fishermen like Tammack Clouston and Bill Sinclair now had to manoeuvre their yawls out to sea between massive armoured ships. The *St Ola* mounted a gun and had two gunners added to her crew. The Commercial Hotel, just across the road from Clouston's pier and the doorstep where George had spent so much of his early childhood, became the NAAFI, where Hughie Brown took a job dispensing beer and refreshments to the troops; Mackay's Stromness Hotel became the headquarters of the Orkney and Shetland Defence Forces. The football pitch, where George's siblings had watched him play so triumphantly a few years earlier, was transformed into a kind of military circus ring, where a regimental sergeant-major from the Indian Army, bronzed and bare-chested, had his fittest soldiers mounting vaulting-horse displays, or forming human pyramids; and an assault course was laid out in a field on the outskirts of the town so that troops could train daily under realistic battle conditions.

Almost overnight, life for the people of Stromness was utterly transformed. A blackout was enforced, and householders were instructed to tape their windows against bomb-blast. They were issued with identity cards and ration books, and housewives like Mhairi Brown went about their errands clutching gas masks, ready to dive, when the siren sounded, into sandbagged air-raid shelters. The leisurely perambulations of the townspeople, which had so absorbed George as a small child, became impossible. The one, narrow, twisting street through Stromness was now a chaos of troop-carriers, dispatch riders, Scammell transporters towing howitzers, mobile 'ack-ack' guns and whistling columns of soldiers, again recalled in *Greenvoe*:

> It soon became apparent that a kind of tension existed between Black Star and Greenvoe. For one thing, Greenvoe lay athwart Black Star's daily supply lines. Hens, sheep, children were forever wandering in front of the urgent lorries that thundered hourly between pier and

site. The track between the huddle of houses was too narrow and eccentric to admit the larger vehicles; it was dust after a week of sun; and a quagmire when it had rained for an hour or two, a necklace of pools. *Greenvoe will have to go*, the engineers said . . .

The older people of Stromness were filled with gloom and foreboding. In such a small community, the loss of every one of the fifty men whose names appear on the First World War memorial at the north end of the town was still painfully felt. One group of men who had served together in the trenches took out of mothballs their khaki overcoats – 'British Warms' – and, in a gesture of patriotism and defiance, began to meet together wearing them for daily walks about the town. But not everyone was downcast. The influx of Irish navvies between 1914 and 1918 had brought sudden prosperity to Orkney. There are stories of shopkeepers literally shovelling their profits into sacks, and when, in the middle of the war, an Orkneyman had made an insulting remark about the Kaiser, a local shopkeeper upbraided him: 'Na, na, say not a word against the Kaiser. He's been a good Kaiser to us.' Once again, in 1939, the tills began to ring, and there were shopkeepers in Stromness – like the grocer, Joseph Evie, in *Greenvoe* – who were not complaining. The younger people, too, felt more excited than afraid. 'We could not understand why our elders looked so stricken,' George wrote, 'for of course we had no knowledge of the Somme and Passchendaele and the war that was to end all wars and the land fit for heroes.'

George was still at Stromness Academy. He had failed his first attempt at Highers and had then stayed on at school for an extra year, drifting from classroom to classroom with no idea what he might do next. The war was a welcome diversion. Lessons were suspended for a fortnight shortly after the beginning of the autumn term, and teams of older children were ferried in relays to the beach beneath the kirk-yard at Warbeth to fill sandbags. The weather was glorious, and they quenched their thirst with limitless free lemonade. Twice a day they were allowed to cast aside their spades, strip off their clothes and run into the sea. Their spirits were high.

As the autumn wore on, however, the reality of war was borne in on them. Scapa Flow had been considered impregnable, but in the early hours of 14 October 1939, Lieutenant Gunther Prien, the commander of a German submarine, discovered a small passage through the defences. 'It is a very eerie sight,' Prien noted in his log as he guided the U-47 silently through Holm Sound. 'On land everything is dark, high in the sky are the flickering Northern Lights, so that the bay, surrounded by highish mountains, is directly lit up from above. The blockships lie in the sound ghostly as the wings of a theatre.' Just after 1 a.m., Prien found himself gliding alongside two battleships, lying at anchor. Into one, HMS *Royal Oak*, he proceeded to order the firing of four torpedoes. Within minutes, she had sunk with the loss of more than eight hundred men.

Stromness woke early to the sound of car engines, whining gears and slamming doors as half a dozen empty taxis wound their way through the town, stopping at each of the seven drapers' shops and departing with every last sheet and blanket. 'It required little imagination and the merest glance at those overloaded taxis heading back to Kirkwall,' Archie Bevan remembers, 'to recognize the huge scale of the disaster.' But, for Bevan, the most painful memory of that morning was the sight of Bob Baker, the Stromness dustman, climbing on to his bicycle to go in search of his sixteen-year-old son, Willie. Willie Baker had been serving on the *Royal Oak* as a Boy Sailor. He was not among the survivors.

The 396 crew who did survive came to the surface with horrifying descriptions of the ship's last moments. As she lurched and began to sink, the electricity had failed, leaving hundreds of men floundering in a darkness occasionally illuminated by racing cordite flash. Many were burned to death; others were trapped and drowned. Divers later described the bodies of sailors lying tangled in their hammocks on the seabed.*

Three days after the sinking of the *Royal Oak*, German bombers descended on Scapa Flow and hit a second ship, the *Iron Duke*. This time there was no loss of life: the ship was manoeuvred into shallow water, where she sank; but the two incidents together had exposed serious strategic flaws, on the basis of which Winston Churchill decided to embark on the formidable task of joining up the small

*Today HMS *Royal Oak* is an official war grave, marked by a green buoy. Every year, a memorial service is held over the spot where she sank.

islands to the south of the Flow with a massive concrete causeway — the Churchill Barriers. The people of Orkney had, in the meantime, become used to the drone of German bombers flying over, and to searchlights criss-crossing the sky at twilight. 'The islands shook,' George wrote, 'with Wagnerian noise.' Lessons had resumed in the middle of the autumn term, and the children now arrived at school in the morning with gas masks slung over their shoulders. When the sirens sounded, they trooped out of their classrooms and into sand-bagged shelters; they trooped back again at the 'all-clear'. But nothing happened. No bombs fell. No bombs, George began to believe, would ever fall. As the beautiful autumn of 1939 gave way to a savage winter of gales and blizzards, the excitement he had felt when the war broke out began to turn to boredom.

So, when at dusk on Saturday 16 March, 1940, the sirens began to wail, nobody paid much attention. Golfers pursued their rounds on the golf course; Mhairi Brown carried on with her weekend shopping. George was at home, smoking and listening to dance music on the wireless. Then, suddenly, Nazi bombs began to rain down on the islands in the most ferocious air raid Britain had so far seen. Well Park shook and shuddered, but it did not occur to George to run for shelter: 'There was too much excitement for thoughts of safety. Even at that age anyhow I remember thinking that I would rather die in the open air than in a black, crowded, claustrophobic shelter.' Above Scapa Flow, the sky was alive with the flash of the anti-aircraft guns, and the air was filled with puffballs:

> The guns stabbed vividly against the dark backcloth of Hoy. The appalling din went on and on; and in the brief intervals we could hear the undulating drone of German bombers. The evening went on, with growing earthquakes and volcanoes. Then, as suddenly as it had begun, the sounds of war ebbed; and after a while the 'all-clear' went.

Scarcely a mile from Stromness, in a hamlet called Brig o' Waithe, a 27-year-old Orkneyman, James Isbister, had watched the air raid from the doorstep of his cottage. His wife and three-month-old son were inside. When a low-flying plane, returning from a raid on Scapa Flow, jettisoned its last bombs just across the road from where Isbister was standing, he was killed instantly. He became the first civilian air-raid casualty of the Second World War.

To the young people of Stromness the death of James Isbister was profoundly shocking. Archie Bevan was one of a group of boys who walked out to inspect the damage the day after the bomb fell, and he remembers it as a melancholy and chastening experience. George too walked over the hill with friends in the spring sunshine, saw the craters and ruins, and handled the bomb fins. 'We felt then,' he wrote, 'a first quickening of the blood – a wonderment and excitement touched with fear. The war was real, right enough, and it had come to us; and it might well come again, and closer.'

A few weeks after Isbister's death, the news came through that France had fallen to the Nazis. Hitler was filmed dancing for joy as he witnessed the signing of the surrender in a railway carriage in the forest of Compiègne; and John Brown was quietly relieved. He himself had been just too old to serve in the First World War, but he had been haunted by descriptions of life in the trenches, and of the carnage on the Western Front. 'Thank God,' George remembered his father saying, 'the boys won't have to go to France.' With the exception of George, all his sons were now caught up in some way in the war. Unhappy, and with no great will to live, John Brown too had decided to play his part. In the autumn of 1939, he had taken a job as a hut tender in the bleak settlement of Lyness on the south-east coast of Hoy, where huge oil tanks were being built into the hillside to fuel the ships anchored in Scapa Flow. Some time before leaving for Lyness he had bought himself a new suit. 'My next suit,' he said, 'will be a wooden one.'

John Brown was sixty-five when, early on the morning of 11 July 1940, he suffered a heart attack and died. His body was ferried back across the water to Stromness and laid out, 'more remote than a star', in a bedroom at Well Park. George remembered being urged forward to touch the dead brow, lest images of his father should linger and disturb him: 'I have never felt a coldness so intense as that touch. He had travelled such a far way from the wells and fires of the blood.' Three days later, John Brown was buried in the kirkyard at Warbeth. It pleased George, in later life, to think of him there, 'a quintessence of dust', enjoying the company of generations of Stromness men and women. 'I wish,' he wrote, 'there was a Thomas Hardy in Orkney to report the conversation of those salt and loam tongues in the kirkyard, immortally.'

Of the immediate aftermath of the death – of his mother's grief and his own – George left no record. Coming as it did, however, at a time when the war was changing life in the islands for ever, John Brown's passing began to represent for him the closing of a chapter not only for his family, but for Orkney as a whole. Nearly two decades later, he published 'Hamnavoe', a poem in honour of his father. Following him as he proceeds on his postal round through Stromness, it is an elegiac celebration both of John Brown and of a way of life that had disappeared:

> My father passed with his penny letters
> Through closes opening and shutting like legends
>> When barbarous with gulls
>> Hamnavoe's morning broke
>
> On the salt and tar steps. Herring boats,
> Puffing red sails, the tillers
>> Of cold horizons, leaned
>> Down the gull-gaunt tide
>
> And threw dark nets on sudden silver harvests.
> A stallion at the sweet fountain
>> Dredged water, and touched
>> Fire from steel-kissed cobbles.
>
> Hard on noon four bearded merchants
> Past the pipe-spitting pier-head strolled,
>> Holy with greed, chanting
>> Their slow grave jargon.
>
> A tinker keened like a tartan gull
> At cuithe-hung doors. A crofter lass
>> Trudged through the lavish dung
>> In a dream of cornstalks and milk.
>
> Blessings and soup plates circled. Euclidian light
> Ruled the town in segments blue and gray.
>> The school bell yawned and lisped
>> Down ignorant closes.

In 'The Arctic Whaler' three blue elbows fell,
Regular as waves, from beards spumy with porter,
  Till the amber day ebbed out
  To its black dregs.

The boats drove furrows homeward, like ploughmen
In blizzards of gulls. Gaelic fisher girls
  Flashed knife and dirge
  Over drifts of herring,

And boys with penny wands lured gleams
From the tangled veins of the flood. Houses went blind
  Up one steep close, for a
  Grief by the shrouded nets.

The kirk, in a gale of psalms, went heaving through
A tumult of roofs, freighted for heaven. And lovers
  Unblessed by steeples, lay under
  The buttered bannock of the moon.

He quenched his lantern, leaving the last door.
Because of his gay poverty that kept
  My seapink innocence
  From the worm and black wind;

And because, under equality's sun,
All things wear now to a common soiling,
  In the fire of images
  Gladly I put my hand
  To save that day for him.

George was in his mid-thirties by the time this poem was published, and by that time he was becoming confident about his loyalty to the past. 'Sometimes,' he would later write, 'I see my task, as poet and story-teller, to rescue the centuries' treasure before it is too late. It is as though the past is a great ship that has gone ashore, and archivist and writer must gather as much of the rich squandered cargo as they can.' At eighteen, however – at the time of his father's death – he was aware less of a devotion to the past than of a craven shrinking from the present and future. As the end of his schooldays loomed, George was gripped by a dread of what was to come next. He had not the least desire to enter any trade or profession, and the idea of nine-to-five employment appalled him. Yet he knew what hopes his parents had had for their children, and his father's death can only have made the prospect of disappointing these hopes more painful. He began to slink about Stromness, depressed and ashamed, 'like a leper'.

The cough that George had developed following the measles had never left him. Added to this, he was now very often dragged down by an overwhelming lethargy, such as he later described in a radio play. 'And what exactly do you feel?' the doctor asks his young patient in *A Seat by My Bed*. 'It's hard to say,' the patient replies, 'but it's as if everything oppressed me – the waves, the cry of whitemaas, the random talk of the streets – all those things, and a thousand others, that usually delight me. To take the smallest decision becomes a wearisome burden. I have to think for five minutes before I force myself to go upstairs. I have to brood for half an hour before I go to the shop round the corner for tobacco.' He was losing his appetite for food, for conversation, even for poetry.

In July 1940, at the age of eighteen, George finally left Stromness Academy and, after a desultory attempt to follow Jackie into the Union Bank of Scotland, took a dead-end job sorting mail in Stromness Post Office. His colleagues in the sorting-room were glad of his company: he had them doubled up with laughter at his imitations of Churchill and Hitler. But both his siblings and his friends were astonished that he seemed to be setting his sights so low. While waiting to be called up, he combined his job in the Post Office with service in the Home Guard, a haphazard, *Dad's Army* outfit intended to offer the town extra protection in the event of invasion. Archie Bevan remembers him, a tall, gangling figure, shouldering arms:

> His first public performance, mounting guard over the telephone exchange, was watched with delight by an appreciative audience of his peers, and with rather less enthusiasm by the officer in charge who no doubt felt that George was hogging the show. But no, George kept a straight face and a straight rifle, stared ahead unwaveringly and clashed his heels in the approved manner. This convulsed his audience. Sixty-five years later I'm still not certain what we were laughing at. George had a reputation for drollery and mimicry of a high order, and perhaps we brought our expectations along with us . . .

While he could put on a good performance in public, however, at home George kept his own company, and spent every penny of his paltry Post Office earnings on cigarettes and paperback books. Ruby was disgusted, and made sure that George knew it. She had a beautiful voice but a sharp tongue, and she lashed out at him, casting aspersions not only on his sloth but also, obliquely, on his sexuality. An estrangement grew up between them that was never fully healed, and for which Ruby blamed herself bitterly in later life: 'I resented his lethargic ways,' she wrote in 1987, three years before she died, 'and what I thought was his indolence. I did not realize how ill he must be. I write this to my eternal shame.'

George's call-up papers eventually came through in March 1941, and he was sent to the hospital in Kirkwall for a medical examination. He did not relish the prospect of life in the Services, except in one respect. Earlier in the summer he had had his bottom teeth – rotted through years of sweet-eating and lack of dental attention – extracted, and he was looking forward to having a new set installed at the King's expense.

Far from letting him join his brother Norrie in the RAF, the doctor who examined him forbade him even to re-enter Stromness Post Office, lest he infect his colleagues. George was ordered, instead, straight to Eastbank, a sanatorium in Kirkwall. He had been classified 'C3': he had tuberculosis.

5

What the Blood Dictates

Sometimes I think . . . recurrent illness is a kind of refuge. When things are beginning to be too much, you suddenly become ill. Not desperately ill, but ill enough to avoid your responsibilities.

GMB, interviewed in 1996

IT IS HARD today to recapture the terror that surrounded TB in the first half of the twentieth century. 'The Captain of all these men of death', Bunyan had called it in 1680, and by the time it was diagnosed in George it was responsible for one death in eight in Britain. Helen Fox, who went to work as a nurse at Eastbank after her sister died of the disease, remembers being shown the lists of men and women admitted to the sanatorium during the twenties and thirties. More than half had not survived. She later married one of her patients, Archie Wylie. He had felt certain, when he was diagnosed with TB, that he would never come out of the sanatorium alive, and as soon as he was admitted his mother had made a bonfire of all his possessions.

So great was the alarm caused by the disease that when, in 1898, the National Association for the Prevention of Tuberculosis (NAPT) was founded, its first meeting was attended not only by leading physicians but also by the Prime Minister, Lord Salisbury, and the Prince of Wales.* But, despite frantic activity and concern, no cure was to be found for almost another half-century. What now seem like common-sense precautions were overlooked. Smoking, which had almost certainly compounded George's TB, was not only permitted in sanatoria but also, occasionally, encouraged: it helped, some doctors believed,

---

*Later King Edward VII.

to stimulate the lungs. In the meantime, the NAPT busied itself with expensive and probably futile initiatives, such as the printing of tens of thousands of 'Do Not Spit' notices to be displayed in railway stations up and down the country; and scientists invented quack remedies. In 1912 hopes soared when a Swiss bacteriologist developed a serum derived from the blood of black horses. Just over a decade later, a professor at Copenhagen University caused a flurry of excitement by devising a system of injecting TB sufferers with gold. On the whole, enthusiasm for this was short-lived, not least because quite a number of patients on whom it was tested died either of shock or of acute metal poisoning; but it was still going strong at Eastbank in the early forties, and it was the first treatment inflicted on George. 'For months,' he recalled, 'this increasingly dense fluid with solid grains held in suspension was injected into the muscle of the upper arm – a painful business. At the end of the course of treatment I was neither better nor worse.'

Ignorance fuelled fear. As time passed, and no cure was found, a suspicion crept in that what TB patients, or 'lungers', were essentially suffering was a form of moral and mental degeneracy. 'Tubercle attacks failures,' pronounced one eminent doctor and member of the Council of the NAPT. 'It attacks the depressed, the alcoholic, the lunatic of all degrees.' Attitudes like this meant that victims of the disease, even once they had been cured and discharged from sanatoria, were often treated as outcasts. Children were instructed not to speak to them; they had great difficulty finding work. And, because TB was widely considered to be hereditary, anyone who had ever contracted it, however briefly, lived in fear of being disowned even by close family and friends. 'Two kinds of suffering have attended me through the battle [to get well in the sanatorium],' wrote one man in an article in the *Western Mail* in November 1938. 'One was the distressful horror of the disease itself. The other is the mental agony born of the knowledge that when I emerge from the fight . . . I am taboo to my fellow men.' For those who were single when diagnosed, the likelihood of marriage became remote.

Here lies a key to the acute physical shyness and lack of confidence that were to afflict George from his late teens onwards. Towards the end of his life he mentioned to a close friend, almost in passing, that he had always found it hard to believe that any woman could ever love him or want him for a husband, because he was so unattractive. Even the sound of his voice was an embarrassment to him. As a boy growing up in a predominantly male household, he had been wary of girls; at the age of nineteen, just as most of his contemporaries were finding girlfriends, and many of them moving away from Orkney, George found himself restricted for the best part of a decade to a limbo exis-tence, confined, very often, to bed. He was weak and skeletally thin, and for a time his appearance to those who did not know him well was shocking. Norrie Brown's future wife, Hazel, first visited Orkney in the summer of 1942. Norrie had tried to prepare her for the fact that George was not well, but she was nevertheless taken aback when she first met him. 'He had a hollow, sunken face, with no bottom teeth,' she remembers. 'He seemed sad and strange and shy beyond belief – shy especially of women.'

Adolescent depression had already caused George to withdraw into himself; now, to cope with illness, he withdrew still further. 'The car takes me to the sanatorium through the morning streets,' he writes of the young patient in *A Seat by My Bed*, who is quickly diagnosed with TB. 'Though everything is familiar, everything is suddenly strange and new – the women in the shop door, the starlings on the pavement, the piece of newspaper blown down a close. I feel like a man going to prison for some nameless crime. I am an exile, and I must will myself to be an exile, so that I can endure this banishment.'

Yet there was a part of George that welcomed exile – that had even, in a sense, invited it. 'I think,' he once wrote in a letter to a friend, 'there must be a secret wisdom inside us all that directs our lives, often against our wills and desires', and he saw this wisdom at work in his illness. Tuberculosis had freed him, for the time being, from all responsibility for his future, and the disease became, from now on, his 'ally', real but also psychosomatic, returning to rescue him at critical junctures from developments in his life that he feared or felt unable to face.

Even the prospect of death left George, 'after a first qualm of dread', calm, almost glad. At a time of war, it seemed to many contemptible for a young man to languish in a hospital ward. One should die in the field, Rupert Brooke had written to John Drinkwater in 1915, not 'coughing out a civilian soul amid bedclothes and disinfectant and gulping medicines'. But for George there was a certain romance about TB. 'How better to die than to take the road that Keats, Francis Thompson, Emily Brontë, had taken,' he wrote, 'and, like them, soon rather than late?'; and a poem written when he was on the road to recovery suggests that he felt almost cheated of an early death:

> At the door of the house called death I knocked
> Seeking admittance, but no one answered.
>> The sound of my knocking
>> Echoed in lonely halls.
>
> . . .
>
> Inside, I knew, was a flowering tree
> Of plenty, nourished with fallen blood.
>> There hung ripe fruit, whose taste
>> Was immortality . . .

As George lay in the sanatorium, wallowing in morbidity and drifting in and out of sleep, Orkney had never felt more thoroughly alive. Having recovered from the initial shock of finding themselves in a windswept, treeless outpost, miles from home, most servicemen were coming to love the islands. The Orcadians, in turn, had taken the troops to their hearts. Though in theory rationing was in force in Orkney just like everywhere else, in practice there was a never-ending supply of beef and poultry, bacon, eggs and cheese. Servicemen boarding the *Earl of Zetland* to go on leave were weighed down by the islanders with local produce for their hungry families further south. A frenetic social life, too, had begun to flourish. The troops organized quizzes, French lessons, debates, mock trials and, above all, dances. 'One could go dancing every night if one so wished,' Ruby remembered. In Stromness, the Town Hall swung to the music of Roy Fox, Jack Payne, and Henry Hall, and a concrete bathing shelter at the south end of the town became a favourite trysting spot. Week by week, the latest liaisons between servicemen and local girls were reported in the troops' newspaper, the *Orkney Blast*, in a column headed 'Romance in Orcadia'. 'Used to their laconic suitors from the farms,' George reflected wryly, the young women of Orkney 'never had such palaver and attention'.

It was not just the young and single who were enjoying themselves. Anne Ridler, poet and former assistant to T. S. Eliot, moved up to Orkney in the spring of 1942 to join her husband, Vivian, who had been posted there by the RAF. The welcome she and her small daughter were given by the local people was so warm that when, years later, she looked back through her wartime diaries, she could hardly believe that she had been in the islands only two and a half months. She was struck by the Orcadians' interest in the arts. Mr Johnson, the Ridlers' Kirkwall landlord, recited Burns by heart after tea; Mr Jackson, the organist at St Magnus Cathedral, gave her organ lessons. And, when she handed over her papers to obtain ration books at the local food office, the woman behind the counter immediately looked up and asked whether she was the Anne Ridler who had edited *A Little Book of Modern Verse.**

Cultural life in Orkney burgeoned as a result of the war. In an effort to keep the troops occupied, ENSA[†] set up cinemas and theatres, and the islanders became used to the sight of West End stars – Gracie Fields, John Mills, Bernard Miles, George Formby – stepping wind-blown down the gangplank of the *St Ola*. Yehudi Menuhin visited the sailors of Scapa Flow and gave a solo violin concert in the garrison cinema on Hoy. First on the programme was unaccompanied Bach, then he took requests from the audience and played music-hall songs such as 'In a Monastery Garden' and 'I'll Walk Beside You'. In Stromness, civilians and servicemen met in a room above Tulloch's Draper Shop to read Shakespeare plays. In Kirkwall, Donald Hewlett, an energetic young sub-lieutenant of the Fleet Air Arm, launched an arts club, and quickly signed up several hundred members. They met in the disused basement of the Temperance Hall, and Dame Sybil Thorndike travelled to Orkney as one of their first speakers. John Gielgud became their patron.

By the autumn of 1940, all these activities could be undertaken in an atmosphere of relative security and peace. Deterred by the density of anti-aircraft fire and searchlights ringing Scapa Flow, the German bombers had bit by bit reduced their forays over the islands. Then, in

---

*Published by Faber & Faber in November 1941.
[†]The Entertainments National Service Association.

the summer of 1941, the air raids ceased altogether, as the Luftwaffe's full force was directed against the Russian front. George remembered wandering through Eastbank on the morning of 22 June and hearing of the invasion of Russia from a clergyman and fellow patient: 'He was, I think, a Congregational minister, and had been on his way to Iceland to minister to the troops when he had a lung haemorrhage. The troopship had put in at the nearest port, Kirkwall, and there the Revd Collins-Williams lay, slowly recovering. "Whom the gods wish to destroy, they first make mad," he said to me, referring of course to Hitler.'

George, too, was by this time recovering, and finding life in the sanatorium surprisingly congenial. Elsewhere in Britain at the time, TB sufferers were being herded into draconian village settlements and training colonies. Idleness, it was thought, might encourage 'loafing' habits and lead to physical and mental deterioration, and patients were compelled to spend their time thoroughly occupied in carpentry or craft classes, or in hard, outdoor, physical labour. But at Eastbank, with its twelve beds for women and twelve for men, the routine was gentle, the food excellent and the atmosphere so buoyant that Margaret Johnston, after a lifetime in nursing, looks back on it as 'the happiest place I ever worked'. There were jewellery-making classes for the women, and rug-making classes for the men, but these George managed to avoid. He was very charming, Margaret Johnston remembers – mischievous, good-humoured and keen on practical jokes – and he had a knack of getting his own way. Soon after arriving, he had persuaded the doctor in charge to give him the only one-bed ward in the sanatorium, and here, after several months of rest and good food, he began the slow process of recuperation:

> First the seat by the bed, while the nurses turn the mattress; next the brief uncertain walk to the toilet; next the half hour in the sitting room, changed from a horizontal man to a vertical man, spilling out your thirty minutes like a miser counting gold; next the stroll to the gate, in your clothes, you and the cow in the farm across the road looking at each other with equal wonderment; then the first real slice of liberty, walking to the town, nodding to folk in the street, looking in shop windows, treading on the cobbles as lightly as a butterfly escaped at last from the high-walled cabbage garden.

Kirkwall is just fifteen miles down a good road from Stromness. Yet, on his walks out from the sanatorium in the late summer of 1941, George seems to have been exploring Orkney's capital for the first time. He was now nearly twenty-one, and the largest building he had ever set foot in was the Auld Kirk in Stromness, built in 1814. When he wandered one afternoon into St Magnus Cathedral, which had stood in the centre of Kirkwall for more than eight hundred years, the experience was overwhelming. The foundations of the cathedral had been laid in 1137, at the orders of Rognvald Kolson, an Orkney earl of sufficient wealth and standing to employ masons from Durham. They worked chiefly in red sandstone, so that entering the cathedral feels rather like stepping into a rose-pink forest. On either side of the nave, seven massive, round columns soar upwards to support first rounded, and then, higher still, pointed arches, giving an impression both of immense height and space, and of powerful, rooted solidity. It is the Durham masons, Eric Linklater wrote, who must take credit for the beauty of the architecture – 'and yet it is a very *native* church, for the old rock of Orkney has been shaped with an extraordinary strength and grace to proclaim the glory of God and yet not lose its persistent kinship with the island cliffs'.

The thrill George experienced as he stepped into the cathedral for the first time was not just aesthetic but visceral. He felt at home in the place, and at home with the Norse generations for whom it had been conceived and built in the days when Orkney was prosperous, independent of Scotland, and Catholic. Around the walls were tombs reaching back well beyond the Reformation, and in a pillar to the left of the altar was the cloven skull of Saint Magnus. The thought flashed through George's mind that, when he died, this was where he wanted to be buried.

But the threat of death had, for the moment, receded. In October 1941, George was discharged from Eastbank. Yet he was not cured, the doctor warned him as he left, and there was no question of his being strong enough to lead a normal life. Mhairi Brown took him back into Well Park and, despite her own poverty, did all she could to look after him. It was believed that cholesterol was good for TB victims, and, after making George's bed in the morning, she brought him up an egg for breakfast, and a small pot of cream. For lunch every day she cooked him three full courses – soup, meat, pudding – and she baked for him in the afternoon. She washed, ironed and mended his clothes, and polished his shoes, and she asked for nothing in return. George was left in peace in his small bedroom, and the apparently empty hours he spent alone there were invaluable to him. 'There was,' he wrote to a friend in 1982, 'an abundance of leisure for literature (reading), for the imagination to be free while the body lay with those light chains on it, and to prepare for creativity to come: but writing was still far off, under the horizon.'

Propped up against his pillows one winter afternoon, George opened for the first time a book that was to affect him more profoundly than any other piece of literature he ever read. The *Orkneyinga Saga* tells the story of three centuries of the Orkney earldom under Norse rule, and is the distillation of poetry, stories and songs handed down from generation to generation over hundreds of years. It seems likely that the *Saga* was set down in Iceland some time in the early thirteenth century, but by whom, nobody knows. This, in itself, immediately recommended it to George who, like Thomas Mann, believed that poetry should be 'anonymous and communal', and who looked back longingly to an age of oral tradition when 'everyone knew the poem, and nobody worried about the author, for in a deep sense they knew that they all contributed to its making'. As he turned the pages of the *Orkneyinga Saga*, he was struck by the same feeling as when he wandered off the streets of Kirkwall into St Magnus Cathedral. He was at home with the language of the *Saga*: a pure, poetic prose, stripped of extraneous detail and description; and the characters whose stories it told struck him as vivid and compelling.

One man intrigued George more than any other. Early in the eleventh century, the earldom of Orkney had been divided between two cousins, Hakon Paulsson and Magnus Erlendson. Magnus, the *Saga* relates, had not only all the attributes one would seek in a ruler and statesman, but also saintly qualities. For many years, he and Hakon got on well enough, but eventually their friendship was undermined by 'men of evil dispositions', and they fell out. In April 1117, the cousins met on the island of Egilsay, purportedly to negotiate peace. It had been agreed that each should bring with him no more than two ships. Hakon, however, sailed to the small island with eight, fully manned and armed. For the sake of peace, Magnus surrendered himself to his cousin. He was executed by Hakon's cook, Lifolf, on Easter Monday, and he walked to his death, in the words of the *Saga*, 'as cheerful as if he were invited to a banquet'. Magnus's body was carried to Birsay, and the poor and afflicted of the islands were soon flocking to it as a place of pilgrimage, and claiming miracles on his behalf. In 1134, he was acclaimed a saint.

Amidst the tales of Viking intrigue and revenge, the martyrdom of Magnus shone out, for George, 'like a precious stone'. 'For me,' he wrote, 'Magnus was at once a solid convincing flesh-and-blood man, from whom pure spirit flashed from time to time.' His death by axe-stroke became the 'still centre' around which much of George's thought and work now began to move.

With a growing feeling for the subjects he wanted to explore, George was writing more and more. Some time during 1942 he wrote a play set in the Viking period. It was his first substantial piece of work, and on completing it he experienced 'a small but agreeable surge of power'. Walking through Stromness the following day, he felt, for the first time, like a free townsman: 'I had made something that I knew in my bones to be good.' He typed it out laboriously on an old typewriter and sent it off to Eric Linklater, who was living with his young family by the Loch of Harray, and he was encouraged by Linklater's kind, constructive response. The lugubrious, melancholy poems of his teenage years, meanwhile, were giving way to more individual, experimental work. Towards the end of his time at Stromness Academy, George had been introduced by an English master, Ian Paterson, to the poetry of Auden, Pound, MacDiarmid and Eliot. He had spent most of his school years believing that poetry was a thing of the past – that 'the mighty harvests had been reaped' – and it was a revelation to him to discover that there was a contemporary, dynamic literary world. Then, during 1944, he found himself enjoying the company of a published poet who moved in literary circles both in Scotland and in London.

While the Nissen huts that had sprung up around Stromness provided housing for the rank-and-file soldiers, more senior officers were given rooms with local people. By chance, the officer billeted with the Brown family during 1944 was a university lecturer as well as an established poet, Francis Scarfe, about ten years George's senior. The months that Scarfe spent in Well Park enriched George's life immeasurably. Together they sat long into the evenings discussing poetry, and Scarfe infected George with his own passion for the work of Dylan Thomas and of D. H. Lawrence. He also introduced him to classical music. In his autobiography, George recalls the day that Scarfe brought over from the large wooden hut that housed the offices and library of the Army Education Corps a small wind-up gramophone, and 78 r.p.m. discs of Mendelssohn's Violin Concerto: 'My ears brimmed with enchantment! There followed "Eine Kleine Nachtmusik", a Mozart horn concerto, Schubert's Fifth Symphony, Beethoven's Eighth and Ninth symphonies. The great outpouring of joy in the choral movement bewildered and excited me.' His spirits strengthened as he listened, and he later believed that music had helped him to opt, inwardly, for life. George had no income at this time except for a small weekly allowance of £1 10s, paid by the government to TB sufferers – and of this he paid £1 each week to his mother. Somehow, however, he scraped together the money to buy his own radiogram and began to build up a small library of 78s. He acquired a recording of T. S. Eliot reading from his poetry, and played it so often and so loudly that Mhairi and Ruby Brown began to go about their housework chanting chunks of *The Waste Land* and *Murder in the Cathedral*.

Most valuable of all, however, were the evenings George spent with Francis Scarfe at the kitchen table writing poetry. Scarfe was an astute critic. He noted, in particular, George's gift for combining 'matter-of-factness and imagination'. More than sixty years on, this is the gift that Seamus Heaney singles out for praise. 'George's writing,' Heaney reflects, 'was crosslit in a way that always appeals to me. On the one hand, there was a daytime reliability to it, these scenes and characters could be lifted from a documentary; on the other hand, they could have been dreamt, there was a gleam of the uncanny at the northern and western horizon.' Warmed by Scarfe's encouragement, George began to write with a new determination and confidence:

> There are no forests in Orkney;
>   Only, blossoming in storms,
> The dark swaying boughs of the sea.

There are no trains in Orkney;
>Only great winds roaring through the land
From the beginning to the end of eternity.

There is no respectability in Orkney;
>Only what the blood dictates
Is done. Spirit and mind are free.

And there are no poets in Orkney;
>Stirred by breeze and blood and ocean
I set the trumpet to my lips. I only.

Between George's moments of resolute elation, however, came moments of despair, when the reality of his situation as a penniless invalid was borne in on him. Early in 1945, Francis Scarfe was ordered to a new posting, outside Orkney; within months of his departure, the war was over. One by one, the Nissen-hut villages were dismantled. Shipload by shipload, the troops left the islands. Soon, the only reminders of the war were the concrete lookout posts dotted about the cliffs – scars on the landscape that time and rain and wind have never mellowed. In Stromness, life shrank slowly back into its old rhythms and, for the younger people at least, there was a guilty feeling of anti-climax. 'Suddenly,' Ruby remembered, 'we were back to pre-war quietness – even loneliness, and a certain flatness.' Ruby had particular reason to feel dispirited. In 1940, she had married Ted Ogilvie, an architecture student from Aberdeen. Shortly after their marriage, he was posted overseas to serve with the Royal Engineers in Egypt, and in 1942 he was killed at the Battle of El Alamein.*

George, too, seemed to his family and friends to be in a poor way. In August 1944, James Twatt, the proprietor of the *Orkney Herald*, had offered him a job as Stromness correspondent, and he had begun to travel every Monday morning to the newspaper's offices in Kirkwall to help correct the galley proofs. But while this helped to fill his time, and while his reporting of local news – 'often delivered more out of imag-ination than fact' – gave him an impish amusement, he knew that

---

*Ruby married again, in 1947, an ex-serviceman, John Ross. To her brother Jackie it seemed that Ted Ogilvie had been her true love, and that she never quite recov-ered from his death.

journalism could never fulfil his real talents and ambitions; nor did there appear to be any prospect of their ever finding a satisfactory outlet. To his friend Ian MacInnes, the chances of George's embarking on a literary career seemed, at this time, to be nil. 'When the war came to an end,' MacInnes remembered, 'George was a very unhappy lad indeed.'

Norrie's wife, Hazel, had the same impression. George and his brother Norrie were close. They had a similar sense of humour and they shared a passion for literature. They liked to recite poetry together and the poem to which they always returned, as if to a refrain, was Tennyson's 'Crossing the Bar':

> Sunset and evening star,
>   And one clear call for me!
> And may there be no moaning of the bar,
>   When I put out to sea . . .

It was poignant to hear George speak these words, Hazel remembers, because, though it was never articulated, nobody was expecting him to survive even to the age of thirty. 'Puir Georgie', Mhairi Brown now called her youngest son; and 'puir' he seemed to nearly everyone.

It took a relative outsider to see things differently. Gerry Meyer, a private with the Royal Army Ordnance Corps, and a former Fleet Street journalist, had been posted to Orkney in October 1940, and had soon after been appointed editor of the *Orkney Blast*. At a dance for servicemen, Meyer met a local girl, Nora Hancox. They were married shortly after the end of the war, and settled in Stromness. The people of Stromness fascinated Meyer, and on some unrecorded date he began to jot down his impressions of a number of them, 'George Brown' included. Meyer's pen portrait of George is fond but not uncritical. In appearance, he writes, George is dishevelled – 'thin and cadaverous with an untidy mop of jet-black hair and ill-assorted dress'. His table manners are atrocious. In person, he finds George generous, loyal, humorous and lovable, but at the same time obstinate, unreliable and lazy. Meyer has no doubt that George is exceptionally talented, with 'deep unknown possibilities'; but he is concerned that sloth and lack of discipline might prevent his talents from ever bearing fruit. George Brown, he concludes, is 'the stuff that failures and geniuses are made of. Who knows?'

6

Tir-nan-Og

But the fairest region of all Hoy is the valley of Rackwick, which lies, shut in with mountains, on the north-west coast of the island. Many say that these few acres are the loveliest in Orkney – and, indeed, on a still summer evening, with invisible larks spilling enchantment into the valley, the magic of Rackwick has power to bind a man's heart for ever.

GMB, *Let's See the Orkney Islands* (1948)

WHEN A FRIEND once confided in George her belief in reincarnation, he was quick to respond that he hoped it would prove unfounded. There had been enough pain in his present life for him 'not to be an Oliver Twist and ask for more'. The years following the Second World War were as painful as any. In a way, George wrote, they were wasted years, 'years that the locusts ate'. He was drifting through what felt like a 'desert of time', dragging out a semi-invalid existence in which the weeks seemed to fold greyly into one another with little achieved, and less to hope for. This is how, removed to the safety of the third person, he described his typical day for readers of the *Orkney Herald*:

He wakens about 9 a.m., after a long, dreamless sleep of nine hours. His breakfast is brought up to bed. He eyes it with distaste – he is never hungry at this time of the morning.

He casts a bleary eye through the bedroom window. It is a rainy morning, and swabs of wind rattle the pane. He pulls the bed-clothes up to his chin, turns over on his other side, and drowses deliciously.

When he awakes the next time, he finds that the breakfast tea is grey and cold. He pours it into a suitable receptacle that he keeps under his bed, and begins to chew, with infinite languor, on the toast and egg, which have already grown cold. From downstairs float the last few tunes of 'Housewives' Choice'.

He is now almost fully awake, and begins to read, his head plentifully propped up with pillows. He reads steadily till half-an-hour after noon; at which time he heaves himself out of bed, fingers his bristly chin, and wonders if he will need a shave to-day. His ablutions are over before dinner, for he hates to have dinner unwashed.

The rest of his day seemed scarcely more productive. In a profile of George in the *Orcadian*, Gerry Meyer described how, on most afternoons, he could be found sitting on a bench at the Pierhead picking up local gossip, a Fair Isle scarf twined several times round his neck, hands sunk low into the pockets of a black overcoat, chin jutting out from beneath a 'black, dishevelled, Maxton-like mop of hair'.[*]

When later in life George looked back on these years, however, it was with gratitude as well as pity; for in the midst of the drift and despondency came 'certain very intense experiences' that profoundly affected the way he thought and wrote. Perhaps the most important of these took place one Sunday in the summer of 1946 when he sailed with a group of friends to the island of Hoy.

Hoy's massive, scarred hills, the Coolags, had been a constant presence in George's life since earliest infancy. Rising out of the sea just a mile south of Stromness, they loom across the water, in the words of Eric Linklater, 'like a lion couchant', impossible to ignore. In winter, they are forbidding, streaked for weeks on end with snow; but on a fine summer evening their lower slopes look lush, emerald green and inviting. Few visitors stay long in Stromness today before being tempted to cross in the *Graemsay* and explore the island. But in the first half of the twentieth century visiting Hoy was not so straightforward. There was no ferry, because the island had no proper pier. Even cattle transported from Stromness had to swim the last 200 yards to shore. When George set foot on Hoy that June morning, it was quite likely for the first time.

---

[*]James Maxton was a leading figure in the Independent Labour Party in Scotland in the early twentieth century, and a passionate campaigner for pacifism during the Second World War. From a low parting on the left, he wore his thick, dark hair swept across his forehead.

In a lorry borrowed from a farmer, he and his friends followed the road that winds westward across the island. He described the journey for his *Herald* readers:

> The scenery through which we were now passing was dark and savage, with immense heather-clad hills on each side of us, and a grim valley strewn with immense boulders and outcrops of rock. But the lonely grandeur of the place was overwhelming. Not for nothing did the Vikings call it 'the high island' – Hoy. There are certainly islands in Scotland much higher than Hoy, but none, I am convinced, is so haunted by the genius of grandeur and desolation.

After five miles the road petered out into a cart-track. A croft came into sight, and then the sea. Finally emerging from the hills, George and his friends found themselves in Rackwick, an immense, green, fertile valley, sloping gently down to a mile-long sandy beach bordered with boulders the shape and size of seals. Reaching into the sea at either end of the beach were towering red sandstone cliffs – the 'Sneuk' and the 'Too'. Between these were enormous views out across the Atlantic. 'The beauty of Rackwick struck me like a blow,' George wrote of that first visit. No other place was ever to move him more deeply. From that day on, the valley came to represent for him a 'Tir-nan-Og' – an earthly paradise, or land of lost content. It was a source of inexhaustible inspiration, and of 'deep, indescribable peace and security'.

Four weeks running, George poured out his excitement about Rackwick in the *Orkney Herald*. It was, he wrote, the kind of valley that Tennyson might have had in mind in 'Morte d'Arthur' when he set the king on the road to his final resting place – a valley

> Where falls not hail, or rain, or any snow,
> Nor ever wind blows loudly; but it lies
> Deep-meadow'd, happy, fair with orchard-lawns
> And bowery hollows crown'd with summer sea,
> Where I will heal me of my grievous wound.

And perhaps, George urged, Rackwick actually was Avilion: no one, after all, has ever known the exact location of Arthur's island valley, and Orkney was one of the distant parts of his kingdom.

For all its loveliness, an air of tragedy hovered about the valley. It was clear that, not so very long ago, it had been home to a thriving community. Its slopes were dotted with stone croft houses: Reumin, Mucklehouse, Burnmouth, Ootroo, Scar. Most had been abandoned. Their doors were falling in, their roofs collapsed, their ploughs and locks and three-toed cooking pots smouldering in 'a slow fire of rust'. Of the handful of people left living in Rackwick, most were old; of four children, two would not reach adulthood. If George could have looked ahead twenty-five years, he would have seen just one farmer left working the valley.

Rackwick began to haunt George's imagination, so that when, more than twenty years later, he came to write about it at length in *An Orkney Tapestry*, he had a clear picture in his mind of the first settlers arriving in their longships, of how they had gradually cultivated the valley, and of how their labours had been intertwined with a life of devotion centred on a small chapel – which never, in fact, existed. He had also formed fierce, eloquent arguments about what had caused Rackwick's close-knit community to fall apart.

In the middle of the nineteenth century, a hundred years before George first saw the valley, Rackwick had a population of 150 working its twenty-eight small crofts. Queen Victoria was still young and happy, and her people followed her in producing larger and larger families. 'The whole nation seemed to burgeon,' George wrote, 'procreation was all . . . The very hens in those years had larger broods.' This remote corner of her kingdom was no exception. In Rackwick, many of the crofts housed families of twelve or fourteen. There were almost more children than the valley could support. While women worked the fields, growing oats, hay, cabbages and bere, and tending sheep and chickens, their men set out at first light to negotiate the ferocious waters of the Pentland Firth. Old photographs show them returning in the early afternoon in yawls slung about with haddock, halibut and cod.

Until 1927, there was no road leading to and from the valley. When a Rackwick woman went into labour, a 'howdie-wife' was summoned from the township of Braebister on the north-west of the island to assist at the birth. When somebody died, the coffin had to be shouldered five miles over the hills to the nearest kirkyard.

Otherwise, the people of Rackwick were almost completely independent of the rest of the world, with their own cobbler, dressmaker,
wheelwright and school. John Bremner, born in the valley in 1899,
has left an account of an 'aura of contentment' and spirit of mutual
support among its inhabitants that makes Rackwick sound like a
miniature Eden:

> If a crofter was behind in his work by reason of ill-health, or other mis-
> fortune, the whole community would turn out to give him a helping
> hand. Whether in the spring, or the peat-cutting season, or in the
> harvest-time, no one ever asked for help in vain. You never knocked
> at a door in our hamlet; had you done so, you would have been looked
> on as a snob. You just lifted the 'sneck', and walked in. And the famil-
> iar greeting would be 'Come thee wis inbye' . . . When the boats
> would return from the day's fishing, the widow's share was first to be
> given. Even the wandering beggars who now and again made their way
> to Rackwick never went away empty handed or hungry. And no one
> was any the poorer for the bounty thus dispensed. In the Hoy district,
> there were a few 'puir boddies' who were always allocated a share of
> fresh fish, from each boat's crew, and it was, in every sense, a true inter-
> pretation of the words of the Bible: 'Cast thy bread upon the waters,
> for thou shalt find it after many days'; in return, these folk gave their
> help freely in the busy periods of the year.

There was, of course, a darker side to this picture, and George was
well aware of it: 'Evil is universal,' he wrote, 'and the simpler the society
the starker it appears.' Life for the people of Rackwick was tough,
and so were they. The land that the women were forced to work was
wet and spongy; the soil almost impossibly light. In the spring, young
lambs were sometimes lost to birds of prey, and in the winter, sheep
were often carried away by high tides. Between May and September,
the valley was plagued with midges. In the men of Rackwick, daily
negotiating the treacherous cliffs and the dangers of the Pentland Firth,
the harsh life bred a canny ingenuity. It was two young Rackwick men,
James Drever and Andrew Thompson, who spotted in the late nineteenth century that the methods employed in the valley for holding up
farming overalls might be adapted to secure women's stockings. They
travelled to America and registered the patent for the clips on suspender
belts.

But this resourcefulness could take a crueller turn. Before the arrival of lighthouses, shipwrecks were common on the coast of Hoy — Rackwick, in Norse, means 'bay of wreckage' — and they were welcomed by the islanders. In *An Orkney Tapestry*, George quotes from an account left by a nineteenth-century journalist, J. R. Tudor, of a freezing night in November 1815, when a Blyth ship, *Albion*, was driven ashore just around the coast from Rackwick near the Old Man of Hoy:

> Only two of the crew were left on the ill-fated craft, all the rest had been washed overboard. Of the two survivors one was lashed to the rigging, the other was lying insensible on the deck. Such was the state of things, when some fishermen from Rackwick, clambering down through a cleft in the rocks, boarded the vessel and proceeded, as was the custom in those days, to plunder the cargo. Having done so, they carried the man who had been lying on the deck, ashore, and left him on a shelf of the cliff, still alive . . . That these savages could easily have removed the man to the summit of the cliffs, and thence to shelter, was proved by their dragging up a companion, who had got drunk on the rum they had found on board. The next day the unfortunate seaman was found dead, as also his messmate who had been made fast to the rigging, and who the wreckers, in their hurry to plunder, had overlooked.

Nor did this ruthlessness prevent the men of Hoy from adopting, when they chose to, a high moral line whose consequences could be equally devastating. On the moors a few miles from Rackwick a white headstone surrounded by a picket fence marks the grave of a girl called Betty Corrigall. Some time in the early nineteenth century, Betty became pregnant by a sailor who then abandoned her. Knowing that both she and her illegitimate child would be social outcasts, she was driven to despair. She tried to drown herself by walking into the sea, but was rescued. Then she hanged herself in her parents' byre. Denied a grave on consecrated ground, she was buried instead on the moor, on the border between two parishes. In his short story 'Betty Corrigall', based on fact, George imagines her burial, and the uncanny rediscovery of her corpse more than a century later:

> The gravedigger consulted a map of Hoy with a thin line going across, then sank in his spade again. And there the gravedigger and the father let down the sodden body of Betty Corrigall, with her head in Voes

parish and her feet in Hoy parish. Then the gravedigger lit his pipe on the windy moor, and the father opened a whisky flask and passed it to him.

And while that generation of islanders withered slowly into death, one after another, and after death rotted more urgently until they achieved the cleanness of skeletons, the deep peat moss kept the body of Betty Corrigall uncorrupted; though stained and darkened with the essences that had preserved it.

Soldiers in the Second World War, digging drains in the moor, came on the body of Betty Corrigall as it lay crosswise with the line of the two parishes. The young men looked with wonderment into a face that had lingered sweet and beautiful from, it seemed, the first springs of time.

Despite the toughness, there seemed to George something essentially good about the rhythm of the Rackwick crofter-fishermen's lives, and the endless cycle of 'birth, love, labour, death' that had gone on unchanged in the valley generation after generation. He had always had a strong feeling for the past. Now, the experiences of a war, coupled with long months lying in the circumscribed world of the sanatorium, had given him a distaste for the future, a suspicion that almost any new development was a development for the worse. What had done for Rackwick, George decided, was 'progress'.

Late but ineluctable, changes in the outside world had begun to filter through to the valley. At the end of the nineteenth century, a Kirkwall merchant, Robert Gordon, had bought five sailing smacks and converted them into floating shops. Once a fortnight, the *Gleaner* sailed into the bay, offering tea and sugar in exchange for eggs, dried fish, cheese and knitted stockings. Gradually, the people of the valley acquired an appetite for 'the gifts of progress': 'rubber boots, primus stoves, novels, religious tracts, lemonade, Tilley lamps, cloth caps, bicycles, fly papers, cough mixture, marmalade . . .' It sounds an almost absurdly innocent list, but George was convinced that in commodities like these lay the seeds of destruction, breeding in the men and women of Rackwick a dangerous sense both of avarice and of inferiority.

'The notion of progress,' George argues in *An Orkney Tapestry*, 'is not easy to take root in an elemental community; the people are conservative, cling hard to tradition which is their only sure foothold and the ground of all their folk wisdom and art and of the precarious crafts by which they lived.' By the beginning of the twentieth century, however, the old ways of life in Rackwick were being fatally challenged. A small school had been built high on one side of the valley. Forty-odd children trooped to their lessons every morning, each carrying a peat to keep the classroom fire going. Over time, George believed, education planted in these children a sense of shame at their 'dung and fish-gut trades'. The boys began to feel that working in an office, or serving behind the counter of a shop, was somehow superior to the arduous round of fishing, ploughing and harvesting. The girls learned that, rather than stay at home to work the crofts, they could move away and train as nurses or teachers. Literature, George imagined, fuelled their unease: 'The novels that dribbled into the valley showed them Sir Sylvester and Lady Jasmine tangled in emotional delicacies very different (and, they tacitly assumed, superior) to their own primitive lustings and delights.'

Newspapers opened their eyes to an enormous new world: 'they began, with a sense of fatuous freedom, to argue in the crofts about Gladstone's Irish policy and free trade versus protection; and the advertisements told them there was no illness, from toothache to consumption, that couldn't be cured with Holbrook's pills; and there was no dark place anywhere that couldn't be mapped and civilised and evangelised'. A gramophone came to Rackwick, 'and the fiddle hung at the wall like a dry chrysalis'. One by one, the young people left the valley; one by one, the crofts were abandoned. 'The notion of progress is a cancer,' George concluded, 'that makes an elemental community look better, and induces a false euphoria, while it drains the life out of it remorselessly.'

Rackwick crystallized for George attitudes that had been forming in him since adolescence. Towards the end of the war, his pieces in the *Orkney Herald*, originally intended to cover Stromness news – measles epidemics, dances, Girl Guide sales – had developed into a weekly column signed 'Islandman', in which he engaged in knockabout polemics about the state of the world and, in particular, of Orkney. Again and again, he warmed to the same recalcitrant theme, resisting almost every initiative on the part of the island authorities, urging his readers to recognize that, by pinning their hopes on prosperity and progress, they were building a future on quicksand. On 8 May 1945, for example, George lashes out against the council housing schemes – like the one in which he was living – springing up around Stromness. 'They are,' he concedes, 'healthy, sanitary, commodious dwelling-houses, and nobody can deny it. But . . . regarded from the outside, no uglier, more insipid, more uninspiring pieces of architecture could be imagined.' In the same piece, he pours scorn on the growing enthusiasm for the installation of a public swimming pool in the town:

> Do I want to see Stromness with a swimming-pool? To be quite frank, I don't. Swimming-pools are primarily intended for inland towns, the inhabitants of which have little opportunity for sea-bathing. In Orkney we have the great Atlantic Ocean foaming at our very doors. Nature has provided us with a bathing-pool that stretches all the way to America.*

This inland-island distinction went deep with George, and he made no bones about his belief that the opening up of Orkney to the rest of Britain as a result of the war had been almost wholly detrimental. 'War changes many things for the worse,' he writes on 25 March 1947. 'One of the most lamentable imports from the south is Suspicion. Life becomes treacherous and slippery when we can no more trust one another. Since 1939 this uncanny state of things has come to pass. Now the doors are locked, back and fore. Robberies, almost unheard of among Orkney folk only a few years ago, are now becoming disquietingly common. The simple trust and mutual confidence that bound the lives of our fathers into such a wonderful unity are now no more.' With the war over, he argued, it was surely time that island life – 'enriched by many thousands of pounds, and a few unwanted children' – should 'flow again in the old channels'.

But the 'old channels' were the last thing that Orcadians wanted. Like Ruby, many of them missed the servicemen, and most felt that the war years had helped Orkney to develop in ways that they wanted to build on, not forsake. The island roads had been improved, and more and more Orcadians now had cars. Farms were slowly becoming mechanized. 'Unique System of Cultivation by Tractor', ran a headline in the

---

*A public swimming pool was finally installed in Stromness in 1969. There are now also swimming pools on Hoy, Sanday, Stronsay and Westray.

Herald in September 1946, and, a month later, 'The New Ferguson Tractor Is Now Here!' Gradually, the plough horses were being put out to pasture.

For Stromness, the most thrilling innovation came in the spring of 1947. 'The time,' reports the *Orkney Herald*,

> was 4.15 last Thursday afternoon, May the first. A small company of local councillors and representatives of the Hydro-Electric Board was gathered in the Alfred Café, Stromness (proprietor Mr Stewart Banks).
>
> Provost Robertson, newly home from the Convention of Scottish Royal Burghs, called upon Councillor Mrs Ella Clouston to do her duty.
>
> Councillor Clouston mounted the stepladder, inserted the main switch, and the café was flooded with light. All present clapped heartily and smiled with gratification. For at that moment, 4.17 p.m. to be precise, the reign of electricity began in Stromness.

Ali Thomson, the lamplighter, had ceased his evening rounds when the blackout was enforced in 1939; and in the course of the war many of the old gas lamps had been damaged by heavy traffic. Now, electric lights were erected along the street. There were no more nights on which Stromness was bathed only in the silver glow of the full moon.

Every step forward fuelled an appetite for another. On maps of Britain, Orkney and Shetland had customarily been displayed in an inset box, floating misleadingly somewhere in the Moray Firth. A movement now grew among islanders to insist that cartographers present the islands in their true position. Literally, and metaphorically, Orcadians wanted Orkney put on the map, and George's backward-yearning views fell on deaf ears.

Unabashed, he continued to hurl criticism not just at the notion of 'progress', but at the degeneracy of his fellow Orkneymen – 'poor remnants of a once mighty race'. They had, George argued, become prim, respectable and mean-spirited; they had lost the vigour and flair of their ancestors. The young people of the islands no longer knew even how to name their children. 'Look up the names of your ancestresses,' he writes in his column on New Year's Day 1946,

> and you will find such homely combinations as Mary-Ann, Maggie-Jean, Bella-Jessie, Georgina, Charlesina, Jamesina, with an occasional Biblical name such as Deborah, Ruth, etc. It's needless to tell you of

the vast change that has taken place in this dark century. Nowadays, when unto us a daughter is born . . . off goes the proud father to the Registrar and . . . calls the poor child Phoebe, or Felicity, or Yvonne, or some similar cacophony.

He himself would do better: 'My family will be named as follows, when they come: Bella, Lizzie, Thora, Ignibiora, Freya, Magnus, Jock, Olaf, Harald, etc., etc. I think, in consideration to my future wife, that I had better stop there.'

Whether George really imagined that he would one day be a married man and a father is not clear; but, given the views on women that he was expressing in his *Herald* column, he would have had some difficulty in finding himself a wife, at least among his readers. The 'ridiculous pampering of women,' he argued, was more than anything else responsible for rotting the twentieth century at its foundations.

> For we stand up to give them seats on buses, though they have legs thicker and stronger than we have. We allow them to take over the pleasures which for a very long time have been regarded as men's exclusively – smoking, beer-drinking, clubbing together. We are even talking about the necessity of giving them equal pay.

Orkney women, he conceded, did have a role in the life of the islands, but they must realize that it could only be played out in 'humble' ways: 'baking bere-bannocks over red peat-fires', brewing ale for their men, bearing children, knitting socks. Instead of which they were now to be found entering pubs, smoking till they were 'blue in the face', taking jobs as barristers and MPs and lamplighters, and wasting their time on frivolous vanities. 'While on the subject of women and their bad habits,' he writes on 15 January 1946,

> I must say that I consider it in the highest degree ridiculous for Orkney girls to smother their faces in rouge, powder and lipstick. In all the world you will never see girls with such lovely flawlesss complexions as the Orcadians. The sickly-complexioned women in cities use these artificial means to give themselves such exquisite colourings as you possess by nature. Believe me, ladies of Orkney, you make yourselves cheap and ridiculous by your unnecessary use of cosmetics.

If Orkney women were to insist on equality with men, George, for one, was determined to see that they paid for it. 'There is . . . one point that I would like to have cleared up with regard to Women's Equality,' he writes on 30 October 1945.

> Do the ladies realize that it is a two-handed weapon? Do they realize that all the chivalry of life is no more? Do they realize that when they go to the pictures, say, with a young man, they will have to pay for their own ticket? Whenever I take one of my many outings to Kirkwall in the bus, I shall certainly not rise to give some 'brozy' country woman my seat. I shall sit tight.

For anyone who knew George in later life – tactful, careful not to offend, shy, almost to a fault, of confrontation – these pieces strike an unfamiliar note. He himself, looking back towards the end of 1948 on three years of 'Island Diary', was surprised by the tone of some of his work, and by his 'peculiar and perverse gift (if you can call it that) of being able to sneer at people in print; a gift which I am quite innocent of in normal conversation'. His remarks, he admitted, had often been injudicious; he had thrown his weight about 'like a young dog who has never felt the stick'.

If some of his provocative pieces are nothing more than exercises in youthful coat-trailing, others betray an undertow of frustration which is not difficult to understand. George was still living with his mother, cosseted, reliant on his TB allowance and on National Assistance, and with little prospect of ever being either practically or financially independent. In the *Herald*, he argued on several occasions that money meant very little to him; that to be poor was 'one of life's great blessings'. But it was a mixed blessing. In *Greenvoe*, George describes two fishermen, Bert Kerston and Samuel Whaness, striding past the house of the state-dependent simpleton Timmy Folster on their way to their boats. 'To think,' Kerston remarks to Whaness, 'that we have to slave our guts out in every kind of weather, and pay national insurance, to keep bloody scum like that!' George knew very well that many of his neighbours in Stromness regarded the recipients of any kind of state assistance if not as 'bloody scum', then as layabouts and spongers.

In another respect, too, he must have had a nagging awareness that he was increasingly something of an oddity. All his siblings, and many of his friends, were now married; but George, nearly twenty-five when the war ended, had never, as far as one can tell, had even the smallest dalliance with a girl. In his autobiography, he touches on this briefly. It was not, he claims, that he had leanings towards his own sex: 'I had no homosexual urges, apart from one, when I admired another slightly older schoolboy in my class, and for a while couldn't have enough of his company and his talk . . . This infatuation lasted for part of one summer, then broke like a bubble.' It was simply, he says, that 'I never fell in love with anybody, and no woman ever fell in love with me. I used to wonder about this gap in my experience, but it never unduly worried me.'

The truth is less straightforward. George certainly did fall in love, later in his life, and was loved in return; and, even in these post-war years, a number of the poems he was writing in private hover around the theme of tortured and ultimately doomed affairs. In May 1945, he wrote a four-stanza poem, heavy with sadness, and addressed to a 'lover' from whom he has been forced to part.* In July, he wrote three verses, equally desperate in tone, and simply entitled 'Love Poem':

> God, what an evening.
> The islands hidden and the sky
> A blur of gray. The passionate blood-drops
> Trembling, falling with the rain.
>
> I walk alone in my cold room.
> The light talk and laughter
> Of women downstairs floats up,
> A wavering blur of sound.
>
> Still, still the rain falls.
> No happiness on earth or in the sky.
> Centred in a blind universe I stand
> And mourn and mourn till my heart breaks.

A year later, George sent this, with a batch of other poems, to a friend. He was gratified when it was singled out for praise: 'The "Love

---

*This poem later appeared in *The Storm* (1954) as 'Song: Rognvald to Ermengarde', but in the original version the title is simply 'The Winds Embrace You My Lover', and there is no indication that the poem refers to these two characters from the *Orkneyinga Saga*.

Poem" you like best is also one of my favourites,' he wrote, 'though for private painful reasons I doubt if I should ever like to see it in print.' What were these 'private painful reasons'? Possibly, George had suffered some secret, unhappy relationship of which there is now no trace. More probably, this poem was painful for precisely the opposite reason: that its subject – the 'lover' to whom he addresses the first poem – was never in fact a lover at all, except in his imagination. There was, he admitted, no shortage of girls to whom he felt attracted, 'but in their presence I was immediately awkward and with-drawn and put on a frown'. Partly this was due to the physical inse-curity that TB had planted in him; very likely it had also something to do with the degree to which he had remained dependent on his mother. With Mhairi Brown such an all-providing presence in his life, it seems possible that it became at first unnecessary, and then difficult, for George to accept the sexual nature of women, particularly younger ones. Better to snipe at them from the safety of his *Herald* column, and to confine his longings to poems that would almost cer-tainly remain unpublished.

No wonder, then, that depression continued to settle on him from time to time, and that at its root lay a sense of bitter self-loathing. ' "I am gall, I am heartburn",'* he quotes to his *Herald* readers one bleak March morning:

> I look on the lean earth, and loathe it; on the dirty sky, and loathe it; on the ill-natured sea, and loathe it. I hate reading, writing, but sitting with my own unquiet thoughts is worst of all. I hate humanity and the things that the spiteful gods make them do. But above and beyond everything I hate myself; everything about me revolts me beyond belief.

But life was not unremittingly bleak. For every one of George's *Herald* columns that is carping, critical or gloomy, there is another that demonstrates his capacity for joy. He writes with delight of the move-ment of clouds over Hoy, of the night sky in winter, thick with stars, and of April ditches bright with daffodils. He describes how, on the first fine day of spring, he bumped into an old school friend who offered to give him a run in the sidecar of his new motorbike. 'The

---

*From Gerard Manley Hopkins's sonnet 'I wake and feel the fell of dark, not day'.

black mould was aflame with tiny crocuses, the wide sky had great gaps of blue torn in it. Swift gleams of sunshine and shadow chased each other over the house-tops, over the fields, over the distant hills and islands, and were gone. All Nature was alive and dancing.' Together they raced to Yesnaby, a dramatic stretch of coastline six miles north of Stromness, where 'the sea and the land are hopelessly entangled', and watched the waves pound against the cliffs. They came home drugged with sun and wind. 'O, but it was glorious to be alive!' George tells his readers. 'The sap of spring-time rose in my own veins, and I was happy.' And, even when depression did descend, he was becoming disciplined in his response to it. Like his father, George had learned to drop a visor of good-humour over low spirits when he was in company; when alone, he persevered in the belief that depression was not only temporary but in some sense illusory – 'no more a part of my life than the shadow on a tree is part of the living organic tree itself'.

He was becoming disciplined, too, about his poetry. One friend remembers George in the years following the war closeted for hours in his bedroom, with words and phrases written on squares of paper and pinned to the wall above his desk. Experimenting with different forms and styles, he was working and reworking his poems. 'None of them, fortunately, survives,' he writes in his autobiography, talking of these years. In fact, many of them do, carefully typed, dated and signed, suggesting a fixity of purpose to which he would occasionally admit. 'I take this business of poetry very seriously,' George wrote to a friend in 1946. 'Journalism means nothing to me at all, except as a means to gain a livelihood.'

Some of his work – like the love poems written in the spring and summer of 1945 – was private and personal; on the whole, however, even at this early stage, George avoided writing about himself. 'My own life strikes me as a gray, uninteresting thing,' he once wrote, and he was not short of other subjects. He was increasingly aware that Orkney offered 'vast tracts of virgin soil to be ploughed up', and Saint Magnus, in particular, continued to work on his imagination. Magnus was becoming such an ally in George's mind that he had begun to address poetry directly to him, beseeching him to breathe new life into Orkney: 'Magnus Martyr,' he implores in one poem,

Pity us poor islanders

. . .

And after these present days of obscurity
Make our islands famous again.
Renew the blood of our children.
And grant us thy peace.

For all the frustrations and limitations of his life, meanwhile, George
continued to feel the love for Stromness that had moved him, at the
age of eight, to write his first poem. During the cloudless summer of
1947, when not a drop of rain fell on the islands for three months, he
began work on the poem that would, over the following decade,
evolve into 'Hamnavoe', in memory of his father. This early version
follows a summer's day in the life of a hermit living in a cell above a
small fishing town – unnamed, but unmistakably Stromness – and
looking down on it at various moments between dawn and dusk:

> At evening the dark sails returned. The harbour
> Spun with life. Gaelic fisher girls
>   Made melancholy croon
>   Over stinking stalls,
>
> And ragged boys ran home, with bunches
> Of burnished herring. From the dance loft
>   Cups rattling, the screech
>   Of a cracked violin.
>
> Hoy gloomed the Sound. One lyrical star
> Prologued night's pageantry. The shawled harlot
>   Crossed the wet field to
>   The bailie's granite house.
>
> Vanity of vanities! By taper light
> I read how, thralled in Time, men walk blind
>   The cloud-dappled alleys of
>   God's eternal city.

George was aware that much of his work at this time was spoiled by
'attempts to be pious which don't quite come off'; but religion was
preoccupying him more than ever. To Ian MacInnes, it later seemed
that living with TB and the threat of early death had given George a

decisive push towards the Catholic Church: 'Struck with a disease which was likely to recur, the Scottish kirk gave little comfort. He therefore substituted another life.' But the war, too, had fuelled George's need to belong to a church that was strong and united. In the spring of 1945, Orkney servicemen and women who had been involved in the liberation of the concentration camps began to arrive home on leave, and to describe what they had witnessed. The *Orcadian* reported that films made of the concentration camps had been watched by several thousand islanders. The newspaper also ran extracts from letters written home by Dr Rena Marwick, daughter of the Provost of Stromness, who was working as a Resuscitation Officer following the liberation of Belsen. 'We . . . are very glad to see an improvement in most of the patients,' she writes in one letter.

> Their mental attitude is definitely better. For example, in the original camp dead bodies meant nothing, or less than nothing – children played over them, other people had to walk over them, or sat and gossiped and cooked beside them, no matter who it was. Last week in one of my wards one patient was very ill and eventually died, and the others actually wept. So, at least, life is considered more valuable now.

The Holocaust was to haunt George for the rest of his life, and his response to it, and to all the horrors of the war, was to urge religious unity on his *Herald* readers. 'If we do not emerge from the fearful "blood baptism" of the past five years cleansed and purified in some degree, then things are in a very bad way with us,' he writes on 8 May 1945. 'I want Stromnessians to worship in one church, and to be moved in their worship to faith, hope and love. Given those three things, there is literally nothing on earth that we cannot accomplish.'

He began, tentatively, to hint at his leanings towards Catholicism. During the war, the Catholic Church had gained a small but significant new foothold in Orkney. In 1941 several hundred Italian prisoners, captured during the North African campaign, had been transported to the tiny Orkney island of Lamb Holm to work on the construction of the Churchill Barriers. It was a bleak, barren, windswept place, and a group of them, led by a painter, Domenico Chiocchetti, asked for permission to ease their homesickness by converting two Nissen huts into a small chapel. The corrugated iron of

the huts was hidden behind a façade of plasterboard, which the prisoners painted with *trompe l'œil* brickwork and carved stone. An altar,
altar rail and holy-water stoop were moulded in cement, and a taber-
nacle constructed from timber salvaged from a wreck, which also
provided iron for two candelabra. One of the prisoners, a blacksmith
called Palumbo, worked for four months on a wrought-iron rood-
screen; others saved up cigarette money from their welfare fund to
send to a firm in Exeter for two heavy gold curtains to hang on either
side of the sanctuary. Above the altar, Chiocchetti painted a
Madonna and Child, basing his work on a battered postcard of
Nicolo Barabina's *Madonna of the Olives* which his mother had given
him when he set out from Italy.

George was deeply moved by the prisoners' achievement. 'The
Italian soldier is a far more spiritual being than his British counter-
part,' he wrote in the *Orkney Herald* on 21 August 1945.

> Where the English captive would build a theatre or a canteen to remind
> him of home, the Italian, without embarrassment, with careful devout
> hands, erects a chapel . . . We who are brought up in the Calvinistic
> faith, a faith as austere, bracing and cold as the winds that trouble Lamb
> Holm from year's end to year's end, can hardly grasp the fierce nostalgic
> endeavour that raised this piece of Italy, of Catholicism, out of the clay
> and the stones . . . The Italians, who fought weakly and without hope
> on the battlefield, because they lacked faith in the ridiculous strutting
> little Duce, have wrought strongly here.

At the time George was writing, it looked as if the chapel might not
survive the coming winter. Battered by wind and rain, it was already
beginning to disintegrate. 'But,' he insisted, 'the faith that created this
thing will endure to the end of the world.'*

During the summer of 1947, George read Newman's *Apologia*, and
was shaken to the core by its 'magnificent devastating logic'. It left him
toying with the idea of becoming a priest. Four months later, he set

---

*The future of the chapel was looking parlous in the late 1950s when, following
enquiries by the BBC, Domenico Chiocchetti was traced to his village in the
Dolomites. In 1960, he returned to Orkney to undertake repairs and restoration, and
the chapel, now a tourist curiosity, receives thousands of visitors a year. Mass is still
said there regularly in the summer months.

to work on 'The Storm', a poem, he wrote, that 'might be taken to represent the soul's flight from evil into the peace of God', but that also explores his own painful heart-searching, and anticipates, in the last two verses, his final reception into the Catholic Church:

> Next morning in tranced sunshine
> The corn lay squashed on every hill;
> Tang and tern were strewn
> Among highest pastures.

> I tell you this, my son: after
> That Godsent storm, I find peace here
> These many years with
> The Gray Monks of Eynhallow.

Who, if anyone, was ever going to read this poetry? 'Ideally,' George argued, when interviewed by a representative of the British Council in 1964, 'I should be trying to communicate with my own people, like the fishermen and the farmers'; and in the years following the war, he was clear that this was the audience he wished, eventually, to reach. 'The modern poets who write exclusively for highbrow audiences are largely wasting any talent they may have,' he claimed in the *Herald*. 'All the great poetry of the world has been written for the common people, who were in the old days mostly illiterate. The crowds who roared with laughter as Burns recited his latest satire in "Poosie Nancie's", the butchers and street sweepers listening to *Hamlet* in the Globe Theatre, Southwark, London, in 1600, the fourteenth-century peasants gathered on the village green to hear the latest ballad from a wandering pedlar-man – none of these knew the meaning of the horrible word "culture". Yet in a score of ways they were more highly cultured than modern possessors of Leaving Certificates, because their response to the great art of poetry was spontaneous and genuine.' He began, for the benefit of his readers, to publish regular 'tips' on how to appreciate poetry, and even how to write it.

The response was less than lukewarm. 'Sir,' wrote the film producer Margaret Tait to the editor of the *Herald*, 'Just who are they in Orkney who feel their lives to be inadequate, and cry out for culture to fill the gaps? The farmers? But their lives are already satisfying for they practise the creative art of agriculture. The business people?

Their lives are quite full of real human contacts. The professional people, the ministers, doctors, teachers, lawyers? They presumably have some sort of liaison with culture already. The housewives and mothers? Family life absorbs most women. The labourers? I don't believe they feel the need of it. That leaves us with the spivs, the eels, the drones and the writers-to-the-newspapers. Is it they who want this culture with a capital "C"?' 'May I very humbly suggest,' concurred Allison Leonard, herself a promising young poet, 'that . . . a surprising number of Orcadians live a full life which is not barren of "intense joy and enrichment" just because they find it in unacademic ways?' George's male readers were less equivocal: 'One feels sorry for this humourless bore, "Islandman",' wrote one, 'whose knowledge is apparently derived mostly from books and profound contemplation of the parish pump, and whose inexperience, lack of travel and immaturity are so clearly reflected in his one-track outlook. He can only see Orkney, having seen nothing else. And, curiously, having seen nothing else, cannot see Orkney. Lack of a comparative background is apparent in all he writes.'

George swung back at his critics with robust rejoinders, but all of them, and particularly the last, touched raw nerves. He knew very well that, try as he might to encourage Orcadians to read and write poetry, the popular image of a poet was of 'a lanky, wild-haired, dewy-eyed, buck-toothed individual, who, too delicate for the storms of this world, fades away in early youth, having sung to the deaf public his few sad lilting melodies'. And keenly though he championed Orkney, railing against the 'almost traitorous' defection of Eric Linklater when, in the spring of 1947, the novelist sold his house by the Loch of Harray and went to live in the Highlands, George recognized that, unless he could get out of the islands, he stood little chance of 'achieving anything spectacular'. He had left Orkney just once, when, as a small boy, he went with his mother to visit his Mackay grandparents in Sutherland. In the autumn of 1948 he decided it was time to leave again.

7

Late but in Earnest

Some kind of ancient wisdom whispers always, 'Stay where you are. What is good and necessary for you will be brought or you will be led to it. Wait. Have patience. What has been written down for you will happen when the time comes.'

GMB, *For the Islands I Sing*

SINCE LEAVING SCHOOL, George and Ian MacInnes had remained close friends. There was one striking difference between them – MacInnes was a convinced atheist – but their bonds had, if anything, strengthened over the years. Both felt a deep love of Stromness, a suspicion of authority, and a sympathy for the underdog; both had a dry, irreverent sense of humour. While he was still at school, it had become clear that MacInnes was a talented artist. Like George, he had made his debut in the *Orkney Herald*, with a series of brilliant caricatures of local worthies, and in 1939 he had enrolled at Gray's School of Art in Aberdeen. The war interrupted his studies but he resumed them in the late forties. When George decided it was time to get out of Orkney, MacInnes was the obvious person for him to visit. In Kirkwall, he boarded a plane for the first time, and flew south to Aberdeen.

Like Norrie's wife, Hazel, MacInnes's future wife, Jean Barclay, remembers vividly the shock she felt when Ian first introduced her to 'Georgie Broon' on Union Bridge. 'I had never seen such a woebegone creature in my life,' she says. Privately, she wondered whether, if George was a typical Orkneyman, she could ever settle happily in the islands. He struck her as feeble and unmasculine, and she noted that Ian was instinctively protective of him. But George did not want protection.

He had come south determined to be independent, and to fill his visit with new experiences. Almost the first thing he did was to insist on catching a train, alone, out of Aberdeen, for no better reason than to give himself his first taste of rail travel.

After a few days, he posted his impressions of the city back to the offices of the *Orkney Herald*. George had an inbuilt suspicion of new places and experiences – 'I am one of those whom novelty depresses,' he once wrote, and for 'depresses' one might substitute 'alarms' – and he was glad to report that Aberdeen not only compared very poorly with Orkney, but also confirmed his prejudices about 'modern life':

> In Orkney every face has its own meaning and its own value. But here the thousands of faces that pass you in the street every hour of every day are merely flickering shadows. You see occasionally a beautiful face, or a compassionate face, or a suffering face; but before you can let it soak into your mind it has vanished for ever in the torrent of humanity. For the most part, however, the faces lack any personality. Modern life has set its unvarying pattern on them: to the Orkneyman they seem curiously hard and unfeeling – a long endless succession of sombre flickering shadows.

At the end of the first week, however, aspects of Aberdeen began to intrigue him. He was fascinated by his first real encounter with trees, and stood a long while watching a silver birch near the wall of the old cathedral shimmering in the breeze. 'A tree,' he told his *Herald* readers, 'has grace and suppleness and strength, it is impossibly fragile and delicate. Nothing in all nature is so perfect and satisfying.' After two weeks, he felt so exhilarated by his new surroundings and independence that he postponed his journey home, and arranged to stay for a further fortnight. 'The spell of the city was beginning to bind me,' he confessed. 'Its noise, its gaiety, its gloom, which had shattered me to begin with, now became curiously attractive. Every morning I woke up with a taste for adventure on my palate. I thought with unsuppressed joy of the long hours of daylight that stretched before me – and, after them, the even more delightful hours of darkness, when Aberdeen really came alive.' He found himself dreading his return to Orkney, and the 'long winter of darkness, loneliness, and cold' that lay ahead.

He went, possibly for the first time, to Mass, and was struck by the devotion of the congregation – 'old blind men and beautiful young women, youths in Air Force uniform and schoolgirls' – as they made their way to the altar rails for Communion. 'I have never experienced anything approaching it in any Protestant church,' he admitted. 'The Catholics have a beautiful faith, and they enter into it with all their hearts and souls.' But even more alluring to George than the Catholic church was the Royal Athenaeum at the foot of Union Street. This was the pub favoured by the art students – among them Alberto Morrocco – and on its walls were Ian MacInnes's paintings of scenes from Burns. Here, George drank himself every evening into a worse state than either MacInnes or any of his friends. Surrounded by men who had fought in the war, MacInnes sensed, he was drinking to give himself courage and to prove that he was tougher than he looked: 'He needed to show the buggers he could take a few beers.'

As a child, George had been unsettled by the effects of drink on grown-ups, impelling them 'to sing and tell extravagant stories, and behave in uncharacteristic ways, such as kissing ladies, laughing uproariously at nothing, or wiping a tear from their eyes'. When, one Hogmanay in the early thirties, he had taken a sip from the yellow-ish liquid in his father's glass, he had found it so revolting that he had taken a vow that, should he live to be a hundred, the 'dreadful drink called whisky' would never pass his lips again. But as he grew up his feelings changed, and by the spring of 1945 he had begun to campaign in the *Orkney Herald* for the introduction of a few pubs in Stromness – 'for the benefit of the male population'. Twice, in 1923 and 1926, the people of Stromness had gone to the polls to decide whether or not the town should remain 'dry'; twice, the 'wet' voters had been decisively outnumbered by those in favour of prohibition. In the course of the war, however, attitudes had begun to ease, and when, on 25 November 1947, the townspeople fought their way through a hailstorm to vote for a third time, the 'wets' finally found themselves in the majority.

One Saturday morning the following May, the Stromness Hotel opened its bar for the first time in twenty-seven years. George went in, downed two glasses of beer, and was hooked. Those first glasses, he wrote, were 'a revelation; they flushed my veins with happiness; they washed away all cares and shyness and worries. I remember think-ing to myself, "If I could have two pints of beer every afternoon, life would be a great happiness."' It was not long before two pints ceased to satisfy. He developed a taste for 'a half and half': a small measure of whisky mixed with a half-pint of beer. The whisky brought out a peculiar nastiness in George. 'It could make him pugilistic, and cruel in his comments,' remembers an acquaintance, Susie Gilbertson, and in later life George himself acknowledged this. But in those early days what he felt under the influence of 'the wee golden ones' was a wild, unaccustomed happiness, relief from tedium and grief, and a sense that life, after all, was full of promise.

Drinkers, like tinkers, inspired in George an envious fascination: 'Sober, waiting for the bar to open, they were apt to be stolid and silent. Drink unlocked their tongues and made poets of them.' The musings of men in their cups enthralled him, and gave him an insight into the workings of the mind and into the Jekyll-and-Hyde make-up of the northern psyche. And his insight was surprising. Drunkenness revealed to George not, as one might expect, how subtle and complex human beings essentially were, but 'how under the drab surface complexities, there exists a ritualistically simple world of joy and anger'.

Very quickly, George was drinking as hard as his purse and guts would allow, sometimes sousing himself so thoroughly in alcohol that he suffered *delirium tremens*. 'There is a state of drunkenness when even sleep leaves the wreck of the body,' he writes in his autobiography, describing one of these occasions.

> All one night I lay in bed open-eyed. I had to force myself to keep my eyes open, for whenever I closed them a sequence of evil depraved faces filed slowly through my brain; each paused as if to note my wretchedness, and passed on; and another hellish face took its place. It was like a sequence of photographs thrown on a screen: all portraits of the utmost frightfulness, hundreds of them. My only relief was to force open my eyes. But my body was so weary that when I lost concentration the eyelids fell, and another file of dreadful faces came in strict order.

George's drinking worried his mother, but she registered her disapproval silently, and even when, day after day, his food turned cold as she waited for him to return from the pub, she continued to cook and care for him. Sometimes friends would shoulder him home in the late afternoon and dump him in the kitchen. Once, he was picked up and escorted back by the police, and thrilled whispers flew about Well Park: 'George Brown was taken home last night in the "Black Maria". . .' He was, he knew, earning a 'certain gray reputation' in the town. 'Had George died then,' says Susie Gilbertson, 'he would simply have been remembered as the local soak.'

In the face of Mhairi Brown's dogged cosseting, however, the likelihood of an early death was diminishing. Friends like Gerry Meyer and Ian MacInnes who sometimes dragged George protesting from the pub were amazed that, despite his feeble appearance, he had such enormous physical strength that they could barely restrain him. He had mental strength too. In some part of himself he knew that, if he were to abandon himself completely to drink, he must cast aside his ambitions as a poet. 'For a long time,' he wrote, 'there was a divided allegiance, drink and writing.' In the end, writing won the day.

George was helped on his way by one of those interventions of 'secret wisdom', or providence, which he later believed had governed the course of his life. On his Monday visits to Kirkwall to edit the galley proofs of the *Orkney Herald*, he had taken to visiting a bookshop, Leonard's. One day, he found a new assistant in the shop, a youngish man, sturdily built, bespectacled and tweed-jacketed, with a bright, direct, quizzical expression. They began to talk, first about books, and then about poetry. Ernest Marwick was the son of a smallholder and travelling salesman from a valley in the parish of Evie, in the north of mainland Orkney. He had a brilliant mind and, had he been physically stronger, he might well have left the islands and made a career for himself as an academic in one of the Scottish universities. When he was ten, however, he had been diagnosed as having a curvature of the spine, and had been forced to leave school and spend hours every day lying flat on his back on a wooden board. It might have broken the spirit of many boys, but Marwick was saved by a passionate interest in Orkney history and folklore, and in books.

By the age of ten, he had already been introduced to many of the classics of English literature through a series of books published and donated to Orkney schools by James Coats, a philanthropic member of the thread-manufacturing family. The series would have been sneered at by succeeding generations, Marwick suspected, 'but it contained the great English novelists and essayists as well as some excitingly unconventional books like [Isaac] Disraeli's *Curiosities of Literature*, in which I revelled. Mr Coats had been wise enough to include Ballantyne, Henty and Marryat. Many people of my age must owe their literary education to this high-minded benefactor.' Lying on his back-board, through his early teens, he continued to immerse himself in these works. Then, one day, his father arrived home on his pony-drawn cart with a tub of junk from a sale. In it, Marwick discovered the complete works of Shakespeare. He began to read, and was hooked.

In Ernest Marwick, George recognized a kindred spirit. They shared not only a love of literature, and of Orkney, but also the experiences of persistent ill-health, which had left both of them prone to depression. As well as being a writer, Marwick was a talented artist and photographer, and for George it was thrilling to be in the presence of a mind that could move with ease 'through a galaxy of artistic and intellectual disciplines'. Although he was only six years older than George, Marwick's learning, and his strict sobriety − he was a Temperance man − gave him an air of authority. When, one morning in the spring of 1946, he divulged that he was compiling an anthology of Orkney verse, and asked George whether he might like to contribute to it, George immediately parcelled up what he considered his eighteen best poems and posted them to Kirkwall.

Marwick was impressed, and George, in turn, ecstatic. 'Your praise,' he admitted, in a six-page, pencil-written letter, 'went to my head like strong wine.' The praise had come at a crucial time − 'a time', George later reflected, 'when a writer is at his most sensitive stage, not knowing if what he writes has any merit or is a heap of words merely, already beginning to moulder'. Over the next five years, he wrote regularly and at length to Marwick, finding in him a steady sounding-board for his views on everything from religion to Rackwick; from the potential pitfalls of the prose poem, to the tediousness of Sir Walter Scott. 'How priggish and stilted is the dialogue!' George writes to Marwick while rereading *The Pirate* in the spring of 1947. 'How irritating to readers in this age of speed is old Sir Walter's leisurely perambulation round a subject before plunging into it! In the 1940s, we scarcely have time to meander through his vast territory.'

The prickly pomposity of George's *Orkney Herald* journalism colours these letters too, but in Ernest Marwick he had found somebody whose opinion and discretion he so respected that he was able, gradually, to remove his mask, and to reveal his private feelings about his work, and his hopes for the future. 'I haven't shown "Swan's Way" to anyone but yourself,' George writes on 24 October 1946, enclosing a long prose poem. 'I don't know, Ernest, whether you approve of this form of literary expression, but the writing of "Swan's Way" one cold night last February was one of the happiest experiences of my life.'

Marwick, in response, both encouraged and restrained. His standards were exacting. 'No work,' George wrote, 'ever left his hands that wasn't as perfect as he could make it.' When George mooted the idea of publishing a collection of his own verse, Marwick advised strongly against it, predicting, accurately, that in later years he might not be well pleased with his early work. On the other hand, he saw that it was important for George to begin to communicate with a larger audience. When George spoke of his admiration for T. S. Eliot, Marwick responded by getting him to organize his thoughts about Eliot's work into a short lecture, which he then read out on George's behalf to a meeting of the Kirkwall Arts Club. It was, the *Orkney Herald* reported, 'certainly one of the best and most learned papers heard for some time'. He encouraged George to send work to the BBC, and although the response to his first offer of a short play was unequivocally discouraging – 'from every angle, No. Too short, too hammy, too anachronistic, too jejune, too impossible . . .' – during 1948, extracts from George's 'Islandman' column were read on the Scottish Home Service.

Marwick also introduced him, in the spring of 1947, to a new publication, *The New Shetlander*, in which over the next few years George published poetry, short stories, book reviews and critical essays; and it was almost certainly Marwick who arranged for George to be commissioned by the publisher William S. Thomson in Fort William to write the text for an illustrated tourist guide, *Let's See the Orkney Islands*, which came out in the summer of 1948. This 64-page book, landscape octavo in card covers, priced four shillings, was George's first published work, and in its short text he touches on all that moves him most about Orkney: the spellbinding loveliness of Rackwick, the central role played by Saint Magnus in quickening the spiritual life of the north, and his hopes that the islands might one day return to the Catholic faith.

As their friendship grew, George was invited to spend weekends and short holidays with Ernest Marwick and his wife Janette at their home in Kirkwall, and to steep himself in an atmosphere that was both new and thoroughly congenial. 'Entering Westermill,' he wrote, 'one was aware of an air of happiness and cleanness and peace that never, with the passing years, turned stale.' In his upstairs study, Ernest Marwick shared with George the fruits of years of private study: 'History, folk-lore, literature . . . folder after folder of carefully researched and lucidly expounded knowledge, entirely original'. Janette Marwick, mean-while, was one of the gentlest and kindest women George ever knew.

George was not the only person drawn to Westermill. It had become, over the years, an unofficial meeting-place for a small band of Kirkwall intellectuals. Among those who congregated there were John Mooney, a historian with a mind so keen and questing that he seemed to George like a small northern Ulysses; Christina Costie, a spinster lawyer, who wrote dialect verse in her spare time, and who had taught herself Norwegian and Icelandic in order to deepen her insight into Orkney's Norse traditions; and John Mackay, a head-master from the island of Sanday, 'whose eyes seemed to glimmer perpetually with mingled intelligence and humour'.

One regular visitor particularly fascinated George: a small, dark, profoundly deaf man with such great whorls of eyebrows that his friends remember him as looking like an owl. Robert Rendall was the bachelor son of prosperous Kirkwall drapers. He had left school just before the outbreak of the First World War, at the age of thirteen, and, like Ernest Marwick, he was largely self-educated. In 1908, when Rendall was ten, Arthur Mee had begun to publish in fortnightly instalments *The Children's Encyclopaedia* – 'the story', as Mee described it, 'of all ages, peoples and things'. Robert Rendall bought it, part by part, sevenpence a time, from Tom Spence's bookshop in Kirkwall, and remained indebted to Mee for the rest of his life. The encyclopaedia was, he wrote, his vade-mecum, leading him into fields of study that he would pursue with passion over the years. Thanks to Mee's inspi-ration, Rendall became an authority on shells, flowers and marine life and a lover of Italy. He was also a painter and archaeologist. One after-noon in the summer of 1929, he had taken himself to the Knowe of Gurness on the north-west coast of mainland Orkney to sketch

Eynhallow Sound. As he was sketching, one of the legs of his stool slipped deep into the ground and, peering into the hole it had made, he saw steep narrow steps leading down into the darkness. He had discovered the Broch of Gurness: one of the strong, circular houses built by the Iron Age inhabitants of Orkney several hundred years before the birth of Christ.

Most notably of all, however, Rendall was a poet. In 1946, George had responded with excitement to the publication of his *Country Sonnets*: Rendall's work was patchy, he felt, but when it was good it was very good indeed. And, although at first Rendall himself seemed rather stiff, George soon realized that 'behind the ludicrously austere mask is the primeval, mischief-loving troll that dances along the edge of cliffs and writes pagan poetry' – and this appealed to him very much.

Before long, George was sending his poems to Robert Rendall, as he had to Ernest Marwick, and receiving in response both encouragement, and courteous, meticulous criticism. 'Your Easter Song raised a mild excitement in my mind,' Rendall writes on 13 October 1947. 'It is so clear and spontaneous in its movement, quite in the manner of the old carols, I thought, and (very slightly) reminiscent of Francis Thompson, but nevertheless wholly your own. I liked it immediately. At first I was slightly confused in the exact meaning of the second line of the first stanza. There is an ellipsis of course, but though your punctuation makes it clear enough when one looks again, at first sight the mind carries over the first line into the second and then after "anointed" the suddenness of the ellipsis seems to throw one (myself at any rate) off the balance. Would you consider having a comma after the first line, and the period after "anointed"? . . .' Rendall was nearly a quarter of a century older than George, and his praise and close attention, coupled with Marwick's, were a spur to him to believe in his gifts, and to move forward. But how?

One spring day in 1949, George found himself on a bus between Kirkwall and Stromness, eavesdropping on a conversation between two teenage girls. They were fantasizing about which film stars they most longed to spend an evening with, and their discussion led George to muse about people he would like to meet. He settled on a shortlist of three. In third place, he decided, he would choose to be introduced to somebody who had won a lot of money on the football pools, to see whether it had really made them happy. As his second choice, he would travel back in time and meet Mahatma Gandhi, who had been assassinated just over a year earlier. But there was no doubt in his mind as to whom he wished to meet most of all. 'There is a man who lives in London and is just sixty years old,' he wrote in the *Herald*.

> In spite of the fact that he is a poet, he is always impeccably dressed. He eats daintily, too, and sips choice wines. He confesses his sins, I suppose, once a week to an Anglo-Catholic priest, and scrupulously observes the feast-days of the Church. In his spare time he throws off poems of a rare and incandescent beauty. He speaks nobly and memorably for all the people of Western Europe living in this tortured generation. On this side of idolatry I admire him, and his name is Mr T. S. Eliot.

Of all the 'modern' poets to whose work George had been introduced in his last year at school, Eliot had remained his hero. But when he put him top of the list of human beings he would like to meet, he was perhaps thinking not only of Eliot the poet, but also of Eliot the publisher of poetry: the publisher who had recognized the talents of W. H. Auden, Stephen Spender, Louis MacNeice, George Barker, Vernon Watkins – a publisher of such authority that he was determining the shape and future of English poetry. If George could only get himself into that office on the second floor of Faber & Faber, and gain an audience with 'the Pope of Russell Square', might there not be a chance of his own work one day reaching a wider public?

It was not to be. George never met Eliot, and there is no evidence that Eliot ever read a single one of his poems. But, as he sat musing on the bus that spring day, George was closer to the kind of breakthrough he needed than he would have dared to hope. Another poet, a close friend of Eliot, was about to step into his life, and to change its course completely.

Looking through copies of the *Listener* in the Stromness library, George had from time to time come across poems by Edwin Muir. He found them, to begin with, strange and baffling – 'and yet they had (it seemed) a secret and exact music'. Then, at the beginning of 1945, he read Muir's autobiography, *The Story and the Fable*. The opening chapters, in which Edwin Muir describes his infancy on the

Orkney island of Wyre, struck George as one of the most beautiful evocations of innocence, and of 'the slow stainings and renewings of time', that he had ever read. He praised the book in the *Herald*, recommending it as essential reading for 'every Orcadian who is proud of his home'. But it was not only as a fellow Orkneyman that Edwin Muir seemed sympathetic and inspiring to George. Muir had come late to poetry – he had not really begun to write until he was well into his thirties; then, when he did start, he, like George, yearned back to his infancy, seeing it as an Eden out of which he had been cast when his family left Wyre, and to which he had never been able to return.

For Edwin Muir, as for George, emerging from childhood had been painful. In *The Story and the Fable* he describes how he experienced, though at a slightly earlier age, a phase of acute guilt, foreboding and misery very similar to that described by George. Like George, also, Muir questioned some of the traditions in which he had grown up. He was fiercely critical of the education he had received at Kirkwall Grammar School, and even more so of the Presbyterian Church. In 1929, he had published a biography of John Knox. It is written with undisguised contempt, and Knox emerges as a terrifying, almost lunatic figure – arrogant, immoral, stupid, vengeful, cowardly and dishonest. Muir shared George's belief that Knox's chief legacy had been to 'rob Scotland of all the benefits of the Renaissance', and to leave the country in the grip of a cold, joyless, life-denying religion – a travesty of Christianity:

> The Word made flesh here is made word again,
> A word made word in flourish and arrogant crook.
> See there King Calvin with his iron pen,
> And God three angry letters in a book,
> And there the logical hook
> On which the Mystery is impaled and bent
> Into an ideological instrument.

By contrast, George sensed that Edwin Muir was a man of compassion, warmth and hope. When Muir's collection *The Voyage* was published in 1946, it made a deep impression on him: it was 'as if a key had been turned in a door, I entered a chamber of pure lyrical meditation'. What appealed particularly to George was that Muir's poems appeared not to be the work of 'one mind working in isolation to impress the world', but had the feeling, instead, of being 'very old, strong, and fragrant, like articles that have taken generations of patience and skill to produce'. He was especially moved by an elegy to Ann Scott-Moncrieff, an Orkney woman who had taken her own life at the age of twenty-nine. In the final verse, Muir recalls their last meeting in Edinburgh a few months before her death:

> Yet 'the world is a pleasant place'
> I can hear your voice repeat,
> While the sun shone in your face
> Last summer in Princes Street.

' "The world is a pleasant place",' George wrote in the *Herald*. 'That is what Edwin Muir remembers as the final message of Ann Scott-Moncrieff before she sought the shades. And that too is what he wants us to believe, in spite of the bitter pains of existence today.'

Edwin Muir was no stranger to the bitter pains of existence. When he was fourteen, his family had left Orkney and moved to Glasgow, then the most overcrowded and slum-ridden of all Britain's cities. Here, within the space of a few years, both his parents and two of his brothers died. He drifted from job to job, until in his early twenties he found himself working in a factory on the Clyde to which animal bones were transported from all over Scotland to be reduced to charcoal. Festooned with slowly writhing fat yellow maggots, the bones gave off a 'gentle, clinging, sweet stench' when shovelled into the furnaces, and on hot summer days this stood around the factory like a 'wall of glass'. The dirt and stench left Muir with a sense of shame that settled within him 'like a grimy deposit'. He would wake suddenly in the night with the chilling realization that his life had gone wrong. Walking beside the Clyde one evening, he wondered idly whether he might throw himself in.

He was rescued by his marriage, at the age of thirty-two, to Willa Anderson, a teacher of Shetland descent working in London. He underwent psychoanalysis, and they lived abroad for much of the twenties, in Czechoslovakia, Germany, Italy, Austria and France. Willa encouraged Edwin in his early struggles with verse, and his *First Poems* was published by Leonard and Virginia Woolf at the Hogarth Press: 'We printed his poems in 1925 with our own hands,' recalled Leonard Woolf, 'and he was the kind of author and they were the kind of poems for whom and which we wanted the Press to exist.'* By the Second World War Muir had published four more books of verse and was well known as a critic and, in collaboration with Willa, as a prolific translator. Together they were responsible for introducing Kafka to the English language. But, despite his success, Muir continued to be dogged both by ill-health and by lack of money, and in the late forties he found himself again at a low ebb. After the war, the British Council had sent him to Prague as Director of the British Institute. In 1948, he witnessed the Communist takeover, and the undoing of all his work, and he was shattered by it. He returned to England and suffered a nervous breakdown.

When, two years later, Muir was offered a position as Warden of Newbattle Abbey, an adult education college half an hour's drive south of Edinburgh, he had no hesitation in accepting. Newbattle Abbey was a small stately home, formerly owned by the Marquesses of Lothian – 'a perfectly quiet place', as Muir described it, 'out in the country, with walks and woods round about'. Both he and Willa were now in their early sixties. They had led a peripatetic life, and had never owned their own home. Privately, Willa Muir hoped that at Newbattle she and Edwin might see out the rest of their days.

As Muir was settling into his new post, in the winter of 1950–1, George joined an evening class – 'out of boredom'. One night, after the class, the Orkney director of adult education, Alex Doloughan, asked him whether he might consider applying for a place at Newbattle, and in April 1951 George wrote to Muir. Muir had seen his work in *The New Shetlander* and had been impressed by it. He replied swiftly: very glad to hear 'from you and from Orkney'; very keen that George should enrol.

That summer, Edwin and Willa Muir visited Orkney, and invited George to join them for tea in the Stromness Hotel. To steady his nerves before the meeting, George downed several glasses of beer; but he was quickly put at his ease. Edwin Muir was small and greying,

---

*The book that the Woolfs hand-printed was in fact *Chorus of the Newly Dead*, in July 1926. *First Poems*, published in April 1925, was commercially printed, by Neill & Co.

with a face that radiated gentleness and serenity. He walked, it seemed to George, 'in a kind of slow glide', and his voice, despite decades of absence from Orkney, retained the tone and rhythm of island speech. He left most of the talking to Willa, who brimmed with wit and gaiety. Before they parted, Muir confirmed that there was a place for George to study for a year at Newbattle, starting in the autumn. In early October, shortly before his thirtieth birthday, with a grant of £150 from Orkney County Council, George prepared to travel south.

Providence, if such it was, had never intervened more decisively in George's life. It is hard to believe that there was anyone better equipped to help him on his way than Edwin Muir, and impossible to imagine a place better suited than Newbattle Abbey to provide him with a stepping-stone from Orkney to a wider world. A full-blown university might, at this stage, have overwhelmed him completely; but at Newbattle – secluded, gracious, romantic, and home to fewer than two dozen students – he was to find a happiness he had never known before. Even the old Lothian motto might have been devised with George in mind. '*Sero sed serio*,' it proclaims: 'Late but in earnest.'

8

One Foot in Eden

Every life, like every civilization, has its golden age. My good
time was the few months between October 1951 and June 1952.
GMB, 'Edwin Muir at Newbattle'

PHILIP KERR, ELEVENTH Marquess of Lothian, was not only a distinguished statesman and man of letters, but a devout Christian and
an idealist. When, in 1930, he inherited his title from an eccentric
cousin, he also inherited four magnificent houses: Ferniehirst Castle
and Monteviot in the Borders, Blickling Hall in Norfolk and Newbattle
Abbey on the banks of the River Esk near Dalkeith. When, ten years
later, he died *en poste* as British Ambassador to the United States, only
two of these passed down to his Lothian heirs. Blickling Hall, with
4,500 acres, was left to the National Trust,* and Newbattle Abbey to
the Scottish Universities. Lord Lothian had spent a happy childhood in
a house on the Newbattle estate and wanted others to enjoy the unusual
atmosphere of a place that had, before the Reformation, been home to
a community of Cistercian monks. In 1937, he had established
Newbattle Abbey as a residential adult education college – a sort of
'college of the second chance', such as already existed in both England
and Wales.† Lothian's plan was to give men and women who had not

---

*Lord Lothian was a leading figure in the 1930s parliamentary campaign that brought
about the Country Houses Scheme enabling owners of historic houses to pass over
their estates, breaking entail and free of duty while retaining rights of residence, to
the National Trust and the National Trust for Scotland.
† Ruskin Hall (later Ruskin College), Oxford, for example, was established in 1899,
albeit with more political intentions, and Coleg Harlech, with the help of the
Workers' Educational Association, in 1927.

been to university an opportunity to step back from their routine lives for a time to study and think and develop their latent talents.

To ensure that Newbattle Abbey College felt as civilized and uninstitutional as possible, he had left the place stuffed with Lothian treasures and curiosities. Over the altar in the chapel was a school of Botticelli *Madonna and Child*; five Van Dyck portraits hung on the walls of the first-floor drawing room. There was a panelled library, and in the entrance hall were a saddle that had reputedly belonged to Robert the Bruce and a water-powered organ designed to be driven by the River Esk. But Lord Lothian was prescriptive in his generosity. Not only were those who came to Newbattle to live in beautiful surroundings; they were to do so unflustered by the prospect of academic hurdles. They were to sit for no exams, and they were to leave the college without paper qualifications of any sort. They were not even to follow specific courses, but to be guided by tutors into attending a selection of lectures ranging across English literature and language, history, philosophy, psychology and economics. 'It was,' writes Bernard Bergonzi, a former Newbattle student, 'an aristocratic gesture that was both generous and condescending, and ultimately impractical.' With no tangible result in view at the end of their studies, it was difficult for men and women to persuade their local education authorities to provide them with grants to study at Newbattle. The college had been set up to accommodate sixty students; in George's intake, there were just twenty-two.

Despite his frustrations with Orkney, and his longing for wider horizons, George travelled south stiff with apprehension. He flew to Aberdeen, and from there caught a train, skirting the east coast through Stonehaven, Montrose and Arbroath to Dundee, crossing the Tay Bridge and then passing on through the rolling, wooded, Fife countryside towards Edinburgh. Between every station, the guard made his way through the train checking tickets, and this unnerved George. He was terrified that he would either disembark too soon, or overshoot Edinburgh and be carried on to Newcastle. He was sharing a compartment with two old ladies and, to distract himself, he listened in on their conversation. One of them was very forthright. She had some time before been seriously ill, but was now in perfect health: 'And, declared she, the cure was *water*.' As the train careered on to the mile-long cantilevered bridge across the Firth of Forth, George confided his anxieties to these ladies, and begged their reassurance. They would 'see him right', they promised; and they did.

Edwin Muir was waiting at Waverley Station with his car – a particular kindness, as he hated driving – and George had a fleeting glimpse of the precipitous Edinburgh skyline before they drove south out of the city. Just past Dalkeith, they turned in through stone gateposts, guarded by weatherbeaten lions, and at the end of a long drive George had his first sight of Newbattle Abbey: vast, battlemented, and, to a newcomer, forbidding. It was a Sunday, and as term was not due to begin until the following Tuesday, only two of the other students had arrived. They seemed friendly enough, George thought, but, as he was shown to the top floor and began to unpack his bags in a high-ceilinged, austere room overlooking a cluster of grey slate roofs, he yearned to be back at home, 'among the sea sounds'.

For the first few days at Newbattle, he remained on his guard – 'cautious and suspicious, ready to beat a retreat to the islands at the first sign of hostility'. He was living, for the first time, surrounded by trees, and through the mellow autumn days he watched the beeches 'rain down leaves in one continuous russet shower'. It was, he thought, 'a very fine show', but he was homesick, none the less, for the 'fluent laterals' of the spare, unencumbered Orkney landscape. Edwin Muir was sympathetic. When he had been forced to move from Orkney to Glasgow at the age of fourteen, and had taken walks into the countryside on Sundays, he had longed to push away the woods so that he might see the land. 'If you are an Orkneyman,' Muir believed, 'you feel the real shape of the world can lie before you only when you are not fussed by these pretty decorations, the trees.' Certainly, for George, trees were no substitute for the sea. 'I think if I lived to be a hundred,' he wrote, 'I would still long for the waves and the whitemaas.' Images of the sea tormented him, and he rushed to collect his post each morning, hoping for letters 'drenched in Orkney sea spray, peatsmoke, ale fumes, wild westerly gales'.

He was critical, too, of the Midlothian climate: it lacked the 'terror' and 'majesty' he was used to in Orkney. Around Newbattle, he wrote, 'the stars are feebler, and the storms punier, and rain a little polite dusting'. The local people struck him as correspondingly drab. Willa

Muir remembered George – 'a shy young man with a soft Orkney lilt in his voice and eyes as blue as periwinkle flowers' – returning from his first foray outside the abbey gates in distress. 'What's the matter with the folk in Dalkeith?' he asked. 'Not a single smile on any face . . . What's *wrong* with them?' And George later wrote, 'When you walk through the streets . . . and see the grim dour look that everyone wears, you might imagine you were on the outskirts of Purgatory. There is something bad and rotten about modern industrialism to give people such hopeless harsh faces.' He posted regular parcels of dirty clothes home to his mother, but for several weeks he felt unable to write to his friends. Then, gradually, the atmosphere of Newbattle began to work on him. He experienced a growing sense of familiarity, a feeling, almost, of homecoming. It was, he wrote, 'like coming to some fruitful place which (in theory) one had always known about, but never expected to see', and he was overwhelmed by a surge of happiness such as he had not known before.

On 5 November, writing in pencil over page after page of thin paper, George poured out his excitement to Ernest Marwick. The abbey itself, with its Cistercian roots, now felt deeply sympathetic to him. The spirit of the monks who had lived there five hundred years earlier had never really left the place, George wrote, and it contributed to an atmosphere that was both stimulating and serene. Beneath the abbey stretched a cavernous twelfth-century crypt, haunted, it was said, by a 'grey lady' put to death for trysting with a monk, and here in the evening the students gathered in armchairs around an enormous fire, and talked about politics and poetry into the small hours. George liked, at such times, to imagine that the students were 'not so very different from those old brothers who, many hundreds of years ago, pored over Aquinas by the light of a candle', and to think of Edwin Muir as their abbot. As he grew older, George would sometimes long for the monastic life – it was, he believed, something to which he would have been temperamentally well-suited. Perhaps this longing, and the convivial, carefree vision of medieval monasticism reflected in so much of his writing, had its roots in those evenings in the Newbattle crypt.

In the centuries since the monks had left Newbattle, the spirit of monasticism had been overlaid with Lothian grandeur and *jeux d'esprit*. Behind the abbey was a formal Italian garden – the most beautiful garden George had ever seen. It had been laid out in the seventeenth century to look like a military uniform with epaulettes and stars, and in its two far corners stood a magnificent pair of octagonal sundials. Beyond it, even older than the garden, grew the largest beech tree in Scotland – an 'arboreal cathedral', it seemed to George. Inside, over the first floor of the abbey, ran a series of beautifully proportioned rooms: a bedroom elaborately decorated for a visit by Queen Victoria, a marchioness's boudoir with a pale green and gold trellised vault powdered with stars, and an immense drawing room with a painted ceiling, Italian marble fireplaces, *chaises-longues* upholstered in oyster satin, a seamless chenille carpet and a grand piano on which the Muirs' son, Gavin, passed his days playing Chopin and Beethoven. The atmosphere in these rooms was thick, George wrote, with the 'incense of old gracious living', and he found it every bit as captivating as the air of 'yet older sanctity' in the crypt. And even in the less formal parts of the house, in the labyrinth of passages and stairs, the walls were covered with paintings. 'The vanished royalty and nobility of Scotland stare down at you wherever you go,' he told Ernest Marwick.

On a more mundane level, the day-to-day detail of institutional life had also begun to intrigue George. Like the nurses at Eastbank, Edwin Muir's secretary, Flora Jack, remembers George as charmingly mischievous. If there was any gossip about a member of staff, he was sure to be the first to know it; he delighted in any 'domestic to-do'. As his initial suspicions subsided, he began to delight, too, in the company of his fellow students. They were a mixed bunch: men and women of different ages and nationalities, and from all walks of life. They included Cedric ('Spike') Mays, a 44-year-old Post Office worker from Middlesex whose wife, Vera, had taken a job in a factory to support him through his studies, and who later paid tribute to all that Newbattle had done for him in a memoir, *No More Soldiering for Me*. Mays describes, among other fellow students, George Innes, an electrical engineer from Dundee, who was studying for entry into the Church, and who wandered about the Newbattle gardens in silence clutching his Bible; David Stanton, a blond, willowy, heavily bespectacled library worker from Nottingham; and a young Yugoslavian woman, Vjera Starcevic, who had worked in the Department of Foreign Affairs in Belgrade as an interpreter, and had endured both German occupation and the imposition of Communism under Tito. Starcevic was almost penniless, and her clothes were threadbare, but from Newbattle she gained a place at Cambridge University.

Rabindrath Chabria's family were refugees from Kashmir, and he arrived at Newbattle with all his worldly possessions: one light suit, two pens and a *Concise Oxford Dictionary*. 'The blast of Scotland's east wind blew through his cotton jacket and pants to set his teeth all a-chatter,' Mays writes, and he became known as the 'blue Indian' because he was almost always cold. Chabria was a devout Hindu, and fascinated George by getting out of bed early every morning, immersing himself in ice-cold water, and then standing on his head to stimulate his circulation. Under Edwin Muir's guidance, Chabria began work on a long essay on 'The Precocious Child in Victorian Fiction', which later earned him a Ph.D. at Edinburgh.

The four who became George's closest friends, however, were all Scotsmen, and all in their mid-twenties. Tom Wilson was a clerical worker from Larbert, and Ian MacArthur a Post Office worker from Stornoway. Both had left school at fourteen, and both went on from Newbattle to study English at Edinburgh University. Bill Drysdale was a miner from West Lothian, and Bob Fletcher a metalworker from Airdrie. Fletcher was dark, heavy-boned and shy, but during that first term George began to appreciate in him 'a deep smouldering passion . . . for the things in life he held dear: "the rights of man", and poetry'. Before Newbattle, Fletcher's only experience of writing had been taking the minutes of trade union meetings every Friday evening. Encouraged by Edwin Muir, he began to develop his talents both as a poet and as a critic, and, on the strength of an essay on *Paradise Lost*, he went on to win a scholarship to King's College, Cambridge. Drysdale also won a Cambridge scholarship, with an essay on Kant, and he, Fletcher and MacArthur all eventually made careers as English teachers in Scottish schools.

One of the great things about Newbattle, George later reflected, was that it made actual the 'might-have-been'. Willa Muir agreed. A whole book, she wrote towards the end of her life, could have been written about the students and their half-stifled longings which found expression in the abbey. But the widening of academic horizons was only a part of what Newbattle had to offer. 'Besides what they absorbed in lectures and discussions,' Willa wrote, 'they learned that their interests could not only come out into the open but could be shared with others. There was a strong sense of companionship.'

If George had taken nothing from Newbattle but that companionship, he believed, it would still have been an experience 'more precious than pearls'. After the solitary, eccentric life he had led for the past decade, he was amazed to find that he could make friends easily, even with men and women whose views and beliefs he did not always share. 'This is not merely a first impression either,' he wrote to Ernest Marwick. 'You know how in small communities little cliques arise, and there are bound to be disagreements and explosions? Well, things may develop that way yet, but I hardly think so. It sounds almost unnatural, but since I arrived I haven't heard one bitter or spiteful word exchanged.' These were the days before the Hungarian uprising, and many of the students were passionate Communists. Tom Wilson kept a poster of Stalin pinned above his bed. George, though he had inherited from his father a vague, Keir Hardie socialism, based on sympathy for the oppressed and exploited, was not much interested in politics. His religious beliefs, however, meant that he felt compelled – 'in the interests of truth' – to combat the 'wilder assertions' of his Communist contemporaries. 'But even then,' he told Marwick, 'there is no ill-nature, and half an hour after the political argument the Communists and the Catholics will be reading Francis Thompson and Shelley to each other.'

Literature, and above all poetry, was the great bond between the men and women who came to Newbattle in the autumn of 1951. Keen as he was to fuel their passion, Edwin Muir was cautious about encouraging any of them to think that they might make a living as writers, let alone poets. 'He sees little future for poets,' George told Marwick. 'Most books of poetry published today sell under 100 copies – every one of them is a loss to the publisher. So the outlook is bleak.' But Muir's warnings did little to dampen their enthusiasm, not least because he himself was such an inspiring example of what a life devoted to literature could be. Even the economics tutor, Kenneth Wood, took to composing poems, and had one published in the *Listener*. In the crypt, evening after evening, George and his new friends read aloud to one another from their own work. 'Here a new poem came to birth, and there a new story, passing from hand to hand round the crypt fire before being delivered to the typewriter or to the flames,' Spike Mays remembered. 'Newbattle was a place of fierce but wholesome criticism.'

Bob Fletcher toiled for weeks on brief, beautiful poems. Bill Drysdale sat up night after night writing a long Shavian play. When, in November, the *Observer* announced that it was running a Christmas story competition, they all set to work and cajoled Flora Jack into typing up their entries. (The *Observer* received 6,700 in all, and the prize of £250 went not to a Newbattle student, but to an almost unknown writer, Muriel Spark, who was living in a bedsit in a rooming-house in Kensington, struggling to support her small son.*)

Edwin Muir lectured three times a week, twice on the Elizabethan dramatists and once on the English language, and, as George told Ernest Marwick, everyone attended his lectures for the sheer pleasure of listening to him. 'For the most part it is a vague aimless drift, like a brilliant man speaking through a half-trance. Then quite suddenly the friendly mist will lift for a few moments, and a whole rich region of English literature lies open, with a brilliant light beating down on it. It is a quite remarkable experience to listen to him.' On the subject of his own work, however, Muir would not be drawn; and certain symbols he used with great power in his poetry – for example, Eden – he refused to discuss with his students, 'as if these symbols were somehow sacred and only for use in the temple of poetry'.

Every Friday evening, a distinguished guest came to talk to the students in the crypt. Professor John MacMurray, who held the Chair of Moral Philosophy at Edinburgh University, spent an hour urging them towards religious belief. 'I am intellectually compelled to believe in God,' he concluded, 'and I am sure that most of you have found something of God here in Newbattle.' There were visits from the novelist Neil Gunn, from the Shakespearean scholar Professor Dover Wilson, from the poets Douglas Young and Francis Scott, and, one evening, from an arrogant young schoolmaster with a growing reputation as a poet. 'His name is Norman MacCaig,' George wrote to Ernest Marwick, 'and I never heard such blistering scorn as he poured on people like Maurice Lindsay, Alexander Scott etc. . . . he said

---

*It was a choice George Mackay Brown would have approved. 'I read a few Muriel Spark novels in hospital and since,' he wrote to the author on 19 August 1992, 'a strange writer, sometimes all candyfloss and sometimes deep sibyl-utterances. Very greatly gifted.'

poetry with Maurice Lindsay was a continual itch, a kind of skin disease, and that you couldn't read ML's poetry if there was an expensive carpet on the floor for fear that you'd be sick all over it. I've rarely heard such masterly sarcasm, and Willa Muir of course laughed her head off all the time.'

If most of these visitors were Scots, Edwin Muir would return from trips to England with colourful vignettes of London literary life: of an evening spent discussing income tax with T. S. Eliot; of Dylan Thomas's deplorable lack of personal hygiene; of the rudeness of Cyril Connolly. Ian MacArthur remembers Muir coming back from a party at which Connolly had taken a dislike to an enormously fat Chinese lady. 'Out, vile jelly!' Connolly had commanded, ushering her to the door. Muir told these tales without a hint of name-dropping or superiority. 'He had a way of speaking to you,' MacArthur recalls, 'that made you feel he was both your father and your friend.' Easily though he moved in the literary world, Muir was, perhaps, even more thoroughly at home with his Newbattle students. Like many of them, he had been forced to leave school at fourteen, and had never had the chance to go to university. He believed passionately in the opportunities Newbattle offered and, like Lord Lothian, was insistent that his students must feel absolutely free from pressure. 'I try to encourage them, always,' Muir says in a one-man play, *Edwin Muir and the Labyrinth*, which George wrote about him after his death:

> Never be hard on them. Never let them feel they're wasting their time. My time as well. The whole treasury of literature is there for them to ransack. Open their minds to the old wisdom, goodness, beauty. Arm them against the gray impersonal powers. They press in on every side. More and more.

Behind the scenes, Muir had to fight for his beliefs. Newbattle was overseen by an Executive Committee, most of whom felt that local authorities giving grants to students in those stern post-war days should be able to show a proper return, in the form of a diploma or degree, on their investment. The views of the committee were fuelled by a double snobbery. They disliked the notion of being in thrall to the whims of a deceased aristocrat, Lord Lothian; but at the same time, Flora Jack believes, they despised Edwin Muir for his humble background and lack of a university degree. As relations grew increasingly strained, they became vicious and small-minded in their efforts to oust Muir. To try his patience, they raised objections even to the most trifling items of expenditure – new light-bulbs, a draining-board for the kitchen. For weeks on end Flora Jack found herself with little to do because Muir was too worn down by his wranglings with the committee even to write letters. He began to suffer acute pains in his chest.

All this Muir did his best to keep hidden from his students, creating around them such an utterly safe haven that the outside world seemed not only remote, but unnecessary, almost unreal. If they left the college at all, it was only to walk a mile up a steep hill to a pub called the Justinlees. 'We were poor,' George writes, 'but in those days you could buy a pint for the equivalent of 6p. And there we crowned the new-found liberality of our days – our widened horizons – with laughter and song!' He remembered walking back to the abbey from the Justinlees one windy night, and watching the moon barging through the clouds – 'like a rugby forward', said Bill Drysdale. By the end of the first term, George was entranced. He flew home to Orkney for the Christmas holidays and, before catching the bus to Stromness, took himself to a Kirkwall bar for a pint of Bass. 'The full wonderment of the winter term at Newbattle broke on me,' he wrote, 'as the yellow circles lessened in the pint glass.'

What was at the heart of this wonderment? Newbattle, certainly, is an extraordinary place. Today, it looks slightly unkempt, and many of its Lothian treasures have been dispersed; yet it retains the atmosphere of the civilized, reassuring oasis that George found in it, and continues to change the lives of the men and women who study there. One element of the magic present in the early fifties is, however, long gone. There was, Edwin Muir wrote shortly before his death, 'some faint air of Eden' about the place then, and his students would have agreed that it was Muir himself who was responsible for it.

Thinking about her husband as she wrote her diary one evening in January 1951, Willa Muir reflected that his poems would live, 'but of himself only a legend'. It was an aspect of Muir's goodness that he was a person without persona. Little survives of him by way of anecdote and, half a century on, it is almost impossible to recapture precisely what it was about this serene, withdrawn, deeply private man that inspired such love. For it was love, George was sure, that his students felt for him, though most would have been shy of the word.

On both Stephen Spender and T. S. Eliot, the overwhelming impression made by Muir was one of 'complete *integrity*', of a pure honesty which Eliot knew to be as rare in writers as in men of other occupations. 'I stress this unmistakable integrity,' Eliot wrote, 'because I came to recognise it in Edwin Muir's work as well as in the man himself . . . I cannot believe that [he] ever uttered one disingenuous word in speech, or committed one disingenuous word to print.' The poet Kathleen Raine was struck by the calm and stillness that seemed to surround not only Edwin but also Willa Muir. Whenever one met them, she wrote, 'they seemed stable and the world moving'. For George Barker, it was this stability that gave Edwin Muir almost visionary insight. He was, Barker wrote, 'like a silent clock that showed not the time but the condition, not the hour but the alternative'.

If these reflections suggest a man removed from the common herd, it is important to note also that what impressed many about Edwin Muir was his almost intense ordinariness: he was loved by very ordinary people, and he loved them in return. Muir suffered fools gladly, George once wrote, because he saw things in them that others were too distracted to see. To some, like Rabindrath Chabria, it seemed that Edwin Muir was, quite simply, 'a saint'; but to George this was somehow to underplay Muir's extraordinary ordinariness. 'No,' he wrote, 'Edwin Muir was no more a saint than the rest of us. People who use that word to describe him – and I've heard a score or more at it – do him a disservice.'

A contemporary news report described Muir as moving among his students like some mild gardener among the plants in his greenhouse, tending them carefully and watching with quiet pride as they took root and bloomed. If there is one adjective his former students use of him again and again it is 'gentle'. Many of the essays they handed him must have been pretty poor, George reflected in a radio conversation after Muir's death; and yet he responded to them with gentleness. He was always kind in his private criticisms, as though he feared he might blast some budding talent with too much honesty.

Gentle, courteous, unassuming: to some who did not know Muir well, all these qualities together gave an impression of weakness. What the students at Newbattle came to understand, however, was that underneath Muir's mild manner lay a core of toughness, ruthlessness even, that had enabled him, from an early age, to plunge himself into the social and political crises of the early twentieth century, and not to be broken by them. He had known greater squalor and deprivation than any of them, but had retained a belief that pain not only fitted into, but actually made possible, a larger pattern of love and compassion:

> One foot in Eden still, I stand
> And look across the other land.
> The world's great day is growing late,
> Yet strange these fields that we have planted
> So long with crops of love and hate.
> . . .
>
> . . . famished field and blackened tree
> Bear flowers in Eden never known.
> Blossoms of grief and charity
> Bloom in these darkened fields alone.
> What had Eden ever to say
> Of hope and faith and pity and love
> Until was buried all its day
> And memory found its treasure trove?
> Strange blessings never in Paradise
> Fall from these beclouded skies.

It was this ability to comprehend both suffering and hope that made Edwin Muir so deeply sympathetic, and that enabled him to emanate kindness to all around him. For this was his great gift. 'It was,' Willa wrote in her memoirs, *Belonging,* 'something he could not help giving out; he radiated it as he walked and breathed, and the whole College benefited.'

Willa herself seemed to most people a more equivocal figure – although never to her husband. Their marriage, Edwin Muir writes in his autobiography, was the most fortunate event in his life; and, more privately, in a letter to a friend, 'We have, almost literally, one heart between the two of us.' But it was, on the face of it, a puzzling match. Where Edwin was slight, neat, quiet, Willa was large, flamboyant, witty and indiscreet. She struck one acquaintance as the Scottish embodiment of a witch – 'one instinctively clothed her in one's mind in a conical Welsh hat' – and the shyer students at Newbattle were thrown into confusion by the crudeness of her jokes. Born in Montrose to working-class Shetland parents, Willa had grown up in a strict, stifling household, and had had to fight, as a girl, to be allowed to move on from school to read Classics at St Andrews University. She was awarded a first-class degree, but she was left for the rest of her life with an impatient disregard for the British class system and for traditional views about women. She delighted in shocking people. At the frequent get-togethers she arranged at Newbattle, she appeared to dominate, regaling the company with pastiches and caricatures and clerihews, while Edwin weaved his cigarette smoke and said little; and she had so few qualms about speaking her mind that Bernard Bergonzi considers her 'the most malicious woman' he ever encountered.

Yet, beneath it all, Willa Muir was, in her own view, and in the view of those who really knew her, 'a soft-centred creature'. Her aggressiveness, consciously cultivated, was her way of masking this, and of enabling her to protect Edwin. He 'was a soft-shell crab', she wrote, shortly before his death, 'and I was his carapace'. Their close friends realized that it was Edwin, apparently unassertive, who really ran their lives and who was by far the steelier of the two. Flora Jack remembers Willa sitting by the front door at Newbattle waiting for Edwin to return from a trip to London. 'You know,' she confessed, 'I'm just no use without him.'

Willa was quietly heroic. Privately, she had sacrificed much for Edwin. An accomplished scholar and translator in her own right, she had allowed him to take credit for much of her work, and had suffered anguish as a result. 'And the fact remains,' she writes in her diary one evening in the summer of 1953,

> I am a better translator than he is. The whole current of patriarchal society is set against this fact, however, and sweeps it into oblivion, simply because I did not insist on shouting aloud: 'Most of this translation, especially Kafka, has been done by ME. Edwin only helped.' And every time Edwin was referred to as THE translator, I was too proud to say anything; and Edwin himself felt it would be undignified to speak up, I suppose. So that now . . . I am left without a shred of literary reputation. And I am ashamed of the fact that I feel it as a grievance. It shouldn't bother me. Reputation is a passing value, after all.

Yet it is now that I feel it, now when I am trying to build up my life again and overcome my disabilities: my dicky backbone, for instance. Because I seem to have nothing to build on, except that I am Edwin's wife and he still loves me. That is much. It is almost all, in a sense, that I could need. It is more than I deserve. And I know, too, how destructive ambition is, and how it deforms what one might create. And yet, and yet, I want to be acknowledged.

Willa had also, in her role as Edwin's protectress, allowed herself to become something of a caricature, and this too was sometimes painful and perplexing. 'I was not born to be a comic figure,' she wrote in 1947, in a poem for Edwin's sixtieth birthday,

> but life has changed me into one at last.
> I hope, my love, you will not find me tedious
> although my double chins are doubling fast,
> and till I die find merriment in me;
> but when I'm dead among the elementals
> I hope you will forget the accidentals,
> remembering rather what I meant to be.

George delighted in the caricature, but he also saw beyond it, understood what Willa 'meant to be', what she essentially was, and what she had done for Edwin. She was, he once wrote, the most generous woman he had ever known. From his window at Newbattle, he would watch the Muirs take their morning stroll around the grounds – Edwin nattily dressed, appearing to glide, Willa hirpling with arthritis – and he was moved by their marriage. But for Willa, George believed, Edwin might never have written a line of poetry: 'Where would you be now . . . without her?' Edwin asks himself in *The Labyrinth*. 'Lost for ever . . . She saved your life and your reason, that dear one. She waited for you at the gate – Ariadne – in the sun. She took your hand. Then you were free.'

The Easter term of 1952 got off to a dramatic start. On the evening of Monday 14 January a storm blew up across Scotland. All that night, at Newbattle, windows rattled, doors banged and chimneys whined. George was unable to sleep. In the morning, the students woke to find that the 400-year-old beech tree had been torn up by its roots. Tourists came to inspect it; some tipped their caps in respect. Looking larky and fogeyish, in tweed jackets and ties, George and his friends posed on it for photographs, perched about its massive trunk like the fairies on the Elfin Oak in Kensington Gardens.

In Orkney, the storm had raged even more ferociously. On the Monday evening, a dazzling display of the Northern Lights spread across the freezing darkness, and the barometers began to plummet. In the early hours of the following morning, a hurricane of a violence never known before or since tore across the islands. The anemometer at Costa Head recorded a wind velocity of 130 m.p.h., and then stopped working. Orcadians were woken from their sleep by a noise Eric Linklater described as 'a hard and solid impact on their ears, a continuous deluge of sound that seemed to hurt the mind'. When daylight came, hayricks, cornstacks and hen-houses lay scattered about the countryside, and drowned poultry bobbed in the waves. On the island of Egilsay, an entire shop had been blown into the sea. When, some days later, George received letters from home, they described the streets of Stromness littered with chimney pots and roof slates, and how in Well Park 'a chunk of iron as sharp as a lance' had come crashing through his bedroom window in the early hours of the morning, and landed on the pillow 'where, normally, my head would have been'.

The storm was followed by weeks of bitter cold. At Newbattle, the boiler failed and for two weeks there was neither heating nor hot water. Bill Drysdale grew a huge black beard – 'like an Assyrian'. The students were sent out across a garden creaking with frost to collect firewood.

In early spring, all this took its toll on George's health and, sweating and shivering, he was forced to take to his bed. He was not well enough to make the journey home to Orkney for the Easter holidays, and Ian MacArthur took him instead to stay with his brother and sister-in-law in Paisley. It was a happy time, and, surrounded by generosity and good-humour, George recovered his strength. But forays out of Newbattle into the 'real' post-war world were unsettling. Paisley struck George as 'seedy and worn ugly with industrialism, like a hopeless woman with twisted hands'. Back at Newbattle at the beginning of the summer term, meanwhile, he and a friend took a trip one day into Dalkeith, and walking up the main street noticed a small knot of people standing in the lobby of a radio dealers.

Television had, that very day, come to the Lowlands of Scotland, and making his way to the front of the crowd George saw for the first time figures flickering across a small screen: ' "Man, man," said an old man at my elbow, "It's wonderful, is it no? Soon they'll be able to see into your very mind." It was a horrible thought.'

Within the abbey walls, however, George could banish such thoughts, and for ten weeks between April and June 1952 he was blissfully happy. He wrote to Ernest Marwick praising the Midlothian climate – clearly preferable to Orkney's, he now believed, 'much warmer, much less temperamental' – and urging him to apply for a place at Newbattle: 'The company is brave and stimulating. The food is good, the trees are in leaf . . . and truly life is sweet.' The early-summer foliage was astonishing to George. The gardens and roadsides were 'lyrical with lilac, juniper, apple-blossom'; and the weather was so fine that the students had given up arguing about politics and spent their days instead tanning themselves on the battlements, and talking about poetry. Edwin Muir gave most of his lectures in the garden. 'The other morning we got a brilliant talk from him on Thomas Traherne,' George wrote to Ernest Marwick on 30 April, 'he who wrote about corn being "orient and immortal wheat" – according to Edwin one of the happiest and most innocent souls who ever lived. And this morning he lectured on the ballads and medieval lyrics, lamenting all the time that delight in nature and ordinary things had almost completely disappeared from life and literature. Dylan Thomas, he thinks, is one of the few people who still have the secret.'

George's own writing was coming 'like a song'. As the months passed, Edwin Muir had become increasingly impressed with his work, recognizing in it 'the real natural grace which is so absent from poetry just now and which poetry needs so much', and a felicity with words that he not only admired but envied. He encouraged George to forget about essay writing – 'I only half believe in prose,' Muir admitted, 'it's a sad fact' – and to bring him poems instead; and some of these he began to send to literary editors in London. J. R. Ackerley at the *Listener* refused one but asked to see more; Janet Adam Smith at the *New Statesman* published George's poem 'The Exile'.

At a safe distance from home, George was at work on a series of free-verse poems, 'rather Chinese in manner', about imaginary

Orkney folk. These had, he explained to Marwick, 'the same end in view as Joyce's "Dubliners", to give a picture of a community'. He was planning to write twelve or possibly even twenty, but what finally emerged was a series of seven, which together conjure up a picture of an island community both rough and tender, tragic and darkly humorous. The best, perhaps, is his portrait of Dr Guthrie, the GP, a clever, quick-tongued, young incomer, pouring scorn on the Orcadians' pride in their racial purity as he sits over his whisky on a Saturday night:

> 'Purity? . . .
>
> First the aborigines
> That howked Skara Brae from the sand.
> Then the Picts,
> Those small dark cunning men
> Who scrawled their history in stone.
> The Celtic fathers followed,
> And many a Pictish lassie, no doubt,
> Felt their power in the bed
> As well as at the altar.
>
> And then the tigers from east over sea,
> The blond butchering Vikings,
> Whose last worry on sea or land
> Was purity of race, as they staggered couchwards
> After a fill of ale.
> Finally, to make the mixture thick and slab,
> The off-scourings of Scotland,
> The lowest sleaziest pimps from Lothian and the Mearns,
> Fawning in the train of Black Pat,
> And robbing and raping ad lib.
>
> But that's not all.
> For many a hundred ships have ripped their flanks
> On Rora Head, or the Noup,
> And Basque sailor lads and bearded skippers from Brittany
> Left off their briny ways to cleave a furrow
> Through Orkney crofts and lasses.
>
> Not to speak of two world wars
> And hordes of English and Yanks and Italians and Poles
> Who took up their stations here:

By day the guns, by night the ancestral box-bed.
Only this morning
At Maggie o' Corsland's I delivered a bairn
With a subtle silk-selling Krishna smile.

A fine mixter-maxter!'

Out of sight of family and old friends, George was also enjoying, tentatively, some of the pleasures of a delayed youth. He had developed a crush on one of the other students, Dorothy McCrory, a tall, dark, buxom woman who had been a shop assistant at Boots in Glasgow before coming to Newbattle. In photographs taken that summer term, he gazes at her longingly, and when he and his fellow students spent one Sunday on the beach at Gullane, they returned sunburned and ecstatically happy: 'desires falling across our bodies like blossoms'. Though it seemed to Flora Jack that nothing came of these desires, she remembers George revelling in flirtation; and nearly twenty years later Dorothy McCrory still lingered in his subconscious. 'I had a dream about Newbattle last night,' George writes one spring morning in 1970, in what turned out to be the last letter he ever sent to Willa Muir. 'I had arrived there suddenly, found myself in a bedroom talking to house-maids who remembered me. Half-familiar students arrived to take me round. There half way up the hall stair stood Dorothy McCrory; so I gave her a kiss, as she was the only one I really recognised. But no, the other students laughed and said that though she looked like D McC she wasn't actually Dorothy McCrory. I woke with a sense of loss.'

Ten weeks steeped in light and laughter was how he saw that summer term at Newbattle: 'Springtime in the spirit, springtime in the world, at one, inseparable.' It was quickly over. On 13 June, the day that Faber & Faber published Edwin Muir's *Collected Poems*, the students packed their cases, gave each other copies of the books they most treasured as parting gifts, and went their separate ways. George's friends bought platform tickets to wave him off at Waverley Station, and he travelled north through unseasonable sleet with a heavy heart. It seemed unlikely that Orkney County Council would renew his grant for another year at Newbattle, and once again the future stretched uncertainly ahead. 'Like the bard,' George wrote, ' "I guessed and I feared".'

9

A Pocketful of Hope

Grace is what I find in all these poems, both the serious and the
lighter ones. Orkney should be proud of this book celebrating
its life, and proud above all that it has produced a young poet of
such high gifts. As a fellow Orkney poet, I salute him and wish
him all the recognition which he so truly deserves.

Edwin Muir, introduction to *The Storm* (1954)

DURING THE SUMMER of 1952, while most of Britain basked in
the sun, Orkney was dismally wet. For every pint of sunshine,
George wrote, the islands got a gallon of rain. In August, George was
invited by the BBC to read some of his poetry on a radio programme
about Rackwick. He found both the process of recording – 'tongue
dry as an old rag with terror' – and the final results appalling. 'You hear
a strange, deep, hollow voice you never heard in your life before . . .
you feel you could kick the person it belongs to. Until suddenly it
dawns that it's your own recorded voice you're listening to. The voice
you impose on people every hour of the day, every day of the week,
every month of the year. The voice you can never hear properly yourself. To an already undermined ego, it is the final shattering blow.'

Most of those wet days he spent shut in his bedroom at Well Park
working on a play about the Orkney legend of Lady Odivere* and listening to Paul Robeson on his radiogram. Not for the first time,
uncertainty about his own future made George jaundiced about the
future in general, and he channelled his anxieties into plaintive,

---

*A woman of noble birth who takes a selkie lover while her husband is away on the
Crusades, and bears him a son, with tragic consequences.

prickly articles in the *Orkney Herald*. 'The slow seepings and rottings' of the twentieth century, he argued, were continuing to spread across the islands, and the outlook was 'grey and forlorn'. As business and trade were increasingly centralized in Kirkwall, the spirit was being sucked from Stromness. When he was a boy, George argued, the Wednesday cattle market had been a high point of the week, the town jostling with apple-cheeked farmers smelling of peats and fields; now, it was 'a pitiful show'. The harbour, meanwhile, seemed practically deserted. 'Nowadays,' he wrote, 'it is a little wistfully that the school-children of the west sing their song, "May Stromness Flourish". For obviously it is not flourishing; it is in a state of most depressing quiescence.' Things seemed no better in the countryside. Farms that had once been pleasantly 'picturesque and insanitary' were becoming 'ugly and convenient'; and, although the islands had never been agriculturally more efficient and productive, farmers were under such pressure to package and export the fruits of their labour that traditional farm produce had become a rarity on Orkney tables. But perhaps most depressing of all, it seemed to George, was the fact that the Orkney townsman and the Orkney farmer were becoming strangers to one another. 'This,' he wrote ominously, 'is not a pleasant trend.'

If these gloomy views were largely a reflection of George's state of mind, they were not entirely so. Life in Orkney was indeed changing, and old, immemorial quirks and customs were steadily disappearing. When Ernest Marwick, also writing in the *Orkney Herald*, enumerated thirty-five things that had disappeared from Orkney life since he was a boy, his list included many of the features that George had loved best: 'Fish drying on wires at the gable-end', 'farm animals on tethers', 'tinkers selling tin pails', 'witch and fairy stories' and – perhaps dearest to George – 'the last of the "characters"'. Eccentrics like Titty Bell and Geordie Chalmers had long since moved on to Warbeth kirkyard, and with them an element of zest and colour had been lost for ever. In the summer of 1939, one-eyed 'Puffer' had walked through the town, ringing his bell and making public announcements heavily salted with local gossip, for the last time. Thereafter, through the war, the ringing of bells was prohibited except as a warning of imminent invasion, and in 1945 Puffer's job was taken over by a man in a van with a megaphone.

The countryside was changing at least as fast as the towns. By 1952, there was hardly a farm still worked by horses. In order to raise money to buy new agricultural machinery, groups of farmers had had to pool their resources and their land, allowing the old, small crofts to be subsumed into larger, more competitive units. One by one, the traditional 'but-and-ben' croft houses were abandoned and fell into ruins. Unaided by government subsidy, meanwhile, fishermen were struggling. The great lobster harvests of wartime had shrunk to almost nothing, and catches of haddock and cod were now menaced by trawlers and seine netters from mainland Scotland. Life for the crofter-fishermen of remote communities like Rackwick had become very hard indeed.

During the summer of 1952, Rackwick's difficulties were compounded by tragedy. On the morning of 10 August, two of the valley's four children – John and Hugh Mowat, aged twelve and nine – left the croft of Moss to play on a homemade raft, and did not return. A search party was sent out, and at dusk the boys' bodies were dragged from the swollen waters of Rackwick Burn. It was not long before the Mowat family, with their two surviving children, left the valley. Catherine Rendall, who had taught the children of Rackwick for forty-five years, locked up her school. For the first time in centuries, the valley was childless. All this took its toll on George's spirits. When, in the late summer, the County Council agreed unexpectedly to give him a grant of £150 for a further year at Newbattle, he could not wait to leave. His love for the islands, he confessed to Ernest Marwick, had 'quite evaporated'.

Not much survives of George's work from the autumn of 1952, but what little is preserved suggests that he did not find it easy to shake off the grimness of the Orkney summer and re-enter the idyll of his first year at Newbattle. In October, he wrote a long poem, 'A Prayer to Two Angels'. Addressed, on the face of it, to two aspects of his guardian angel, the 'bright' and the 'dark', it is in fact an examination of the conflicting dynamics in his own nature. The 'bright angel' enables him to feel gladness and peace in the face of criticism and hurt, and equanimity about his poverty and the uncertainty of his future. But it is the 'dark angel' – angel of 'love, death, poetry' – that is his more constant, and not unwelcome, companion. It follows him, 'hand on sword-hilt', wherever he goes, entering into him every so often – 'like a ghost into a child' – to bring glimpses of the paradise that awaits him beyond the grave. Of the dark angel, he begs just one thing: that he should be allowed to live long enough to write five really good poems. Granted this, he will be 'acquiescent' when the sword is finally unsheathed.

George's death wish, albeit in a conditional, postponing form, had returned. By Christmas, his health was beginning to suffer. Edwin Muir had encouraged him to try for a Cambridge scholarship. George dismissed the idea out of hand. 'A medical examination is called for before you're admitted,' he wrote to Ernest Marwick, 'and . . . I couldn't possibly leap that hurdle.' He managed to get home to Orkney for the holidays, and to return to Newbattle for the beginning of the spring term, but he was then almost immediately forced to take to his bed, sweating and exhausted. He was too weak to pick up a book, and coughed so relentlessly that he felt like a shell pounded by the sea. Willa Muir installed him in the spare bedroom of the Warden's flat, and nursed him until he was strong enough to make the return journey north. In Well Park, Mhairi Brown took over.

At first, the days passed pleasantly enough. Lying on his bed, George devoured 'book after book after book, gluttonously', and even wrote again to the BBC asking whether he might do some work for them. He was invited, in response, to prepare a series of talks on 'Trends in Orkney Agriculture' for their schools programme. He turned the offer down flat. 'It seems to me,' Ernest Marwick noted in his diary, 'that if he cannot write fine literature, he will refuse to write at all.' Instead, George poured what energy he had into letters to his Newbattle friends, painting vivid pictures of life in Stromness. 'There has been some excitement in our little town today,' he writes to Flora Jack on 23 March 1953. 'A large Grimsby trawler lost her way in last night's thick fog, and grounded on some reefs off Hoy. If the crew had kept their heads and stayed put, they would have been all right. But, poor men, they got into the ship's lifeboats, and the heavy ground swell upset one of them. Seven men altogether were drowned, the others were saved. I saw them this afternoon bringing some of the bodies into the harbour.'*

---

*The trawler to which George refers was the 411-ton *Leicester City*. She had been at sea for twenty-two days, and was returning to Grimsby from the Icelandic fishing grounds with 1,300 kits of fish.

He thought perpetually of Newbattle – 'the crocuses and daffodils will be coming up along the river bank now' – and begged for news. He was determined that he would be well enough to travel south for the summer term. For all Mhairi Brown's efforts, however, George's health deteriorated. His 'ancient ally' had returned, and in early April, the doctor ordered him back to Eastbank. For more than a year, this once again became his home.

In the decade since George was last in the sanatorium, there had been a breakthrough in the treatment of tuberculosis in the form of three powerful new drugs: streptomycin, PAS and INAH. With the help of these, a young Scotsman, Dr Brodie, about George's age and good-humoured and positive, was determined to rid the islands of the disease. On the whole, this meant that the atmosphere was bright: few of the patients were now threatened with death. But to George, over-come with nostalgia for Newbattle, Eastbank seemed part torture chamber, part charnel house.

His day began at 6 a.m. with an injection of streptomycin into the shoulder, followed, very often, by a blood test. 'I had to summon all my virile strength to keep from giving vent to scream after piercing scream, while they searched about in my arm with a syringe to find a suitable vein,' he wrote to Flora Jack. 'At last they found one, and got their blood, after which I collapsed among the pillows bedewed with sweat.' In the course of the rest of the day, he was 'perpetually set upon by sadistic women with needles', and was expected to swallow thirty crimson tablets 'as big as peppermint drops'. These wreaked havoc on his intestines and made his eyes bloodshot and sore. He felt sure, he told Ernest Marwick, that these trials were being visited on him in retribution for the happiness he had experienced at Newbattle. He was worried about the future.

George yearned for sleep, and for silence, but he was sharing a room with a garrulous man whose wife visited twice a day, and who never switched off his radio. This so played on George's nerves that once, when he was left alone, he took the set and smashed it against the wall. The radio was not the only aggravation. In the interest of keeping up patients' spirits, the hospital was regularly visited by the Salvation Army, who positioned themselves immediately outside George's window. He found their performances not only untuneful and depressing – they repeatedly played 'Abide with Me' – but also revolting. The band would stop every so often, unscrew their instruments, and blow out accumulations of saliva on to the ground a yard from where George was lying. 'If I had known I must come home to this,' he admitted to Flora Jack, 'I believe I would have set my teeth and stayed on in the Abbey, but then we never know what's in front of us.'

There was worse to come. When, after some weeks, it seemed that George was not responding properly to the new drugs, a more savage treatment, involving sawing open the ribcage, was mooted. He was flown south to be examined by specialist surgeons at Woodland Hospital in Aberdeen, a place so horrible that Eastbank seemed 'Arcadia' by comparison. He wrote to Ernest Marwick on 19 October:

> I have been here, in a long lofty 12-bed ward, ice-cold, and diabolical with cleanliness and efficiency, for a full week now, enduring various tests to see if I am fit to undergo this grisly operation. If they decide, by means of their esoteric rituals, that I am fit for it, I'll be kept here. Only God forbid . . . I'm beginning to revolt against all this beastliness carried out in the sacred names of medicine and science. The other day they spreadeagled a young Shetland lad and shoved a long tube with a lighted bulb at the end of it down his throat and probed about with it among his bronchial tubes. The whole business was indescribably agonising, according to the boy, who lies in the bed next to me.

In the end, George was forced to endure neither a bronchoscopy, like the young Shetlander, nor the twelve-hour rib-sawing operation. He was flown home, and the only lasting effect of his spell in Aberdeen was to make him happier, by comparison, with life at Eastbank. By September, he had gained a stone and a half in weight, and settled into 'a kind of drowsy contentment . . . not caring overmuch what happens'. On fine days, his bed was wheeled out on to the men's veranda, where he took part in long games of Monopoly. He began to enjoy the company, in particular, of two of the older patients: Davie Fox – a Kirkwall man, and a Catholic – and a farmer, Jimmy Sinclair, whom he later considered one of the few truly happy people he had ever met. Sympathetic to George's need for silence, Dr Brodie had had him moved into the single-bed ward, looking out across a field and the rooftops of Kirkwall to the spire of St Magnus Cathedral, with a glimpse of Scapa Flow beyond. Here, he told Flora Jack, he so relished his solitude that he sometimes crooned to himself with delight.

Alcohol was strictly forbidden in the sanatorium – although as a special concession, on 2 June, each of the male patients had been given one bottle of beer to drink while they listened on the radio to the Coronation crowds cheering through the London rain. By the autumn, however, George had become adept at helping his brothers and friends to smuggle in whisky, and he puffed constantly on a pipe to mask the smell. Four Kirkwall ladies, Mrs Shearer, Mrs Tinch, Mrs Garden and Miss Bain, were now in charge of occupying the patients with handicrafts, including 'candlewick, leatherwork, basketry, embroidery, dress-making, jewellery-making and tatting'. From all these George had contrived to be excused by undertaking to launch and edit a quarterly hospital magazine, *Saga*, written almost entirely by himself. He was also working on a play, and was pleased with it. 'I murmur it to myself,' he told Flora Jack, 'alone in my small ward, like a bee humming over a flower.'

In September, inspired by George's experiences, Ernest Marwick had left with his wife to spend a year at Newbattle. In his absence, Robert Rendall became a frequent visitor, using George, as he had used Marwick, as an audience for his poetry, and thereby reawakening George's own desire to write. 'I must tell you about Robert Rendall and his new sonnet,' George wrote to Marwick, just after Christmas 1953. Rendall had turned up at Eastbank in the early afternoon, flushed and agitated, speaking chiefly to himself about images and rhymes that were tormenting him, and that he felt unable to put down on paper. He left as abruptly as he had arrived, but in the evening, after the bell had sounded warning visitors to be gone, he appeared again. 'He had all the symptoms of a *drunk man* – flushed face, shining eyes, uncertain gait – and for a while he couldn't even speak, having come loping up the road like a greyhound. He had just, he said, written a poem. The vague ideas floating about in his mind had suddenly crystallised, and the poem (a sonnet) had been born with almost fantastic ease. He had just sat down after tea, and typed it out. And then he said he would read it out, and he did, in a purged exultant voice.' The poem, 'Renewal', was, George wrote towards the end of his life, one of the most perfect sonnets he knew. When Rendall finally left his bedside, 'wrapped in his singing cloak', George sank back against his pillows 'in a backwash of jealousy'.

Another regular visitor, at George's request, was Father Smith, the priest from the Catholic Church in Kirkwall, a fellow pipe-smoker and lover of poetry. At Newbattle, George had taken himself two or three times to Mass in Dalkeith, and had been disappointed. He had found it difficult to follow the Missal, and the long silences and whispers of the Tridentine rite, and the hymns and the worshippers with their rosaries seemed strange to him. But he had been moved, none the less, by the devotion of the working-class women – 'here they found beauty and peace in the midst of drab lives' – and his belief that, in spite of all, the Catholic Church was guided by the truth had continued to grow.

This second spell at Eastbank was, if anything, even more crucial than the first to George's religious development. 'I think,' he once wrote, 'that the work of some writers is shaped by a few over-mastering images'; and it was during these months in the sanatorium that one particular image began to work on his imagination. It was the image of man's life as the seed that is cast into a furrow, and that must die in darkness and silence before new life can spring from it. As George pondered this, it seemed to illuminate the whole of life for him, making everything simple and marvellous. In so far as it comes from St John's Gospel, the image is Christian, but what compelled George was that it seemed to encompass the entire sweep of history, so that Christianity arrived as a consummation rather than a contradiction of what had gone before: 'It included within itself everything. From the most primitive breaking of the soil to Christ himself with his parables of agriculture and the majestic symbolism of his passion, death, and resurrection.' All around him in the Orkney cornfields the image was embodied. It would remain at the heart of his thinking and writing for the rest of his life.

The image, of course, had particular significance for George as he lay in the sanatorium, hidden away like the buried seed, apparently achieving nothing as the weeks and months passed. In his play *A Seat by My Bed* the young patient, as he falls asleep, feels that he is 'one with the drifting snow, the hungry birds, the buried seeds, deep down near the beating heart of the world'. He hopes that, while he sleeps, 'some new brightness, some new blessing' is being woven into his body's darkness, and that darkness and light together will create 'a new man and a new world'. This was George's own experience. In the spring of 1954, after nearly a year at Eastbank, he began to feel a surge of hope and energy. In March, Allison Tait, the gifted poet and singer whose father owned the Kirkwall bookshop where George had first met Ernest Marwick, died in childbirth at the age of twenty-eight. George, in response, wrote an elegy. It is governed by the image of the seed, and in style it seems to mourn not only Allison Tait but also Dylan Thomas, who had died aged thirty-nine the previous autumn. But, despite these two untimely deaths, the poem ends on a note not of lament, but of triumph:

> The Magnustide long swords of rain
>   Quicken the dust. The ploughman turns
>   Furrow by holy furrow
>   The liturgy of April.
>   What rock of sorrow
>   Checks the seed's throb and flow
> Now the lark's skein is thrown
>   About the burning sacrificial hill?
>
> Cold exiles from that ravished tree
>   (Fables and animals guard it now)
>   Whose reconciling leaves
>   Fold stone, cornstalk and lark,
>   Our first blood grieves
>   That never again her lips
> Flowering with song we'll see,
>   Who, winged and bright, speeds down into the
>   dark.
>
> Now let those risers from the dead,
>   Cornstalks, golden conspirators,
>   Cry on the careless wind
>   Ripeness and resurrection;
>   How the calm wound
>   Of the girl entering earth's side
> Gives back immortal bread
>   For this year's dust and rain that shall be man.

As George grew physically stronger, so his spirits rose; but his friends, and especially Edwin and Willa Muir, were also responsible for his improved morale. Since seeing him off on the train home from Newbattle, Willa had kept in constant touch with letters full of bracing wit and affection. 'You must know,' she wrote, when George was at a particularly low ebb, 'that you have friends scattered like points of light in the darkness.' Edwin Muir sent regular parcels of books: Kafka's short stories, Osbert Sitwell's autobiography, Alain-Fournier's *Le Grand Meaulnes*. In accompanying letters he kept up a discreet but dogged pressure on George not to give way to despair, and to count his blessings. 'Forgive me for preaching,' Muir had written shortly after George left Newbattle, 'but let me say that you are lucky in one way, that you have a gift that most people pass all their lives without having, and that even in Orkney, even without the atmosphere which would help to nourish it, it is yours, and you can do something with it, to our good and your own.'

Privately, in earlier years, George had dismissed the predictions of both his Classics master John Cook and the poet Francis Scarfe that he would one day make his name as a writer; but affirmation of this nature from Edwin Muir was harder to ignore. It was hard, too, for George to disregard Muir's well-calculated insistence that his gift had been given to him not just for his own enjoyment, but for the enrichment of a wider public. Confined to the sanatorium, he decided that the time had come to bring out a collection of his work, and in June 1954 the Orkney Press published *The Storm*: twenty poems between buff paper covers, with illustrations by Ian MacInnes.

'For the islands I sing,' George proclaims in the Prologue, and his love of the islands is at the heart of the collection. In 'The Road Home', he celebrates the expanse of history and prehistory against which Orkneymen live out their lives; in 'The Tramp' he delights in the glorious freedom of people on the fringes of society; in 'Rackwick' he distils into ten lines his feelings for the sea valley; and in 'Saint Magnus on Egilshay' he imagines the blessings showered on the islands in the wake of the martyr's death:

> But O, what love came then! Grass, vole, and flower
> Twined in a riot through the acre of death
> And larks cut lyrical nests deep in its turf.

Parched loin, and stringless tongue, and pearl-blind eye,
And poor daft Sigurd, reaped life from that death,
Loading their broken barns. There Time's harsh breath
    Closed in a fall of song.

The passion of the more serious poems is counterbalanced by the tender, comic affection of poems like 'Them at Isbister', in which George offers a vignette of the lives of an old crofting couple, Janet, with 'bright eyes / And thick brisk hands' and Robbie, 'useless with rheumatics'.

When Janet rails at Robbie
He rarely bothers to answer.
Sitting by the honeysuckle in July
Or under the tilley in December,
He is well contented.
He knows when it will rain
By the pains in his legs.

When a letter comes from the youngest boy
They peek at each other over their spectacles,
Spelling out the clumsy words far into the evening.

The dog barks in amazement.

When a butterfly knock comes at the door
Robbie says, 'Damn me, it's the minister.
But let him in.'

He gropes for his pipe.
Janet scurries to hang the kettle on the hook
And cries a welcome to the rattling sneck.

The Storm was roundly applauded in the local papers, its reviewer in the *Orkney Herald* predicting that in years to come George Mackay Brown would be ranked in a class with Edwin Muir. Muir himself would have been not only pleased but flattered by this. At George's request, he had written an introduction to *The Storm*. It was the only time in his life that he agreed to do such a thing, and he confessed that he found it difficult. The result was generous and moving. George, he wrote, had 'the gift of imagination and the gift of words: the poet's endowment'. His poetry was imbued with 'a strangeness and a magic rare anywhere in literature to-day'. Muir explained that he had first read many of the poems in *The Storm* at Newbattle, and that he had been struck then by their 'fresh and spontaneous beauty'. Reading them again, he found himself impressed as well 'by something which I can only call grace. Grace is what breathes warmth into beauty and tenderness into comedy; it is in a sense the crowning gift, for without it beauty would be cold and comedy would be heartless.'

Copies of *The Storm* are now rare and very expensive* – and, George later thought, 'greatly to be shunned'. In the summer of 1954, however, he not only pressed ahead with publication against the advice of Ernest Marwick, but also paid for it out of his own pocket. He cannot, at that stage, have been unhappy with the quality of his work. But something else worried him. One afternoon, shortly after *The Storm* was published, his Eastbank companion Jimmy Sinclair took George to see his farm in the parish of Rendall. Sinclair described how, over the years, he had brought acres of tough, intractable, stony land under the plough. George was moved, and unsettled. How much more satisfying and worthwhile, he reflected afterwards, to see green fields where once there was bog 'than to do something new with the language, like T. S. Eliot'. Sinclair's fields were real, animals could feed on them, and crops could flourish. By contrast, he feared that the achievement of many writers, Eliot included, was simply to provide 'a field for a few barren intellectuals, with that sowing which poets like to call "eternal", flattering themselves'.

T. S. Eliot, once George's hero, had become in his mind a suspect figure, the embodiment of all that most unsettled him about poets and their craft. One wild winter morning in the sanatorium, George had settled down to write to Ernest Marwick. He set out his letter in rhyming couplets, replete with frustration about the state of the world, and particularly of poetry. His old enemies, prosperity and respectability, come in for their regular thrashing and, towards the end, Eliot is depicted as a vain, fastidious old phoney:

> In a London office Eliot sits,
> Prince of intellectual wits,

*Only three hundred copies of *The Storm* were printed, and the type was immediately dismantled. When, a fortnight after publication, the book had sold out, it was impossible to reprint.

Writing his few lines every year
Between a wry grin and a tear,
Wearing his bowler and his spats
Sampling cheese and petting cats . . .

George sees him as exerting a dangerous influence on poetry, making it a thing of the head, not the heart, and the preserve of intellectuals.

To the end of his life, George had a horror of the notion of 'kultur' (he often spelled it with an aggressive 'k'). Because his imagination encompassed such an enormous sweep of history, he considered culture a newish concept, one whose effect had been not just to distort but to turn on its head the proper purpose of art, by dropping 'a great chasm between poet and people', thereby destroying communication. If he had to stand on one side of the chasm, George had no doubt that he would rather be numbered among the ordinary people than the intellectuals – the 'gray horde'. And, if he was to devote his life to poetry, he was clear that it must be with the aim of making hard lives beautiful by imposing 'a meaningful pattern' on them, and not of tit-illating the vanity of clever, comfortable minds. Yet here he was, aged thirty-three, publishing a collection of poetry that he knew very well would not appeal at all to most of the people whose lives he wished to touch. He felt distinctly uneasy about this. If ever he brought out another collection, he promised Marwick, it would be different – 'simple and forthright and such as a crofter or fisherman would read and remember with pleasure'.

'I am sitting down trying to overtake time': many of Edwin Muir's letters to George begin along these lines. Time, despot and gaoler, is the great enemy in Muir's poetry, and by the summer of 1954, harried by the Executive Committee at Newbattle, and troubled by the pains in his chest, he was beginning to suspect that his own time was running short. George, too, was feeling threatened by time, but for the opposite reason. In June, he was finally released from Eastbank. He was still weak. 'I get hideously tired,' he told Ernest Marwick, 'by walking even a short distance'; and he had been discharged with a warning that a part of his lung would be out of action for the rest of his life, and that he would never again be truly fit. Once more, the years yawned ahead of him.

Although he still had a term's grant in hand, there was no question of George's being strong enough to return to Newbattle. Instead, he settled back into what looked very much like his old routine, sleeping till noon, drinking himself every evening into 'that delightful condition where the frontier between truth and imagination is hazy and ill-defined'. He had resumed his weekly column in the *Orkney Herald*, and was using it again as a punch-bag against which he could vent his frustrations with modern living and modern man. He marvelled at the 'really ingenious ugliness' of the new houses that had begun to scab the Orkney landscape since the war, and deplored the 'brittle, celluloid manners' of young Orcadians, and their utilitarian, grasping attitudes to life. 'What brisk hard-headed common-sense dehydrated little manikins we are nowadays,' he writes in September 1955, 'strutting around with our cheque-books!'

During 1955, the first televisions began to arrive in the islands. They were slow to catch on, partly because they were so expensive (a 14-inch portable set cost over 50 guineas, and an average Orkney farm wage was still less than £10 per week) and partly because the nearest transmitter was 250 miles away at Meldrum in Aberdeenshire, so that most programmes had to be watched as if through a blizzard. George was full of gloom about the havoc that 'this startling box of tricks' would wreak on Orkney homes, making those who watched it mechanized in their speech and reactions and habits. 'Will it give a death-blow to the already dying art of conversation and story-telling? Will it cause the dust to gather even thicker on the fiddle on the wall? Will it make books and reading old-fashioned? Will it give our sons and daughters a still greater thirst for the bright lights of the city, and so accelerate depopulation? Or will it bring great new knowledge and glory to the islands of the north?' he asks. 'I think I hear the trows on the hill-tops sniggering sarcastically and withdrawing deeper among their shadows.'

Mhairi Brown was now in her mid-sixties, and George was not the only one of her children causing her concern. Shortly after he was discharged from Eastbank, his eldest brother Hughie suffered a heart attack and nearly died. (Hughie later described to his siblings how, the night after the attack, the toddler ghost of their brother Harold, who had died of measles in infancy, appeared beckoning at the foot of his bed. 'Not yet!' Hughie pleaded, and Harold receded into the shadows.) George, nevertheless, was welcomed back into Well Park, where his mother once again cooked and washed and cleaned for him. He was still so domestically helpless that when Mhairi Brown left for a few days' holiday in the spring of 1955 he found himself unable to boil an egg or make a piece of toast, and was forced to sustain himself almost entirely on milk. His shoes, which Mhairi normally polished until they 'shone like the hooves of a unicorn', grew drab and dull, the fire remained unlit and his bed became such a hideous confusion of 'independent coils of sheet and blanket' that he could hardly bear to sleep in it.

Newbattle, George had once told Ernest Marwick, had provided him with some of his happiest memories: whatever happened, these could never be taken away. As the months went by, however, it began to look as if George's time there was nothing more than a memory, and was to have no tangible, lasting effect on his life at all. And so, but for the determination of Edwin Muir, it might have turned out.

In the summer of 1955, Muir finally succumbed to the bullying of the Executive Committee, and resigned the Wardenship of Newbattle to take up a post as Charles Eliot Norton Professor of Poetry at Harvard University. Here, to their surprise, he and Willa found themselves bowled over by the urbanity, generosity and optimism of the American people. 'I expect all nations make up a sort of caricature of other nations,' he wrote to George. 'At any rate, the America we've come to know is not in the least like the America we were told we would find. The people do not *eat* and *drink* excessively, they do not hustle, or clap you on the shoulder, or speak out of the corner of their mouths. They are kind, considerate, intelligent, tolerant, excellent company – but kind, above all.' He was spending a lot of time in the company of Robert Frost, now eighty-two, and 'a great and wise man', proud that his mother had been of Orkney stock. 'We Orkneymen,' Frost would begin his conversations with Muir, taking his arm.

Despite the distractions and demands of a new country and a new job, Muir continued to write regularly to George. The previous summer, he had sent copies of *The Storm* to a number of his friends, and George, in response, had received a grand sheaf of letters of appreciation, including one from E. M. Forster. G. S. Fraser had broadcast a number of poems from *The Storm* on *New Poetry*, on the Third Programme, and Alexander Scott, discussing the collection on *Arts Review*, had spoken of the 'luminous images' that could only have been written by a poet who had 'mastered his craft'. In 1955, Scott was appointed editor of a new literary quarterly, the *Saltire Review*, and poems and articles by George began to appear regularly in its pages, alongside work by Norman MacCaig, Eric Linklater, Edwin Morgan and Stevie Smith. Janet Adam Smith was publishing George's work in the *New Statesman*, and in 1956 his sonnet 'The Old Women' appeared in *Encounter*.

From Harvard, meanwhile, Edwin Muir sent a handful of George's poems to the literary editor at *Harper's Bazaar*, who immediately offered $130 to publish three of them. Muir urged George to keep sending him new work, and was fulsome in response. 'I admire these poems of yours more and more the more I read them,' he wrote in the spring of 1956. 'You have a feeling for words which I sincerely envy . . . The genius is there, my dear George, and I wish you all that it offers you.' He singled out for particular praise 'Thorfinn', a poem based on the true story of a Stromness lad, a known poultry thief, who had rowed out beyond the harbour one evening, supposedly to collect his lobster creels, and drowned:

> Heart sick of the land
> Where troubles grew with every grass blade
> And every rose gushed from a septic root
> And every casual car was the Black Maria,
>
> He rowed his little boat behind the holm
> To take the purple samurai of the flood.
> Cornless they range, the lobsters.
> By weeded rock and plangent pool
> God puts in their beautiful claws
> Sweet algae and tiny glimmering fish
> The dropping surfeits of the rich Atlantic
> Ravelling its rivers through the corn-patched Orkneys
> And shrinking, twice a day.
> (To their peril they eat man fodder:
> Explore a casual fishgut hole, they're snared
> In a tarry mesh, drawn up, and drowned with air.)

Whether it chanced, the Owner of these lobsters,
Grown sour at Thorfinn as any bristling poultry man
Turned a salt key in his last door of light;
Or whether Love, abroad in a seeking wave
Lifted him from the creaking rowlocks of time
And flung a glad ghost on a wingless shore:

No one can tell.

　　　　A crofter at early light
Found an empty boat stuttering on the rocks
And dawn-cold cocks cheering along the links.

In the summer of 1956, 'Thorfinn' was published in a short-lived but distinguished magazine, *Nimbus*, in which it appeared alongside work by W. H. Auden and William Empson. It was the first of George's poems to be read by Ted Hughes, then just twenty-five and recently married to Sylvia Plath, and it struck him as a 'marvellous, fresh, new thing' quite unlike anything he had ever read before. 'Reading it again now,' Hughes said, speaking as Poet Laureate in 1991, 'I can see that it really went into me. I can see all sorts of little hints and suggestions in this piece that I've taken myself.'

Despite Muir's advice that he should stick to poetry, George was also experimenting with short stories. Sometimes, he found, an idea for a poem would simply turn into a story as he began to write, and vice versa. One fine morning in the summer of 1955 – a summer so hot that it seemed to George that the children of Orkney spent more time in the sea than on dry land – he sat on a bench on a hill behind Stromness and wrote 'Tam'. It is the tale of a crotchety old cobbler whose three luscious daughters – 'clustered in age round the sweet number twenty, like three wasps round a squashed plum' – seduce their second cousin one after another through one glorious night, as he stays with them before sailing for the 'nor'-wast'. Like much of his best work, this story came singing effortlessly off George's pen, giving him a sense of 'sweetness and power' that is infused in the writing.

Depression, at such moments, seemed mercifully distant; but it had continued to plague George, on and off, and in the spring of 1956 it returned with a vengeance. On 24 March, pulling pints in the British Legion Club, Hughie Brown suffered a final, fatal heart attack. His death shocked the community. Dark, good-looking and charming, Hughie had been the least bookish and the most vigorous and obviously attractive of all the Brown boys. George was devastated: it was he, after all, and not Hughie, whom fate was supposed to have singled out for an early death. For several weeks, he felt exhausted and distracted, unable even to write his *Herald* column, the 'tide of the spirit . . . shrunken, ebbed far out'. The atmosphere in Well Park was grim: Mhairi Brown had now seen not only her husband but two of her five sons laid in Warbeth kirkyard. No wonder that by May George felt the need to escape. He applied, and was accepted, to spend one final term at Newbattle.

Once again, the abbey worked its magic. As he lay in bed on his first night, listening to the waters of the Esk 'singing out to sea in the darkness', and the wind stirring in the trees, George felt the clouds of *Morbus orcadensis*, that had threatened to engulf him, lift. He longed to be able to stay within Newbattle's protective walls for ever. 'Here, I am perfectly happy,' he confessed to Ernest Marwick. 'I only wish it was 600 years ago, so that I could have taken vows and become a monk (one of the Browningesque kind that keeps a secret still buried under the beech tree).'

Yet, without Edwin Muir, an essential ingredient was missing from the life of the college, and the students that summer term lacked the flare and spirit of George's earlier companions. They were quiet, and studious, and very very nice, he told Ernest Marwick, but the publican at the Justinlees was depressed by their lack of interest in drink. Through the month of June, George believed that he had fallen in love with a female student from Aberdeen, and murmured lines of Shakespeare into her ear. But the general atmosphere of sobriety and diligence provoked a wild, rebellious streak in him.

One evening, the students were visited by a poet and BBC producer, George Bruce. Bruce was immediately struck by George. 'I knew from the first moment I met him,' he later reflected, 'that here was a person of the deepest possible spiritual resource.' He invited George to contribute to a radio programme about Edwin Muir. A fellow student, Edward McLaughlan, agreed to accompany him to Edinburgh for the recording, and, when it was over, the two of them set out with George's £9 payment on a pub crawl. They arrived back at Newbattle plastered, just as some important visitors were leaving, and the following morning, as he nursed a wretched hangover, George was ordered to pack his bags and leave. In the end, under pressure from the other students who threatened to depart *en masse* if George was expelled, the Warden relented; but the threat of expulsion had served as a salutary shock. The prospect of returning indefinitely to Orkney, without either qualification or plans for the future, was, George realized, terrifying. Before heading north at the end of the summer term, he had secured a place to study English literature at Edinburgh University, starting in the autumn.

That summer, Edwin and Willa Muir visited Orkney for a holiday. They called on George one beautiful afternoon in a hired car, and the three of them drove to a spot just beneath Brinkie's Brae, and stood looking out over a magnificent view of Scapa Flow, Hoy, Orphir and Stromness, before going on to the Standing Stones Hotel for tea. They sat together a long while in the hotel garden: 'All around was the blue and green of a good summer afternoon in Orkney.' When Edwin asked for the bill, the proprietress, Mrs Heywood, 'sent word that for the poet and his guests the delicious meal was free'.

This was to be the last time Edwin Muir saw Orkney. His ambitions for George were yet to be realized, but he had planted in him a spirit of optimism and resolve. Without the encouragement of this extraordinary man, George later reflected, he might never have become anything more than a local journalist. 'It was Edwin Muir who turned my face in the right direction: firmly but discreetly – and gave me a pocketful of hope and promise for the journey.'

10

The Muse in Rose Street

The idea of the Muse who brings out the best in artists is ancient, of course. Some modern poets have their Muse, a woman who transfigures their work and guides them like a star, *stella maris*. This girl was actually called Stella. I met her one summer evening in The Abbotsford, together with someone else who has become a nameless shadow.

GMB, *For the Islands I Sing*

THE BIOGRAPHY OF an artist, George once wrote, is really a pattern of those experiences and images that enter deeply into his consciousness and set the rhythm and tone of his work. With this in mind, it seems worth recording one small moment in his early, uncertain days as an undergraduate in Edinburgh. Sitting in a pub called the Greyfriars Bobby, having a pie and a pint of beer for lunch, and turning the pages of Bede's *Ecclesiastical History of England*, he came upon the image of an old monk alone in a cold cell, writing by candlelight. It both enthralled and disturbed him. From childhood, George had been nudging towards an acceptance of what he called a 'monkish disposition', a desire to spend much of his time alone. But, while he relished solitude, he hated loneliness: he felt it 'like a pain'. Around him in Edinburgh he watched the other students come and go, couples often hand in hand. He envied them.

To his fellow undergraduates, George Brown must have seemed an odd figure. He was now thirty-five – nearly twenty years older than many of them – and though his shock of black hair and very bright blue eyes gave him, at a distance, an appearance of puckish youthfulness, close up he was worn-looking, thin, hollow-cheeked and painfully shy. His clothes looked as if they had suffered years of neglect, one acquaintance remembers, and he himself gave rather the same impression. His scarred lungs meant that walking even short distances exhausted him, so that on weekdays, after breakfast, as hordes of students trooped from their digs in Marchmont across the Meadows to the university lecture halls, George joined a queue of Edinburgh housewives and waited for a 39 bus.

For the first half of his first term he observed Edinburgh through a cloud of misery. It was, he told Ernest Marwick, a 'stand-offish city . . . I shudder whenever I hear those young things newly up from Edinburgh public schools, and their cold metallic confident accents. A lot of them go round in bowler hats, swinging umbrellas. Truly I think the Communists, or the Jehovah's Witnesses are right – we are getting near the end of the present set-up. A city that breeds such people is at the edge of a crumbling crag.' He found the English course gruelling – 'forget about sweetness and light, work till you sprout grey hairs' – and Marchmont, where he was lodging, deeply depressing: 'It's a warren of students . . . simply swarming with them, and fusty old poverty-stricken landladies who vote Tory.'

At every turn, George felt brought up short by buildings. It was like being snared in a stone web. Compared with Orkney, where all the buildings were scoured clean by salt wind and rain, Edinburgh seemed filthy. 'Auld Reekie' was still a coal-powered city, and the façades of institutions like the Royal Academy and the National Gallery of Scotland, now pewter-coloured, were then black. The novelist Candia McWilliam, who grew up in Edinburgh during George's undergraduate years, remembers moving about the city in autumn and winter under a continual pall of smoke, breathing air the colour of old vellum. Everywhere, inescapable, was the smell of coal. It collided in the air with the thick scent of fermenting hops from the breweries; and when there was no wind, and the air was damp, smog descended suddenly, so dense sometimes that you could hardly see your finger if you held it before your nose. Leaving his lodgings one smoggy October evening, the man who lived in the room below George stepped unwittingly into the path of a bus, and was killed.

All this induced in George a kind of despair. He knew he could not go back to Orkney: for all his homesickness, he had begun to wither there for lack of direction. Nor did he see that he could ever be happy in Edinburgh. He would stick it out as long as he could, he wrote home, but the chances of his completing the four-year course were slim.

Yet as the autumn wore on, just as at Newbattle five years earlier, depression began to give way to a tentative excitement; and, just as at Newbattle, it was in part the past that came to George's rescue. Even in his early days in Edinburgh, the sight of the castle towering over the city on its rock had thrilled him. As the weeks went by, he felt his pulses racing as he wandered down the Royal Mile and thought of the men and women who had walked there before him: Burns, Mary Queen of Scots, Knox, Hume, Scott, Stevenson. He became fascinated by the story of an Edinburgh dustman's daughter who had died in obscurity in 1925. He heard of her first one Sunday when he went to listen to John McCormack, a scathing anti-Catholic, speaking at the city's open-air arena, the Mound. McCormack's rant that afternoon focused on Margaret Sinclair, a girl brought up in an Edinburgh slum earlier in the century who had entered a Poor Clare convent and who, despite an early death, had become an inspiration to Scottish Catholics. McCormack poured scorn on Sinclair's lowly origins – ' "Why," he cried, "her father was *a scaffy!*" '* – but the effect of his words was precisely the opposite to what he had intended. Margaret Sinclair became for George from that day on a heroine, and he prayed for her intercession for the rest of his life.[†]

The ghosts of sinners as well as saints enthralled George – of Deacon Brodie, the impeccable town councillor who had moonlighted as a burglar, and of Burke and Hare, the Victorian murderers who kept Edinburgh's medical students supplied with bodies for dissection. It fascinated him that the city that had given birth to *Dr Jekyll and Mr Hyde* was itself a Jekyll-and-Hyde place, where magnificence and middle-class respectability existed cheek-by-jowl with low-life, poverty and sleaze. In Princes Street, housewives shopped in hats and gloves, but propped outside shops like Jenners were limbless, begging ex-servicemen. At the top of the Mound, gowned advocates and bankers

---

*Lowland Scots for a scavenger or street cleaner.

[†]Margaret Sinclair was declared Venerable by Pope Paul VI in 1976, and Catholics all over Scotland continue to pray for her canonization. Her many advocates include Sir Jimmy Savile, whose mother attributed to Margaret Sinclair her son's recovery from a serious illness as a small baby.

in bowler hats arrived for work every morning at the law courts and the Bank of Scotland. Down below, in the Grassmarket, drunks with florid faces knocked back Blue Billy, a mixture of meths and Brasso. 'They did not often wear shoes,' Candia McWilliam recalls,

> and had no understanding of cars, which occasionally blethered down the black sweep of setts, as the deep, orderly Edinburgh cobbles are called, granite dovetailed with the precision of igloo blocks. The drinkers would freeze when a car came as though at Medusa's passing. Most of the men had been at sea, in the war or on the fishing boats. Tears came to them, after so long being awash with the drink, with a tidal ease.

Edinburgh appears rarely in George's work, but when it does the 'schizophrenia . . . that goes right through the city from top to bottom' is intimated. In *Greenvoe*, he paints a nostalgic picture of the monotonous but reassuring lives of the McKees – a middle-class family living in a neat, terraced house in Marchmont Square. But, beneath the façade of innocent respectability, there is mounting anguish as alcoholism takes hold of the adored only child, Simon.

Towards the end of his first term, George admitted rather grudgingly in a letter to Edwin Muir that he was beginning to see some good in Edinburgh. During his second term, as spring arrived, and the gaunt streets and squares blossomed with greenness, he found himself falling 'suddenly and lastingly' in love with the place. And, as his perceptions of the city changed, so too did his feelings about the people he was meeting there. The 'fusty old poverty-stricken landladies' of Marchmont, many of whom were widows of the two world wars, gradually began to seem to George brave, valiant characters. One of his own landladies, Mrs Thomson, had not only lost her husband to the great flu epidemic of 1918, but had also sat at the bedsides of her two daughters as they died, one of TB and one of food poisoning. She was unbroken by these experiences, and unembittered. She was the kind of powerful, indomitable, humorous woman – not, in some ways, unlike Willa Muir – whose company George relished. With two other undergraduates, a black dental student from British Honduras and a Norwegian engineer, he lived in her care in 'a web of strength and laughter'.

Among the students, too, George was forming lasting friendships. In later life, he remembered most warmly of all the company of John Durkin, a former miner, joiner and signalman who had made his way, after George, to Newbattle, and who eventually became head of English at Telford College of Further Education. They had in common feelings of eternal gratitude to Edwin Muir, a wry sense of humour, and a combined passion for poetry and pubs. Durkin remembers George as 'beautiful in drink'. While others in their cups fell into argument, George drifted instead into gently self-mocking, lyrical introspection. 'I am much more concerned,' he once murmured to Durkin, as a student dispute raged around them, 'with a sightless fish in the depths of my being'; and often he quoted Yeats:

> I must lie down where all the ladders start
> In the foul rag-and-bone shop of the heart.

Durkin's parents and many siblings lived in Fountainbridge and their house became a second home to George. It was the first Catholic family he had known, and what appealed to him – surprisingly, perhaps, for those to whom Catholicism is inextricably associated with a sense of guilt – was its complete freedom from the feelings of scruple and rebuke that his own Presbyterian ancestry had bred in him. Durkin himself had ceased to practise his religion, but his cradle-Catholicism had given him a rootedness and assurance that George envied.

George was hesitating still on the brink of conversion. In Edinburgh he began to go weekly to Mass at the Catholic chaplaincy in George Square, joining the Catholic undergraduates as they gathered, like the first disciples, in an upper room. He also had regular meetings with Father Barrett, a Jesuit, in Lauriston Place, though whether he was receiving formal instruction is not clear. While George was as careful and conscientious in his approach as any convert, doctrinal nicety left him cold. 'My mind doesn't work logically, only imaginatively,' he admitted; and it was literature, rather than intellectual argument, that finally broke down his defences.

Here, to his surprise, he found that the university English course had much to offer. George's experiences of force-feeding at school had left him with a lifelong ambivalence about the teaching of literature, and even about books. 'In general,' he states frankly in his autobiography, 'I do not *like* books.' In a letter to Ernest Marwick at the beginning of his first term, he had made it clear that what had brought him to Edinburgh was principally the need for diversion and change: 'It's all a game, really: I have no ambition towards academic honour whatever.' To begin with, the English department seemed as unedifying as every other aspect of Edinburgh life – 'a factory for turning out M.A.s like sausages', overseen by 'very sad dim souls' haunted by the ghosts of Saintsbury, Grierson and Dover Wilson. 'The mills of knowledge grind ponderously and inexorably in the brain,' he writes to Ernest Marwick on 23 October 1956. 'The trouble is to keep them from grinding down the heart too.'

By the following spring, George had changed his tune. He was being forced to read books he would never otherwise have opened, and some that seemed least appealing as he embarked on them ended by yielding the most extraordinary riches. To begin with, for example, he dismissed Anglo-Saxon and Middle English as 'a frightful waste of time, nerves, and energy'. Before long, he discovered that this was a period of literature in which he felt thoroughly at home: firmly rooted in the four elements and the five senses, and underpinned by the kind of profound and simple spirituality he was seeking for himself. Particular phrases and passages, like Chaucer's adoration of the Virgin – 'Withinne the cloistre blisful of thy sydis / Took mannes shape the eterneel love and pees' – stopped him dead in his tracks. Sitting 'alone and apart with the miracle of words' like these, he told Ernest Marwick, left him triumphant and rejoicing.

And, if it was true that many of his tutors were rather long in the tooth, George began to discover that they were not all so 'sad' and 'dim' as he had at first suspected. Dr George Kitchin was in his late seventies, and officially ten years into retirement, when he was brought back to the university to oversee the small tutorial group in which George had been placed. Small, bright-eyed, amused by life, Kitchin seemed to George like an eighteenth-century Edinburgh eccentric who had strayed into the wrong era:

> He punctuated our stammering efforts to grasp the riches of literature with salty benign remarks. He would praise the beer brewed in the brewery just below our high tutorial window in Minto Street, where we

were supposed to be deep into Pope or Chaucer. Sometimes he seemed to drift off into a light sleep, but would wake soon, his mind vivid with the rhythms and images we were splurging in: a dozen or so mature boys and girls; and I the oldest one among them, a kind of stepping-stone between themselves and the sceptical wisdom of Dr Kitchin.

If he seemed, in some respects, a character from the past, Kitchin was also very much alive to his own time, passionately concerned with social justice, quick, perceptive, good at grasping what people were really about. Although his main area of study had been the Metaphysical poets, he had also been one of the first to call attention to the achievements of Hugh MacDiarmid, and it is a mark of George's respect for Kitchin that he chose, early on, to show him some of his own poetry. Kitchin, who had a gift for knowing when rules should be bent, decided, in response, to allow George very often to hand in poems in place of essays. None of the other students knew about this; nor, almost certainly, did the rest of the English department. As a result of the marks Kitchin gave these poems, George found himself at the end of his first summer term placed second out of an English class of three hundred.

Not all his tutors found it so easy to build up a rapport with George. Winifred Maynard was three years his junior, and one of the youngest members of the department. She sensed that everything about her – her sex, her youth, the fact that she was English – made George ill at ease, and in the four years she knew him they never got beyond terms of guarded politeness. Throughout this time, George seemed to Maynard like a fish out of water in Edinburgh. 'He never really seemed to be at home in the university environment,' she reflects, nor did he appear to fit comfortably into any group.

The truth was that the group to which George felt drawn was not one that Winifred Maynard would ever herself have mixed with, or even necessarily encountered. In the centre of Edinburgh, behind and parallel to Princes Street, ran Rose Street, a dark, cobbled alley, half a mile long and with thirteen pubs interspersed between shops selling old silver, bric-à-brac and second-hand books. During the day, it was a cheerful place. Margaret Tait's 1956 film *Rose Street* shows children playing hopscotch and tag, and racing their bicycles over the cobbles. But, after dark, prostitutes loitered in the shadows, and few respectable women would have chosen to spend time there. Certainly, they were not made welcome: 'Females Not Admitted' stated notices in many of the pub windows, or, more ambiguously – though not intentionally so – 'Women Not Supplied'.

What drew George to Rose Street was that poets and writers and all the hangers-on of the arts were known to gather in its pubs. They particularly favoured Milne's, one of the shabbiest of the bars, run with brilliance by a genial landlord, Bob Watt. Here, on a Saturday night, Edinburgh poets – Sydney Goodsir Smith, Tom Scott, Norman MacCaig, Robert Garioch, John Tonge – were joined by shifting groups of poets passing through from Glasgow and the west: Iain Crichton Smith, Alexander Scott, Charles Senior, Tom Wright. In their time, T. S. Eliot, Dylan Thomas and Sean O'Casey had all visited Milne's; and, while George was in Edinburgh, W. H. Auden and Stevie Smith turned up one night and sang together at the bar.

'Men of sorrows, and acquainted with Grieve' was how Edwin Muir described the Rose Street poets, and there is no doubt that, to those who frequented Milne's, the greatest excitement was the possibility that Hugh MacDiarmid (*né* Christopher Grieve) might travel in from his home at Biggar in Lanarkshire. MacDiarmid's status as a poet has remained disputed in England, but in Scotland the author of *A Drunk Man Looks at the Thistle* was already, in his own lifetime, a legendary figure. If Scottish poets in the fifties and sixties felt they were riding high, there was a general acceptance that it was MacDiarmid they had to thank for it. Combative, Anglophobic, a nationalist but a modernist, an ardent propagandist almost single-handedly responsible for the revival of the Scots language, he had given his followers a new confidence in the part Scotland had to play in world affairs. MacDiarmid was, in the words of Compton Mackenzie, 'the most powerful intellectually and emotionally fertilising force Scotland has known since the death of Burns'. Those who could claim to have rubbed shoulders with him in Milne's bar had on others the effect Robert Browning evokes in his poem 'Memorabilia':

> Ah, did you once see Shelley plain,
> And did he stop and speak to you?
> And did you speak to him again?
> How strange it seems, and new!

George could afford to drink only at the weekends. During his first term in Edinburgh he had begun to take himself to Rose Street on Friday and Saturday evenings, and to sit over two-shilling pints of McEwan's heavy at the bar in Milne's, observing the other poets through the smoke and beer fumes. He never dreamed that he would join them, and in some ways it is surprising that he felt drawn to them at all. George came to dislike writers as a species. 'I think,' he once wrote, '[they] should be heard but seen as rarely as possible – in general they're not very interesting people, in themselves.' But, by the time he made this comment, he was himself a well-known and established poet, and seeing his work between hard covers had lost its thrill. In those early Rose Street days, barely published and unknown, he was still fired by a determination to make his name, and fascinated by others who had done so.

Those gatherings in Milne's are immortalized by one who often observed them, Alexander Moffat, in his painting *Poets' Pub*. It is an apocryphal celebration of a meeting that never took place, painted in 1980, long after the Rose Street scene had broken up. Seated around a small table are Hugh MacDiarmid, Norman MacCaig, Sorley MacLean, Iain Crichton Smith, George Mackay Brown, Sydney Goodsir Smith, Edwin Morgan, Robert Garioch and Alan Bold. Moffat shows the poets, though crowded close together, absorbed not in conversation but in their own thoughts; and, if there is a single unifying figure, it is neither MacDiarmid nor MacCaig, but Sydney Goodsir Smith. Smith, it seemed to Moffat, was '*the* great character of all the poets', and the one whom the others would have chosen to put at the centre. George would certainly have agreed.

Sydney Goodsir Smith, the son of an eminent professor of forensic medicine, was, despite a public-school and Oxford education, a poet who wrote exclusively in Scots. These days his work is little read outside Scotland but in the fifties and sixties he was regarded as formidably talented. Edith Sitwell described him as one of the few young poets to whom the word 'great' could be applied, and, as well as being a poet, he was an accomplished painter. What drew people to Smith, however, was not principally his artistic gifts but his genius for life. Generous, convivial, a bon viveur and brilliant raconteur, he had also a melancholic streak. In photographs, he sometimes wears an expression of bloodhound sadness, and his melancholy made him sensitive to others in difficulty of any kind. It was he who first noticed George sitting alone at the bar in Milne's, and invited him to come over to his table for a drink; and it was thanks to his generosity and encouragement that George was able to report to Ernest Marwick in the summer of 1957 that he was now on friendly terms with 'most of the Scottish poets . . . and a host of minor luminaries'.

In later years, George would look back on those evenings in Milne's as among the happiest of his life. If he seemed strange and shy to the other undergraduates, and to some of his tutors, he came powerfully into his own, eased with drink, among the Rose Street poets. 'Refreshingly and deeply entertaining', is how one Milne's friend, a librarian, Hugh Mackay, remembers George: 'the wittiest man I ever knew'. To another, a photographer, Paddy Hughes, who became a lifelong friend, George seemed not just 'unforgettable' but 'charismatic'. If Sydney Goodsir Smith was the great Rose Street raconteur, George quickly became admired for his lightning, hilarious one-line interventions into conversation, and for a wit that was both sharp and utterly without prejudice or malice. George's particular gift, the poet Stewart Conn has written, was to be able 'to put at ease, despite his shyness, those who might otherwise have remained awkward in one another's company'. He was a unifying presence.

Unassuming, apparently free from vanity, George also struck his companions as having a steely centre, an absolute confidence in his ability as a poet, and a solid self-assurance. In his long poem *Kynd Kittock's Land*, Sydney Goodsir Smith offers a glimpse of George, dogged and forceful, in the company of the other poets:

> And Brown leads wi' his Viking chin
> And winna be rebukit.

He could hold his own in arguments about poetry, the Cold War, Scottish independence, Marxism or pacifism; but he also had a knack for diffusing argument with humour. And, if the theorizing and speculation about poetry became too high-flown, he was able deftly to bring the conversation back down to earth. Like Dylan Thomas, the poet Stanley Roger Green reflects, George understood that poetry was not a competition. In Milne's bar, this was a healthy corrective.

Yet despite being, as Alexander Moffat remembers him, 'the warmest and most approachable of the poets', George remained fundamentally mysterious to many of his drinking companions. 'You could never get into his soul,' says Stanley Roger Green. In *Poets' Pub*, though physically central, he is portrayed as the outsider. This was absolutely intentional on Moffat's part. He wanted to show George apart from the others, 'and I know this might sound ridiculous, but to emphasise his unique spirituality'.

George was conscious of keeping a part of himself private, and of remaining, to some extent, an onlooker. In his short story 'Sealskin', he imagines the life of a talented Orcadian composer, Magnus Olafson, as he travels in cultured circles round the cities of Europe in the late nineteenth century. Olafson is fundamentally different from the artists whose company he keeps. He has selkie blood, and cut off from the sea and the islands, he lives in increasing confusion and unhappiness.

> He often felt, in moods of depression, that he was caught up in some meaningless charade in which everyone, himself included, was compelled to wear a mask. He would take part in their passionate midnight arguments about socialism, the ballet, anthropology, psychology, and he would put forward – as well as his clumsiness with German or French allowed him – a well-ordered logical argument. But deep down he was untouched. It didn't seem to matter in the slightest. It was all a game, to keep sharp the wits of people who had not to contend with the primitive terrors of sea and land. So he thought, while the eyes flashed and the tongues sought for felicitousness and clarity all around him. He was glad when the maskers had departed and he was alone again, among the cigarette ends and the apple cores . . .
>
> And his guests would say, going home in a late-night tramcar, 'Is he not charming, this Magnus? And how shy! And underneath, such talent!' What they were describing was the mask; few of them had seen the cold dangerous Orphean face underneath.

For all George's protestations that his work contains almost nothing of himself, there is surely an autobiographical strain in this.

At 10 p.m. precisely on a Saturday evening, Bob Watt closed his bar. If the company was good, and the conversation in full spate, a group of poets would then very often decamp by bus to Norman MacCaig's house in Leamington Terrace, carrying bottles of beer and whisky.

Here they continued their drinking and discussion into the early hours. George later looked back fondly on these nocturnal gatherings, and wrote with gratitude of the welcome and encouragement given him by MacCaig. It is clear from letters, however, that at the time George's feelings towards MacCaig were complicated. There was a tension between them, and a suspicion on George's part that MacCaig disliked him. The dislike, for a while, was mutual.

George had noted MacCaig's 'masterly sarcasm' and sharp tongue when he had come to lecture at Newbattle. It is possible that, by the time they met again in Edinburgh, he felt that these traits had developed into an arrogance which he found off-putting. Certainly, friends remember George referring to MacCaig in gently puncturing terms behind his back, as 'Castlemain XXXX MacCaig', and worse. Apart from poetry, the two men appeared to have little in common. MacCaig was suave, handsome, educated in the Classics and thoroughly at home with urban life, while George remained, throughout his six years in Edinburgh, duffle-coated, Orkney-accented and distinctly unmetropolitan. In one important respect, however, their tastes coincided, and it seems likely that this coincidence, rather than their differences, was the source of the friction between them.

One evening during the summer term of 1957, drinking at The Abbotsford in Rose Street, George was introduced to a girl called Stella Cartwright. He was now nearly thirty-six; Stella was just twenty, tall, buxom, beautiful, with a great mass of wavy blonde hair swept back from her face, blue eyes and honey-coloured skin. Those who remember her, and there are many of them, often turn to classical paintings in their attempts to describe Stella when she was young. She was like a creation by Rubens, they say, or by Botticelli. She was, on the face of it, the kind of woman who might have reduced George to a paralysis of inhibition; but there was something about her that struck him as so open and alive and unaffected, and so much at home in the male world of Rose Street, that he felt completely at ease in her company. They talked and talked, connecting immediately on such a deep level that they did not bother to sketch in for one another the more superficial details of their lives. Stella, at that first meeting, took George for a fisherman.

When, some time later, George and Stella met again at a party at Norman MacCaig's house, they found themselves still talking among the empty bottles and cigarette ends long after the other guests had left, and Norman and his wife Isobel had gone to bed. 'I remember nothing of our dialogue,' George writes in his autobiography, 'but the laughter and delight of being in her company.' As dawn broke over Edinburgh, Stella discovered that she had run out of cigarettes. As soon as the shops opened, George went out to buy her another packet: 'It was a joy to give her things.' Stella had awoken in George 'a delight I had not known before'; she, in his presence, felt a sense of security and happiness that had eluded her since early childhood. Both experienced a feeling of homecoming.

Stella Cartwright, the only child of a difficult marriage, had grown up in a bungalow in Juniper Green on the south-west outskirts of Edinburgh. Her mother, Winnie, a nurse by training, was dutiful and devoted, and a neat, fastidious housekeeper; but Winnie and Stella were very different characters, and relations between them tended to be strained. Stella was much closer to, and more like, her father, Jack, who was employed as an architectural draughtsman by the Ministry of Works. Jack's father was the butler at Aberuchill, a turreted, fairy-tale castle in the Perthshire highlands, and here Stella spent long holidays as a child. Her cousin Bill Cartwright recalls that being in Stella's company was always refreshing and enlivening. He remembers her deep love of nature and the countryside, and her swift, instinctive response to any creature in pain.

Aberuchill remained for Stella a kind of Garden of Eden: it was as dear to her as Rackwick was to George. For, though she was to spend most of her life in Edinburgh, she was never essentially an urban creature. At the weekends, when she was a child, she and her father had tramped for miles across the Pentlands. Both had good, strong voices, and as they walked they liked to sing old hymns, neither piously nor mockingly, but with a vigorous *joie de vivre* – 'Workmen of God', 'Hills of the North', 'Emmanuel'. They were proud of one another.

Jack Cartwright was a gifted man – a good painter, an accomplished pianist – and people were easily charmed by him. But he was frustrated that he had not made more of his gifts, and frustration made him volatile. Anne Leith, Stella's closest friend at school, remembers being introduced to Jack for the first time, and her instant, instinctive, seven-year-old's response: 'I thought, "You are charming, and handsome, and very, very foolish." ' He was unreliable with money. Stella was often anxious about whether he would manage to pay her school fees, and she describes in a letter to George having to accompany her mother to a moneylender to pay back his debts. And he was a drinker. On Saturday evenings, after the pubs closed, Jack would regularly bring groups of friends home to 37 Baberton Crescent; they would drink and sing around the piano until the early hours, and then collapse insensible in Winnie's immaculate living room.

Stella grew up with drink. Like Simon McKee in *Greenvoe*, she seems to have had her first taste of alcohol when she was a child, suffering from a cold. Unlike Simon, who was given spoonfuls of wine to aid his recovery, Stella was offered a nip of whisky, and it took a hold. By the age of fifteen, she was praising the joys of whisky-drinking to her friends at the Mary Erskine School for Girls. They were amazed, Anne Leith remembers; but then they were used to being amazed by Stella. In the strict, regimented life at a school originally set up for the daughters of poor merchants, she had stood out from the day she arrived as a colourful, talented, fearless girl whose spirit was not to be curbed. Like her father, she was a gifted painter, but Anne Leith remembers her time and again being sent by Mr Webster, the art master, to stand alone next to the sink where the brushes were washed because she refused to paint as he wanted her to. She was also naturally musical and, though not strictly academic, she had a flair for literature. She read widely and independently. In a sixth-form exercise book, she kept a list of the authors she was reading, and they included Gorki, Zola and Manzoni, as well as Joyce, V. S. Pritchett, Somerset Maugham, Lewis Grassic Gibbon and George Douglas Brown. By the age of sixteen, she had developed a passion for the poetry of Norman MacCaig.

The education at the Mary Erskine School was designed to equip girls to apply themselves to solid careers for a few years, before settling down as competent wives and mothers. Stella Cartwright was never going to fit this mould. She left school in the summer of 1955 and, while her contemporaries embarked on training to become teachers, academics, laboratory technicians and physiotherapists, Stella took a job as a receptionist at F. C. Inglis, a photographic studio in Dean Street, Edinburgh. If it was unequal to her talents, the job had its advantages. The manager of the studio, David Oliver, was prepared to turn a blind eye if on a Monday morning Stella was not in a fit state to come to work. Increasingly often, she was not.

Jack Cartwright had long frequented the Rose Street bars, and when Stella turned sixteen he had begun to take her with him on his drinking sprees. Not everybody was pleased by the appearance of a woman on this very male scene, and not everybody was impressed by her. John Durkin, for one, failed ever to appreciate Stella's appeal: she was not beautiful, it seemed to him, it was just that she was the only woman around. But on most of the drinkers, and particularly on the poets in the Abbotsford and Milne's, her effect was mesmerizing.

In his poem 'The Muse in Rose Street', Sydney Goodsir Smith recalls the first time he set eyes on Stella. It was a Friday night, and he was sitting drinking amidst the gossip and clink of glasses, when the door swung open and in, among a crowd of students, she stepped. She struck him as almost unearthly – 'A lassie frae the mune' – and when she smiled at him, he was overwhelmed. Charles Senior describes the empowering effect on men of even one blink from 'that richtfu' queen' in 'Verses on a Rose Street Muse'. For George, the titles of these poems described Stella perfectly: 'it was on *poets* that this extra-ordinary girl cast her spell.' ('Poet after poet,' John Durkin concurs, 'and never a bricklayer or a joiner in between.')

To Stanley Roger Green, it seemed impossible not to be attracted to Stella: 'Her physical power was irresistible, almost transcendental. She seemed built for love.' Even Hugh MacDiarmid, Green believes, though nearly fifty years Stella's senior, had 'frustratedly lustful' feelings for her. But Stella's appeal was not purely physical. 'In a world of deniers,' George once wrote to a friend, 'she is what D. H. Lawrence called a life-giver.' She had a natural, infectious gaiety that was both unselfconscious and uncontrived. 'She laughed a great deal,' George wrote, 'not the empty half-nervous spasmodic spillings of many young women, but out of a deep well of humour that was forever renewing itself.' She had also what she herself described as a 'nerve-ending' response to art, a gift for understanding people, and an unbridled generosity towards anyone who was suffering in any way. At school, the other girls had turned to Stella for counsel, especially in love. But the qualities that had made her a natural agony aunt to her friends at Mary

Erskine led her into situations more complicated and dangerous among the poets of Rose Street.

For all her gifts and beauty and radiance, Stella was entirely unprotected by guile or sophistication. Kulgin Duval, a book dealer who lived in Rose Street in the late fifties and early sixties, remembers her as being entirely without vanity, and exuding great innocence. Hugh Mackay, who first met Stella in 1960, agrees: 'She was, in a pre-Freudian sense, infantile; and in the sense that she was not at all vain, she was anything but a *femme fatale.*' Stella knew there was a star inside her, says Mackay, but she found it hard to have confidence in it; and her bright, laughing exterior masked a deep vulnerability. To enable herself to shine in company, she relied on drink, and particularly on whisky. At first, there seemed no danger in this. Stella had what Hugh Mackay describes as 'a good working relationship with alcohol'; and there was no shortage of men willing to keep her glass filled.

Shortly after leaving school, Stella had become a regular guest at Norman MacCaig's impromptu Saturday-night parties in Leamington Terrace. Like many women, she was infatuated with MacCaig, and he was fascinated by her. She carried in her handbag a clerihew he had written for her, which friends remember as running: 'You placed me on a pedestal / according to my lights / but what you didn't know, my dear / I have no head for heights.' To what extent MacCaig lost his balance over Stella remains a matter for conjecture among those who knew them.

Beyond any doubt is the fact that, not long after her arrival on the Rose Street scene, Stella embarked on an intense affair with the poet Tom Scott. An ex-Newbattle student, tall, red-headed, quick-tempered and passionate, Scott was nearly twice her age when they met, and had been married for some years. This was not the first time that he had been unfaithful to his wife but, as one friend puts it, if his other dalliances had been flashes in the pan, Scott's affair with Stella was an inferno; and, when his marriage ended in divorce, Stella was cited as co-respondent. Scott's poem 'The Paschal Candill', in which he praises the woman who has led him by the hand 'Throu midlife's forests, whaur nae licht wes leamand', was written for Stella. As his divorce went through, he bought a flat in which he hoped to settle down with her. But his intensity and possessiveness had begun to frighten her, and she enlisted her father's help in bringing the affair to an end.

In the early days of Stella's friendship with George, Scott had not yet accepted her rejection, and he shadowed her about Edinburgh, a brooding, Heathcliff presence. George was unsettled by this: he would peer through the windows of the Rose Street bars and, if he spotted Scott inside, would take himself off to drink elsewhere. He was becoming gradually aware, perhaps, that he was beginning to replace Scott in Stella's affections. Outwardly, little had changed. In the months following their first meeting, George and Stella did not pair off in any obvious way. Both still joined the groups of drinkers in Milne's and the Abbotsford on a Saturday night, and their friendships with others flourished. Those who saw them regularly, however, were aware that there was a particular bond between them, and Stella's other admirers, in particular another librarian, John Broom, became distinctly jealous.

Years later, Stella would long to read again the letters and poems George had written to her as they first got to know each other. Lovelier letters, she claimed, no girl ever received. Sadly, not just for Stella but for posterity, Winnie Cartwright had destroyed them in a fit of exasperation at the chaotic state of her daughter's bedroom, and of her life. What remain, however, are the letters George wrote Stella in later years. Many of them look back on their days in Edinburgh, and give glimpses of the times they spent together – walking in the Pentlands, sunbathing by the sea at Cramond, sitting on Stella's bed in Baberton Crescent reading poetry, kissing one wet Saturday afternoon beside the Water of Leith and, when the rain got too heavy, sheltering in a disused railway hut, drinking beer, kissing again.

It was not a full-blown affair, and given George's acute physical shyness, and Stella's experiences with Tom Scott, this may have suited both of them very well, at least for a time. What is evident, both from George's later letters to Stella and from hers to him, is the extraordinary closeness between them. They were, as Stella notes, alike in many ways. Both were troubled by 'deep chasms and crags in the psyche', and both were prone to depression. At the same time, they shared a delight in life's absurdities, and an unusual capacity for joy. 'Dear George, it is so strange,' writes Stella in one undated letter, 'our souls seem to fly together joyously over mountains and seas while each of us in our mutual ways suffers agonies.'

In Stella, who, for all her gregariousness, felt easily out of step with the world, George's love could ease a great burden of loneliness: 'Do not think it phoney, but I feel the essence of you – almost within me, and it touches me, so that I feel like weeping tears of gratitude . . . Often I feel cut off from everyone and from the world as a whole. At such times I think of you . . . and know that souls can and do communicate.' On George, Stella's patience and sensitivity had the effect of soothing mental turmoil:

> Cargoes of alien pain
> Tenderly she transmutes
> To quiet things

he wrote in one of a sequence of four poems dedicated to her; and, in a letter written when their Edinburgh days were long past, 'Dearest Stel, How often I wish I could talk to you for an afternoon – you know, when things get all difficult and knotted up, and only such gentleness and understanding as you have can unravel them.'

This sense of being profoundly understood by another human being, perhaps for the first time in his life, had an invigorating effect on George's poetry. During his first year as an undergraduate in Edinburgh, he had found writing a struggle. The demands of the English course, he complained to Ernest Marwick, meant that he had no time for his own work; and urban living left his imagination dislocated. During the second half of 1957, however, in the months following his first meeting with Stella, he was building up a sheaf of new work; and in the late autumn he posted the best of it to Edwin Muir. The Muirs had returned from America the previous year, and were now living in a small village near Cambridge. On the back of Edwin's Harvard earnings, they had been able, for the first time, to buy their own home, Priory Cottage. But money remained a problem, and despite the fact that they were both now approaching seventy, and in poor health, they were obliged to keep working hard, writing and reviewing. Edwin found this daunting. 'I confess,' he wrote to T. S. Eliot, 'that sometimes I have a slightly sinking feeling, knowing that now I have nothing to do but write, and must depend upon it.' He missed his students and, as he moved into old age, he admitted to being far more excited by other people's literary endeavours than by his own.

The package Muir received from George towards the end of 1957 thrilled him. He read the poems again and again before writing to tell George that they had left him with 'a vivid sense of delight such as I feel from hardly any of the other poetry that is written now, and not only that but beauty as well. I admire these poems more than I can say.' Earlier in the year, he had suggested that George might send some of his work to a London publisher. Now, he determined to take the matter in hand. Rejecting the idea of Faber & Faber – 'Eliot is growing old' – Muir instead approached the Hogarth Press, the firm which Leonard and Virginia Woolf had founded in 1917, and which had, since 1946, been under the management of the publishers Chatto & Windus. He wrote specifically to Norah Smallwood, a formidable member of the board as notorious for reducing her staff to tears as she was admired for battling on behalf of her authors 'like a tigress for her cubs'. There was a sense of urgency in Muir's letter: he enclosed a stamped addressed envelope to expedite a reply and when, after a month, none was forthcoming, he wrote again. All was well. Norah Smallwood had been impressed by George's poems, and so too had her colleagues Ian Parsons and Cecil Day-Lewis. One afternoon in April 1958, George returned to his Marchmont lodgings to find a letter from the Hogarth Press inviting him to sign a contract, and offering an advance of £10. He was exultant – 'I had never dreamed that such a thing could ever be'; Edwin Muir was delighted. The advance was modest, Muir conceded, but then he had had no advance whatever for his first collection of poetry. All in all, he told George, this was 'Great good news'.

The publication of *Loaves and Fishes* was finally announced in the spring of 1959, in a Hogarth Press catalogue that included Laurie Lee's *Cider with Rosie*. It was warmly received. In the *Spectator*, Frank Kermode described George as 'a most deliberate and admirable artist', and both John Wain in the *Observer* and G. S. Fraser in the *New Statesman* said that this was a poet whose progress they would now be watching closely. 'Out of the ruck,' announced Sydney Goodsir Smith in the *Weekly Scotsman*, 'a name is beginning to emerge.'

Of Stella's response, there is no record, but there can be little doubt that she welcomed *Loaves and Fishes* with at least as much enthusiasm as the critics. She was perceptive about George's work – she it was who admired his gift for writing with 'involved detachment' – and she believed in him as a poet. 'If any poet deserves to be paid for his labours, you do,' she once wrote when he was struggling to make ends meet. 'For what you do in making beautiful thought-pictures and songs of the spirit is worth more, much more, than all the bloody commercial travellers in the world are paid.'

But the irony was that the more George was given reason to hope that he might make a future as a poet, the more remote became the possibility of a future with Stella. During George's undergraduate years his brother Norrie was also living in Edinburgh, teaching English at Portobello High School, and on Sundays George very often went to visit him and Hazel and their three daughters for lunch. On one of these visits to Oxgangs, Hazel remembers, he confessed that he was desperately in love with Stella, but that practical difficulties made it impossible for him to see how he could ever marry her. He was worried, principally, about his inability to support her financially. The sales figures for *Loaves and Fishes*, particularly in America, were gratifying; but George's credit with the Hogarth Press a fortnight after publication stood at just 17s 4d – 'or about 10 fish-&-chip suppers'. It was hard to see how he was going to keep himself, let alone a wife.

Then there was the question of where he and Stella might happily settle. 'You love the sea and I love the hills and oft the twain shall meet,' Stella writes in a letter to George in April 1960; but, though she was happiest in the Perthshire highlands, Edinburgh and Rose Street had a siren appeal for her. Hugh Mackay feels sure that, had Stella married George, she would have remained faithful to him, just as Jack Cartwright, for all his good looks and weaknesses, had remained faithful to Winnie. At the same time, Mackay suspects that, removed from Edinburgh and from all who loved and admired her there, Stella might have drooped and 'dwined', like one of the selkie women in George's stories, only really at home in the sea, but forced instead to live on dry land.

For George, however, putting down roots in Edinburgh was out of the question. Every time he went to Orkney for a holiday, he found it more of a wrench to return to 'the long gowns and the Lucky Jims' of the university. By the end of his third year, he was also becoming gradually disillusioned with the Rose Street scene. Individually, he was fond of his fellow poets; and Charles Senior, in particular, had become a close friend and confidant. But, as a group, George found them navel-gazing and self-obsessed: 'The only one who is genuinely interested in seeing things produced – other than his own – is MacCaig,' he writes to Willa Muir on 2 July 1959. 'The others are sunk in dreams of their own genius.' George's undergraduate years had confirmed him in his belief that Orkney was the only place where he could properly exercise his gift as a poet; and to this gift he had no choice but to be loyal. 'It isn't a unilateral thing,' he once explained to a friend. 'You can't disown it: it won't disown you.'

Compounding these practical difficulties was a consideration more subtle and intractable. George had seen for himself – in Edwin and Willa Muir, and in his own parents – how fruitful and strengthening a good marriage could be. Yet scattered through his writing are hints that he was suspicious of the tendency of women to entrap men, to draw them into their own element, and to reduce them to a state of emasculated foolishness. In 'The Story of Jorkel Hayforks', George tells the tale of a Norwegian sailor who sets out from Bergen with a crew of six, among them a poet, Finn. In Shetland, Finn is seduced by a woman, Brenda. When the crew sails on to Fair Isle they are obliged to leave him behind.

> They say that Finn made no more poems after that day. Brenda bore him twelve children. He died there in Shetland before there was a grey hair in his beard. He was drunk most days till his death, and he would drink from no cup but Brenda's. He was totally dependent on her always. It was thought rather a pity that such a promising poet should make such an ordinary end.

George's ambitions were not conventional: he was not much interested either in fame or in money. But an 'ordinary end' was not what he was after.

George's time in Edinburgh had been punctuated with bouts of bronchitis and spells in hospital. Early in 1960, he seems to have suffered a serious physical breakdown; and, in the middle of the spring term, he left Edinburgh for Orkney to recuperate. Stella wrote to him frequently, and her letters are full of love and concern and longing for his return. 'You are a presence in my heart, and do not ever quite disappear,' she wrote two days after his departure. 'I have been very unhappy very often, sweet, and you, I think, have not always bubbled with joy. But you, by being you, and by loving me, have changed a lot of that.' And, six days later,

> Dearest George, If only I could be beside you to love you, comfort you and cherish you beyond everything and everyone else in the world. All these things I do from where I am; but if one loves (rather is *in* love *with*) someone it is hard to stay put quietly when one knows there is something wrong. Dearest love, try to feel me beside you, think me close to you and believe in me. Right now I am as near to you as your own right hand – attached and capable of any ministration of love. Darling, get better and come back to me . . . for (God help us) we seem to need each other.

What George wrote in return, we cannot know; but, though Stella thanks him for saying 'such sweet things' in his replies, her letters also suggest that George's troubles are as much psychological as physical, and that he has been suffering from religious, and sexual, qualms. Stella had been reading Lawrence Durrell's *Alexandria Quartet*, and in one letter she quotes at length from *Justine*, from a passage in which Balthazar warns his followers of the dangers of scruple:

> None of the great religions has done more than exclude, throw out a long range of prohibitions. But prohibitions create the desire they are intended to cure. We of this Cabal say: *indulge but refine*. We are enlisting everything in order to make men's wholeness match the wholeness of the universe – even pleasure, the destructive granulation of the mind in pleasure.

'It seems there is a load of truth in this,' Stella urges, 'and it is part of what I have always believed – so I draw your attention to it, dearest George.'

Perhaps George was moved by Stella's arguments; perhaps the fact that his undergraduate years were drawing to a close concentrated his mind. In the late spring, after returning from Orkney, he took a bus out to Juniper Green and, having secured Jack Cartwright's blessing, dropped to his knee and asked Stella to marry him. She was overjoyed; her parents were greatly relieved. Though Stella was just twenty-three, they had become uneasy about her lack of direction, and about her appetite for alcohol. In Orkney, away from the taverns and temptations of Rose Street, they foresaw a safe, if frugal, future for their only child.

But it was not to be. How long George's engagement to Stella lasted, and how and when it was finally called off, we do not know. In the autumn of 1960, in the Edinburgh University magazine *Gambit*, George published his 'Four Poems for Stella': short, beautiful pieces, brimming equally with love and with anguish. On the facing page is a sad little poem by Stella herself, 'Parting'.

The scruples and psychological blockages that had afflicted George earlier in the spring had proved, in the end, insuperable. Years later, Stella confided to a close friend that their engagement was finally called off because George had found himself unable to consummate their relationship. Her letters bear this out. 'As you said recently, we might have been married for almost two years now,' she writes to George in March 1962. 'Did you not find me physically attractive or what, honey?'

It is a leading question, but, if George replied to it, his reply was put out with the rubbish by Winnie Cartwright. Among those prepared to venture replies on his behalf, meanwhile, there is no consensus, but a multitude of theories, all in some way compelling, none entirely satisfactory.

David Campbell was a friend and contemporary of George at Edinburgh University, and knew the Rose Street scene, and Stella, well. To Campbell, it seems futile to consider George and sexuality in conventional twentieth-century terms. Like a number of others who had grown up in the remoter parts of the British Isles, Campbell believes, George had simply never absorbed 'the Freudian, Western thing'. He was essentially asexual.

Kulgin Duval and his partner Colin Hamilton, who got to know George in Edinburgh and who remained among his closest friends, see things differently. Like themselves, they believe, George was fundamentally homosexual, though perhaps unable to admit it, even to himself. They often discussed the matter with their friend Edwin

Morgan, who knew George later in his life, and he agreed. 'It seemed to me,' Morgan writes, 'that gayness, if I can put it this way, hovered over or around George,' although 'he was totally closeted and inhibited and possibly in denial to himself about it'. Neither Duval nor Hamilton nor Morgan offers any concrete proof, or cites a single homosexual encounter on George's part, but all three point to the fact that George felt 'unthreatened and unfazed' in the company of homosexuals, and believe that throughout his life his closest friendships were with other men.

To the women who knew George well, this is simply not true; and certainly, among his surviving correspondence, there is nothing to match the intimacy of George's letters to Stella Cartwright. Their relationship may never have been physically consummated, but George revealed himself to Stella as to no one else. And Stella was by no means the only woman to whom he felt drawn. One woman to whom George became close later in his life feels that, to understand his sexuality, one has to appreciate the long shadow that his teenage tuberculosis had cast over the succeeding decades. It had left him not only convinced that he was ugly and essentially unlovable, but also permanently short of energy. He had had to choose whether to devote what little energy he had principally to his work, or to serious relationships. He could not have had both. Ultimately, he chose his work, and to live, in consequence, with what Edwin Morgan saw as 'a loner's lack, a loner's darkness'.

Perhaps the key to reconciling all these different perceptions lies in this essential aloneness: the aloneness to which George had felt drawn from childhood, but for which he sometimes cursed fate. It meant that, when he did develop close friendships, he had the time and the mental and emotional freedom to form unusually deep bonds with people. It was easy for friends to interpret these bonds as a reflection of George's likeness to them — for homosexual friends to assume he was fundamentally homosexual; for a number of women to feel sure that beneath George's shyness and inhibition lay a yearning for heterosexual union; for the many religious who were impressed by the understanding of monasticism reflected in his work to assume that George Mackay Brown was a writer with a vocation to celibacy. They were all, in a sense, right: all seeing aspects of a truth that George himself probably never fully disentangled.

In the early summer of 1960, in sweltering heat, George had sat his Finals. In July, Mhairi Brown travelled down from Orkney for the degree ceremony in the McEwan Hall. Edinburgh billowed with black gowns and beaming mothers. 'A proud day, a proud day,' an elderly man commented as George walked by carrying his degree diploma in its red cylindrical box. For George, it had been a far prouder day when he 'first laughed with Stella over one of the fine old oak tables in The Abbotsford in Rose Street'.

I I

Grief at Every Milestone

It hurts me to think of you being unhappy, Stella. I think of how
happy we might have been together, there was such tenderness
and quiet joy. And certainly these good things won't pass away,
when the totality of things is reckoned.

GMB, letter to Stella Cartwright, 1965

EDWIN MUIR HAD not lived to see the publication of *Loaves and
Fishes*. In the summer of 1958 he was suffering from water on the
lungs. He made light of it – 'I think in a few months I shall be in better
health than I have been for years,' he wrote to George on 15 October;
but, in a scribbled postscript, Willa intimated that the situation was
grave. She was distraught, and herself unwell, and, because neither of
them was able to work, money became desperately short. Willa wrote
out cheques without daring to consult the bank. On Christmas Eve,
in the offices of the Hogarth Press, Norah Smallwood dragooned her
staff into writing letters to everybody they could think of in the literary world, urging them to contribute to a fund to help tide the Muirs
over. It was hoped that, with the support of T. S. Eliot, they might be
awarded a Civil List pension, to begin in the spring. On 3 January
1959, Edwin Muir died.

George felt Muir's absence painfully in the succeeding months and
years. In his letters, Edwin Muir had had a gift for helping George to
rise above the difficulties of the present, and to believe in a bright
future. In the months following his graduation, in particular, he could
have done with a shot of Muir's quiet, steadying courage.

After years of prevarication, it looked as if George might finally be
about to confront the world of 'getting and spending' that he had

avoided for so long. His university grant had been paid under the National Teachers' Training Scheme, and in September 1960 he had no choice but to return to Edinburgh to enrol at Moray House College of Education. He quailed at the prospect. 'The thought of teaching is deeply depressing,' he wrote to Kulgin Duval. 'I know it isn't for me – all uselessness and waste . . . Pray for me.'

In some ways, it is surprising that the idea of teaching so appalled George. Orcadians, like Italians, have a reputation for adoring children, and George was no exception. In Orkney, he frequently dropped in on friends such as Gerry Meyer and Ian MacInnes in the early evening to tell their sons and daughters bedtime stories. In Edinburgh, Norrie's three girls, Allison, Pam and Ros, remember him as the perfect uncle, gently subversive and irreverent when he came on his Sunday visits; full of interest in all that they were doing. Ros remembers George performing solemn marriage ceremonies on her dolls, and cutting out pictures of the Beatles for her scrapbook. Once a week, after Brownies, she would trip up the stairs with a couple of friends to visit him in his lodgings. One little Brownie took such a shine to George that she walked across Edinburgh to visit him when she heard he was staying with Norrie and Hazel.

Children were one thing, however; teaching quite another. In the autumn of 1960, George was placed by Moray House at Boghall School in Bathgate. The pupils, on the whole, were the sons and daughters of miners, and it is clear from a letter George wrote to Ian MacInnes that he liked them very much, and found it satisfying when he succeeded in firing them, for the first time in their lives, with an enthusiasm for poetry. When conventional children's poems, like 'Vagabond' and 'Sea Fever', left them cold, he turned instead to the ballads, and scored a rollicking success with 'Sir Patrick Spens'. The excitement the children got from experiences like this was not frivolous, George believed, but something that would help them to define for themselves 'what it means to be a man among other men in the world'. What he could not bear was to be obliged then to break the spell, to move from enjoyment to analysis – as if poems were nothing but a number of 'stinking frogs' legs to be cut up and examined' – and to watch his pupils turn 'cold and stiff' in the process. In his first week at Boghall School, George told MacInnes, he had come to a number of radical conclusions on the subject of education, all of them so thoroughly opposed to the Moray House philosophies that he recoiled at the thought of continuing his training.

At the root of George's unhappiness was something more than just a suspicion of formal education, deep though this went. He knew very well that what he was meant to be doing was not teaching poetry, but writing it. He was now nearly forty, and everything in him rebelled against any further compromise or delay. He need not have feared. Always dependable in times of crisis, ill-health came swiftly to his rescue. In the middle of November, George collapsed with chronic bronchitis. Suspecting a recurrence of TB, the university doctor ordered him to leave Edinburgh immediately and indefinitely, and he was transported by ambulance to Tor-na-Dee, a sanatorium on the banks of the Dee near Aberdeen.

Before departing, George asked Sydney Goodsir Smith to keep an eye on Stella. Although their engagement was now formally over, she and George remained as close as ever. Stella wrote to him regularly at the sanatorium – sweet, quirky, morale-boosting letters, urging him not to worry overmuch about Moray House, and not to be depressed about his future.

In fact, within days of his arrival at Tor-na-Dee, George's spirits had begun to rise. Life in the sanatorium, he told Ian MacArthur, was surprisingly congenial: the food was good, the doctor in whose charge he had been placed was kind and interested in literature. He had been given a room to himself, two storeys up, looking over the Dee to the fields and hills beyond, and here, restored by drugs and rest and solitude, he was immersing himself in Orkney history. George had asked Ernest Marwick to advise him on good books about the Reformation in Orkney. He was still feeling his way towards Catholicism, but everything he read fuelled his belief that the Reformation had struck a death blow to the life and spirit of the islands. Even the Orcadian tendency to depression, he decided, was a symptom of the fact that, since the middle of the sixteenth century, ordinary islanders' feelings of awe and mystery had been denied proper expression.

As a result of his reading, George began to develop the idea of a short story based on the imaginary expulsion of an old priest from his Stromness parish at harvest-time in 1561. Father Halcrow is aware of his flaws – 'I fish too long at the rock, I pray only a little, I drink too much of the dark ale that they brew on the hill' – but he is a holy man, and it is with a sense of 'immense oncoming evil' that he sits down to record how he has been turned out of his church by the ministers of a new religion:

> Yesterday began the cutting of the oats at the Glebe. The kirk lay like a foundering ship in long windy surges of corn. The first thing I saw when I looked out at the door was John Riddach my servant sharpening his blade on a red whetstone at the end of the barn.
>
> After Mass (the usual women were there, seven of them, with heads covered) came three strangers into the kirk, to whom I (putting out the candles) remarked that they were too late, the Mass was over for that morning, but they were welcome to bide in the kirk for as long as they liked. In truth I was anxious to get down to my boat, there being mackerel in Hoy Sound that day. 'The Mass is over,' I told them.
>
> 'The Mass is over for ever,' said one of the men.

George was also reading about seventeenth-century Orkney, and the crops of witches who had been put to death in Kirkwall under Earl Patrick Stewart. He was working on a play – *A Spell for Green Corn* – and starting to piece together in his mind a short story tracing the last hours of Marian Isbister, an innocent country girl, condemned to death for witchcraft through a combination of lust, jealousy and pure malice on the part of the men who know her. On the afternoon before her trial, Marian Isbister sits in her prison cell and confides her anguish to an older woman, Janet Bourtree:

> MARIAN : It is the common thing to be first a child, and then a maiden, and then a wife, and then perhaps a widow and an old patient woman before death. But that way is not for me.
> JANET: There is much grief at every milestone. A young girl cries for a lost bird. An old woman stands among six graves or seven in the kirkyard. It is best not to tarry overlong on the road.
> MARIAN: Yet with John the shepherd I might have been content for a summer or two.

At her trial the following day, however, John the shepherd, Marian's sweetheart, proves her most cowardly accuser, and after a night of unspeakable torture, during which the nails are drawn with pincers from her fingers and toes, and her head is shaved, she is led through Kirkwall to her death:

> Because her toes were blue and swollen after the extraction of the cuticles, she could not walk but with much difficulty. Therefore they bound her arms and carried her out on to the street. There was much laughter and shouting at sight of her naked head. Every alehouse in town had been open since midnight, the earl having decreed a public holiday. All night people had come into the town from the parishes and islands. There was much drunkenness and dancing along the road to Gallowsha.
>
> As she hobbled through the Laverock with her fingers like a tangle of red roots at the end of her long white arms, and her head like an egg, some had pity for her but the voices of others fell on her in a confusion of cursing and ribaldry and mockery, so that the holy words of Master Andrew Monteith could scarcely be heard.

Mentally, George had put not only miles but centuries between himself and his teachers' training. An escape, it might have seemed to the Moray House authorities, but to George it was the opposite. 'For the imagination,' he had once written, 'is not an escape, but a return to the richness of our true selves; a return to reality.' He felt invigorated by his writing. It was, he told Ian MacInnes, gaining 'in slow patience and power'. He was determined to keep at it until he was wholly satisfied: 'It'll be clean and crisp to the core, or I disown it.'

As winter turned into spring, however, worries from the outside world pressed in. Stella was in a poor state. 'The smiler with the knife', as George called whisky, was beginning to have the upper hand with her and, as well as drinking too much, she was smoking heavily and afflicted by regular bouts of bronchitis which left her despondent. She was, George admitted to Hugh Mackay, 'a constant and tormenting worry', and he dreaded to think what the future might hold for her. Her unhappiness left him with faint feelings of guilt. 'She is bound to suffer,' he wrote to Charlie Senior, with whom he corresponded weekly, 'since she can't conceive what it is to have malice or evil intention, and that is the air most of us breathe naturally.'

The Moray House authorities had not released George from their grasp. They had arranged that once a week a Mr McNaught – 'a man with a crusading zeal for Education' – should drive out from Aberdeen to tutor him in the sanatorium. 'He must find me curiously apathetic and uncooperative,' George joked to Ernest Marwick. 'I catch a puzzled look on him sometimes.' But McNaught's visits unsettled him more than he cared to admit. By comparison with this brisk, enthusiastic, professional man, George felt himself no more than 'a focus of stagnation' in a busy world. 'I know that's the wrong way to look at it,' he wrote to Senior. 'One should be a still point of peace – but always the unseen pressure is there, "Get better, so that you can be once more part of the *real world* of profit and loss." To me it's a world of sick shadows, that "real world".'

George re-entered the 'real world' in March 1961, determined at all costs to part company with Moray House. 'Make a mess of it,' Stella had suggested, and this is what he did, entirely losing control when left in sole charge of a classroom full of children. By the end of May, the authorities had conceded that he would never make a teacher. His relief, however, was tempered with anxiety and further guilt. Norrie, the brother on whose support and sympathy George had always relied, was angry with him for not persevering with his training. Norrie himself was now suffering from such acute heart trouble that he had been forced to give up work. He feared that his three daughters would soon be fatherless. George, the uncle they adored, was setting them a poor example.

Nor did George have any idea what he might do next. 'Employers shy away from middle-aged consumptives,' he wrote to Ian MacInnes, 'especially (for some reason) if they have a degree.' In the spring of 1961, he had written to George Bruce, asking for a job at the BBC. Bruce's response was kind, but unequivocal. Had George any expertise or training at all? Could he even type? Without some qualification, there was no question of his being offered employment at Broadcasting House. He had applied, at the same time, for a university grant for postgraduate study, and had been turned down.

Towards the end of 1961, as he turned forty, penury forced George back to Orkney, and to his mother's house. It was a double homecoming. After twenty-five years of exploring and pondering his religious beliefs – a process he later likened to gathering jewels – he was finally received into the Catholic Church. On 23 December, he was baptized at the Church of Our Lady and St Joseph in Kirkwall, and at

Midnight Mass the following evening he received Communion for the first time. He experienced no special emotion or illumination – 'a feeling of inevitability only'. Nor, outwardly, did his conversion change his life in any way. Father Cairns, the parish priest in Kirkwall, had hoped that, at this solemn juncture, George might finally be persuaded to curb his drinking. In fact, it is clear from George's letters to his Edinburgh friends that he was spending as much time as ever in the Stromness pubs. His particular drinking companions were Attie Campbell and Billy Evans, both of whom worked on the *Pole Star*, the coal-burning ship that serviced the Orkney lighthouses. Campbell was a lovable raconteur and quipster; Evans had a quick mind, and a memory well stocked with verse. He could quote at length from an enormous variety of poets, from the Scottish-Canadian ballads of Robert Service to the work of Andrew Marvell, George Herbert and Thomas Traherne.

When the *Pole Star* was in harbour, Evans, Campbell and George would sit for hours at the bar of the Stromness Hotel. 'Great fun there yesterday,' George writes to Charlie Senior after one of these sessions. 'A warden from Strangeways jail, Manchester, here on holiday (why Orkney?) and an itinerant Irishman called Paddy (what other?) who has been in Durham jail among others. The talk drifts on to hanging, and I swear I never spent such a droll and grisly hour listening to the pair of them. Not one technical detail of the noble and ancient craft of execution was omitted.' George had been putting the final touches to his short story 'Witch'. Perhaps it was this conversation that enabled him to describe so hauntingly the last moments of Marian Isbister at the hands of the hangman, Piers.

> They came to Gallowsha by a steep ascent. There beside the stake waited Piers with a new rope in his hand. With courtesy and kind words he received Marian Isbister from her jailers, and led her to the stake.
>
> PIERS: My hands are quick at their work. Thou hast had enough of pain. Only forgive me for what I have to do.
>
> Marian Isbister kissed him on the hands.
>
> At this, some of the crowd shouted, 'The witch's kiss, the witch's kiss!' But Piers answered, 'I do not fear that.'
>
> It is usual on such occasions for the sentence to be read out first, and thereafter ceremonially executed on the body of the criminal. But the

clerk had not uttered three words when Piers secretly put the rope about the neck of Marian Isbister and made a quick end. Those standing near saw her give a quick shrug, and then a long shiver through her entire body. She was dead before the clerk had finished reading from the parchment. Most of that great crowd saw nothing of the strangling.

Mhairi Brown was upset by George's drinking. 'Some Catholic you are!' she would comment, as he sat at the kitchen table in Well Park trying to recover from a hangover, and because she was a woman naturally free of scorn or sarcasm the rebuke haunted and shamed him. George himself was worried. Again and again, in letters to friends, he describes the weariness and guilt he suffers after heavy drinking sessions, and more than once he admits that it is only lack of money that keeps him the right side of ruin: 'When I think of drink, I thank God I'm poor.'

And yet what was he to do with his life? The chances of his making a go of his poetry seemed, once again, slim. In March 1962, George posted a collection of work to the Hogarth Press. Without Edwin Muir to champion his cause, it took some courage to do this, and he attempted to mask his nervousness with a covering letter bristling with brittle self-assurance. 'History and ceremony' were the main themes of this collection, George explained, and though some English readers might be unfamiliar with the events he had chosen to write about – the Battle of Largs, for example, fought out bloodily on a beach in south-west Scotland in 1263 – they would find that his poetry gave more insight into the human condition than the *Daily Express*'s reports on Kennedy and Khrushchev. 'I have tried a few experiments with rhythm,' he went on. 'Of course (as T. S. Eliot says) there is no such thing as *free verse* for the man who is concerned to do a good job. Free verse attracts all kinds of charlatans and poetasters by its apparent lawlessness – "anybody can do it" . . . But in fact for a writer with no sense of rhythm it is a deadly trap.'

Leonard Woolf and Cecil Day-Lewis were not convinced and, after a careful reading, sent a civil but uncompromising letter declining publication. 'Your saga-esque and runic kinds of poem leave me cold,' Day-Lewis confessed when George pressed for an explanation. The poems in which George had attempted a contemporary idiom had struck Day-Lewis as 'badly flawed by outcrops of dead metaphor'.

George retaliated with three furious pages of red-ballpoint protest. These poems, he insisted, were far better than the ones Hogarth had chosen to publish in *Loaves and Fishes*. They had 'rhythmic virtuosity', and 'the kind of vision you don't find in those little crucifixions of the ego that pass for poems in so many slim volumes nowadays'. He accepted Day-Lewis's verdict 'in the spirit of a man found guilty by the jury who knows, nevertheless, that he was nowhere near the place at the time'. But accept it he must.

In Edinburgh, Stella was in an equally bad state. She too was drinking heavily, and recklessly. On one occasion, after mixing whisky with Benzedrine, the drug she had been prescribed for her bronchitis, she ended up in hospital. A note of hopelessness entered her letters. She longed, she wrote to George, to be able to help people, and make them happy – 'yet I seem to bring such sorrow'. She dreamed of a life that was 'joyful, free, useful'; instead, she was miserable, bound to the whisky bottle, often unable to work. Even Rose Street, and its poets, had begun to lose their allure: among the 'hypocritical mire' of Edinburgh, she told George, the 'goodness and beauty' of his poetry shone out like a star.

It is clear from her letters that the feelings between Stella and George were still intense. 'For you and I (je crois),' she writes, 'it is possible, maybe inevitable, that we could be in love with other people, but still always love each other.' On 13 April 1962, Stella arrived unexpectedly on the *St Ola*, and stayed for two weeks in Stromness. This was a happy fortnight for her. She was overwhelmed by the beauty of Orkney – 'the sparkling and startling colours of sea and sky and moorland really made me unable to speak often' – and she fitted comfortably into life at Well Park. Mhairi Brown became fond of Stella. She made a point of seeing her on her subsequent annual trips to Edinburgh; and the affection was mutual. Years later, Stella mentioned wistfully in a letter to George how she often wished that she had been born with the 'lovely temperament' of his mother.

For George, Stella's visit was more complicated: it was a time, he writes in his autobiography, of 'confused happiness and pain'. About a dozen Stromness men had fallen in love with her, he told Charlie Senior, 'and they keep plaguing me with enquiries as to her wellbeing, likely time of return, etc.' The fact that she seemed so perfectly at home in Orkney, and in Well Park, can only have made him question whether they might have tried harder to make a future together.

But, by the time of that spring visit, both Stella and George had already, on the face of it, gone their own ways. Stella, after fighting off the advances of John Broom, had become engaged again, this time to Hugh Mackay. George was spending increasing amounts of time with a Stromness girl fifteen years his junior, Sylvia Wishart. He had first taken note of Sylvia when she was just twelve. Reporting for the *Orkney Herald*, George had been struck by one of her paintings in a local exhibition: here, he predicted, was 'a gifted child artist of whom Orkney will not be ashamed in the years to come'. He was right. By 1960, when George spent the winter at Tor-na-Dee, Sylvia Wishart was working on a postgraduate diploma at Gray's School of Art in Aberdeen, and from here she began to visit him regularly at the weekends. George was fascinated by her changing moods: one moment she was as subtle and withdrawn as the Mona Lisa, he told Ian MacArthur; the next she was as boisterous as Eartha Kitt. They had much in common. Like George, Sylvia was drawn to Catholicism; and, like him, she loved Rackwick more than any other place on earth. By the autumn of 1962, Sylvia and George were seeing each other every evening and, as often as their funds would allow, catching a lift with a fisherman to Hoy at the weekend.

Mhairi Brown, who longed to see George settled with a dependable wife, may have hoped that here at last was a potential daughter-in-law. But the fact that his mother was beginning to show signs of old age only exacerbated George's anxiety about the future, and his feeling that, however grim the prospect, he must find some way of earning a living. In the early summer of 1962, following his rejection by the Hogarth Press, his financial worries became acute. Friends rallied round. Willa Muir, herself short of funds, sent George £50, and gave him a year's subscription to *Encounter* to raise his spirits. Tom Scott, his old rival in love, offered to write to T. S. Eliot and Kathleen Raine to ask whether they might secure George a grant from the Royal Literary Fund. Besides the practical implications of pennilessness, the fact that he seemed incapable of supporting himself had begun to tell on George's nerves. 'It's more than awful,' he wrote to Tom Scott, 'living on the National Assistance pittance, and enduring all that poking and prying.'

He began to explore the possibility of applying to the Commercial College in Glasgow, and training to become a librarian. 'This will qualify me to spend the rest of my life among books,' he wrote to Flora MacArthur,* 'a thought which terrifies me.'

Once again, at the eleventh hour, George was spared. His old tutor, Dr Kitchin, had followed George's progress with interest since his graduation, and he now arranged for Edinburgh University to offer him a grant for postgraduate research on Gerard Manley Hopkins. It was a typically imaginative move on Kitchin's part. He recognized from the outset that George would never produce a thesis on Hopkins; but he felt that, provided with a grant and a couple of years' shelter from the 'cold winds of the world', he might stand a chance of concentrating sufficiently on his own work to establish himself as a poet. In the autumn of 1962, George travelled south to Edinburgh, and took up lodgings with John Broom in Bathgate.

'Inscape in the Poetry of Gerard Manley Hopkins' was the subject of the never-to-be-written thesis, and Winifred Maynard was the tutor appointed to oversee it. It was a frustrating task. She was privy to Kitchin's ruse, but she hoped, none the less, that some aspect of Hopkins's own interests – Duns Scotus,† for example, and his feelings about 'quiddity' – might fire George's imagination sufficiently to inspire some original, investigative work. She hoped in vain. Week after week, George appeared punctually for his tutorials; but often, even in the mornings, he was too drunk to make proper conversation, and Maynard had to send him away. When sober, he seemed so 'buttoned-up' that she found it impossible to get through to him. And, despite her best efforts, all George could be persuaded to produce were short, under-graduate-style essays in response to individual Hopkins poems. 'In my whole life,' Maynard reflects in retirement, 'I have never taught anyone so signally uninterested in following up research leads.'

It was not that George was uninterested in Gerard Manley Hopkins. 'No English poet ever fell upon the language with such skill, sweetness and boisterous daring,' he writes in his autobiography; and

---

*Flora Jack had married Ian MacArthur in June 1954.
†John Duns Scotus, thirteenth-century Franciscan philosopher, who distinguished between the 'quiddity' (what-ness) and 'haecceity' (this-ness) of things.

he admired Hopkins's heroic, lonely fight to turn the melancholy tide of late Victorian poetry with poetry full of energy and gladness. In all sorts of ways, too, this passionate, shy, tormented Jesuit was a kindred spirit to George. They shared a capacity for joy, particularly in nature; and they had both known the near-despair Hopkins expresses in his dark sonnets:

> O the mind, mind has mountains: cliffs of fall
> Frightful, sheer, no-man-fathomed. Hold them cheap
> May who ne'er hung there.

But academic dissection of Hopkins's work seemed to George to have been all but exhausted. 'The Yanks have done all the scholarly and pedantic stuff,' he wrote to Tom Scott. 'No room to put in another spade.' And the very fact that he loved Hopkins's poetry so much militated against his subjecting it to analysis and theory. 'I've a feeling,' he wrote to Charlie Senior, 'it's best to leave the great dead where they are with the eternal light on their brows; not soil them with our vain breath from below.' Towards the end of 1963 George confessed to his friend Ian MacArthur that, while he was grateful to 'inscape' for keeping him out of the poorhouse for two years, he had still not the faintest idea what the word meant. In the spring of the following year, Winifred Maynard had no choice but to recommend that his grant should not be renewed.

By the summer of 1964, George's prospects looked as bleak as ever. He had tried, and failed, to persuade the Edinburgh authorities that he might usefully follow up his work on Hopkins with research into Robert Henryson, or the Scottish Ballads, or even Edwin Muir. He had applied for a job in the university library, and been turned away. In the meantime, as he wrote to Stewart Conn, financial and family and personal difficulties 'keep piling up'.

Stella's situation appeared to get steadily worse too. Her engagement to Hugh Mackay had been called off,* her parents had thrown

---

*Hugh Mackay had decided, in the end, that he could not go ahead with it. It has remained a source of anguish for him that, had he married Stella at this point, he might have saved her from the tragedy into which her life now began to descend.

her out of 37 Baberton Crescent, and she was living in a dark, damp basement flat in Fettes Row. She and George had continued to see each other during his postgraduate years, and when they managed to stay away from Rose Street, there was still affection and humour between them. In the course of his studies, George had fallen out with John Broom, and had moved to live in a basement room sublet from a Glasgow writer, Edward Gaitens. Stella visited him from time to time to take 'the top layer of dirt off the kitchen'. George, in return, cooked for her: 'Menu for Dinner,' he wrote in a note before one of her visits:

Oeuf fricasse
Sausage fricasse   I hope 'fricasse'
Bacon fricasse   means 'fried'
Tomato fricasse   for that's what it's
Thé   going to be
ou
Café

But, if they drank together, George and Stella now almost inevitably ended up fighting; and, though George recognized that friction and confrontation could be a part of love, these fights alarmed him. 'There are different kinds of fighting,' he believed. 'There's a creative kind, positive and healing strife, and hard fusion. And there's the discharge of black hatred; and that's the kind that frightens me, though I know I'm one of the poles that generates the voltage.' George's first surviving letter to Stella is written in the aftermath of a raging, drunken argument: 'We have given each other a lot of wounds just lately,' he writes. 'I hurt you, you hurt me. Why this should be, when at the root of it all we have such affection for each other, I just don't know . . . If you want to see me, I will meet you anywhere and at any time, but *please*, not in a pub.'

Within the Brown family, too, there were troubles. In June, George's mother travelled down from Orkney for what had become an annual visit to Edinburgh, to see Norrie and Hazel and her granddaughters, and to buy herself a new pair of shoes. These visits to Oxgangs were generally a time of delight for all concerned. Unlike George, Mhairi

Brown loved travel and cities, and nothing made her happier than to catch a bus to Princes Street and spend a morning wandering around the shops. 'Marks and Spencer's was a cave of pure enchantment to her,' George wrote in a memoir of his mother, several years after her death.

> 'I think,' she would say, 'I'll take the bus down to Malcolm Spencer's.' (She had a habit of getting names wrong, as well as common expressions: small lingual aberrations possibly stemming from her ancestor-rooted original tongue.) Her three Edinburgh granddaughters, who loved her, would explain gently, 'It isn't Malcolm Spencer's, Granny – it's *Marks and Spencer's.*' 'Oh, is it?' she would say. Then a couple of breakfasts later, she would announce once more, 'I just love that Malcolm Spencer's shop – I think I'll take a ride down to it in the bus before lunch.' Looks of happy exasperation on three girls' faces.

But, when Mhairi arrived in Edinburgh in mid-June 1964, the atmosphere was strained. Norrie's health had continued to cause concern. One evening during his mother's visit, he excused himself from the conversation and went to tidy his desk. Before going to bed, he showed Hazel precisely how his papers were organized. In the early hours of the following morning, he suffered a heart attack and, by breakfast-time, Mhairi Brown had lost the third of her five sons. George was devastated. Stella took him for a walk by the sea at Cramond to help him compose himself but when he arrived at Oxgangs in the afternoon he was still in a state of uncontrollable distress. It was the first time his niece Ros had seen a man in tears.

In early July, George returned with his mother to Orkney. The weather in the islands that summer was dismal; and, despite visits from Charlie Senior, Paddy Hughes and Sydney Goodsir Smith, he sank into a slough of despair. Again, he moved back into Well Park; again, he began to draw National Assistance; again, he turned to drink for consolation. He had nothing to look forward to, he told Stella, but 'a futureless future (without money or prospects or any worthwhile objective)'.

In fact, things were a great deal more hopeful than they seemed. George's postgraduate years had been dogged by ill-health; but the reprieve from the 'real world' that Dr Kitchin had secured him had paid off in precisely the manner intended. If George had achieved little by

John Brown (back left) with fellow Stromness tailors, c. 1920. Seated immediately beneath him is his brother Jimmy, whose suspected suicide in March 1935 precipitated George's first serious depression

The view across Stromness Harbour to Hoy

George (centre row, far left) with his class at Stromness Academy, 1926–27. Ian MacInnes holds the slate inscribed 'Infants'

George, c. 1930, with his mother – 'the most naturally cheerful woman I have ever known'; with his father, c. 1926 (John Brown used his tailoring skills to 'make down' his old Post Office uniforms into clothes for his sons); and in a pushchair, surrounded by his siblings, (left to right) Jackie, Hughie, Norrie and Ruby

Students at Newbattle, 1951–52: (back row, left to right) David Hamilton, Dorothy McCrory, 'Spike' Mays, Bob Fletcher, Rabindrath Chabria; (front row, left to right) George Mackay Brown, Vera Starcevic, Bill Drysdale, Tom Wilson, Helen Tulloch, Margaret Darge. *Below*, Alexander Moffat's painting *Poets' Pub*, 1980: (left to right) Norman MacCaig, Hugh MacDiarmid (seated with pipe), Sorley MacLean, Iain Crichton Smith, George Mackay Brown, Sydney Goodsir Smith, Edwin Morgan, Robert Garioch and (foreground) Alan Bold

George, c. 1968: in repose, Ernest Marwick wrote of him at this time, he had a look of 'agonised maturity'. *Below*, George in the sea valley of Rackwick, his 'Tir-nan-Og', c. 1960: from a composite photograph by his friend Paddy Hughes

Edwin and Willa Muir at Newbattle, 1951; Norah Smallwood, George's editor at Chatto & Windus for a quarter of a century; Ernest Marwick in his study at Westermill

'I think there must be something in Graves's idea of a living muse': Stella Cartwright and, below, Nora Kennedy (left) and Kenna Crawford

George and Peter Maxwell Davies in Rackwick on the afternoon of their first meeting, 12 July 1970. *Below*, George with Gunnie Moberg in Stromness, June 1991

way of new insights into the poetry of Gerard Manley Hopkins, he seems during this time to have come to a better understanding of himself, of the constraints life had placed upon him and the opportunities it now offered, and of the real nature and purpose of his own work. In the short story 'Sealskin', George describes how, as Magnus Olafson tours around the cities of Europe, he is preoccupied with images of the Orkney island of Norday, where he spent his childhood:

> All these years he had carried Norday with him wherever he went, but his memory had made it a transfigured place, more like a piece of tapestry than an album of photographs. The great farmhouses and the small crofts had appeared, in retrospect, 'sunk in time'. The people, viewed from Paris, moved like figures in an ancient fable, simple and secure and predestined, and death rounded all . . .
>
> It was in a fable that these people seemed to move; and Magnus thought that if each man's seventy years could be compressed into a short time, his laborious feet, however plastered with dung and clay, would move in a joyous reel of fruition.

During his postgraduate years in Edinburgh, Orkney had worked on George's imagination in just the way he describes here. Urban living, George believed, had infected much of the culture of the twentieth century with sickness and despair: 'Think of Beckett, Bacon, Burroughs, all the sick writers and the anti-artists; their works are the symptoms of a deep and (it may be) incurable malaise. Even with the stories of a talented writer like Muriel Spark, you ask over and over again, "What does this come out of? What is she trying to say?"' In celebrating the old ways of island life in his writing it was his task, by contrast, to sound a clear, if unfashionable, note of hope.

Spurred on by Cecil Day-Lewis's rejection, for which George later felt nothing but gratitude, he had set to work again. New poems homed in on him, sometimes one a day, and he was quietly confident that they were the best he had yet produced. Shortly before Norrie's death, George had summoned up his courage and sent forty-seven poems written out by hand (he was, he confessed, too poor to have them typed) to the Hogarth Press. 'They are all about Orkney,' he explained in a covering letter; and in many of them the lives of ordinary people were gathered into the 'joyous reel of fruition' that he would later describe in 'Sealskin'. Among the poems, for example, was 'The Funeral of Ally Flett', possibly inspired by the drowning of George's fisherman friend Andy Goodsir at harvest-time two summers earlier. In it, he evokes a small island community by looking at seven different ways in which men and women choose to pay their respects to a man who has died before his time:

> Because of his long pilgrimage
>   From pub to alehouse
>   And all the liquor laws he'd flout,
> Being under age
>   And wringing peatbog spirit from a clout
> Into a secret kettle,
>   And making every Sabbath a carouse,
> Mansie brought a twelve-year bottle.
>
> Because his shy foot turned aside
>   From Merran's door,
>   And Olga's coat with the red button
> And Inga's side
>   Naked as snow or swan or wild bog cotton
> Made him laugh loud
>   And after, spit with scunner on the floor,
> Marget sewed a long chaste shroud.
>
> Because the scythe was in the oats
>   When he lay flat,
>   And Jean Macdonald's best March ale
> Cooled the long throats
>   (At noon the reapers drank from the common pail)
> And Sanders said
>   'Corn enough here for every tramp and rat',
> Sigrid baked her lightest bread.
>
> Although the fleet from Hamnavoe
>   Drew heavy nets
>   Off Noup Head, in a squall of rain,
> Turning in slow
>   Gull-haunted circles near the three-mile line,
> And mouthing cod
>   Went iced and salted into slippery crates,
> One skipper heard and bowed his head.

Because at Dounby and the fair
   Twelve tearaways
      Brought every copper in the islands
Round their uproar
      And this one made a sweet and sudden silence
Like that white bird
   That broke the tempest with a twig of praise,
The preacher spoke the holy word.

Because the hour of grass is brief
   And the red rose
      Is a bare thorn in the east wind
And a strong life
      Runs out and spends itself like barren sand
And the dove dies
   And every loveliest lilt must have a close,
Old Betsy came with bitter cries.

Because his dance was gathered now
   And parish feet
      Went blundering their separate roads
After the plough
      And after net and peat and harvest loads,
Yet from the cradle
   Their fated steps with a fixed passion beat,
Tammas brought his Swedish fiddle.

This time, the reaction from the Hogarth Press was positive, and in the autumn of 1964 Cecil Day-Lewis sent George a contract for a new collection of poems, *The Year of the Whale*.

12

Heaven and Hell Play Poker

PETER ORR: Does poetry bring you more happiness than anything else?

GEORGE MACKAY BROWN: The greatest happiness I know under the circumstances in which I live.

GMB, Interview, 1964

GEORGE'S VERSE WAS now appearing regularly in the *New Statesman*, the *Listener* and the Scottish poetry magazine *Lines Review*. He was sufficiently well-regarded that in October 1964, as part of a joint enterprise between the British Council and Harvard University, he was paid to travel to Edinburgh to record for posterity his thoughts about his work. The recording session was an ordeal. Peter Orr, the British Council representative sent to interview him, reflected years later that seldom, if ever, had he met a writer 'apparently so unprotected by the poetic persona which more sophisticated authors assume for their public encounters'. He had to calm George with several shots of Glenfiddich before beginning to question him formally, and George's voice on the tape is distinctly slurred. His opinions, however, are clear and forceful. Asked whether poetry matters to him more than anything else, George's unhesitating answer is 'Yes'. And, though he baffles Orr by claiming to care nothing for critics or fame or a wide readership, when asked whether he would like a niche for his work in posterity, George reveals an unusual but striking ambition. 'It depends who remembers it,' he says. 'If the kind of people I was sympathetic towards, if they remember it maybe seven or eight or nine generations hence, that would be tremendous.' Seven or eight or nine generations – two hundred-odd years: few writers' work lives longer than that. George's unassuming modesty, Orr concluded, concealed a character of great strength and determination. Here was a poet who 'would not easily be deflected from a particular course once it had been plotted in his mind'.

As Christmas approached, George was not short of commissions. The *Glasgow Herald* had published a number of his short stories and, at the BBC, George Bruce had begun to broadcast his poetry, short stories and essays on a regular basis on the radio programme *Scottish Life and Letters*. His work was also beginning to attract attention from his peers outside Scotland – both Kathleen Raine and Stephen Spender wrote out of the blue to express their admiration – and even abroad. The American writer and editor George Plimpton, a noted talent-spotter, commissioned a number of poems from George for his literary quarterly, the *Paris Review*. They appeared in its pages alongside work by writers such as V. S. Naipaul, Italo Calvino and Philip Roth. Peter Davison, director of the Atlantic Monthly Press, wrote to tell Norah Smallwood that he considered George 'the most exciting new voice since Ted Hughes', and when, just before Christmas 1964, George received payment for four poems published in the *Atlantic Monthly*, he could hardly believe the size of the cheque. (The astonishing thing about American editors, he remarked to a friend, was that they calculated their payments 'per line'. Perhaps, he joked, he could develop a lucrative, staccato style specifically for the American market.)

In the spring of 1965, George found himself able, for the first time in years, to live without the aid of National Assistance or a university grant. This financial independence, and the feeling that he was no longer 'a nuisance in the world', pleased him very much. Then, in August, *The Year of the Whale* was published. The reviews were excellent. 'Nobody I know of, anywhere, writes poems like these,' Norman MacCaig reflected; and he praised George's gift for capturing 'the miraculous reciprocations of love – when it's reciprocated – and its withering loneliness when it isn't'. Reviewer after reviewer confessed that they had not been satisfied with just one reading of the poems, but had found themselves drawn back to them repeatedly: 'They are Bruegel-like,' wrote the publisher Giles Gordon. 'They are lovely and one goes on and on reading them. Phrases sing in your head and images assail your vision days later.' Kathleen Raine wrote again to George, to tell him of the joy it had given her to read 'real' poems, 'wedding the inner experience of the soul to the places of the world, Orkney and its history'. The poet Kevin Crossley-Holland described how *The Year of the Whale* had taken his mind off a devastating toothache as he waited in Guy's Hospital in the middle of the night to have a molar extracted. In Queen's University, Belfast, the collection left a young lecturer, Seamus Heaney, with 'a feeling of being newly wakened, of the lens widening'. In a letter to George, Heaney confessed that he had read *The Year of the Whale* 'with delight and (probably) envy'.

Success bred determination. 'From now on,' George wrote to Stella in November 1965, 'only the best counts.' Ernest Marwick, in a letter to Willa Muir, expressed his excitement at the discipline and application with which George now approached his work. He was beginning to develop the routine he would keep until the end of his life: settling down straight after breakfast, and writing for three or four hours without a break.

Sometimes, these sessions were a battle – 'the mind full of bustle, fret, anxiety, half-fulfilment'. In *The Year of the Whale*, George had published the much-anthologized poem in which he defines the poet's true task as 'interrogation of silence'. But silence was hard to come by in 6 Well Park. Inexhaustibly generous and gregarious, Mhairi Brown kept the small house filled with friends and family. Almost every morning, her neighbours Mrs Tulloch, Mrs Wishart and Mrs McLeod gathered around her kitchen table with cups of tea, and then for an hour or more the house was 'crammed with words'. In the afternoon, Mhairi rested, and through the bedroom door George could hear her 'snoring like a circular saw'. In the evenings, she watched television, and he had to battle against the background noise of *Z Cars*, *Dr Who*, *The Monkees*. During school holidays, meanwhile, the household was swelled with troupes of visiting grandchildren. 'Pam has taken a craze for playing Ludo,' George wrote to Charlie Senior in August 1965. 'I grow sick of the rattle of dice.'*

On the whole, nevertheless, during the autumn of 1964 and for the year following, George was writing with ease and excitement. It was invigorating, he told an interviewer from the *Sun*, to be away

---

*Pamela Brown was the daughter of Norrie and Hazel.

from Edinburgh where the 'talk of culture was absolutely killing'; and he wrote to Senior of the excitement he felt that 'what talent I have is flowering'.

Shortly before Christmas 1965, the BBC broadcast a talk by George in which he tried to encapsulate for an urban audience what it was about Orkney that so fired his imagination as a writer. He spoke of the rich contrast between the slow, dependable rhythms of agriculture and the 'stark perpetual drama' of life at sea; and of the sense, everywhere and inescapable, of history stretching back thousands of years – a history, often, of violence and cruelty, but shot through, since the death of Magnus Erlendson on Easter Monday 1117, with the 'bright thread of sanctity'. He explained how the clear, hard light of the islands made it impossible for an Orkney writer to be troubled by the kind of obscurity that seemed to him to bedevil much of twentieth-century literature. In Oban, Iain Crichton Smith listened to George on the radio, and was moved. 'You sounded to me,' he wrote, 'like a poet who has found the way he must go.'

Anxiety about the future, which had cast a shadow over George for so long, was finally receding and, as it did so, he was writing with renewed delight in his surroundings. In letters to friends outside Orkney, he described the changing weather and seasons with a combination of precision and rejoicing reminiscent of the journals of Gerard Manley Hopkins. 'The darkness of winter is over land and sea,' he wrote to Charlie Senior one December afternoon, 'days of stillness followed by ferocious gusty days. But O, what starlight! And the moon tangled in sounds and firths.' And in May, as the 'throb of early summer' began to go through the islands: 'The light now is beginning to take on that magical midsummer quality. I walked out last night between supper-time and ale-time and it was marvellous, first stars coming out and a kind of primrose glow all along the north.' Whenever he could find a fisherman to give him a lift, George spent the weekend in Rackwick, wandering along the beach between the great red cliffs, and through the fields and tumbled crofts, 'like a leaf in the wind'. He was working on the idea of an anthology tracing the history of the valley through the centuries, and throughout the spring and summer of 1965 Rackwick poems were tumbling from his pen. By the end of the year he had written more than a hundred.

In December 1965, quite unexpectedly, the Scottish Arts Council wrote to offer George a bursary – 'enough to keep me in ease for a whole year'.* Following the success of *The Year of the Whale*, meanwhile, the Hogarth Press had expressed interest in publishing a collection of his short stories, and for the first half of 1966 George was busy corresponding with Norah Smallwood about the fourteen stories to be included. 'Orkney is a small green world in itself,' he wrote in a foreword. 'Walk a mile or two and you will see, mixed up with the modern houses of concrete and wood, the "old farmhouses sunk in time"; hall and manse from which laird and minister ruled in the eighteenth century; smuggler's cave, witch's hovel . . .' The stories he chose for his first collection reflect this landscape, ranging across the centuries. But whether set in Orkney's Viking past, or in the twentieth century, all are written with the same quiet feeling for the human condition, and for what he would later describe as 'the bitter ordinances of time'.

In 'The Wheel' George gently lifts the lid on the life of Robert Jansen, an elderly man whose long-term sailor companion, William Walls, has been dead two years. Jansen cannot accept his friend's death, and every Saturday evening he unsettles the small island community in which he lives by walking about, knocking on doors, asking in a coarse throaty voice, 'Has Walls been here tonight?' At the end of his rounds, back in his little stone house by the sea, he takes a scrap of newspaper from a drawer in the dresser. Putting on his glasses, he reads carefully, for the umpteenth time, a report of how the body of William Walls was found at low tide among the rocks under his pier. Then he proceeds, as always, to lay the table for two:

> Robert carefully replaced the cutting in the drawer. He put a spoon of sugar and a spurt of milk into each cup. He took two eggs out of the box and broke them into the pan; then, after a moment's hesitation, he broke a third egg into the pan.
>
> 'Walls is always hungry for his supper on a Saturday night, after the drink,' he murmured. 'What a man for eggs!'

---

*The bursary was for £750, and, perhaps to assuage his guilt at having remained dependent on his mother for so long, one of the first things George did when it arrived was to buy Mhairi Brown a washing machine and spin-drier for Christmas.

A Calendar of Love, published in February 1967, was an overwhelming critical success. Reviewers praised the 'spare, beautiful
accuracy' of George's prose, and the 'strange and fierce and quietly
truthful' quality of his stories; and, as with *The Year of the Whale*, many
of them felt moved to return to the book again and again. 'I find
myself, even with the clock against me, lured to re-read for half an
hour,' wrote Hilary Corke in the *Listener*. '*A Calendar of Love* looks
like one of the few really solid achievements of the year.' More gratifying still, perhaps, were the letters that George now began to receive
from unknown members of the public. 'I am a very ordinary reader,'
wrote Alexander Kelly from Barnes, 'so my opinions are worthless as
a literary critic. May I simply say as a *human being* that I have found
the reading of your stories an experience that has enriched my life?'

It is a recurring theme in George's writing that what we strive for
hardest rarely yields what we long for most. Now, as he began to achieve
the success he had worked towards for nearly forty years, he was more
than ever aware of the constrictions of his circumstances, and of loneliness. 'I used to think it would be heaven to be a writer,' he told an
interviewer from the *Weekend Scotsman*, 'but . . . all the thrill now is in
the actual writing – to see the thing in cold print afterwards gives you
strong feelings of remorse, inadequacy and exposure.' The mornings at
his desk were the happiest parts of George's day, and when poems came
singing easily from his pen he felt 'full of interior rejoicing'; but in the
afternoons and evenings, he told Stella, he often felt desperately alone.

In the spring of 1965, George had asked Norah Smallwood
whether *The Year of the Whale* might be dedicated to the young artist
Sylvia Wishart. In August, on the day of the book's publication, his
friendship with Sylvia 'expired in a violent flare-up'. Initially, this left
him less miserable than he might have expected. 'So now,' he wrote
in a jaunty letter to Stella, 'I see I'm cut out only to be an old bachelor drinking pints at sunset at the door of pubs and wondering who
will wash my shirt next week.' But, as the months went by, the limitations of his solitary state were borne in on him. 'You should
know . . . that it's impossible for you not to love,' he wrote to Stella
on 11 November. 'As for me, I think now I'm quite incapable of it.
So I plunge into a vortex of work, and in fatigue, and in some species

of small creation (for poetry and all art is a poor thing, set beside love)
I get contentment (of a kind).'

For consolation, and to relieve the perplexity he felt at the twists of
fate, George turned to 'the smiler with the knife'. His letters at this
time are filled with references to lost weekends, often extending over
four or five days, to hangovers which left him stale and weary, to the
backwash of remorse that set in after every alcoholic splurge 'like the
ebb tide in Hoy Sound', and to the mixture of dread and powerless-
ness with which he anticipated each new bout. 'The thought of
whisky harrows me to the skeleton,' he told Stella.

Hogmanay was always a dangerous time. On New Year's Day 1964,
George had woken to find his sheets drenched in blood: he had put his
fist through a window the night before. The following new year, on his
way to bed after a heavy night, he stopped beside the small bookcase
on his mother's landing, seized the books from the shelves, and hurled
them, one by one, down the stairs until they lay strewn in the hall 'like
shot birds'. George then tumbled after them, breaking a number of ribs.

When he could keep himself in check, George's sessions with Attie
Campbell and Billy Evans in the Stromness Hotel were convivial and
fruitful, fuelling him for his next stint at his desk:

> At noon he went to the inn.
> Voices, smoke, shadows. He sifted
> One heavy hard gleam from the gossip.

But increasingly, during 1965 and 1966, George was drinking himself
into a state in which he became abusive and violent, leaving behind a
trail of bitterness and bad feeling. 'What perverse demon lures me into
such folly?' he asked Charlie Senior. 'All I know is, I cause unhappiness to myself and others, and yet there seems to be some pattern in
it, as if a regular binge was necessary for the complete picture.'

To Ian MacInnes, it seemed that George was on the verge of squan-
dering his life and his gifts in drink. There were, however, two things
keeping him from ruin. The first was his weak constitution, which
meant that, in the words of one friend, 'his legs tended to go faster than
his head'; the second was his writing. Without this, George confessed
to Charlie Senior, he would almost certainly be an alcoholic – 'one of
the poor ones, a winey'.

Stella, in Edinburgh, had no such purpose into which to pour her energy and gifts, and by 1965 she had become a slave to drink. She begged George to look on her as a caution: 'George, my dear, dear friend, please take a warning . . . don't abuse alcohol. I would *hate* to have you in the state I am in.' In the summer of 1965, as American troops moved into Vietnam, and the Beatles screamed 'Help!', Stella was admitted to hospital. She was suffering from 'needles and pins and lack of balance, and impaired eyesight, the shakes, palpitations, dizziness', all of which were diagnosed as symptoms of neuritis, brought on by alcohol. She was frightened, and afflicted with a sense of guilt. 'George, pray for me,' she begged, 'I don't want to die yet – not before I have remedied some of my sins of omission.'

George had never ceased to pray for her. As Stella had once predicted, their love for each other was not diminished by their loving others, and even when George was spending every evening and weekend with Sylvia Wishart, Stella had remained constantly in his thoughts. He wrote to her regularly, letters full of affection and reassurance. 'Be good and patient, dear Stella,' he had urged, shortly before midnight on New Year's Eve 1964. 'There will be sweet waters and gentle winds about you soon. May your good angel watch over you in 1965 and always.' A few weeks later he wrote: 'A lot of white thoughts and blessings go from Stromness to Fettes Row, a continual flight. That basement must be bright with doves.' In May 1965, on the eve of Stella's twenty-eighth birthday, George lit a small candle he had saved from the church on Easter night – 'a little silent visible prayer that you may be all shining; mind and spirit'. And in June, just before she was admitted to hospital, he wrote: 'Keep well. What would our world be without Stella? A poor dark lonely place.' 'Not a morning or an evening passes that I don't think of you,' he assured her in November. 'In gratitude for the past, in hope for the future.'

But it was hard to keep this hope alive. In letters to friends George had begun, perhaps subconsciously, to refer to Stella in the past tense: 'She was so good,' he wrote to Charlie Senior in October 1965, 'she deserved so well of life because of the sweetness and gaiety she brought to it – and all she gets in exchange is ashes.'

That autumn, after failing to turn up for work one Monday morning too many, Stella was sacked from her job at F. C. Inglis. She was, in George's words, 'unhappy, sick, destitute', and spells in hospital now became a regular part of her life. She had little faith in the likelihood of anyone in the medical profession getting to the root of her problems. 'Could a psychiatrist cure you?' she asks herself in a poem scribbled on a scrap of paper:

> Could he, Impartial Brain,
> Understand that Heaven and Hell
> Play Poker in your soul?
>
> So pure, in purity afraid.
> From traitorous freedom aching to be free
> To place a human hand upon a human hand
> And be.

In February 1966, Stella wrote tearfully to George from Ward 1A of the Royal Edinburgh Hospital to say that her life had been a failure, not just for herself but for all who had ever known her. George replied, gently bracing:

> You must not talk of your life being wasted. No person can say his life is a failure until the moment of death, and even then it is for God to say. Perhaps you – and this applies to me and a host of others – have gone about some things in a wrong way, not intending any evil. It is hard often to know the right way to act in this confused world. But this must be a comfort to you, dear – I'm speaking as one who has benefited often from your kindness and love and sweet nature – you have given much happiness to people who were hungry for it. This is the greatest gift of all, charity, deep disinterested love of one's fellowmen; a far higher gift, believe me, than the gifts of art or music or poetry, marvellous though they are. Treasure your gift, dear Stella, for this would be a darker and a sadder world without you.

George's hatred of 'culture', and of the twentieth-century tendency to worship the arts as a substitute for religion, had hardened during his years in Edinburgh; but when he tells Stella that her gift is more precious than any artist's, he does so with particular feeling. Culture, he believed, had been Stella's undoing; and the company of the Rose Street poets 'a poison' for her. 'The horrible heresy of Bohemianism,' he wrote to Charlie Senior. 'If only she had married early some decent man and had a half-dozen kids, and to hell with art and poetry.'* When one of the psychiatrists at the Royal Edinburgh Hospital suggested to Stella that she should 'tear up her old life by the roots', George found himself agreeing. 'I sometimes think it might be better, for her sake,' he confessed to Senior, 'if we gently & gradually . . . broke off all communication.'

Yet George relied on Stella just as Stella relied on George. He was by now adept at putting on a bright face – a 'mask' – when he left his writing desk and moved among the folk of Stromness. Stella was perhaps the only person to whom he felt able fully to unburden himself, to confess his anxiety about his drinking habits, and his dread of the depressions that continued to plague him despite his success. 'Nothing but rain and low clouds and increasing darkness,' he wrote to her during a week in which he had sold four short stories to magazines, 'and the silver wings of the spirit furled in despondency.' Writing to Stella, George admitted, gave him courage.

For Stella retained, even in her lowest moments, a generous spirit; and, though she was an irregular correspondent, when she felt George was in trouble she was able to draw on what he called 'her old sweetness', and to respond with intuitive compassion and perception. 'My dearest George, Why are you sad?' she writes on 6 August 1965. 'Are you lonely in a way? You struggle alone with many emotions that probably nobody can help you with – or so it seems . . . You are surrounded by beauty in Orkney and I know this can put an edge not only to joy, but to suffering. However, you come back to the beauty which is God, and lasts.'

In the summer of 1966, George mentions in a letter to Stella that he is working on a short story about a girl called Celia, whom he is basing largely on her. Celia is a beautiful but vulnerable creature, acutely sensitive to pain. She is also an alcoholic. 'I drink because I'm frightened,' she explains, when she is finally persuaded to talk to the minister.

I'm so desperately involved with all the weak things, lonely things, suffering things I see about me. I can't bear the pity I feel for them, not

---

*The irony is that, when she was just eighteen, Stella had very nearly married a Polish refugee, Leszek Beldowski, who might have given her just the kind of life that George describes. In a poem, 'Why, What Happened?', she later cursed her decision to allow Beldowski to leave her, blaming it, in part, on the fatal lure of the Rose Street poets.

being able to help them at all. There's blood everywhere. The world's a torture chamber, just a sewer of pain. That frightens me.

Yesterday it was a gull and a water rat. They met at the end of this pier. I was pinning washing to the line when I saw it. The gull came down on the rat and swallowed it whole the way it would gulp a crust of bread, then with one flap of its wing it was out over the sea again. I could see the shape of the rat in the blackback's throat, a kind of fierce twist and thrust. The bird broke up in the air. It screamed. Blood and feathers showered out of it. The dead gull and the living rat made separate splashes in the water.

It seems most folk can live with that kind of thing. Not me – I get all caught up in it . . .

In exchange for alcohol, Celia prostitutes herself among the men of Hamnavoe, ruining her chances of marriage to a decent crofter, Ronald Leask, who loves her. Towards the end of the story, however, she experiences some undefined *coup de grâce*, and rediscovers a faith she had lost in childhood. We are left believing that all will be well for her.

But the chances of a happy ending to Stella's story were now slim. Some time during 1966, she embarked on an affair with Sydney Goodsir Smith, and moved into a flat he owned in Dundas Street. It might have proved a happy match. Smith was the sort of steadying, kind, older man George felt Stella needed; she, meanwhile, was able to lift him out of melancholia, and make him laugh until he wept. But Sydney Goodsir Smith was committed to another woman, an English teacher called Hazel Williamson. During 1967, as he wrote and published reams of love poetry to Stella, his 'Seal Baby', friends waited in trepidation for Hazel to discover what was afoot.

Stella's situation filled George with despair. He saw no end now to the 'hideous spiral of drinking', and he knew very well that her affair with Sydney Goodsir Smith could only, in the end, compound her misery. In the autumn of 1967, a friend, Betty Grant, reported to him that she had been to a party at Stella's flat, and had come away shocked by the atmosphere of 'hopelessness and decay' both in the place and in its inhabitants. 'The air inside 27 Dundas Street gets more murky,' George wrote to Charlie Senior on 28 September, 'it's like the setting for some kind of inevitable tragedy.'

13

Involved with Mankind

No man is an island, and all that we ever say or think or do –
however seemingly unremarkable – may set the whole web of
existence trembling and affect the living and the dead and the
unborn.   GMB, *Scotsman*, 1986

MHAIRI BROWN NEVER quite recovered from the death of Norrie.
Physically, she had always been delicate, but from the autumn of
1964 onwards George's letters to friends refer frequently to her failing
health. She was afflicted with crops of boils, which her doctor seemed
at a loss to treat effectively; she spent more and more time in bed. In
the summer of 1967, she arrived back from her annual visit to her
granddaughters in Edinburgh agitated and unwell. She had fallen in
the corridor of the Edinburgh–Aberdeen train, she told George, and
hurt her head. Then one evening, shortly after her return, he found
her rummaging through a chest of drawers. 'Somebody,' she muttered,
'has been stealing my clothes.' It was an allegation so bizarre, from a
woman so naturally gentle and buoyant and full of trust, that George
knew at once that something was seriously wrong: 'It was like the
touch of a chill finger on the heart.'

From then on, her decline was rapid and distressing. During the late
summer and autumn she suffered a series of small strokes, and it was as
though somebody was working their way through the corridors of her
mind, switching off lights. She sat for hours on a chair in the garden
looking ahead with a hurt, baffled expression and, when neighbours
came to visit, she could not recognize them. It seemed, George wrote
later, 'as if she was learning a part in a frightening play, and a part totally
unsuited to her: a Beckett tragedy rather than the pastoral comedy that

she had played with such natural grace and gaiety all her days'. Periodically, she broke her silence with eruptions of anger, most often directed at George. He responded harshly, hoping to shock her back to her old self, and he then felt overcome with sadness and remorse.

In September 1967, Orkney basked in a glorious Indian summer. George, however, longed for the 'yellow beast' to leave the sky, and for winter to close in on the islands. Adding to the strain he already felt on account of his mother, July and August had brought desperate letters from Stella. The neuritis in her legs and feet was so bad that she could hardly walk, and, at thirty, she now wrote in a large, laboured, shaky script, like an old lady's – 'not due to booze,' she assured George, 'but tiredness and pain'.

In October, John Broom wrote to ask whether Stella might come to Orkney for a holiday. She had a new doctor, who had blithely pre-scribed 'rest and hope' as the most likely cures for her troubles, and Broom, unaware of Mhairi Brown's state, thought that a fortnight's cosseting in Well Park was more likely than anything to provide these. George was forced to explain that his mother was, in a sense, no longer living in Well Park, but rambling instead through what he described as 'some land of Lear and Carroll', her wits and memories and per-ceptions 'twisted . . . into confusion'. He had abandoned his own work and was throwing himself, for the first time in his life, into cooking and housekeeping. He was struggling on the one hand to deal with the dirty laundry piling up around him ('like bad weather in the offing', as he had once described it), and on the other to 'urge and reason with a mind that has lost compass and anchor (and that has covered me with goodness all my life)'. He was exhausted. If the sit-uation did not ease, he told friends, he felt he might collapse.

In late October, Mhairi Brown was taken by ambulance to Eastbank where she became increasingly disoriented and distressed. 'She was learning the confused, mysterious language of the dying,' George later wrote, 'through which we could guess at nameless (and doubtless imaginary) dreads.' George himself had become no more than a 'shadowy vaguely hostile stranger' to her. At lunchtime on 3 November, her family were summoned to her bedside. 'The sister-in-charge held her pulse. Time passed. At last the sister said, "Now there's no pulse . . ."'

Ten days later, alone in Well Park, George wrote to Willa Muir:

It's very lonely here now but there's a kind of happiness in the house too because I have the feeling that a notable victory has been won for goodness. I'm always sorry that you didn't meet Mhairi Sheena Mackay, because as so many folk have expressed it in recent letters to me, she was a lovely person. (She knew nothing about books or art or religion at all.) I have faith that the goodness of people like Edwin and her is not lost at all, and is not just gathered up in heaven (though it is that too) but when their small faults and frailties are purged away their sweetness will infuse itself into the lives of the living also. So I believe and so I pray for their souls and the souls of all good people.

Friends like Ian MacInnes now considered George's situation with increased apprehension. Mhairi Brown's death might just be the making of him, they felt, but without her support he might equally well slide into drunkenness and despair. George too recognized that his future was precarious. His mother had left an estate of less than £5: he had to choose whether to sink or swim. As Christmas 1967 approached, in place of the profusion of decorations with which Mhairi Brown had always festooned 6 Well Park, he placed a single, red candle in the comb of the china cockerel on the chimney-piece: an emblem of a new austerity. Over Hogmanay, for the first time in years, he remained sober. 'Real winter in Orkney now, very cold, very wet,' his letter to Willa Muir had ended. 'Still, I must walk the ¾ mile to town and back again for errands – I'm the householder now and must plan prudently ahead.'

George's resolve was fuelled by a sense of guilt. In an essay written in the early eighties, he reveals how his mother often visited him in dreams in the years following her death, and how nearly always she seemed displeased. These dreams were more than a replaying of the painful memories of the summer and autumn of 1967. George was acutely aware of the distress he had caused through his drinking, of having lingered on at home long after he should have flown the nest, and of not having enough to show for the years of leisure his mother had afforded him. There is no record of Mhairi Brown's reactions either to *Loaves and Fishes* or to *The Year of the Whale* but, when *A Calendar of Love* was published just months before her death, she had commented that there was 'Nothing in it but pubs and drinking'. For all her sweetness, she had been ambitious for her children to better themselves – to 'get out of the rut'. George felt he had failed her.

In fact, as his mother died, after an apprenticeship that had lasted nearly a quarter of a century, George was on the brink of becoming one of the best-loved and most critically acclaimed poets and story-tellers in Scotland. In June 1967, he had sent off a parcel of new stories to the Hogarth Press, and the reaction from Norah Smallwood and Leonard Woolf was swift and enthusiastic. Privately, Cecil Day-Lewis posted the stories to Charles Causley in Cornwall, and in response received a letter brimming with praise. Like Francis Scarfe before him, Causley noted George's gift for conjuring up 'a world that's at the same time both foreign and wholly familiar'. He admired his ability to make people and places 'intensely real, recognisable', and his 'hard, clear, salty prose'. 'I don't know anyone writing in this particular genre today,' Causley concluded, 'who comes within a thousand miles of him.'

When *A Time to Keep* was published in 1969, the reviews struck the same high note. George was described as 'the most powerful story-teller since Lewis Grassic Gibbon', 'precise, poetic and dazzling', a writer possessed of 'the magician's touch'. If it had been a common theme among reviewers of *A Calendar of Love* that they felt moved to read the stories again and again, Paul Bailey was one of a number of reviewers of *A Time to Keep* who admitted that the book had brought him close to tears. 'Celia', in particular, with which George had chosen to open the collection, was singled out for praise. For the poet and critic Robert Nye, it remains the finest piece of writing George ever produced.

The relentless toughness of island life is shot through in all the stories in this collection with humour, gaiety and celebration – and so it had been in *A Calendar of Love*. What is new in *A Time to Keep* is George's treatment of people: for the first time, his characters really convince, and though they are drawn warts-and-all, he handles every one of them with compassion, finding goodness in unexpected places. 'These stories are written without the slightest trace of sentimental-ity,' wrote Alexander Scott, reviewing *A Time to Keep* in *Lines Review*, 'but they show the cruelty of life as being everywhere and anytime chastened by a charity of such loveliness as to seem more than mortal.' Scott went on to speculate on the effect that George's becoming a

Catholic had had on his work. The quality of grace that Edwin Muir had described in his introduction to *The Storm* had always been present, he argued, but George's Catholicism had now given his writing a firm, philosophical underpinning.

One story in *A Time to Keep* reads like an apologia, allowing George, under the cover of fiction, to explore his feelings about the richness at the heart of the Catholic faith. 'A Treading of Grapes' is composed of three imaginary sermons, each delivered on the same spot, each based on the gospel story of the wedding at Cana. The first is preached at some indefinable point in the twentieth century by the Revd Gary Watters. It is a slick but soulless piece. No real 'miracle' took place at Cana, Watters states, but because Jesus – 'the best organiser, the best planner who ever lived' – was present, he was able to warn the stewards that the wine was running out in time for them to lay in more supplies. Watters appears to speak into thin air: there is no sense that he is really communicating with a single person listening to him.

In the next sermon, delivered in the late eighteenth century, the presence of individual members of the congregation is painfully felt, as Dr Thomas Fortheringhame uses the wedding at Cana as an excuse to rail against the evils of drink:

> 'Magnus Learmonth, you in the second pew from the back, at the wedding you made for your third lass Deborah at Skolness at the back end of Lammas, all the guests lay at the ale-kirn like piglets about the teats of a sow till morning, to the neglect even of dancing; and two women in this same district came to themselves next morning in the ditch of Graygyres. Bella Simison, you do well to hang your head there at the back of the Kirk – it argues a small peck of grace. Andrina of Breck, you were the other defaulter – don't look at me like that, woman! – you have a brazen outstaring impudence commensurate with your debauchery . . .'

Only when it comes to the third sermon, preached by Father Halcrow in 1548, on the eve of the Reformation, is the miracle understood in all its fullness. Christ turned water into wine, Halcrow explains to his small flock, as an expression of his desire to transform ordinary lives into something infinitely precious, and to make even the humblest men and women heirs to his kingdom. ' "So then, princes," 'Halcrow proclaims, ' "(for I will call you Olaf the fisherman and Jock the crofter no longer but I will call you by the name the Creator will call you in the last day) princes, I say, I have good news for you . . ."'

Although George had found a fullness of faith in the Catholic Church, in his assessment of individuals he was never sectarian, and very often his greatest sympathies lie with unbelievers. In the title story, 'A Time to Keep', a Rackwick crofter struggles to provide a decent life for his new wife, Ingi. He is a man of few words and, like George's father, detests gossip and false sentiment. On Sundays, he steers well clear of the church, and when Ingi dies in childbirth, he drives the keening women from his croft, and refuses – as George's father had refused – to have his son baptized. Privately, when the women have left him, he seeks his own kind of benediction for the new child:

> I took the sleeping baby from the cradle and carried him outside. The first stars shone on him. I carried him down over the fields to the beach. We stood before a slow darkening heave of sea. A fleck of spindrift drifted on to his cheek. The wind had lain in the south-west since before his birth and Ingi's death. He slept on in my arms, with the bitter blessing of the sea on him.
>
> 'Be honest,' I said, 'Be against all darkness. Fight on the side of life. Be against ministers, lairds, shopkeepers. Be brave always.'

If George's faith had helped him to write like this, giving him an underlying assurance that 'all shall be well, and all manner of things shall be well',* so, surely, had Stella Cartwright. The tenderness he conveys here had first found expression in his letters to Stella, and the experience of having loved her, and been loved in return, had given him the courage to carry it into his work.

It was, on Stella's part, a pelican giving. The more she enriched the lives of others, the more attenuated her own life became. She was jobless and, in between her meetings with Sydney Goodsir Smith in Milne's and in the basement flat in Dundas Street, she was lonely. Knowing, in some part of herself, that her affair with Smith could not

---

*These words of the fourteenth-century mystic Dame Julian of Norwich were very dear to George, and he quoted them often in letters to friends.

end happily, she began to idealize the memory of her time with George, and to look to him for a kind of strength and hope he could not possibly provide. 'George Mackay Brown is a F—ing better poet than any of you bastards,' she spat at Sydney Goodsir Smith as he shook her out of a drunken sleep one morning, and she begged George to take care of himself. Just to know he was there, she said, enabled her to keep going.

George, in response, urged her not to lose hope. She must always remember, he wrote, that wherever she went and whatever happened, she carried about with her 'the essential Stella that is rarer and richer than any diamond'; she must believe that there would be fruitful, happy times ahead. 'Be patient for a little while longer,' he writes to her in hospital on 23 November 1968. 'You've had a long winter of it but soon the wee snowdrops will come up and then the crocuses, and the nests full of broken shells and birdsong and dear Stella will be happy once more. Wait for it – it's almost here.'

From time to time, George had suggested tentatively that at the root of Stella's troubles was a *genuine religious sense* which she had never been fully able to express. She reminded him a lot, he had once told her, 'of that truly good woman in Graham Greene's novel *The End of the Affair* who came at last to truth and beauty and God through the shifting fantasies that we all have to endure every day'. If only she were a Catholic, he urged, she might find some firm ground under her feet, and might see the world 'shot through with a new beauty'. Would she not talk to a priest?

Stella did her best. She took herself one afternoon to the Jesuit church in Lauriston Place. She walked up and down on the pavement outside it. She was on the point of ringing the presbytery bell when it occurred to her that it was teatime: her call would be an inconvenience – and anyway, she had nothing very clear to say. She walked away.

As Stella's life drifted downward, George was struggling to come to terms with a growing reputation. He was as little interested as ever in conventional success. When George Bruce wrote from the BBC to tell him how warmly *A Time to Keep* had been received on *Arts Review*, and promised to keep a tape of the programme for him to listen to when next he came to Edinburgh, George's response was polite but firm: 'I think I won't be in Edinburgh very soon, so it would be as well to dispose of the tape you have been so kindly keeping for me. We will hear all these things in heaven.' When *A Time to Keep* went on to win the Scottish Arts Council prize, he appeared equally nonplussed. Karl Miller, then editor of the *Listener* and one of the judges, travelled by train with George from Glasgow to Edinburgh after the presentation of the prize. George seemed guarded and on edge, and took regular nips from a flask of whisky. Miller found it impossible to tell whether he had been pleased to receive his £1,000 prize cheque or not.

Uneasy though it made him, however, the attention of the public was becoming an inescapable part of George's life. On his rare visits to Edinburgh, he found himself invited to dine at the 'posh houses' of complete strangers. In Orkney, the morning post brought numerous requests: from the archivist at the National Library of Scotland, asking to acquire George's manuscripts; from the BBC, inviting him to judge their student verse competition. Literary agents wrote recommending their services; editors tried to lure him away from the Hogarth Press.

Shortly after his mother's death, George had had a letter from the publisher Giles Gordon asking whether he might like to write a book about Orkney for Victor Gollancz. It was not the kind of work he much enjoyed, George confessed to Charlie Senior, 'But it should bring in a couple of hundred quid or so, and will take me to parts of the islands I haven't been to before'.* Even within Orkney, George remained surprisingly untravelled: to the end of his life some of the islands he writes about most often – Eynhallow, for example – he had visited only in his imagination. But Giles Gordon's commission, in the end, involved no travel at all. As George turned it over in his mind, what he had at first envisaged as a general guide to Orkney began gradually to offer the possibility of a weaving together, through poetry, prose and drama, of particular events, places, legends and people that had shaped the Orkney character, to create a work that would be at once a celebration and a jeremiad.

---

*In January 1968, George received an advance of £250 for *An Orkney Tapestry*. Considering that his annual rent when he moved into Mayburn Court, his final home, less than a year later was just £34 16s, this must have seemed a handsome sum.

Since his early days writing for the *Orkney Herald*, George had mellowed somewhat in his attitudes to progress and the modern world. Science, he had admitted in a letter to Ian MacInnes from Tor-na-Dee sanatorium, 'wears the old Janus-mask': on the one hand, it had led to the atom bomb, but on the other it had produced a cure for TB, without which George would almost certainly not have been alive in the late sixties. But he had only to step outside Well Park to feel sadness and anger at the 'gray wash of uniformity' moving inexorably over island life. The beautiful main street of Stromness, uncoiling 'like a sailor's rope' from the north to the south end of the town, had not been designed to carry heavy traffic and, under the weight of cars and lorries, the old blue Cairston flagstones were breaking up. As they did so, they were replaced with concrete squares. 'Time is not in love with concrete,' George wrote, and the street increasingly looked as if it was 'scabbed with some strange sickness'.

Listening to people chatting as they went about their chores, meanwhile, George was aware of the old Orkney speech becoming infected by hideous, vapid southern vocabulary. Housewives talked about 'privatization', and their 'gut-reactions' to events; at the Pierhead, or in the pubs, instead of the old yarns and stories, men felt obliged to discuss current affairs, and to exchange second-hand opinions on Vietnam, or interest rates, or heart transplants. And, as darkness fell, an eerie glow now shone from the downstairs windows of almost every house in the town as, family by family, Stromness huddled round *The Virginian* or *Softly, Softly* or *Top of the Pops*. Television personalities like Fanny Cradock and Inspector Barlow, it seemed to George, had become more 'real' to some of his fellow townsmen than their flesh-and-blood neighbours on the outlying farms. If, in response to Giles Gordon's commission, he could awaken Orcadians to the way things were going, and at the same time stir in them some pride in their roots, perhaps he might inspire a rearguard action.

After his sober Hogmanay, George began work on *An Orkney Tapestry* in January 1968. He was writing at length, for the first time, both about Rackwick and about Saint Magnus, about Orkney lore, and about the islands' rich traditions of poetry, from the ballad singers of the seventeenth century to Robert Rendall. Rendall was a less important poet than Edwin Muir, George acknowledged, but one who deserved to be remembered. He had died the previous summer, and in his last days George had visited him at Eastbank, in the same ward in which he himself had lain fourteen years earlier:

> His mind had been ranging among old half-forgotten things; now he remembered seeing London slum children coming back from a day in the country with their hands full of wild flowers. He read, with great labour, the poem he had just written about them.

> *On a London Street* 1932

> Faded flowers in fist,
> A chain of slum children
> From summer fields long missed.

> Not now can squalor stain
> The pure bright image
> Of that fair green domain.

> In mute defiance
> Young eyes have glimpsed
> God's glory in dandelions,

> His miracle of leaf and blade,
> Bud and blossom,
> All that He has made.

> One fine day Ian MacInnes wrapped him in blankets and carried him into his car and drove him round the familiar roads. Summer was wakening everywhere. That was the last time his eyes saw the islands.
> A few days later he was dead – gathered, with the wondering children, among endless fields and flowers.

George had never worked harder than in those early months of 1968, nor enjoyed his work more. When in February a young friend whose poetry he admired wrote to complain that the writer's life was too tough for him, George urged him to persevere, even though it might lead him into poverty and loneliness and long periods of obscurity. 'That's the way poets are tried and tested,' he insisted. 'It's worth it.'

An Orkney Tapestry was not his only source of excitement that spring. George was discovering that he found housekeeping surprisingly satisfying. Washing clothes gave him 'a great sense of achievement – like

writing a small lyric'; concocting soups and stews was 'endlessly interesting', and small tasks like chopping vegetables could be powerful
weapons in keeping depression at bay. And, while relishing his new
independence, he was also preparing to go abroad. On the same day
that he had heard from Giles Gordon, George had received a letter from
the Society of Authors offering him a scholarship to be spent on foreign
travel. The scholarship would normally have been for £500, but this
year the committee* had decided to split it equally between George and
Stevie Smith ('I rather hope,' George wrote to Kulgin Duval, 'I don't
have to travel with her'). This suited him well. He had no desire to
travel far. There was, in fact, only one country he was curious to visit,
and that was Ireland.

In the days of Norse rule, before the Orkney islands were annexed
to Scotland, Orkney and Ireland had been closely intertwined. In the
eleventh century, Sigurd, Earl of Orkney, had led an army of islanders
across the Irish Sea to fight with Sigtrygg, King of Dublin, against
Brian Boru, High King of Ireland, at Clontarf.† It was a long, bloody
battle, fought on Good Friday, and Brian Boru's victory sealed the
future of both Ireland and Orkney as Christian, rather than pagan.
Clontarf, George believed, had been as critical to the course of
European history as Lepanto or Waterloo or Stalingrad, and it was
more vivid in his imagination than any of these. Seamus Heaney,
whom George planned to meet in Belfast, understood this. People in
London might have considered George eccentric, out of the swim,
Heaney says, 'But in a sense I think that his confidence was that he
dwelt in an older kingdom, and London hadn't been quite discovered
yet.' When George caught the ferry from Stranraer to Larne in May
1968, he was following an ancestral path.

He was accompanied by the photographer Paddy Hughes, whom
he had first met in Milne's, and who had remained one of his closest
friends. After disembarking from the ferry they set off in Hughes's
clapped-out Morris Traveller, following the coast road through Antrim
and Donegal to Galway and Connemara. George was invigorated. He

---

*Janet Adam Smith, Walter Allen, Maurice Cranston, Richard Findlater, Karl Miller
and Winston Graham.
†Now a suburb of Dublin.

sat in the passenger seat, almost oblivious of Hughes, quoting chunks of Yeats, and he wrote in high spirits to Charlie Senior: 'Connemara is the weirdest wildest sweetest place, one huge moor littered with gray stone and bogs and lochans where you could swear not one human family could live, and yet there are happy well-fed people everywhere, and new houses going up everywhere in the apparent wilderness.' Compared to the Scots, he felt, the Irish seemed full of hope and high spirits: 'If an independent Scotland could achieve what Ireland is doing for its people, I'd be a Nationalist tomorrow.'

On the second day in Connemara, however, the car broke down. Steam poured out of the bonnet. Stranded, and surrounded by an excess of space, George panicked. Once the car was mended, he insisted that they take the quickest route back to Dublin and then north to Belfast, where they had arranged to spend an evening with Seamus Heaney in the Ulster Arts Club. Heaney brought with him a friend, David Hammond, and when, in the early hours of the morning, Hammond burst into song, George responded by reciting, in a fine voice, the ballad of 'The Queen's Maries' which Ruby had sung to him as a child:

> Yestreen the Queen had four Maries,
> The night she'll hae but three;
> There was Marie Seaton, and Marie Beaton,
> And Marie Carmichael, and me.*

'It was a chanting, more than a singing,' Heaney remembers; 'and more a haunting than a chanting.'

Heaney was delighted with the conviviality. George was, he felt, 'elevated at being across the water'; but he also recognized, beneath his high spirits, an essential privacy. 'There was a genuinely attentive,

---

*The ballad tells the tale of Mary Hamilton, Scots maid-of-honour to Catherine, empress of Peter the Great, who had an affair with Ivan Orlof, an aide of the tsar, and murdered their illegitimate child secretly. Imprisoned at the Petropaulovsk fortress, charged with the death, and tortured, she confessed and was executed on 14 March 1719, as the tsar watched. This story appears to have been conflated with that of the four Maries who served Mary Queen of Scots. One of these four, a Frenchwoman, had a child by the queen's apothecary, and, having killed it, was hanged for the offence in Edinburgh.

intuitive, sympathetic quality to George,' Heaney reflects; 'a courtesy that came in part from the common culture of the islands, partly from his own nature. But there was a core of solitude as well, a still receiving station away inside, as quiet as a pool on a moor.'

The next morning, George's need for solitude asserted itself. Heaney had been keen to introduce him to some of his students at Queen's University, and had planned a party; George lost his nerve at the prospect. He sent Paddy Hughes to offer his apologies. This was neither moodiness nor whim on George's part, Hughes recognized, but a nervous condition over which he had no control.

The following day, they headed for home. It had been George's first and last experiment with foreign travel, and he was relieved to get back to Orkney. It was early June, the weather was lovely, and the islands were spilling over with light. 'The midsummer sunsets leave me awed,' he wrote to Willa Muir. 'I find it impossible to attempt to describe them: it would take an Edwin or a Wordsworth.'

If George's life was ever like that of the monk whose image in Bede's *Ecclesiastical History of England* had so enthralled him as an undergraduate, it became so now. He had always known that he would have to move after his mother's death and, on a fine day in September 1968, a group of friends gathered to help him 'flit' to a council flat a few hundred yards from Well Park in a converted distillery across the road from the Stromness Museum. It was a first floor flat, comprising two bedrooms, a bathroom, a small kitchen and a living-room with a view of the harbour, and it was reached by a set of outside steps bordered by an iron railing. The flitting complete, George stood behind the railing outside his new front door, pulled a lock of black hair over his brow, stuck two fingers of one hand under his nose and held out the other in a Nazi salute. 'This,' he shouted to his friends in the street below, 'is my last territorial claim on Europe.'

Later that autumn, George described his life in Mayburn Court in a letter to Stella:

My new house is away up on top. I can see the sea down below. I sit here day after day like an old awkward owl. Hardly a soul comes near me. You can't blame them – they don't get much of a reception – the tenant squinting at them and wondering what they're after and more

or less hinting that he has work to do and would they call again . . .
The kids look at me as much as to say – 'That crusty old devil!' . . .

Stella was once again in hospital, and in an attempt to cheer her up
George exaggerates the oddness and loneliness of his life. He was, in
fact, surrounded by friends in Stromness. Within five minutes' walk of
Mayburn Court were both Archie Bevan and Ian MacInnes and their
families: households 'full of children, music, sudden eruptions of
gaiety and distress'. In the summer of 1968, Charlie Senior had moved
to Stromness, and set to work establishing a tiny bookshop on the
main street. Norrie's daughter, Allison, had married a scientist, Fraser
Dixon, and, shortly after George settled in Mayburn Court, they also
moved to Stromness, to a house in the centre of the town. George
called in on them when he was shopping, and plied his great-nephews
and great-niece with sweets. In the evenings, he was frequently visited
by Jimmy Isbister, an alcoholic and beachcomber, who would arrive
with offerings from the shore. George was particularly fond of Isbister:
complicated, depressive, near-destitute – a reflection, perhaps, of what
he himself might have become, but for his writing.

Yet, if there was no shortage of company when he wanted it, it is
also true that in his early years in Mayburn Court George relished his
solitude, and thrived on it. In repose, Ernest Marwick noted, George's
expression was now one of 'agonised maturity'; but, a year after Mhairi
Brown's death, Marwick also commented in a letter to Willa Muir that
George seemed happier and healthier than he had been for a very long
time. George himself described in letters to friends how he had come
to love his own company. When he heard a knock at his door, his heart
sank. If callers insisted on coming in, he found himself wondering irri-
tably how long they were going to stay, and looking to see whether
they had stamped mud into his new rugs. Alone in his little flat, meanwhile, he enjoyed an ongoing, private dialogue with himself. 'One of
the characters, the violent one, is always hurling abuse at the innocent
foolish one, like "O you bloody fool!" and "O you are one stupid
bastard!"' he told Willa Muir. 'And frequently I go off into secret
spasms of laughter . . . I'm not going off my head – it's just that I'm
crossing the choppy ferry between A-Merry-Blade and A-Crusty-
Old-Bachelor.' George was certain now that he would never have

either a wife or children of his own, and this, he confessed to Willa Muir, was a relief to him: 'the thought of such responsibilities really would drive me round the bend'. He felt his days flying 'swifter than a weaver's shuttle'. All he wanted was to be left alone with his books and pens and paper.

Throughout the autumn of 1968, *An Orkney Tapestry* was cascading from his pen 'by fizzes and leaps, like a jumping firework'. He was also struggling with a long sequence of poems about Rackwick, which had him 'tossed three times a day between despair and joy', and he was turning over in his mind ideas for a play. And if sometimes the going was tough – 'like smashing your bare foot against a stone' – there were other times when the writing came so easily that he felt as if the words were flowing on to the paper in front of him almost of their own accord. He worked steadily every morning in his small kitchen, sitting with his back to the window at the same Formica surface on which he ate his breakfast, writing in longhand with a cheap ballpoint pen on to blocks of Basildon Bond paper. In the afternoon, when the weather was fine, he often walked a mile or so around the coast to the kirkyard at Warbeth. In the evenings, he sat in a rocking chair by the fire in his living room – a rather dark room, cluttered with books and manuscripts.

On Saturdays, George took a busman's holiday and wrote nothing but letters. If the knocking of unexpected visitors at his front door was an irritant, the rattle of the letterbox and the swish of post on to his hall floor was always a delight. He read his letters sitting in his rocking-chair, and found that his friends became 'actual and dear' to him in the act of replying to them. So much so, in fact, that communicating by letter was, in many ways, preferable to George than seeing and speaking to people in the flesh. Certainly, it was almost impossible for friends to persuade him to journey outside Orkney to visit them, persistently though some of them tried.

To Willa Muir, in particular, it would have meant a great deal to have been able to see George again during these years. Her life, since Edwin's death, had been wretched. She felt that she scarcely existed – 'I am now really dead, with Edwin,' she wrote to a friend. 'What is left is a shell, or a core.' Her identity, she felt, was 'tenuous'. Her grief was exacerbated by poverty, arthritis, and a rift with her son. Gavin

Muir had married in 1960, and he and his wife had moved into Priory Cottage outside Cambridge with Willa. Almost immediately, there were rows, and in the spring of 1963 Willa felt compelled to leave and to accept an offer from Kathleen Raine of the basement flat of her house in Paultons Square, Chelsea. This became Willa Muir's home for nearly five years, and she pressed George with all her feisty charm to come and stay with her, even going so far as to buy a sleeping bag in readiness for his visit. 'Please note that no man is an island even though he lives on one: your movements involve other people's movements too!' she writes on 6 April 1968. 'It's no use your wailing you would be *alone* coming to London, you wouldn't be alone; you'd be met at the airport to begin with and taken in charge by friends!'

George felt deeply for Willa, and the thought of her 'isolation in the heart of the biggest city of the world' appalled him. But the notion of travelling alone to London appalled him more and, though he did not refuse her invitations outright, it is clear that he never seriously considered doing so. Instead, he wrote regularly, and what Willa Muir described as his 'lovely little Dutch interior pictures' of island life did much to lift her spirits. Corresponding with George not only kept her in touch with Orkney, where she hoped that Edwin's ghost might be roaming,* but also allowed her to give vent to a wit and maternal affection that now had little outlet. She sent George Vitamin C tablets as a curative for exhaustion ('Take them dissolved in liquid, preferably not whisky'), and recommended he buy drip-dry shirts. She warned against his becoming too isolated from 'the lovely stir and bustle of life', and poured scorn on his claim that a wife would be a burden to him. She confessed that his poetry made her weep, and she rejoiced in his literary success, and in the integrity of his work: 'Your stories and poetry, George, come out of a whole way of life, not like the Londoners' products which at best come out of country weekends! Or drug sessions! So false they won't last. Yours will.' Often, her letters were full of anguish, but in the spring of 1970 her spirits seemed to

---

*Although she came, reluctantly, to believe that his ghost was not roaming at all. 'For months after his death I waited, in an agony of expectation, for some sign . . . from him . . . and none came,' Willa wrote to J. Mary Bosdêt on 11 October 1959. 'I am now trying to live with the bleak fact that he has vanished, with his unique store of memories and experiences.'

rise. She had left Paultons Square, and after an unhappy spell in a nursing home in Cambridge was about to move with a niece to a house in the countryside near Dunoon. 'My beloved George,' she writes on 20 April, 'I think you had better go on praying for me – if you can be bothered. I might live to see 81 yet . . . The savage winter seems to have snarled away elsewhere now, and the green world is returning.' A few weeks later, on 22 May, she died.

Regularly and affectionately though he wrote to friends like Willa Muir, George's most frequent and intimate letters were still reserved for Stella. At the beginning of 1969, he had written light-heartedly suggesting she make five New Year's resolutions:

   i. No Milne's, No Howard's
   ii. Get married
   iii. Go Among the Hills
   iv. Have Baby
   v. Be part of the World.

The wrong side of the coin had turned up so often, he urged, that, with the next spin, she would surely find peace and happiness at last.

    In fact, the next spin of the coin was the cruellest yet. One evening in April 1969, Stella walked to Rose Street to meet Sydney Goodsir Smith in Milne's. Later, she wrote a poem, 'Closing Time':

> I went into the pub to-day,
> you were not there
> I thought you late.
> unusual.
>
> I ordered you a whisky mac
> and a vodka for myself.
> you did not come.
>
> I asked the barman
> 'What's the time?'
> he said, 'it's nearly closing time.'
>
> You never came.
> you could not come.
> would never come again.

It seems that Hazel had finally discovered what was going on between Sydney and Stella, and had insisted that he put an end to the affair. Stella, in response, fled to an unmarried aunt, Flora Cartwright, in Perthshire. Throughout May, Sydney Goodsir Smith wrote to her almost daily, trying to persuade her that all was not lost. But there is a desperate air about his letters. With one, he encloses a final 'Seal Baby' poem, begging Stella to sleep, and never dream of him. It seems clear that he knew, in his heart of hearts, that everything between them was finally over. What Smith was now forced to admit to Stella – what others had tried to tell her, but he had always denied – was that he had in fact been secretly married to Hazel for more than a year.*

For Stella, this discovery was devastating. Sydney had not only broken her heart, she told George, but had shattered her belief in human nature. In June, she was admitted to the Crichton Royal Hospital in Dumfries, and here she spent most of the summer, having her brain tested with 'a great electrical device', and arranging little bricks in patterns for analysis by a psychologist. She begged George to pray for her: 'Don't let anyone run away with the easy idea that my troubles are all due to drink – it is the other way round. I have seriously tried to help and comfort people as best I could, but how much good I've ever achieved will never be known. Very little I expect.'

In late August, she was discharged. Hugh Mackay offered her temporary lodgings; otherwise she felt deserted by all her old friends. In Milne's, Bob Watt the barman refused to serve her. She was still only thirty-two, and she challenged George to tell her what she had done to find herself 'thrown on the rubbish heap' so young. 'I feel suicidal,' she wrote. 'No money no health no friends and no future. To bloody hell with everything.'

Many people in receipt of such a letter would have felt compelled to act: to travel to Edinburgh and somehow to attempt a rescue. But for George there was no question of visiting Stella in her distress; indeed, the more desperate her life became, the less inclined he seems

---

*It was generally believed that Stella and Sydney Goodsir Smith never saw each other again, but in 1974, just months before Smith died, they were spotted together in a pub in Juniper Green. Both were laughing till the tears rolled down their cheeks.

to have been to see her. Perhaps he feared that, exposed to Stella's misery, he too might be sucked into the downward spiral; perhaps, more ruthlessly, he felt a need to protect the ideal image of her that had so enriched his work. Unable to face her in person, he tried instead to share with her, on paper, beliefs from which he himself would draw increasing strength as the years went by. 'Dearest Stel,' he wrote in response to her letter,

> You've got to have a rhinoceros hide to endure many of the things that are said and done. Poor Stella, it is hard for a sensitive soul like you. However one hardens oneself (and one has to, just to keep alive) the heart remains vulnerable. Be brave. Be loyal to yourself.
>
> Dear Stel, not many people have to walk such a hard road. One feels desperate with solitude often; then it is salutary to know that one is not alone, but is 'involved with mankind'.* And that means, as I understand it, that whenever you are brave, enduring, uncomplaining, then the whole world of suffering is helped and soothed somehow. This is sacrifice, and fulfilment and renewal: an incalculable leavening.

The more solitary George's life became, the more profoundly he understood that he was 'involved with mankind'. Edwin Muir, in his poetry, had yearned back to a mythical time when the human race lived in unity:

> Long since we were a family, a people,
> The legends say; an old kind-hearted king
> Was our foster father, and our life a fable . . .

For George, this unity was ongoing: human beings were connected in a web of existence, deeply responsible for one another. He might have neither wife nor children, he once wrote, 'but in a sense, *everyone* is the writer's concern. The whole of humanity is his family and he must participate in their joys and *ennuis* and sufferings, otherwise what he does would be as meaningless as an endless game of patience.' If he never much enjoyed discussions of current affairs, he followed the news attentively. In private conversations, Ernest Marwick noted, George's wit and mimicry were interspersed with 'well considered, devastating' comments about the state of the world, and his letters refer to the horror he

---

*From John Donne, Meditation XVII.

felt in response, for example, to the Moors murders, the ongoing agony of Vietnam, the street battles in Londonderry, the injustice of apartheid rule in South Africa. Most horrifying of all to him, as countries like Israel and India joined in the scramble to acquire atomic weapons, was the possibility of nuclear war. He expressed his concern by passing it, as Seamus Heaney has written, 'through the eye of the needle of Orkney'; but the concern is none the less present in his work.

In the autumn of 1969, George put the finishing touches to a six-part cycle of poems about Rackwick. The cycle begins in the ninth century, with the arrival in the valley of a tribe of imaginary Norwegian fisher people, fleeing some unnamed horror. In the middle four sections, George follows them down the centuries as they become 'fishermen with ploughs', yoked to a hard life that sees a man, even on his wedding night, forced to rise before dawn and go down to his boat:

> Midnight. The shoal drifts
>   Like a host of souls unborn, along the shore.
>   The tide sets from the west.
> His salt hand shifts
>   From tumults of thigh and breast
>   To the hard curve of an oar.

In the early twentieth century, the people begin to succumb to the blandishments of progress: roads, tractors, medicine, schools. The valley is deserted, and the wider world then engulfed in nuclear holocaust. But, in the final section, a chorus of women describes how, sailing north past ruined, blackened lands, they have discovered a 'sweet green gap' in the cliffs of Hoy. Life in Rackwick begins once more.

George posted off his poems to the Hogarth Press in trepidation. There were so many of them, he told Stella, and they were 'so bizarre in parts', that he rather doubted Norah Smallwood would be able to publish them. In fact, both she and her colleagues immediately recognized that parcel as containing George's most remarkable poetic achievement to date. Ian Parsons wrote to congratulate him, and to say how deeply honoured he would be to publish the poems; and when, after some delay, *Fishermen with Ploughs* finally appeared in the summer of 1971, the reviews were fulsome. Here, wrote Peter Porter in the

Guardian, was the most effective use of the saga style since early Auden. George Mackay Brown, Porter insisted, could never again be either overlooked, or relegated to 'a regional pantheon'. He was, quite simply, 'one of the consummate masters of poetry in Britain today'.

There would from now on be some who questioned George's confinement to Orkney. Wouldn't it be marvellous, asked Maurice Wiggin, reviewing *Fishermen with Ploughs* in the *Sunday Times*, if George Mackay Brown could transport himself for a while to some squalid, urban wilderness like Shepherd's Bush, and learn to sing a new song – 'if only a scream of horror'? George argued hard against such critics: Orkney was a microcosm of the whole world, and the material it offered him was inexhaustible. 'There are stories in the air here,' he claimed. 'If I lived to be five hundred there would still be things I wanted to write.' Yet those close to him were aware that attacks on his insularity unsettled George more than he let on, and it meant much to him when others joined him in rebutting them. For Ted Hughes, speaking in 1991, George was as connected to the modern world as any other writer: 'It's just that he's retreated to a point where he can see it in an internal reflection, a very clear simplification, a penetrating simplification, that he could never achieve if he were in the middle of the hurly-burly with the whole thing going around him from day to day, disrupting him from moment to moment.'

Seamus Heaney supports this view, and enlarges upon it. 'My hunch is that if George had made a move to "develop", that's when we'd have sensed a weakness. Orkney wasn't just a setting, wasn't just material,' Heaney argues.

> It was his gateway to the completely imagined. There's a poem by Yeats, for example, called 'The Collar Bone of a Hare', a really strange scenario in which the poet finds a hare's bone beside the water and pierces a hole in it and turns it into a kind of do-it-yourself lorgnette, one that magics the world every time he looks through it. Well, George had only to look out over the garths and the crofts or the boats in the harbour at Stromness for the magic to begin to work. It wasn't photography. It wasn't sociology. In fact, you could say that George's Orkney was also a bit like Yeats's 'instructors', those spirits who spoke to him through his wife's automatic writing; they came, they said, to give him metaphors for poetry. And that's what his island and its lore

did for George. His work constituted itself into and out of this world in equal measure.

Others appreciated that, by drawing his boundaries closely about him, George was achieving a depth and scope elusive to most twentieth-century poets. 'Lately, I have hesitated to buy volumes by "moderns" except perhaps Hughes,' the writer and social activist Naomi Mitchison wrote to him after reading *Fishermen with Ploughs*, 'because they are so entangled and inward-looking and their private worlds are not, it seems to me, worth the trouble of exploring. And again, so many have so little feeling for the overtones of words or for the rhythm of waves and work and dance, that they are unmemorable. Yours, on the contrary, are memorable and throwing a new light on to large, real, outward things . . . You have done something for us all.'

By 'all', of course, Mitchison meant all serious readers of poetry; but, as Ernest Marwick had once commented, 'the fear of poetry in Scotland is even greater than the fear of religion'. Poetry readers were never going to be more than a small, select group. Four years after it was published, despite outstanding reviews, *Fishermen with Ploughs* had sold fewer than 1,500 copies. Within a fortnight of publication in the summer of 1969, meanwhile, sales of *An Orkney Tapestry* had topped 3,000. One particular copy, bought in Charlie Senior's bookshop the following summer, was to have a swift and dramatic effect on the future of its owner, and of Orkney.

14

Words of Resurrection

Slowly the sun heaved itself clear of the sea. The cliff below was alive with the stir and cry of birds. The sea moved and flung glories of light over Quoylay and Hrossey and Hellya, and all the skerries and rocks around. The smell of the earth came to them in the first wind of morning, from the imprisoned fields of the island; and the fence could not keep it back.

GMB, *Greenvoe* (1972)

PETER MAXWELL DAVIES, known to all as 'Max', was thirty-six when he took a holiday in Scotland in the summer of 1970. A phenomenally prolific composer and *enfant terrible*, he had burst upon the British music scene in the late fifties – when the tougher scores of Vaughan Williams were still considered radical – with work that was explosive, atonal and iconoclastic. During 1969 and the early months of 1970 he had produced such a torrent of new work that he was exhausted. Added to this, in the spring of 1970, he had lost most of his books and possessions to a fire at his cottage in Dorset. He crossed the Pentland Firth to Orkney aware that a phase of his life had come to an end.

Max opened *An Orkney Tapestry* in the evening, in a hotel bedroom in Kirkwall, and read the first chapter with mounting excitement. By 3 a.m. he was still reading, transfixed. The vividness of George's imagery, combined with the plainness of his prose, suggested tunes and rhythms, so that, as he turned the pages, he felt an 'extraordinary closing in of two worlds: the potential musical world, and the world that George had established'.

Underpinning George's world were beliefs that were both new to Max, and also sympathetic. He had thought a great deal about the importance of ritual; but George, in his conviction that art should be embedded in the lives of ordinary farmers and fishermen, had gone a step further. Max was struck, too, by George's approach to religion. In the 'Rackwick' chapter of *An Orkney Tapestry*, George had included a poem in which he sees the fourteen stations of Christ's Passion and death reflected in the cycle of the agricultural year:

> *Condemnation*
> The winter jar of honey and grain
> Is a Lenten urn.
>
> *Cross*
> Lord, it is time. Take our yoke
> And sunwards turn.
>
> *First Fall*
> To drudge in furrows till you drop
> Is to be born
>
> *Mother of God*
> Out of the mild mothering hill
> And the chaste burn.
>
> *Simon*
> God-begun, the barley rack
> By man is borne.
>
> *Veronica*
> Foldings of women. Your harrow sweat
> Darkens her yarn.
>
> *Second Fall*
> Sower-and-Seed, one flesh, you fling
> From stone to thorn.
>
> *Women of Jerusalem*
> You are bound for the Kingdom of Death. The enfolded
> Women mourn.
>
> *Third Fall*
> Scythes are sharpened to bring you down,
> King Barleycorn.

The Stripping
Flails creak. Golden coat
From kernel is torn.

The Crucifixion
The fruitful stones thunder around,
Quern on quern.

Death
The last black hunger rages through you
With hoof and horn.

Pieta
Mother, fold him from those furrows,
Your broken bairn.

Sepulchre
Shepherd, angel, king are kneeling, look,
In the door of the barn.*

Max had difficulties with institutional religion, but George's Catholicism − down-to-earth, unjudgemental and encompassing a profound belief in the unity of creation − was inspiring to him. Above all, he was moved by George's retelling of the story of Saint Magnus. This, it seemed to him, cast an 'enchantment' over Orkney: an enchantment he wanted to explore for himself, in his music.

The following day, in 'a hyper state of tiredness and receptivity to experience', Max caught the ferry to Hoy. Among the handful of other passengers on the *Watchful* that morning was George's old friend Kulgin Duval, and in driving rain they got chatting and shared a flask of whisky. Duval was on his way to see George, Archie Bevan and his family, who had all gone over to spend the weekend in the Muckle House in Rackwick. He invited Max to join him.

From then on, Max recalls, 'everything happened as if preordained'. The rain continued to sluice down and, when he and Duval reached Rackwick, the valley was sunk in a deep haar,† through which they could hear the sea pounding. Duval introduced his new friend to the

---

*'From Stone to Thorn' was the first of George's works to be set to music by Peter Maxwell Davies.
†A sea fog.

group – 'a slight small dark active man,' George wrote later, 'with intense smouldering eyes'. They liked him; and he immediately took to them. George seemed 'as good as his book: very alone, very intense', with a lilting, gentle voice which confirmed Max's desire to set his work to music. 'What was clear from that very first meeting,' Max says, looking back, 'was that George had a beautiful personality. I can think of no other way to describe it.'

During lulls in the conversation, Max sat silent and alert, entranced by 'the Aeolian harp effect' of the sea crashing in on the cliffs. He had decided, instantly, that Rackwick was a place in which he wanted to compose music. After they had all shared a hearty lunch of stew and red wine, he set about examining the ruins of a croft down by the shore, and discussing the possibility of restoring it. George had a better idea. Pointing up through the haar, he indicated what looked like a rubble of stones on a high cliff: a deserted croft, doorless, roofless and feet-deep in sheep dung, with enormous views over the Atlantic.

Bunertoon was to become Maxwell Davies's home for twenty-four years.[*] At first, he 'sat about, listening to the sounds of the birds and the wind, getting to know myself very well'; then new music began to pour out. Much of it was inspired by his experiences in Rackwick: in the second movement of his cello concerto,[†] for example, he depicts with a sudden flashing of violins a sight he caught one morning as a shoal of mackerel swam into the bay; much of it was based directly on George's work. 'And even in the purely abstract work,' he says, 'I can sense George's presence.'

But Max's life in Rackwick was taken up with more than music. He helped Jack Rendall, who was now the only farmer in the valley, to cut peat, gather driftwood and deliver lambs in spring. He took his turn at coastguard duty, and walked through the hills on Sundays to play the organ in Hoy church. George once commented, in a BBC programme about his life, that he worked 'in the tremulous hope that what I write are words of resurrection, and not of death'. By portraying the decline of Rackwick with such powerful eloquence in *An*

---

[*]He moved into Bunertoon in 1974, after it had been restored. In 1998, he moved again, to the Orkney island of Sanday.
[†]Strathclyde Concerto No. 2 for cello and orchestra.

Orkney Tapestry, thereby drawing Peter Maxwell Davies to the valley, he had helped to sow the seeds of its rebirth.

By the time of that first meeting with Max, George was engaged on a piece of writing unlike any he had undertaken before, and one that was less a lament for the past than an uncanny foreshadowing of the future. As light relief after completing *Fishermen with Ploughs*, encouraged by Norah Smallwood, he had set to work on what he at first envisaged as a comic novel. It was to cover one summer week in a fishing village on the imaginary island of Hellya, capturing, with a fine balance of affection and sharp observation, the dynamics at work in a small community. As Jo Grimond* later commented, the Orkney George depicts in *Greenvoe* is no more like 'real' Orkney than Shakespeare's England is like real England, or than the real Ireland is to be found in Yeats; and yet the novel is more evocative of the place than any 'real' description could ever be. Similarly, with one notable exception, the characters are not drawn in any psychological depth, yet in deft brushstrokes George succeeds in communicating his own poignant fondness for the inhabitants of Greenvoe, with all their small failings of vanity and snobbery, lust, loneliness and regret. Here, for example, is the hen-wife, Bella Budge, alone in the moments following the death of her rough-tongued sea-dog brother, Ben:

> What did you do with a dead man? What were the duties of the living towards the dead? It was a long time, twenty years, since Bella had performed these black ceremonies . . .
>
> She bent over the shape in the bed.
>
> Ben had been five years younger than Bella but now this very ancient wisdom was graven on his face; she felt like a girl in the presence of a stone idol. Ben lay there very old, very remote, very strange.
>
> An ancient answering wisdom rose through her as she looked at him. Of course she knew what to do. The voice of the first elegiac woman in the island, a dweller in a stone place, murmured to her mildly.
>
> She took the zinc bucket from the corner of the lobby and went out to the pump, and filled the bucket with water. Fog rolled heavily through the hills.

*MP for Orkney and Shetland, 1950–83; leader of the Liberal Party, 1956–67.

Gino, the simple-minded, motherless boy from the farm of Blinkbonny, plays alone in the corner of the classroom while the other children do their lessons:

> Gino Manson placed a cut-out photograph of a lion next to a cut-out print of the Eiffel Tower, and at the other side placed a cut-out coloured clown. This juxtaposition pleased him very much. He smiled gently in every direction but his felicity was private.

While Johnny, the Indian pedlar, calls on the nervy spinster schoolmistress, Miss Inverary, who is agonizing over whether to succumb to the advances of Ivan Westray, the ferryman:

> *Pyjamas*, I say softly, *for your future husband. Paisley pattern*. She shakes her head bitterly. I close the case. I kneel on it. I am about to strap it up. *I will take the Paisley pattern*, she says suddenly. (She will not mention the word pyjamas, because of its connection with bed, therefore sex.) *It is for a present*. Two guineas. She puts a last look on me before she shuts the door: the kind of look that henceforward all men will have from her – hard, hurt, fascinated, baffled. Where will her youth and her beauty be next summer? Ghosts, half forgotten.

As George worked on the novel, one character, a fragile, elderly lady, began shyly to assert herself in his imagination, and to demand to be explored more fully. Mrs McKee is the mother of Greenvoe's alcoholic minister. She is not a native of Hellya, but has moved to the island to help her son Simon escape the strain and scrutiny of an Edinburgh parish. The spectre of Simon's alcoholism is constantly with her. She sits alone in the manse, surrounded by heavy, Victorian furniture, and by memories so painful and overwhelming that wherever she moves the rooms seem to crepitate with shadows and accusers, feasting on 'the remnants of her life'. She is gentle, generous and blameless; but regularly, every three months, the manse at Hellya becomes in her mind a courtroom, and ghosts gather to put her on trial for imaginary wrongdoings.

> Afternoon was always the quietest time in the village. The fishermen were still at sea. The crofters had not yet unyoked . . .
> In the manse parlour old Mrs McKee knew without a shadow of a doubt that with her it was once more the season of assize. On every

bright and dark wind they came, her accusers, four times a year; they gathered in the manse of Hellya to enquire into certain hidden events of her life. The assize lasted for many days and generally covered the same ground, though occasionally new material would be led that she had entirely forgotten about. All the counts in the indictment had to be answered in some way or other. This was the summer assize; it was a shame that all these beautiful days (not that she ever went out much to enjoy the weather) must be wasted with charge and objection and cross-examination. Moreover, the tribunal was secret; nobody in the village or island knew about it but herself, not even her son Simon who was the parish minister; though Simon shrewdly guessed, she felt sure, that something preoccupied his mother sorely on such occasions; and moreover – this was very strange – the assize usually assembled when Simon was bearing or was about to bear his own little private cross. For a few days, sometimes for as long as a week, the manse was an abode of secret suffering.

George very quickly grew to dislike most of his work, and *Greenvoe* was no exception. To the end of his life, however, he would some-times take the novel off the shelf and 'over a glass of whisky . . . commune for half an hour' with Mrs McKee. 'She is a consolation,' he wrote. 'We have things we can say to one another.'

Mrs McKee is a complicated mixture of the sweetness and generosity of Mhairi Brown, and George's own neuroses and feelings of guilt. For George, as for Mrs McKee, trivial anxieties could become over-whelming, and in his imagination these anxieties, like Mrs McKee's, assumed physical shapes, so that he describes them in letters to friends as 'birds', 'bats', 'ravens', 'dragons', 'imps'. Depression had continued to dog him, on and off. In many Orcadians, the long, dark winters are responsible for bringing on the '*Morbus*'; more difficult for George, often, was the relentless light at the height of the Orkney summer, when the sun barely sets, and even at midnight there is 'a glow under the northern horizon, like a banked-down forge'. This could leave him feeling painfully exposed: 'Autumn has come, thank God, with coldish winds and big blue-and-white surging skies,' he wrote to Stella towards the end of August 1969. 'That hot summer nearly drove me mad. I was in that particular emotional state when every day the sun probed my wounds like a long golden spear.'

The winter that followed was cold and, as snow fell incessantly over the islands, *Greenvoe* flowed along 'like a river in spate'. By 9.30 every morning, George was settled at the Formica surface in the kitchen and here, oblivious to the rattle of the fan heater at his feet, he worked hard until lunchtime. 'I wrote steadily for 3 hours this morning,' he reports in a letter to Roger Harris, a young poet who had first visited Orkney in the early sixties, and with whom he corresponded regularly for several years, '2000 lovely words.' As the novel romped ahead, the people he was creating began to seem as real to George as those passing in the street below and, more than ever, he dreaded disturbance: 'I just want to be at peace,' he told Stella, 'left alone, hidden away.'

George was aware that a number of the characters in *Greenvoe* bore resemblance to people he had known, or heard about. Timmy Folster, Greenvoe's meths-drinking beachcomber, is very close to his friend Jimmy Isbister; while Gino Manson is unmistakably similar to a boy who had been in George's year at Stromness Academy, dressed always in a sailor suit, and dumb from birth. George's father had told him, when he was small, of a Stromness girl with a large brood of children, each by a different man, and she appears in *Greenvoe* as Alice Voar. In creating Simon McKee's spinster aunt, Flora, George was perhaps thinking of Flora Cartwright, the aunt to whom Stella had fled after discovering that Sydney Goodsir Smith was married. Ernest Marwick, when he saw a draft of the novel, warned George that there had once been a ferryman, like Ivan Westray, who had had an affair with a schoolmistress and left her in 'a certain condition'. The ferryman's Christian name had been Ian, and so, in the original manuscript, was Westray's. Just before the novel went to press, George worked his way through the proofs inserting a 'v' every time the name appeared.

What never occurred to George as he wrote was that a number of reviewers would see *Greenvoe* as an attempt at an Orcadian *Under Milk Wood* – would assume, for example, that Alice Voar was Polly Garter by a different name, and Ivan Westray a northern Nogood Boyo. But the comparisons are superficial. Mrs McKee, *Greenvoe*'s central character, has no equivalent in *Under Milk Wood*. And, whereas *Under Milk Wood* is suffused with a sense of permanence and peace, what gives *Greenvoe* its tension and energy is the knowledge that the small island community faces flux and change.

Almost unwittingly, George found that what had started out as a comic novel developed a darker side. From the second chapter onwards, streaks of cruelty and violence creep in. Schoolchildren, resentful after a day of incessant rain and times-tables, vent their anger on Gino Manson, forcing him to lie on his back in a puddle while they splatter him with mud. The laird's granddaughter, Inga, on holiday from her English boarding school, is raped by Ivan Westray in the cabin of his boat. And there is a growing awareness that hovering over the community of Greenvoe is some vast, unspecified threat. A stranger moves into the hotel. By night, he makes coded notes about the local people, their physical attributes and defects, their homes, their farmland. Hellya is being sized-up as a base for 'Operation Black Star' and, in the final chapter, heavy machinery moves in. The island is probed and tunnelled. Bulldozers flatten first the village of Greenvoe, and then, one by one, the outlying farms:

> The Glebe went down in a brief clatter of stones. Nothing stood there by nightfall but the wooden box-bed where generations of Browns had loved and died and been born. Then the navvies broke it up and carried it to the bogey stoves in their huts; for the nights were growing chilly.
>
> The farm of Isbister shuddered some days later. The two gable-ends tottered and leaned towards one another and embraced for the first and the last time. The black hearth-stone stood among the ruins. The smell of living lingered for an hour, then mingled with a wind blowing out to sea, and was lost . . .
>
> Rossiter died in a cloud of dust. The labourers had never seen such quantities of stour as rose from the disordered stones, as if the finest purest grains of sand had been used to cement them. The men in the bulldozers covered noses and mouths with handkerchiefs. Rossiter died in cold dry whispers. The ghost of the house drifted seawards.

Greenvoe, and the farming and fishing rhythms by which its people have lived since time immemorial, is destroyed. Hellya is deserted. Only in the last few pages of the novel is there a flicker of hope that life might one day return to the island.

The apocalyptic final chapter of *Greenvoe* was prompted, in part, by a nagging sense of menace that George himself had felt while writing, and when the book was published in May 1972 he found himself hailed as a minor prophet by fellow Orcadians. Six months earlier, North Sea oil prospectors had begun to turn their attentions to Orkney. Rumours flew around the islands: Kirkwall was to become an international port for heavy tankers; a disused Second World War airfield at Skeabrae was to be redeveloped as an airbase for jumbo jets from Texas; part of the parish of Orphir – an area of extraordinary pastoral beauty – was to be taken over for the construction of oil platforms; the Bay of Houton, on the south coast of mainland Orkney, was to be dammed as a dry dock, and Midland Hill to be mined to provide the necessary stone. 'There's an awful breathless hush in Orkney at the moment, as we wait for the real 20th century to break over us,' George wrote to Roger Harris. 'The Oil Man Cometh. I heard yesterday that they want Garson farm. I hope that isn't true.'

Then, at the beginning of 1973, Occidental Petroleum made what they described as the 'greatest oil discovery of all time': the Piper Field, 100 miles east of Orkney and rich enough to provide the United Kingdom with one quarter of all its energy. As work began on the biggest oil-production platform ever built, Flotta, a tiny island not unlike Hellya, with a population of eighty, was identified as the site of a £25 million tanker terminal. Construction workers were flown in, and farms demolished. By Christmas 1975, Jo Grimond's wife, Laura, reported that the island looked like the Somme battlefield, roads a foot deep in mud. The people of Flotta protested in vain. To cheer them along, the chairman of Occidental, Dr Armand Hammer, arrived in a private jet and, smiling broadly – for the Flotta terminal was shortly to be producing 60,000 barrels of oil a day – presented the islanders with a cheque for £25,000 towards the building of a new community centre.

By now, Orcadians faced a more deadly threat. In the summer of 1973, geologists working for the UK Atomic Energy Authority announced the discovery of a 'uranium corridor' worth millions of pounds on one of Orkney's most beautiful stretches of coastline, between Stromness and the cliffs of Yesnaby. Permission was sought to drive exploratory boreholes hundreds of feet into the cliffs; again, farms and farmland came under threat. If Orcadians had been divided over the issue of oil – many seeing it as an essential new source of income and employment for the islands – over uranium, and the threat of radioactive contamination, they were united in their opposition. Hundreds marched in silent protest through the streets of Kirkwall. Peter Maxwell Davies set to work on *Black Pentecost*, a bitter polemical symphony based on *Greenvoe*, and on *Yellow Cake Revue*, an anti-nuclear cabaret which he performed for the locals in a pub in Stromness. A delegation of Orcadians travelled to London to lobby the House of Commons. Gradually, Westminster lost heart. Visiting the islands shortly after becoming Prime Minister in 1979, Margaret Thatcher promised the Orkney people that they had nothing to fear. The uranium issue was in 'cold storage', she assured them: 'For the moment, we have enough to meet our needs.' For the moment. 'The uranium is slumbering among its rocks, and the oil is dribbling among seals and sheep and sea birds,' George wrote to Roger Harris in the spring of 1979. 'What will Stromness be in fifty years' time?'

15

A Place of Burnings and Ice

So Magnus Erlendson, when he came up from the shore that
Easter Monday, towards noon, to the stone in the centre of the
island, saw against the sun eleven men and a boy and a man with
an axe in his hand who was weeping.

GMB, *Magnus* (1973)

B Y THE TIME *Greenvoe* was complete, George had been published
under the Hogarth Press imprint of Chatto & Windus for more
than ten years. In all that time, the only person from the firm to have
set eyes on him was Hugo Brunner. Brunner combined his work as a
Chatto editor with a directorship of Caithness Glass, and had therefore been able to nip across from Wick to Orkney for a few hours in
the spring of 1970. He had returned to the Chatto offices in William
IV Street with a bottle of Highland Park whisky* and with glowing
reports of George's charm and wit and gift for friendship. He had
taken to him at once.

Norah Smallwood envied Brunner his visit. Since Edwin Muir had
entrusted George to her care, she had nurtured his talents with
wisdom and skill. Terrifying to some who worked with her,
Smallwood was, nevertheless, one of the most remarkable publishers
of her generation. Privately, she was a lonely and a tragic figure. One
afternoon just before Christmas 1943, she had left the office early to
meet her husband off a train: he was serving in the RAF, and had two
days' leave. When, after an hour, he failed to appear, she went home
and found a telegram waiting for her. Peter Smallwood had been

---

*'It really is marvellous stuff,' Norah Smallwood wrote to George, 'and two thim-
blefuls before I leave the office and plunge into the maelstrom of homeward-bound
commuters have a very euphoric effect.'

killed in action; his body was never recovered. From that moment on, publishing became her *raison d'être*, and her authors – Dirk Bogarde, Henry Green, Compton Mackenzie, Iris Murdoch and V. S. Pritchett, to name but a few – became her surrogate children. 'To us writers,' Iris Murdoch wrote after her death, 'she was a combination of comrade, leader, mother, business partner and muse.'

Although they had never met, George had won a special place in Norah Smallwood's affections, and she in his. 'Dear Mr Mackay Brown', 'Dear Mrs Smallwood', their letters open, and the correspondence that travelled between Trafalgar Square and Stromness has an *84 Charing Cross Road* charm: two worlds gradually revealing themselves to one another, as two people write with a growing but unspoken tenderness. When, in the spring of 1969, a Bloomsbury book dealer wrote to Smallwood to say that George's short stories had enchanted him more than anything he had read for years, she admitted in her delighted reply that George Mackay Brown was her 'particular care'. And when, a year later, Hugo Brunner returned from meeting George, she became determined that she should meet him too. At the beginning of 1972, as the publication of *Greenvoe* approached, she wrote to George to propose that, if he would travel south as far as Edinburgh, she would like to offer him his first full-blown launch party.

The prospect of a party did not thrill George. He was always anxious that people encountering him for the first time would feel disappointed, or worse. 'Perhaps we'll meet some day,' he once wrote to a woman with whom he corresponded over several years, and who had developed a soft spot for him through his letters. 'Then the scales will fall from your eyes, and you'll see what a frail selfish ugly beast you've been writing reams to.' He was unnerved, too, at the notion of being put on show. In the spring of 1971, David Campbell, a friend from university days, had tried to persuade George to read some of his poetry at the Edinburgh Festival. 'Oh no, David, I couldn't do anything like that,' he had responded. 'I look too much like Pinocchio.' But churlishness was not a part of George's nature, and, after making it clear to Norah Smallwood that he must not be asked to read from his work – 'the thought . . . turns me on a gridiron' – nor required to '*reply to toasts*', he agreed that the party should go ahead. By April, he was busy compiling Norah Smallwood a list of Edinburgh friends to whom she might send invitations.

Notably absent from the list was Stella Cartwright. Since the end of her affair with Sydney Goodsir Smith, relations between Stella and George appear to have become strained. Apart from occasional wild binges, George now had his drinking more or less under control. He was working hard, living with discipline, taking full responsibility for himself and for his future: surely Stella, with all her gifts, could do the same? A bat-squeak of impatience entered his letters as he parried her protests that everything good was now over for her, and that her childhood and upbringing had somehow condemned her to a life of misery. 'I do feel for you, dear Stella, in your unenviable situation,' George writes on 17 February 1970.

> But then your mother is not a villain . . . She has had much to endure
> and to condone. None of us can ever justify ourselves entirely by putting
> the blame on others. This is to enter deeper into the tunnel. The begin-
> ning of the return to the light is to say: 'Here I am, in such and such a
> situation, and I alone am to blame for it, because my will is free. And I
> have had dealings with other people, and in this and that it seems to me
> that they let me down and did not act as they should have acted. But in
> the clear light of eternity I alone am responsible for my actions. And now
> I wish to drag myself out of this rut where I have fallen'. . . And, my
> dear Stella, with all your kindness and sweetness and gentleness you can
> do it – the clue is in your hand – you will stand in the full sun once more.

What she needed, George believed, was a job – 'it is good for none of us to just hang around wondering' – ideally one in which she could give her compassion its head, and lose her suffering in the suffering of others. 'Dear Stella, *surely* there must be a job for you *somewhere* in Edinburgh,' he urged, adding pointedly that there was no work for women in Orkney. But jobs were hard to come by, and the only employment Stella could find was with the cosmetics company Avon, cold-calling on Edinburgh housewives, peddling beauty products. George was appalled. 'Selling cosmetics: what kind of a job is that for a girl like you, helping the bad old world to plaster her face!'

Because she was paid on commission, moreover, and because she was still drinking, Stella was constantly in debt. She began to ask George for money; and this was a mistake. It was not that George could not afford to help her. His needs were modest, and his income now comfortably outstripped his expenditure. But the anxiety he had felt about money as

a child, compounded by years of poverty, had left him financially cautious almost to the point of meanness. 'I am,' he once admitted in a letter
to a friend, 'rather tight-fisted by nature.' Also, of course, he knew that
whatever money he gave Stella would go immediately on drink. Once
or twice, he sent small sums; then he drew the line. Stella was deeply
hurt. 'Of course there is no need to help me to the extent of £10 when
I am in the most awful trouble,' she writes in March 1970. 'I have given
something (a lot I feel) of myself to you. Money is of no interest to me
except now: when I am in debt. About half (at least) of the poets in this
country owe me a lot more than money.'

Not for the first time, George felt that Stella might ultimately be
happier if she could sever her connections with the past. His letters
slowed to a trickle, but without the desired effect: 'Dearest George, I
am hurt and sad that you do not speak to me,' Stella writes on 20 July
1970. 'Maybe I am too old and plain for your notice . . .' She was now
thirty-three.

The *Greenvoe* launch party was considered a huge success, a champagne reception for sixty at Gladstone's Land, a renovated sixteenth-
century merchant's house, followed by a dinner attended by Compton
Mackenzie at Prestonfield House. George fulfilled Norah Smallwood's
best expectations, and she was delighted now to be able to supply a full
physical description when readers wrote to her enquiring about his
work. His hair, she admitted, was rather unkempt – 'it is very curly,
and the salt winds of Orkney are not conducive to producing a West
End style' – but he was 'extremely well built', and his outstanding features were 'a pair of brilliant, large blue eyes and a very, very firm chin.
He would have made a splendid figurehead on one of the Norsemen
ships he writes about.'

For George, however, the evening was a trial. He was nervous
about deploying his cutlery correctly, and feared that he might drink
too much. As often, when ill at ease, he kept up a low hum – an echo,
perhaps, of the gentle, tuneless crooning he had heard from his mother
as she moved about her housework – to fill gaps in the conversation.
He was relieved to get home.

Yet even in Stromness it was becoming increasingly difficult for
George to escape his public. The success of his work, together with

his passionate attachment to Orkney, led to regular requests for interviews for radio, television and newspapers. These left him feeling
'probed and peered into and exploited'. He argued repeatedly that his
life and work were no more interesting than anybody else's. 'Writing
is a trade like any other trade,' he insists in a television programme
made about him in 1970. 'Making a good table, making a good loaf
of bread, making a good poem or story – what's the difference?' And
it was clear to anyone who met him that he gave himself no airs, but
lived at eye-level with the community in Stromness: that he was, as
Seamus Heaney puts it, 'in no way like Larkin's "shit in the chateau",
or Yeats in his Galway tower', but rather 'a man in a council house,
going in for his dram with the locals, writing his letters in longhand,
turning in copy for the Orkney newspaper'.

Yet precisely because George's life remained, in a sense, so normal, the
privacy enjoyed by most normal people was denied him. Having bought
copies of his books in Charlie Senior's shop, visitors had only to ask in
the street to be pointed towards Mayburn Court, and in the summer
George was now besieged. Strangers battered at his door wanting books
signed, or poems uttered into tape recorders, or deep discussions about
Kafka, or William Burroughs, or the existence of fairies. And because
he had inherited from his mother a deep, Gaelic hospitality – Mhairi
Brown's courtesy had extended to thanking all visitors for their calls, no
matter how unwelcome – George felt compelled to invite them in.
'Then,' as he explained in a letter to Roger Harris, 'the routine is that
both parties sit down and talk about books, inspiration, future prospects
etc for twenty minutes: a thing which I abhor.' And all the time, he confessed to Kevin Crossley-Holland, he suspected that the shyer folk, the
ones he might really have liked to meet, never came near him at all.

The morning's post, too, brought endless requests: that George
should travel to Cardiff to address a conference of Celtic writers, to
London to read at the Poetry Society, to Edinburgh to judge a
students' verse competition, to Aberdeen to spend a term as writer-
in-residence. Within a year of its publication, a dozen sixth-formers
from different parts of Scotland set to work on extended essays on
Greenvoe and wrote to George with lists of questions, to which he sent
encouraging, detailed replies. He reckoned that, during the summer
of 1972, more than a hundred people had knocked at his door wanting

him to sign their copies of *Greenvoe* – 'and also, I suspect, to have a good look at the queer fish that spawned it'. He began to feel, he told Norah Smallwood, like 'some kind of summer peepshow'.

George needed silence and solitude now more than ever. North of mainland Orkney is the small, green island of Eynhallow, surrounded by ferocious waters, and inhabited only by seals and sea birds. On it are the ruins of what some believe to have been a medieval monastery. George found himself wishing that the monks were still living there, and that he could escape from Stromness for a time and 'slip in with folded hands'.

After finishing *Greenvoe*, he had started work on the most ambitious and soul-searching piece of prose he was ever to undertake: a novel about the life of Saint Magnus. George had twice before written at length about Magnus, once in *An Orkney Tapestry*, and again in a play, *The Loom of Light*. On both occasions he had 'sweated blood' in the process. As he explained in letters to friends, he faced the double difficulty that he was writing for a generation indifferent to the notion of sanctity, and that he himself had no idea what sanctity essentially was – 'it's only that, when certain facets of it are turned to me, I get a flash of beauty off it'. This 'flash of beauty' he felt compelled to explore and to communicate.

It was tough going. By the end of most mornings, through the winter and spring of 1972, George felt that he had been battering his brains out, and by early summer the manuscript of his new novel looked 'like a gory battlefield'. He was, however, invigorated. He felt himself growing in determination and patience as he confronted difficulties, and developing a will as hard as granite as he outfaced them. 'And it sometimes happens,' he wrote to Roger Harris, 'that the stone breaks into flower in your hand.' He was confident, and would remain so until the end of his life, that *Magnus* contained some of the best prose he had ever written.

In exploring the nature of sanctity, George was examining the concept of sacrifice: What was it? Why was it necessary? What went through a man's mind as he chose, at particular moments in his life, to forsake the things he loved and desired for some greater good? In imagining himself into the mind of a twelfth-century earl, George was also asking tough questions about his own life, and about the purpose of the sacrifices he himself had made. This is what gives *Magnus* its power and poignancy.

It is recorded in the *Orkneyinga Saga* that Magnus, despite being married, chose to live a celibate life, and, when George first read this as a young TB patient in 1949, he appears to have thought little of it. Magnus was simply not attracted to his Shetland bride, Ingerth, he had explained to readers of the *Orkney Herald*. He had looked at her and felt 'disgusted'. A quarter of a century on, his relationship with Stella now woven into his experience, George began to contemplate a truth more subtle and profound. Magnus, in this novel, feels sexual desire as strong as any other man's and, when he and his wife are left alone together after their wedding feast, he longs to consummate the marriage. Yet he has been troubled by a recurring dream, a dream 'intermeshed with his diurnal existence', in which he has felt himself invited to a marriage feast greater than his own, 'the marriage feast of Christ with his church'. If he is to accept this invitation, he must channel his love for Ingerth into a wider love for the whole of creation.

> Magnus looked at Ingerth hopelessly. He shook his head. The bed lay between them white and unbroken.
>
> Magnus slept in his own room. He dreamed. He was in a place of burnings and ice. 'No,' said the voice of the friend beyond a fold of green wavering fire, 'but there is love indeed, and God ordained it, and it is a good love and necessary for the world's weal, and worthy are those who taste of it. But there are souls which cannot eat at that feast, for they serve another and a greater love, which is to these flames and meltings (wherein you suffer) the hard immortal diamond. Magnus, I call thee yet once more to the marriage feast of the king.'

Magnus tries, one evening, to explain to his friend Hold Ragnarson what has happened; but an element of his sacrifice, as of George's own perhaps, is that even those closest to him cannot begin to understand it:

> Hold Ragnarson smiled at the deep sincerity of his friend – expressed in falterings and sudden fluencies – and at the beauty of the images he uttered, as they walked together along the cliff verges of Marwick that sunset. He smiled with simulated understanding, but in truth he was more perplexed than ever.

Magnus Erlendson is no plaster saint. In the years following his marriage to Ingerth, he devotes himself to war against his cousin Hakon

Paulson, with whom he shares the earldom of Orkney. By the time the two earls meet to negotiate peace on the island of Egilsay on Easter Monday 1117, Orkney has been despoiled by decades of conflict, and the islanders are starving. Magnus is now well into middle age, and the faith that meant so much to him as a young man has wavered. Yet when Hakon arrives for the peace talks with eight ships, fully armed, and Magnus's men beg him to abandon the meeting and turn home, Magnus refuses.

According to the *Orkneyinga Saga*, in the early hours of the morning, on the day of his execution, Magnus heard Mass in the small church on the island of Egilsay. George imagines him kneeling at the back of the church, overcome with feelings of abandonment, and lassitude, and bitter cold. The Mass seems nothing more to him than the movements of an old man muttering 'dead foreign words'. Seeking distraction and comfort, however – 'as some old story might comfort a child on a winter night' – Magnus tries to enter into the mystery of what is supposed to be happening at the altar. As he does so, he finds himself once more drawn into a dream, a dream that takes the form of an invitation. He is invited again to a marriage feast, and told that if he can only make his way through streets of slaughterhouses to a weaver's shop, he will find that a wedding coat has been woven for him.

As the bell rings at the consecration, Magnus is shaken out of his dream. He is clear now about what he must do. 'His mind took the small infusion of peace that comes after every hard decision. He offered all that he had left: the peace and the pain.' He emerges from the church knowing that he will not leave Egilsay alive, but knowing also that his death at the hands of his cousin will bring peace, after years of war, to Orkney.

At the point of Magnus's execution, what was already an ambitious novel becomes more ambitious still. In an attempt to imbue the sacrifice made by Magnus with universal significance, not confined to a particular place or time, George swings the narrative from twelfth-century Orkney to Nazi Germany, and the hanging of a Lutheran pastor from a meat hook in a concentration camp.

Norah Smallwood was delighted with *Magnus*, and it became the Hogarth Press's Booker Prize submission for 1973. But George knew very well that it would never enjoy the popular success of *Greenvoe* and, as he had predicted, some reviewers were baffled by it. 'A weird tale, well told, with strong poetic leanings,' wrote one, hedging every bet. 'This is a story for those who like something out of the ordinary.' Ernest Marwick was right when he wrote that *Magnus* eluded conventional analysis, that it was a novel whose success could only be judged in terms of the impact made on the hearts and minds of individual readers. And this impact was, at its best, immense. For Peter Maxwell Davies, *Magnus* remains George's greatest achievement. Shortly after its publication, Max began to work on the idea of establishing an annual arts festival in Orkney and when, in the summer of 1977, the first St Magnus Festival took place, the centrepiece was his opera *The Martyrdom of St Magnus*, based on George's novel and performed in St Magnus Cathedral. John Betjeman, who had visited Orkney in 1970, and had met George briefly, wrote, nearly five years on, to thank George for the delight *Magnus* had given him. And for the novelist Jacky Gillott, reviewing it in *The Times*, *Magnus* was quite simply 'the most beautiful contemporary book I have ever read'. Occasionally, Gillott wrote, one comes across a novel of such imaginative force and beauty that all stiff critical precepts have to be laid aside: 'Such a book can make the reader's mind depart his body briefly. Such a book is *Magnus*.'

On New Year's Day 1974, George Mackay Brown was appointed OBE.* Letters of congratulation flooded in. Norah Smallwood, who had herself been appointed OBE a year earlier, wrote to tell George of a chapel in St Paul's Cathedral reserved exclusively for members of the Order: 'You and I must go there one day – who knows what ghosts we might not see.' Stella confessed that she had wept with happiness when she saw George's name in the honours list, and cautioned him to take a friend when he travelled south to collect his medal from the Queen, 'as no man alone is allowed into the pallace [*sic*]'.

But there was no question of George's travelling south. Since finishing *Magnus* the previous spring, he had been suffering from acute agoraphobia. Walking through Stromness, shopping, he would find himself suddenly terrified that the houses on either side of the street

---

* 'When I get a peerage,' he later joked in a letter to Kulgin Duval, 'I think I'll choose Lord Hamnavoe of Rackwick.'

were about to collapse and crush him. At times, the terror became so crippling that he doubted whether he would ever be able to leave Orkney again. The affliction was capricious. As George later explained to Dr Michael Curtis, a London GP with whom he corresponded, it was like living with a dragon. Sometimes, for weeks on end, the dragon slept, and he felt reasonably at ease.

The poet and critic Jay Parini, then a postgraduate student at St Andrews University, visited Stromness during one of these periods of release. George met him off the *St Ola*, showed him about Orkney and took him to the Braes Hotel above Stromness for a drink. He was attentive and generous, quick to smile and 'gentle with my vast igno-rance', Parini remembers. 'He had one of the sweetest temperaments I have ever encountered.' Yet Parini was aware that George was 'somehow willing conversation and human contact', and he was con-scious of a 'sense of foreboding behind the eyes'. George lived in con-stant dread of the dragon's stirring, and of the next 'swing of the horny tail'. Then, it was as if a door closed in his mind, and was bolted and padlocked. He gazed across the water to Hoy, and wondered how he had ever dared travel there. Some days he remained shackled to Mayburn Court, unable even to post a letter or shop for food. Confined to his flat, and to 'a prison of the self', he wondered whether he was on the verge of madness.

Magnus, so thrilling in the writing, had taken an enormous psycho-logical toll; and its publication left George with a sense of deathly anti-climax. 'All that winter of labour and invention,' he wrote, 'to lie at last between narrow boards!' In the spring of 1974, as Britain was brought almost to a standstill by the miners' strike,[*] he sank into a state of nervous depression in which even trivial circumstances became part of the machinery of a nightmare.

George had known these dark times, on and off, for nearly forty years now. He knew that there was nothing to be done but to sit them out – to 'thole' them – and to work hard while he waited for the clouds

---

[*]George felt great sympathy and admiration for the miners. 'Who among us would spend his working week toiling in the black veins of the earth?' he asks in the *Orcadian* on 14 March 1974. 'Society in the past has not rewarded the miners adequately, to put it mildly. Yet, in spite of everything, the mining communities of Scotland . . . remain the most cheerful and generous of people. If any folk deserve to be well paid, it's them.'

to lift. He had plenty to work at. In the autumn of 1974, Hogarth published both a new collection of short stories, *Hawkfall*, and a volume of Orkney stories for children, *The Two Fiddlers*, for which Ian MacInnes provided the illustrations. George, meanwhile, was putting together a collection of poetry, *Winterfold*, and a second children's book, *Pictures in the Cave*, and starting to build up his fourth volume of short stories, *The Sun's Net*. He was also engaged once again in local journalism. The *Orkney Herald* had been published for the last time in January 1961. A decade later, in 1971, George had started to produce a weekly column, 'Letter from Hamnavoe' in the *Orcadian*. Each 400-word piece turned on some small subject: a childhood reminiscence, the weather, his terror of rats, his feelings about decimalization. George no longer aimed to engage in polemic or political argument, but simply 'to entertain a small community of 1,600 townsfolk – possibly a scattering of other islanders – also to kindle home thoughts in the minds of the thousands of Orkney folk who live outwith the islands but keep in touch through the pages of the paper'. This was perhaps the only kind of writing through which George fulfilled his youthful determination to communicate with the ordinary people of Orkney, the crofters and the fishermen. No matter what his state of mind, he never failed to turn in his copy.

While writing, George could hold his depression at arm's length, and the words flowed from his pen 'like raindrops off a farm gate'. Yet his very fluency was becoming a source of anxiety. In letters to friends between the spring of 1974 and the summer of 1976, he worries that he is becoming an automaton, 'a machine that churns out poems, stories, articles to order'. Again and again, he compares himself to a spider, compelled to 'spin his web or die'. *The Sun's Net* opens with 'A Winter Tale', a story in which George lifts the masks being worn by three professional men – a doctor, a teacher and a minister – as they go about their lives in a dwindling community on the imaginary island of Njalsay. The story is set in the short, dark days running up to Christmas, and each of the three characters is struggling with some thorn in the flesh known only to himself. For the doctor, the most sympathetic of the three, the thorn is homosexuality; for the teacher, some unspecified but progressive nervous disorder which is gradually causing his limbs to shake and buckle. The minister is locked in a marriage that has turned cold. He works on his Christmas sermon late into the night in order to be sure that his wife will be sound asleep when he joins her in bed, but as he considers what to say to the few islanders who still come to church, he is forced to recognize that his faith has largely deserted him. George, too, was suffering from a feeling that his professional life was becoming a sham, that his writing was nothing but 'lies'. When he read new work that he really admired, like Seamus Heaney's *North*, or Ted Hughes's *Crow*, he felt overcome with the pointlessness of his own efforts.

By the autumn of 1975, along with drugs for his agoraphobia, George was taking regular doses of Librium, a sedative that made him 'drowsy and content like a lotus-eater'. Between doses a sense of futility persisted. In May 1976, the BBC broadcast an *Omnibus* programme about George's life and work. Filmed wandering along the beach at Warbeth, he looks agonized. 'I feel old and weary and near the end,' he admitted to a friend, Patricia Crowden, on 18 June. A week later, in a letter to Roger Harris, he confessed that he was 'tired of years of writing' – but what else could he do?

Claire Tomalin was literary editor of the *New Statesman* during these years, and was keen to commission poetry from George. Among the work he sent her was 'The Poet', a fourteen-stanza piece about a man thirled to a gift that fate has thrust upon him, that he would never have elected for himself, and that he has grown, almost, to hate. Its conclusion is bleak:

> They will take it from your widowed hands at last,
> That harp.

> Think not that one line or one phrase will be ever remembered of it,
> That stone.

There are grains of consolation for the poet along the way: 'A kind listener in the street' lightens his pain; 'remembered love' nurtures his vision. But there are indications that George's own 'remembered love' – his love for Stella – had by this time become so painful that he wished almost to cauterize it from his memory. It may be that he had by now discovered that Stella had been selling his correspondence to an Edinburgh book dealer to raise money for drink. Certainly, following their fracas about money, George's letters to Stella had become much less frequent and, when he did write, they were cooler in tone.

Where once he had signed off with flourishes of affection, and small fences of kisses, his letters now ended simply 'Love, George'. Between 3 November 1974 and 9 November 1975, he appears not to have written to Stella at all.

At the beginning of 1975, the Edinburgh publishing house Canongate wrote to George to ask whether they might include some of his work in an anthology of Scottish love poetry that Antonia Fraser was compiling for them. In a letter to Kulgin Duval, George protested at the oddness of this request: 'I have never been in love in my life.'* In the autumn of 1975, and again in February 1976, he managed to overcome his agoraphobia and travel to Edinburgh to visit friends. He avoided seeing Stella on both occasions.

On the evening of 16 March 1976, Radio Scotland broadcast *Earth Gold, Sea Silver*, two fictional dialogues by George Mackay Brown. In the first, a female journalist travels a long way to interview a celebrated author in his sitting-room overlooking the sea. Perplexed by the author's repeated insistence that he has no wisdom or insight to offer the world, and that many of his works have been 'fakes', she turns to the portrait of a beautiful girl hanging on his wall. The poems the author has written about this girl are well known: surely his love for her, at least, is real and enduring? Again, the journalist is rebuffed. The love has passed away, the author insists:

> If I remember her now, I see a shadow only. I remember nothing but pain – a pain as great at least as birth or death. The pain of first desire, the pain of tuning our two instruments to one another, the pain of discovering this and that in her, the pain of her absences, the pain of her returns . . . When I try to think of her (as I do sometimes, on a summer night, when I'm sitting alone here, above the sea, with a pipe and a glass of whisky, and the past floods in like a slow lingering tide over the rocks of the present), when I try to summon her ghost only a shadow comes, and seems to stand over there beside the window. It is a shadow without speech or fragrance. And I sip my whisky and I wonder. And when I look again, the shadow has gone into the thickening shadows of night. And, 'Thank goodness,' I say, '*that* pain is dead . . .'

---

*Four of George's poems – 'Country Girl', 'Fiddler's Song', 'Wedding' and an extract from 'Lord of the Mirrors' – were in fact included.

16

A Rack of Flowers

Do not expect a kind of love I am not capable of giving to anyone. Perhaps that supreme thing is kept from many writers and artists: 'the muse' demands all that there is . . .

Study to see me as a frail creature in the grayness of common day: occasionally stirred to put a few words into a pleasant pattern, no more.

GMB, letter to Nora Kennedy, 1977

IN 1976 BRITAIN sweltered in the hottest summer of the twentieth century. With temperatures in the nineties, and tempers frayed, the Notting Hill Carnival descended into violent race riots, and 350 policemen were wounded. Reservoirs in the south of England dried up, exposing clay beds cracking in the heat. The Prime Minister, James Callaghan, appointed a Minister for Drought. When, on the last day of August, a few drops of rain finally fell, crowds watching cricket at Lord's rose in the terraces and cheered.

The north got off more lightly, but Scotland too had its share of the extraordinary weather. Forest fires swept across Inverness-shire, and the roads through the Highlands twinkled as the tarmac melted in the heat. In Orkney, the sun shone day after day.

In early July, George spent a long weekend in Hoy with friends, Peter and Betty Grant, whom he had met when he was an under-graduate, and who had travelled up from Aberdeen to stay with him nearly every year since 1963. Rackwick that summer was brimming over with light and warmth. Betty cooked enormous meals, George collected buckets of water from the burn and wandered about the slopes of the valley with the Grants' two-and-a-half-year-old son, Alan. He described, in his *Orcadian* column, knocking on the doors

of ruined crofts, spinning stories about their imaginary inhabitants for
the little boy:

> 'Can we come in, Margaret-Anne?' (Margaret-Anne was a fairy. She was
> not at home that day.) . . . 'Are you home yet, old Willie?' (Old Willie
> goes to the sea and fishes.) But no, old Willie was not yet back from his
> lines; when he did come in, he would leave a fish on our doorstep.

The company of children was a delight to George. He returned to
Stromness with his spirits greatly restored.

Another visitor to the islands that summer was Nora Kennedy, a
Viennese jeweller and silversmith, almost twenty years George's
junior, and recently separated from her husband. She had come to
Orkney from Edinburgh, where she had lived for the past ten years,
and had bought and renovated a cottage, Dyke-end, on the island of
South Ronaldsay. She first saw George in the Royal Hotel in
Stromness. The 'Tennessee Waltz' was playing in the background, and
he was drinking with friends at the bar. His whole appearance, she
remembers, gave an impression of fragility, and she felt protective
towards him. A few days later, she knocked on the door of 3 Mayburn
Court to ask whether he might sign her copy of *A Spell for Green Corn*.
George asked her in. After chatting for a while over cups of tea, they
arranged to meet again for dinner at Tormiston Mill, a restaurant
opposite Maeshowe. Nora felt drawn to George, and he to her. 'I
think of you with much tenderness,' he wrote on 28 July, when she
had to return briefly to Edinburgh. 'You are certainly a unique person,
so gifted and intelligent and kind; I have not met anyone quite like
you before.' As with Stella, years earlier, he found himself longing to
give Nora small presents of books and poems and cards.

On all sorts of levels, George felt Nora to be a kindred spirit. A poet's
art, he had often written, was very like a jeweller's; and, despite her
broken marriage, it pleased him that she was a cradle Catholic. Her
foreignness, too, was appealing. After months of depression, weariness
and imprisonment by agoraphobia, the company of a young Austrian
woman without Orkney roots was refreshing. And he felt instinctively
protective of her, just as she had of him. 'There is a deep sadness in you,
in repose, that I would love to lighten,' he wrote to her; 'or else to have
explained to me, even by silence.'

Casting aside his rigid work routine, George soon arranged for taxis to ferry him almost daily the hour's journey east towards Kirkwall, and then down across the Churchill Barriers to South Ronaldsay, and Dyke-end. This corner of Orkney was completely new to him. The cottage was secluded, surrounded by fields of ripening crops, and less than a minute's walk from the most beautiful small beach he had ever seen: it was 'a golden-gray crescent' of sand, he wrote in the *Orcadian*, and 'The sea that breaks on it is green and cold and translucent'. Here, they spent afternoon after hot afternoon together, chatting, picnicking, playing with Nora's black kitten, Gypsy.* 'What a happy day that was at Dyke-end,' George writes on 18 August 1976, 'the friends and the food and drink – the green beautiful wide cornfields – the beach! It will be one of my happiest memories.' There was more to this happiness than sunshine and good company. Between George and Nora there was a powerful, and mutual, physical attraction.

When Nora was obliged, intermittently, to return to Edinburgh, they exchanged frequent letters. 'I kiss your eyes, your hands, and your hair,' Nora writes on 25 August. 'Perhaps you can feel that I love you more all the time.' George, in response, was only slightly more restrained. He missed her desperately, he wrote; he found a letter a poor substitute for a kiss. Alone in Mayburn Court, he turned over the memories of the times they had spent together, and waited impatiently for her return. Nora had brought an extraordinary sweetness into his 'dull life' – and, more than that, she had touched him with 'enchantment'. 'I love you, dear,' he writes on 29 August, 'and I treasure all the happiness we have had: I accept the pain too. I send many kisses.'

Beneath the excitement, there were, from the beginning, hints of nervousness on George's part at the intensity of their feelings for each other, and at the direction in which this was leading them. 'I hope you will understand,' he had written in his first letter to Nora, 'when I say that, in a sense, I'm glad you're not staying in Stromness permanently – I would burn out quickly in that flame. (On Sunday, I was an utter wreck.) Yet I long to see you and talk to you, always.' Two weeks later

*George later published a volume of his witty and touching letters to this 'Very Special Cat': *Letters to Gypsy*, Balnain Books, 1990.

he admits: 'You have taken me into regions where I never thought to go. I am half-enchanted, and half-afraid.' With Nora Kennedy, at the age of fifty-four, George had embarked on what was almost certainly the first, and only, consummated affair of his life, and his reactions were complicated. In the autumn, he confided obliquely in Roger Harris: 'Strange things have been happening to me lately – pleasant and disconcerting. I am trying to adapt new rhythms to the set selfish rhythm of a middle-aged bachelor: difficult. Yet it seems I am writing better because of those new experiences. There is pain also. It is a curious kind of rack of flowers to be stretched out on, so late in the day.'

So far as his writing was concerned, there is no doubt that Nora Kennedy had done George a great service. As the heatwave passed, and autumn settled on the islands, he returned to his work with an energy and enthusiasm he had not known since writing *Magnus*. For some time before Nora's arrival in Orkney, he had felt unable to write poetry; now it began to flow from his pen in astonishing profusion. 'The verse fairly erupted from me in the fortnight of mid-October,' he told Roger Harris. 'I just had to sit down in front of a sheet of blank paper, and either let a few words drift across the mind, or picture (vaguely) a situation – and the poems (if you can call them that: early days yet) began to write themselves. It was exhilarating and uncanny, like being (I suppose) a medium at a seance.' He relished the drawing in of the evenings, and the prospect of sitting at the Formica surface in his kitchen, 'mining ore all winter – finding the sun in darkness!' and, by the early spring of 1977, he was able to report to Kulgin Duval that he had had the most productive winter of his life. 'I think now I am writing for you,' he told Nora, 'and that seems to raise me to new heights.'

With his return to work, however, strains began to emerge in their relationship. For all his sweetness, Nora reflects, George was 'harder than diamonds' inside. His discipline and utter dedication to his work were formidable, as he himself was well aware. 'I know I am very selfish,' he wrote to her. 'Over the years I have developed a settled routine, and any alteration upsets me in a hundred subtle ways.' Nora realized that, if they were to have any future together, she would have to share George not only with his public – who continued to batter on his door at all hours, often disregarding the small note requesting that he be left in peace until 2 p.m.* – but also with the characters in his imagination. When his writing was going well, these could absorb him utterly, so that in his treatment of Nora he became distant and distracted. 'Sometimes George seemed to think of nothing but how to please Nora,' says a friend who observed them together; 'at other times he was locked up in his shell.' In the course of the autumn, an unhappy note began to enter Nora's letters. She complained that George was 'cold and unthinking', that he treated her with 'busy coolness', that he failed even to attempt to understand or love her properly.

George tried to make light of these concerns: 'Do you really want me to say over and over again "I adore you!" . . . and "Darling of my life!" . . . and "Heart's joy", letter after letter, with variations? Well, you are too much of a real person to waste all that drivel on. I won't and I can't do it.' In fact, he knew that it was not just a change in style that Nora wanted from him, but something more profound: a kind of love and commitment that he was simply unable to give to anybody. 'It may be – this is only a theory,' he writes to her on 5 October, 'that a writer puts most of his emotions into his writing, and has only a little warmth to bring to everyday life. To put it at the lowest, he squanders his energy among shadows and figments. It *may* be, there's an element of truth in it. Thomas Mann knew that; he always insisted that in every artist there's an element of the fake and the charlatan.' These emotional limitations had physical implications. 'Dear Nora,' George writes on 30 October, 'you realize as much as I do that there are many unresolved things between us, and they are so acute at times that they give rise to doubts, to say the least.' He mentions 'physical difficulties', and is aware that Nora must find these deeply frustrating: 'And there is no cure for it. And as for me, it leaves me drained and exhausted.' He asks himself whether, if they were to abandon their physical relationship, Nora could still love him: 'A troubled and doubtful echo comes back.'

Over Christmas, Nora stayed for nearly a fortnight at Mayburn Court. George introduced her to his family and friends: to the Dixons, the Bevans and the MacInneses, and to Gunnie Moberg, a Swedish photographer who had recently moved to Orkney with her

---

* 'Writing – my job – is almost impossible these days for people,' George complained in a letter to Patricia Crowden, 17 July 1976.

husband and four sons. 'All my friends like you so much,' George told Nora. 'There are half-a-dozen houses in Stromness where you will always be welcome.' But, as the days went by, Nora and George began to 'rasp on each other's nerves'; and, by the time she left, George was nervous and depressed.

Towards the end of 1976, Jeremy Rundall, radio critic and travel correspondent of the *Sunday Times,* had died suddenly in Oxford. Rundall had loved Orkney, and had asked that George should scatter his ashes there. On 9 January, on a clear wintry afternoon, with shadows of snow clouds on Hoy Sound, George carried the ashes to Warbeth beach and performed this melancholy task. By the evening, when he settled down to write to Nora, he was at such 'a low ebb of the mind' that every thought was 'like a piece of lead travelling through the brain'. His affection for Nora had not diminished: 'There are so many things I like and admire and cherish in you: your extraordinary kindness, intelligence, sweetness, sensitivity to the beautiful things in life, both natural and artistic. These things are so rare in the world.' But he was unsettled by the local gossip that now surrounded their relationship, and he felt more uneasy than ever about the relationship itself. 'I know how the physical reality must be a bitter hurt to you,' he wrote. 'Me it drains of all energy – even such as it is – and it fills me with shame at my shortcomings and inadequacies.'

By the end of February, George's mental state had deteriorated further. He had always been open with Nora about his tendency to depression, but now he began to describe something more sinister. 'It's as if the foundations of my mind were being upset,' he wrote to her. 'It's frightening, often. I think so much of mental asylums, or suicide. And yet I'm so much afraid of what eternity will hold for me!' Together, he and Nora seemed about 'as miserable as two skylarks in a cage'. He feared that they might grow at last to hate each other, and, because Nora was so dear to him, the thought of that was terrifying.

This fear was not realized. George never ceased to feel affection for Nora Kennedy. In 1978 she moved to a house in Stromness, and she remained an inextricable part of his life. When, in 1981, the poet Dennis O'Driscoll visited Orkney, George left him in no doubt about Nora's importance to him. If ever she was in difficulty, meanwhile, George felt for her deeply. 'Poor Nora,' he writes to a friend on

4 February 1988, 'she has a generous and gentle side to her nature which most people are either too stupid or too insensitive to appreciate.'*

After those few idyllic weeks in the summer of 1976, however, the magic had given way to a more mundane reality, and George's letters to friends reflected a wearying, repetitious round of reproach and remorse in the months and years that followed. 'Nora was here yesterday,' he writes to Roger Harris on 17 March 1978. 'There was (as nearly always) a fight followed by a reconciliation.' And in the spring of 1979: 'I don't know what to do about Nora. Last night there was a violent scene about next to nothing. It's always happening. Yet I feel a constant care & tenderness for her.'

Under these strains, the depression that had settled on George in the spring of 1977 proved almost impossible to shift. 'The weather is bleak and cold,' he wrote to Roger Harris in December of that year, 'and so are my spirits, most days'; and, early in 1978, 'I am very upset and apprehensive about nerve storms that gather and burst about my head every now and then – the world is then a huge dark minefield, one longs for oblivion.' For some time, George pinned his hopes on a belief that he was suffering from the male menopause, and that soon he might pass into a 'sterile carefree' old age. In fact, from the beginning of 1977 onwards, depression was to dog him constantly for the best part of a decade, rising and falling like a haar, 'making life "a tale told by an idiot", and a malevolent idiot at that'. There were weeks and even months on end when his days seemed 'a long tissue of boredom and meaninglessness', and even more acutely painful times when everything he looked at, thought about or touched, seemed 'suffused with anguish'.

Throughout these years, George relied on drugs – Valium and Limbritol – to help numb the mental pain; but his chief weapon in the face of depression continued to be his own steely self-discipline. 'True heroism,' he had once written to Stella, 'is to try to live this one day well, whatever the circumstances', and during these years George was a hero of day-to-day perseverance. However low his spirits, he kept up his working routine and in Stromness he shopped and chatted and saw

---

* George's enduring devotion to Nora was demonstrated in his will. He left her a life interest in 3 Mayburn Court, which he bought from the council in 1989.

old friends wearing a mask so effective that, to the end of his life, many who felt they knew him well remained unaware of what he was suffering. Neither Norrie's widow, Hazel Brown, nor George's brother Jackie knew anything of his depressive tendencies until after his death. Gerry Meyer, whose friendship with George dated back to the early days of the war, only once had an inkling of them. He had mentioned to George that he was feeling very low, and he was struck by the expression of pain and recognition that flickered across George's face in response.

Very occasionally, his mask slipped. In the summer of 1978, George was visited by Renée Simm, the retired proprietress of an Edinburgh art shop. She was twenty years his senior, and had written to him after picking up a copy of *Letters from Hamnavoe** in a station bookshop. They began to exchange weekly letters, and she travelled regularly to Orkney to see him. On one of these visits, she remembered calling in at Mayburn Court and finding George in the grip of a depression so agonizing that he was unable to sit still, but paced up and down the room, as his father had done, muttering that it would be best if he ceased to exist. 'All / Life death does end,' Gerard Manley Hopkins had written, casting about for comfort in one of his dark sonnets. Repeatedly during these years, in poems like 'Countryman' and 'Bird in the Lighted Hall',† George too dwelt on the briefness of life.

Depression was fuelled by feelings of guilt. Ever since he was a teenager, George had been troubled, periodically, by the groundless but persistent sense of wrongdoing that he explores in the character of Mrs McKee. His affair with Nora Kennedy aggravated this. George's writing reflects contradictory feelings about sexual expression. On the one hand, he seems to envy, and approve of, characters who live unfettered by restraint or scruple. The sadness he feels for lives that are lonely and loveless – for spinsters 'shedding / Shadow from flesh, until / With a last seedless sift / The dark bridegroom has his will' – is palpable. On

---

*In the summer of 1974, Brian Murray, Adviser in English to Ayrshire Education Committee, had persuaded George to publish a collection of his weekly pieces for the *Orcadian*. *Letters from Hamnavoe*, published by Gordon Wright, appeared in 1975. It was followed by two further collections: *Under Brinkie's Brae* (1979) and *Rockpools and Daffodils* (1992).
†Both in *Voyages* (1983).

the other hand, he had a profound feeling for the virtue of chastity. In *Magnus*, he had written of the dangers of 'lust unsanctified and uncreative', binding those who indulge in it 'upon a wheel of torment that will carry them down into uttermost burning depths'. After his relationship with Nora began, though he continued to go to Mass in Kirkwall every Sunday – sitting on the end of the back pew, near the door, to quell his agoraphobia – George ceased to receive Communion. Relations with the Jesuit parish priest, Father Herbert Bamber, a man for whom he felt fondness and respect, became strained. Letters to friends, meanwhile, conveyed a sense of self-loathing: 'The sun is flashing off the snow on to the back of my head as I sit writing in the kitchen,' he tells Roger Harris on 3 February 1979, 'and all that brightness makes me feel what a filthy creature I am.'

At moments like this, George longed to run away. In the autumn of 1979, he received a letter inviting him to spend the following summer as writer-in-residence at Melbourne University. He had had many invitations of this kind, and had always dismissed them out of hand: Newbattle, he insisted, was the only place where he would ever consider taking up a residency. This letter reached him at such a low ebb, however, that he seriously considered moving for a time to Australia. Again and again, he toyed with the idea of writing to the Abbot of Pluscarden, a Benedictine monastery in Morayshire, to ask whether he might come and live as part of the community for a year: sealed off in a monastic cell, he felt, he might finally 'face the truth' about himself. And often, in his letters to Dr Michael Curtis in London, he talked of his need for a long break from Orkney – 'so that I can learn to see things in wholeness and harmony again'. But he did nothing about it, and his inaction became a further source of self-reproach.

In fairness, it was not easy for George to leave Orkney. He was still suffering, periodically, from agoraphobia, and he was not in good health. Every winter brought severe bronchial problems. In the spring of 1981, he was admitted to the Balfour Hospital in Kirkwall with fluid on the lungs, and his condition was considered so serious that he was given the Last Sacraments by Father Bamber. He remained in hospital for two weeks, and the warmth and company and routine did much to lift his spirits. 'Everyone here is so utterly kind and compassionate,' he wrote to Renée Simm on 23 March, 'and even the constant stir and

hum, like a beehive, sounds cheerful and friendly compared to that
sterile little cell I inhabit at Mayburn Court.' Out of hospital he went
to convalesce first with his sister-in-law Hazel Brown, and then with
the MacInneses. Back at home, however, his spirits quickly began to
sink. His illness had left him apathetic. 'Laziness is my constant companion these days,' he wrote to a friend in April, 'and she is accompanied often by her dark sister Depression.' June brought the St Magnus
Festival, and he was overwhelmed by the number of strangers who
knocked at his door. 'It becomes a burden,' he admitted, 'when all
one's body and mind are crying out, "Rest! – let me rest!" '

The festival was something of an annual trial to George, bringing
to the fore all his old prickly suspicion of 'culture' and its devotees,*
but, while he never himself gave a public performance, he arranged
every year for fellow poets to come north and read from their work.
In the summer of 1982, Seamus Heaney travelled to Orkney and
recited his poetry to a packed audience in the Pier Arts Centre in
Stromness. Although Heaney did not stay at Mayburn Court, George
was, in effect, his host: he introduced Heaney to the Bevans and to
the photographer Gunnie Moberg. He drank with him, and arranged
that he should be taken out by Ian MacInnes's daughters to walk
around the Ring of Brodgar in the midnight sun. 'I had the time of
my life,' he says, looking back. But, just as in Belfast more than a
decade earlier, he was aware of great privacy, and even pain, beneath
George's courtesy: 'There's something that Ted Hughes said once that
seems to me to apply very purely to George. Hughes said that poetry
derived from the place of ultimate suffering and decision in us, and
despite George's social sweetness and his geniality and kindness and
deference as a social creature, you did recognise that there was solitude there . . . that there was a place of suffering and decision.'

Suffering there certainly was. On 24 June, as the festival came to an
end and Heaney headed home, George unburdened himself in a letter
to Dr Curtis.

---

* 'Tonight, alas, a meeting of the St Magnus Festival Committee at Hopedale,' George
writes to Kulgin Duval on 25 March 1982. 'They go on so long! If it wasn't for
Archie's ale, I think I'd begin to scream.' And to the author, on 25 June 1992, 'The
St Magnus Festival finished last night – I almost breathed a sigh of relief as too much
kultur [sic] throws me off stride, and I can't do my own work.'

> Some days I go around feeling like suicide – only I'm too much of a coward to do anything against myself. But it's as if life was a drained honeycomb – there's no sweetness or relish or joy anywhere; and every thought is like a thorn.

Suicide may never have been a real possibility for George, but there were times when he sought comfort by toying in his imagination with the notion of ceasing to exist. At the beginning of 1979, he had started work on a play. His plan was to trace the adventures of a nameless girl as she moved mysteriously through time and space, with a mission to search out and cancel the root of human conflict before atomic war destroyed the world. After working on it for some time, he decided that the play should in fact be a novel, and four years later he completed *Time in a Red Coat*. The story begins with the birth of a princess in China at the time of the Mongol invasion. Never appearing to grow old, she travels westward, seeking out the 'dragon' of war, armed only with a flute and a bag of coins. ('The flute,' George explained in an article in *The Independent*, 'symbolises the healing power of art – the small treasure for the proper alleviation of suffering.') The more conflict the girl encounters, the more her white coat becomes stained red and black, and yet at every episode in her journey through the centuries she meets a child – 'a sweet, pure promise that indeed all shall be well'. Finally, she comes to Orkney, and grows old at last.

Time in a Red Coat was, George realized, 'more a sombre fable than the novel that people expect to read nowadays', and it was not an enormous success either critically or commercially. George, however, remained proud at least of parts of it. After the book was published, he admitted that the chapter that gave him the greatest satisfaction was one in which a soldier, hideously wounded, lies one night in a pigsty on the outskirts of a burning village, choosing, in his deep subconscious, whether to live or to die. Death, at first, seems the more seductive option but, as the night wears on, the soldier begins to 'ache' with sadness for all the good things that he must leave behind him. At dawn, on the point of dying, he decides to claw his way back to life.

In describing that long night, and the soldier's final decision to live, George was drawing on his own experiences. If depression is the keynote of his letters during these years, one is aware also of 'gleams and fragments of joy' penetrating the gloom, and of a recognition, even in the bleakest moments, that life is not without delight. 'I had an unpleasant experience this morning,' George writes to a friend on 11 June 1982. 'For weeks I've been channelling all my vague depressions into this novel, *Time in a Red Coat*. This morning the depression brimmed over and clogged mind and writing fingers. I said to a friend who came, "If Death was to come for me this afternoon, I'd give him a welcome". . . And yet, the ache of leaving the good things of life!'

For all his longing to run away, Orkney, and the turning seasons and changing weather, were unceasingly beguiling to George. He describes, in letters, his thrill at walking through Stromness on a freezing night under a sky alive with the Northern Lights – 'great shoots and ferns rooted in the north and reaching to the zenith', and the delight he finds in looking out of his kitchen window on a cold, still winter's morning – 'snow over Orkney, bright cracking frost. The clouds cargoed with more snow, moving through magnificent skies of blue and pale gold.' With the arrival of spring, his spirits lift: 'Isn't it lovely being in April?' he writes to a friend in 1982. 'The very word is one of the most beautiful sounds in the language.' And, two weeks later, 'It has been bitterly cold in Orkney for days, but yesterday and this morning were crowned with sunlight, and one's heart "dances with the daffodils".' In 1981, the Hogarth Press published *Portrait of Orkney*, a collection of photographs by Werner Forman accompanied by text in which George considers the islands in themed chapters – 'People', 'Land', 'Sea', 'Stone', 'Lore'. . . The book has none of the polemic of *An Orkney Tapestry* but George's passionate love of his surroundings remains intact.

Even in low spirits, meanwhile, George continued to read, and the discovery of new talent was a source of tremendous excitement to him. In 1978, at the age of eighty-two, Naomi Mitchison published her first collection of poetry, *The Cleansing of the Knife*. George thought it wonderful – 'passionate, earthy, beautifully wrought' – and for weeks afterwards, he was writing about it in letters, urging friends to read it. During the bitter last weeks of 1980, meanwhile, when he felt that the cold and darkness had frozen the sources of his own imagination, he discovered the work of Flannery O'Connor, the American novelist and short-story writer who had died aged forty in 1964. Her stories were tragic. 'One flinches from the awful inevitable cruelty of what's happening,' George wrote, 'at the same time as one is hugely impressed by the marvellous skill of the story-teller. I suppose – poor young woman – the shadow of sickness that darkened her life and finally blotted her out, inevitably made her tales so very sombre. Still, what a superb talent!'

For consolation, he returned again and again to his old favourites – Evelyn Waugh's *Brideshead Revisited*, Lytton Strachey's *Queen Victoria*, the novels of E. M. Forster and, above all, the novels of Thomas Mann. 'If ever I feel suicidal I will read Mann,' he had written to Roger Harris in the late sixties, 'for then I will no longer be a blind meaningless suffering cipher but a necessary stitch in a most amazing fabric.' Between 1976 and 1985, George reread *The Magic Mountain* three times.

Television, too, was a surprising source of comfort. For all his inveighing against it, George had installed a set in Mayburn Court, and it was so much a part of his life that when, in 1978, he was asked to prepare an entry for *Who's Who*, he slipped 'watching TV' between 'ale tasting' and 'reading' in his list of recreations. And, even if there is something in his argument that television had contributed to the breakdown of community life in Orkney, in his own case it drew him out of the confines of his imagination, and helped him to engage with a wider world. On Monday evenings George watched *Horizon*. He then liked to discuss the subjects covered in the programme – immunology, evolution, volcanoes – with his niece's scientist husband, Fraser Dixon. He enjoyed the afternoon quiz show *Countdown* and, in the spring of 1979, he was gripped by David Attenborough's *Life on Earth*. Three years later, in May 1982, he hardly moved from his television during Pope John Paul II's visit to Britain. George had warmed to Karol Wojtyla ever since his election as pope in 1978. He felt him to be a truly good man, and it appealed to him that, like Rognvald Kolson, nephew of Saint Magnus and founder of St Magnus Cathedral, this pope combined holiness with a love of climbing mountains, of skiing and, above all, of literature and poetry. As he watched John Paul II celebrate his open air Mass for 70,000 young people in a rugby stadium in Edinburgh, he was overwhelmed with happiness: 'Such radiance, such goodness. Old and decrepit as I am, I wanted to shout for joy like the kids at Murrayfield!'

A successful session at the Formica work surface in his kitchen could still, sometimes, give George the same sense of exuberance and exhilaration. When he believed that he was writing well, he told

Renée Simm, it was 'the most glorious feeling' that life could give. But this feeling was no longer to be relied upon. George had always been a fierce self-critic, constantly revising his poetry, and steadfastly refusing to permit the reprinting of poems to which he had taken a scunner – 'The Funeral of Ally Flett', for example – in subsequent collections of his poetry. During these years, his dissatisfaction with his own work became extreme. More often than not, he wrote, his writing had 'a taste of ashes'; and while, in the decade after his mother's death, new work by George had poured out of the Hogarth Press, his output in the ten years that followed was comparatively thin. In the spring of 1982, George posted to Norah Smallwood the collection of poetry that would eventually be published as *Voyages*.* In an internal note, the poet D. J. Enright, now a director of Chatto & Windus, registered his concern that the poems were not up to George's previous standards. The following year saw the publication of *Andrina*, George's fifth, and possibly weakest, collection of short stories.

In the early seventies the publication of a new book had lost its thrill for George; in the second half of the decade, it became a positive torment. His writing, once 'a pure seeking past a swarm of symbols', now seemed a means of avoidance and deception. He looked over his unpublished manuscripts with 'unease and almost despair'. As he explained in a letter to Hugo Brunner at Chatto, it was not simply that he believed his work was worthless – that, he could bear – but that he felt it to be in some way 'a pollutant'. The piles of poems and short stories sitting like shaggy haystacks around his living-room would become, if published, 'incriminating documents' to be used against him. Embedded in works already published, meanwhile, and particularly in his poems, were 'thorns', invisible to readers but infinitely painful to himself. What was at the root of these 'weird delusions', George could not say, but there were times when they possessed him so completely that he feared that his road was 'winding straight to the nut-house'.

It was not easy for George to admit to these feelings, and he did his best to make light of them – 'I am, most of the time, more a Sir Toby Belch than a Hamlet,' he assured Norah Smallwood. Between the

*Dedicated to Nora Kennedy.

lines, however, he sought Smallwood's reassurance that she had known other authors suffer in a similar way. This she was unable to give, but what she could and did offer George in response to his difficulties was sensitivity and a steady nerve. Friends like Kulgin Duval and Colin Hamilton had, from time to time, suggested to George that he would be better off with a more commercial publishing house, and with an agent. But amassing money, when he had few needs and no dependants, had always seemed futile to George, and during the late seventies and early eighties, when trouble struck, his loyalty to Norah Smallwood was amply repaid.

These were difficult years for Norah Smallwood, too. In 1979, she turned seventy. She was unwell and crippled with arthritis. Unable to countenance retirement, she clung on at Chatto & Windus and, to those who had to deal with her day to day and face to face, her unhappiness manifested itself in volatility and anger. To others in distress, however, and particularly to her authors, her own suffering enabled her to respond with sympathy and generosity. She made it clear to George that she would put no pressure on him to publish while the prospect unsettled him, but, at the same time, she urged him gently to try his hand at new forms. In 1977, she suggested he write an autobiography, and though he was adamant that this was something he would never do – an autobiography, he insisted, was nearly always the forging of a mask of self-flattery – she repeated the suggestion four years later. Even when proposing new projects, meanwhile, she managed to convey the fact that she cared about George's health and happiness more, even, than about his books. 'If ever anybody should not feel that nothing's worthwhile, it is you,' she wrote, when he was in the depths of a black depression at the beginning of 1980:

> Your contribution to other people's enjoyment is considerable, more than most, and I am not referring only to your writing. But I think it is one of the disadvantages of getting older. One does ask oneself all too often what's it all in aid of and what in the world has one achieved? . . . Do you find it's better when Spring comes to stay? Or does the simple beauty make it worse? It can be that way.

It is hard to overestimate the importance of correspondents like Smallwood in keeping George on the right side of morbidity and despair during these years. He had continued to set aside a whole day each week for letter-writing, and he had a clutch of correspondents, most of them women, with whom he kept in regular contact. His letters are neat, set out carefully on the page, with a wide margin to the left in which he added notes and reflections in the evening after they were written, before taking them to the post.

Many of his correspondents, like Dr Curtis, or Sister Margaret Tournour, a Sacred Heart nun and gifted wood engraver, George never set eyes on. With others, he exchanged letters for years before meeting them. This suited him well. He was, in his own view, 'no great shakes at talking'; but, gathering his thoughts 'slowly and considerately, on a blank sheet of paper', he found himself able to confide in strangers in a way he would almost certainly not have done in normal conversation.

Jenny Robertson, an Episcopal clergyman's wife and fledgeling poet, first wrote to George in 1977, to tell him how moved she had been by *Winterfold*. They began to exchange weekly letters, hers full of the hurly-burly of parish and family life, George's a series of sketches of the past week in Stromness. Amidst the news, they shared their private anxieties and sorrows – Jenny's over her teenage daughter, Aileen, a victim of early schizophrenia, George's about his depressions, and the strain of his relationship with Nora. They bolstered each other not only with practical advice and encouragement, but also with spiritual support. On 11 June 1982, George ends a letter to Jenny with the words written by Saint Thomas More to his daughter Margaret Roper on the eve of his execution: 'Pray for me, as I will for thee, that we may merrily meet in heaven' – adding, in the evening, in his revising pencil, 'But I hope we'll meet before that!' On 4 November he writes: 'I light a candle for you in my mind every day, when I remember to pray. Don't forget me either; I'll need them.'

There was, however, one correspondent for whom George reserved an openness and love that were unique. Whatever coolness had come between him and Stella Cartwright in the early seventies had, by the end of the decade, disappeared. From the autumn of 1977 onwards George was once again writing to Stella regularly, with warmth and conspiratorial affection. 'Some day,' he muses on 29 October 1977, 'we must publish, very privately and expensively, *Poems from GMB to*

SC . . . Then my other girl friends will tear the hair out of my head! But I don't care.'

George's involvement with Nora Kennedy must surely have played a part in rekindling his feelings for Stella. The fact that he was for a time, in the eyes of the world, coupled to Nora may have left him feeling less exposed to, and responsible for, Stella and her troubles, and therefore, paradoxically, freer to express love and compassion for her. As strains developed in his relationship with Nora, meanwhile, George began to idealize the memory of Stella, just as she had idealized him in the course of her affair with Sydney Goodsir Smith. Stella, in Edinburgh, spent much of her days now dwelling on memories of her time with George – 'especially the happy crazy carefree ones'. George's letters hint again and again at a wistful longing that somehow the two of them might turn back the clocks and rewrite their story with a happier ending. 'I wish we could meet,' he reflects on 13 October 1978, 'and put all our troubles in a heap on the table, then throw them out of the window and let the wind take them. Then we could start again, as clear as crystal!'

When they did meet, on George's infrequent sallies out of Orkney, what resulted was less a crystalline new beginning than a revisiting of old demons. In October 1979, George visited Renée Simm in Edinburgh and asked whether she might drive him to see a friend in Morningside. On the way, he asked her to stop the car outside a licensed grocer's: he wanted, he said, to buy a box of chocolates, and he emerged from the shop with a package tucked inside his jacket. Renée dropped him by the entrance to a basement flat, and arranged to meet him back at her own flat later in the afternoon. When George failed to appear, she went out to look for him. What had taken place during his meeting with Stella he did not reveal but, long after darkness had fallen, Renée found him wandering the streets in a daze – maudlin, drunk.

Stella was not always on the bottle. Periodically, with an enormous effort of will, and with the support of friends like Hugh Mackay, she checked herself in for a spell in the Andrew Duncan Clinic in Edinburgh. She had not lost her charm and charisma, and she enjoyed a kind of guru status among her fellow alcoholics. She would emerge from the clinic determined to start a new life. 'Home and *dry*,' she writes triumphantly to George after one visit. She had inherited her father's gift for painting, and George encouraged her to spend as much time as she could at her easel, and to make something of it. For a few weeks, her letters remain coherent and full of hope.

The hope never lasted long. Stella avoided admitting to George that she was drinking again, but her handwriting offers a clear index of her state: from being firm and strong, it becomes straggly, and often so illegible as to be indecipherable. Some letters are criss-crossed with shopping lists – 'Optrex, cat litter, cigs . . .' – others posted in envelopes so wildly addressed that it seems a miracle that they ever found their way across the Pentland Firth.

In the periods when she was drinking hard, it seemed even to those who most longed for Stella's happiness that in order to maintain a friendship there was nothing for it but to drink with her. In 1974, Hugh Mackay had moved from Edinburgh to work as a librarian in Hawick, but he remained a devoted friend to Stella and every weekend he travelled up by train to be with her. On Friday evenings and Saturdays they drank together, and then, amidst the tragedy of her life, Stella was able to recapture something of the gaiety and hilarity of earlier days: 'she never became less than herself' is how Mackay puts it, looking back. On Sundays, in preparation for work, he sobered up, tidied the flat and did some cooking to see Stella through the week.

Between Mackay's visits, Stella's life was bleak. She was almost entirely reliant on what she called 'Social Insecurity', and because of her neuritis she was often bedridden, and lonely. Like George, she sometimes feared that she was going mad; and, like George, she sometimes longed for oblivion. In one poem, written in early autumn, she describes lying at night listening to the leaves falling from the trees – 'Such happy, dying, lucky things'. In another, her loneliness is exacerbated by imaginary company:

> It seemed that there was
> Someone sounding
> At the window
> Last night.
>
> I thought it might be you
> It was only the wind.

Of those who had loved Stella in her Rose Street days, almost all had either moved away, or moved on. Stanley Roger Green remembers visiting her for the last time in 1974. He knocked on her door, and stood for some minutes waiting for a reply. As he was turning to leave, the door was opened and Stella, now in her late thirties, appeared on a Zimmer. 'The party was over,' he says.

Three people had remained loyal to Stella. John Broom had moved to Orkney in the early seventies, and had taken up the post of librarian in Stromness. He had long known that his desire to marry Stella would never be fulfilled, and he was scarcely in touch with her. In the mid-seventies, however, he bought a flat in Comiston Gardens, Edinburgh, in which he allowed her to live rent-free. Hugh Mackay not only continued to visit her at weekends but also paid Stella's heating and telephone bills. The telephone was a vital prop. When things were bad she would ring Mackay at all times of the day and night and pour out her anguish for hours on end.

And then there was George. For years, after leaving Edinburgh, he had encouraged Stella to believe that, just around the corner, a bright future awaited her. The painful, baffling experiences were just shadows, he urged; her 'real' life would soon begin. By the mid-seventies, it would have been not only futile but cruel to pretend that the tide would ever turn in her favour. Instead, in letters and poems, George consoled both Stella and himself with a belief that one day, in a better world, the two of them would be together. 'Some beautiful summer morning,' he wrote on 26 March 1981, when he was in hospital in Kirkwall, and Stella in a rehabilitation unit,

we will walk out among the dew and the roses and the birdsong . . .
Meantime, a little poem to cheer us both up.

Storms
Toss leaves, lives, loves.
Everlasting
Loom of darkness,
Let your shutters fall silent soon.
April will throw over us green light and golden light, the year's coat
of song.

Less than a year later, in January 1982, Stella was in hospital again. She was gravely ill with a viral infection, and the doctors were doubtful about her chances of recovery. George telephoned the hospital every day* and, fearing that this might be his last opportunity, poured his feelings into another acrostic poem for Stella's forty-fifth birthday:

So, once, in the 50s
There was this crazy chap, high among clouds,
Edinburgh-bound.
Laurel-seeking he was, out of Orkney.
Long and salt his throat
Among the stanzas that starred the howffs of Rose Street.

Could he not bide forever in that beautiful city?
A sweet girl, one day,
Rose, a star, to greet him.
To him, she was sweeter than rain among roses in summer,
While poets like columns of salt stood
Round the oak Abbotsford bar.
I, now
Going among the gray houses and piers of Stromness
Hear that voice made of roses and rain still; and see
Through the stormclouds, the remembered star.

It was, Stella wrote, the most precious gift she had ever received and the loveliest of all the poems George had written for her; but it was not the last. There were birthday acrostics again in 1983 and 1984. 'Some day,' George writes on 7 June 1984, 'we must print all Stella's birthday poems in a little book and launch it upon the world. Everyone will say, "They Liked Each Other More Than a Little" . . . They sure did, people, and still do.' His letters now were full of longing: longing for Stella as muse – 'Two days now of sun. I must go and sit at some pier, and watch the waves. I wish you could be there, on a fish-box, talking to me, through the sea music' – and longing simply for her company. 'The sun is weaving winter cloth-of-gold as hard as it can before the winter night comes down,' he writes late one

---

*After his own spell in hospital in the spring of 1981, he had been persuaded to install a telephone at 3 Mayburn Court.

afternoon in the autumn of 1984. 'Wish I could walk with you along the coast. I think of you every day, dear Stella, with love.'

George was now writing to Stella regularly, so it seems unlikely that the letter he posted to her at the Rehabilitation Unit of the Astley Ainslie Hospital on 16 November 1984 was his last; but it is the last that survives:

> Dearest Stella, I'm sending a few words from the wild windy Orkneys to my dear friend: hoping that she is warm and not feeling *too* low in that hospital . . .
>
> Nothing much happens to me, but words. I am like a spider making endless webs . . .
>
> But I am always thinking of you, dear Stella. May your good angel look after you well. Best regards to Jack, and Hugh.*
>
> To my Stella, much love,
> George xxx

Stella's mother, Winnie, had died suddenly earlier in the year. Jack Cartwright could now hardly bear to see his daughter. Hugh Mackay spent Christmas with Stella and then, through the early weeks of 1985, took the Friday evening train from Hawick to be with her in Edinburgh. He remembers nothing unusual about the weekend of 30–31 March. Early on the morning of Tuesday 2 April he received a telephone call. Stella had suffered a brain haemorrhage and had been found dead by her home help.

*Jack Cartwright and Hugh Mackay.

17

A New Star

All the sweet dear good things in life happen unexpectedly.
                    GMB, letter to Kenna Crawford, 1987

F OR HUGH MACKAY, the shock of Stella's death was overwhelming.
He thought of William Cory's 'Heraclitus':

> I wept as I remember'd how often you and I
> Had tired the sun with talking and sent him down the sky.

Stella's anguished telephone calls in the early hours of the morning
had sometimes tried him to the point of collapse, but the silence, now
that she was gone, seemed almost unendurable.

George appeared to fare better. He does not seem even to have considered travelling south with John Broom for Stella's funeral[*] and he
did not refer to her death either in letters or in conversations with
friends. His mask was adamantine.

Alone in the kitchen at Mayburn Court, however, he found himself
unable to write. To shift the block, and to help ease and clear things
in his own mind, he did what he had told Norah Smallwood he would
never do, and began to map out an autobiography. *For the Islands I Sing*
was not originally intended even for posthumous publication[†] and this
perhaps explains the uneven treatment that the book gives to the
various phases of George's life. The fifteen years between 1970 and
1985 are skimmed over in fewer than four pages. There is not so much

---

[*] The funeral took place on 5 April 1985 at Warriston Crematorium, in Edinburgh.
[†] On 16 May 1985, George writes in a letter to Kulgin Duval that he is working on
an autobiography – 'not for publication'.

as an oblique reference to Nora Kennedy. She and George remained close, though no longer, in any conventional sense, a couple.

By contrast, George dwells at some length on his feelings about education, about Gerard Manley Hopkins, about Catholicism, and about drink. Significantly more space is devoted to Stella Cartwright than to any other individual, and a celebration of the grace and radiance with which she had enlightened the lives of a whole generation of Scottish poets forms the heart of the book. 'Somewhere in the great music, she is lost,' George writes,

> but lost is the wrong word, of course. She wrote nothing herself, but what she truly was, her rare lovely unique essence, is a part of the literature of Scotland.
>
> May it be well with her, who loved and suffered so much.

From Stella's death onwards, there was a consciousness on George's part that his own end could not now be far off. 'One knows that one is growing older,' he writes in an essay commissioned in the spring of 1985, when he was sixty-three, 'but for a decade or so in middle age, time – that was a treasury to be squandered ignorantly in youth – is still no burden. Body and mind and spirit are still in accord. Then, quite suddenly, in the space of a year or so, one becomes aware of mortality.' Minor physical frailties began to accumulate. George's eyesight was failing, he suffered from gout – which led him to speculate wryly on the possibility of some unknown aristocratic ancestry – and from rheumatism. He was often breathless; he found it hard to sleep. In an early poem, he had written of 'the brightening/Blizzard of age', and mentally he was now troubled by a sense that, for all his years of solitude and pondering, he had little to offer by way of answers or certainties. 'Do you get wiser as you get older?' a BBC interviewer asks George in a programme made about his life in 1991. 'No,' he answers, unhesitating, and looking, for once, straight at the camera. 'You don't get wiser at all. You get a bit more disillusioned, I think, and that can be quite disconcerting.'

A great number of the friends who had meant most to George were now long gone. Driving through the parish of Rendall on a beautiful day in July 1977, Ernest Marwick, who had been suffering from depression, had swerved off a straight road and crashed fatally into a farm steading. One icy morning in February 1975, Charlie Senior had been found in his cottage, sitting dead at his desk. Attie Campbell had died in 1967: he had contracted cancer of the lip through mending tarry fishing-nets. 'Where are the never-to-be-forgotten friends that I drank with twenty years ago?' George asks. 'I go into a pub nowadays and sit alone over my beer.'

There is, however, quite another side to this gloomy picture. Reading through the hundreds of letters George wrote to friends in the last ten years of his life, the note of decline and dénouement is easily balanced by one of renewed vigour and appetite for life. Spurred on by the feeling that time was now short, he produced, during this decade, some of his most outstanding work. And, after the agonies of the previous ten years, he seems finally to have come to terms with the hand that providence had dealt him. When, in 1991, as his seventieth birthday approached, the *Scotsman* asked George for a poem, he was able at last to consider his life with equanimity:

> To have got so far, alone
> Almost to the seventieth stone
>   Is a wonder.
>   There was thunder
>
> A few miles back, a storm-shaken
> Hill and sea, the bridge broken
>   (The bright fluent
>   Burn a bruised torrent.)
>
> But all cleared, larks were singing
> Again, the April rain ringing
>   Across the sown hills,
>   Among the daffodils.
>
> The road winds uphill, but
> A wonder will be to sit
>   On the stone at last –
>   One star in the west.

'Alone', in the first line, is powerful; and alone, in a sense, George had remained. Yet he had been sustained along the way by an extraordinary capacity to draw strength and inspiration from other human beings, particularly from women, and this, in his last decade, did not desert him. One evening in the early spring of 1986, a girl called Kenna Crawford stepped unexpectedly into 3 Mayburn Court. 'I don't know what you did to me,' George wrote to her some time after that first meeting, 'but it was like opening new springs in my heart that I had thought to be long dried up. I have a great deal to thank you for.'

Kenna was twenty-seven, a friend of Nora Kennedy, and an artist, whose long childhood summers on the Hebridean island of Coll had given her a deep love of the natural world. She was unaffected, open-hearted and very beautiful. As George later admitted, when she first called on him he was 'confused at so much beauty coming suddenly into my house'. For Kenna, too, that first meeting was confusing. She had a sense that George Mackay Brown – whose work she had known from her schooldays – looked at her as if she was 'almost celestial', and she was not far wrong. Some months later, George sent her a poem, 'A Writer's Day: 21 April 1986'. It describes a poet toiling fruitlessly all day, so that at sunset he is sitting still before two blank pages. Then:

> The latch lifted. A stranger came in
> So beautiful
> She seemed to be a woman from the sea.

'I hope you like it, Kenna,' he wrote, 'it's about yourself. Why "21 April?" That's the day I first set eyes on you.'

Kenna had arrived in George's life almost exactly a year after Stella's death, and there were likenesses between the two women that went beyond the shape of their names. When, in his autobiography, George had described Stella as a girl with 'honey-coloured skin' and a 'sweep of bright hair', he could as easily have been writing about Kenna, and when Kenna first saw a photograph of Stella she was amazed and slightly unnerved by their physical similarity. Describing the effect that Kenna's visit had had on him, George uses precisely the same vocabulary he had used in writing about Stella: Kenna had 'brought a radiance' with her to Orkney, and 'left a rare sweetness and fragrance behind'. And, as he began to write poetry for Kenna, he returned repeatedly to the old stellar imagery. Kenna is, again and again, 'a star', even specifically, in one poem, 'A new star, sea-brimming, over the islands'. George never spoke about Stella to Kenna, but these parallels were not lost on him. Here was the woman that Stella might have been, free from the shadows of Rose Street and the curse of drink.

There was, however, more to Kenna's appeal than this. The day after their first meeting, she and George had lunch together in Nora's garden overlooking the sea. Reaching across the table and taking Kenna's sketchbook, George wrote an impromptu poem, 'Kenna's Return to Orkney'. He used 'return' in two senses. He hoped desperately that Kenna would visit again, and soon. 'Please, please come back,' he pleaded in a letter after she had left, and at the thought that he might never see her again he felt his heart flutter and sink. But he also believed that this first visit had been, in some sense, a homecoming:

> Now she has found a way
> From Edinburgh, back to the hills and seas
>   Of her people, and discovered
>   Seals on the shore, waiting . . .

Kenna Crawford had Orkney ancestry. Her paternal great-grandmother had been born and brought up on Hoy. Her grandmother had been called Isabella Budge: the same name that George had given one of his characters in *Greenvoe*. Kenna, George felt, had arrived in Orkney in response not just to an invitation from Nora Kennedy, but to a summons from the past. 'There's no doubt,' he writes to her on 17 May 1986, 'that your ancestors were waiting – have been, this long while – to welcome you. And would keep you, I'm sure, if they could.' And on 11 July, from Hoy: 'I think Rackwick has been waiting for you and for your sweetness and bonniness for a long time.' He encloses with this letter a blade of thatching grass, a buttercup, an eyebright and a sliver of stone from the wall of a ruined Rackwick croft. He felt, he explained to Kenna, that she belonged to Orkney, and Orkney to her. George had often written of his belief in the unity of creation – 'We and earth and sun and corn are one'. Kenna Crawford, with her elemental beauty, seemed an embodiment of this belief:

> . . . That dear one
> Is gold of our corn,
> She's Orkney's rain and spindrift . . .

As soon as Kenna departed, George began to write to her regularly. In November 1986, he invited her to be his guest of honour at a dinner in Edinburgh given by the Scottish Arts Council to celebrate his sixty-fifth birthday. He was not much looking forward to the occasion, but with Kenna at his side – 'one flower in that garden of intellectual thorns' – the evening would be transformed for him. To George's irritation, when the evening came, he and Kenna were seated at different tables. He wrote her a tiny poem on his place card, and delivered it to her the following morning.

It might have been overwhelming for a girl in her twenties to receive such attention from a famous, elderly poet, but Kenna from the start felt completely at ease in George's company. 'I simply saw him as a dear friend,' she says, looking back. 'And although he expressed his love for me very clearly in his letters, somehow I never felt under any pressure to reciprocate.' Her replies to George's letters were unselfconscious and uncomplicated, full of news about her life in Edinburgh. Sometimes she enclosed little drawings of seals, or photographs of places she loved. Into one letter she folded the feather of a golden eagle.

Just before Christmas 1986, Kenna left to spend a year in New Zealand. In the months that followed, George continued to write to her at least once a week. Distance made him, if anything, less tentative in his expressions of love:

> Many a day I feel lonely, thinking of you – I have a pang at the heart and a catch at the breath, remembering how beautiful you are and how moved I was – and am still, and will be always – by the mere sight of you in Orkney 18 months ago, and your words and gestures; and how it set my whole being trembling, with love and hope and delight . . . I'd thought those feelings were dead in me long ago, blown away like old dust of roses. And then you come on the scene, Kenna Crawford, and there's a marvellous quickening of roots in the earth again.

'All my love', his letters end; or 'Yours forever'; or 'My love for always, George xxxxxxx'.

Kenna, travelling around New Zealand and living out of the back of a van, was not easily able to reply, but her letters, when they came, brought George ecstatic delight:

> What happiness yesterday in this house! I had to go to Kirkwall to do a small recording at Radio Orkney. When I came back, there was a big

letter waiting with New Zealand stamps on it. O dear dear dear Kenna, what joy to read it! Those beautiful photos – I fell in love with you all over again. I was so very happy I could have danced and sung – I think maybe I did, a few steps, a few bars . . . It was so lovely of you to write – it was worth all the long winter of waiting. I look and look at the pictures and my heart spills over with delight . . . I will treasure them always – and your very sweet kind beautiful letter. (Don't be shy about the way you write – it's good and suits you – and I can sense the true gold underneath . . .)

Spurred on by the image of Kenna, and a longing to make beautiful things for her, George was now writing more furiously than ever. He had only to think of Kenna and the power flowed to his pen. She drew poems from him 'like a snake-charmer bringing a cobra out of a basket'. She was a source of 'pure inspiration', a muse more powerful even than Stella. 'I have to thank you for filling my lamp of verse with oil continually, though you're so far away,' he writes on 12 May 1987. 'No woman has ever been so good to me in this way before.'

A small clutch of verses in *The Wreck of the Archangel* is officially dedicated to Kenna, but many other poems, not only in this collection but also in the posthumously published *Travellers* and *Northern Lights*, were originally written for her and posted to New Zealand. Other poems enclosed in Kenna's letters from George have never been published. On 7 March 1987, he described for her a dream in which he had been visited by every lovely woman he had ever known. It ends:

> They come to me in sleep
> These women, all. I dreamed
> That, weeping, I folded two wintered hands.
>
> At daffodil time came Kenna.
> Her kiss
> Opened the door to the corn and the honeycombs.

There was one piece of work, however, that George kept to himself. On 1 May 1987, he wrote a poem about a worthy, dependable Hamnavoe merchant who confounds his island community by committing suicide. Looking through the shop ledgers to try to discover the cause of the merchant's despair, a fellow townsman finds that in the entry for 1 May the neat handwriting falters, and among the meticulous lists of deliveries and sales there is the beginning of a description of a girl of extraordinary beauty who has passed the shop window in the early morning:

> . . . He thought,
> Turning the last blank pages
>   How a dry stick
>
> Must have quickened that May morning
> And dared not disclose the madness
> But launched out secretly, at sunrise
>   Under a star, to bury the rose
>   In salt chasms beyond Hoy.

George was aware that his love for Kenna was a kind of 'madness' and that eventually his feelings for her would have to be buried. Despite this, the thought of her filled him not with despair, like the merchant's, but with an energy and *joie de vivre* that spilled over into every area of his life and work.

In June 1987, while Kenna was still in New Zealand, Gunnie Moberg persuaded George to travel to mainland Scotland for her son Colin's wedding in Nairn. The previous spring, George had been asked to write something to mark the 850th anniversary of the founding of St Magnus Cathedral. He set to work on the text for a *son et lumière* tracing the unfolding of events after Magnus's martyrdom in 1117: the miracles that clustered about him as the poor of Orkney and Shetland brought their sufferings to his burial spot, his canonization, and the building over centuries of St Magnus Cathedral, the 'great ship of stone' that was to carry Orcadians through history with Magnus at their helm. *A Celebration for Magnus* was performed on 20 August 1987, the feast-day of Saint Rognvald, founder of the cathedral. It was then lavishly published, with photographs by Gunnie Moberg and Giles Conacher, Benedictine monk and Guest Master at Pluscarden Abbey, and paintings by an artist friend of George, Simon Fraser.

It was Simon Fraser with whom George stayed for the wedding of Gunnie's son Colin McPhail, and one afternoon he, George and Gunnie visited Pluscarden. For George, who so rarely left Orkney, to meet a monk living under a vow of stability* was, as Father Giles reflects, 'an event so unlikely that the odds against its happening were like those against a random DNA match; but happen it did'. George had long dreamed about Pluscarden as a place where he might find silence and tranquillity, but the mood that afternoon was more hilarious than contemplative. Father Giles brought out a sponge cake so delicious that the four of them ate the whole thing at one sitting. He and Gunnie then embarked on competitive joshing about the difficult circumstances in which they worked as photographers. Gunnie had no darkroom but her kitchen, and developed her photographs in the sink; Giles Conacher had not even a sink but a biscuit tin. George stood by, greatly amused. He enjoyed others' sparring, and had an impish gift for encouraging it while saying very little. As they drove away, Father Giles was left with the impression of a man 'lovable, simple, open' – 'fully Christian, fully cultured and fully human'.

At the party after Colin's wedding the following day, flushed with drink and delight, George led Gunnie in an unsteady but glorious waltz around the marquee. When the music stopped, he confessed that it was the first time in his life that he had danced.

In the autumn of 1987, Kenna returned from New Zealand, and before Christmas she went to spend a month at 3 Mayburn Court. During the day, while George worked, Kenna wandered on the beaches, and in the evening she returned with shells and fossils which she laid out on the living room floor. She cooked for George, and introduced small changes to his domestic routine. He had always washed his hair in Fairy Liquid; she bought him his first bottle of shampoo. She slept in the small spare bedroom, and, physically, she and George got no closer than holding hands; but in Stromness there were raised eyebrows. George revelled in this. He drew on it five years later when, in his novel *Beside the Ocean of Time*, he described the gossip that crepitates among island women when Sophie, 'a beautiful girl, with a great mass of golden hair', steps off the ferry one spring

*Benedictine novices take three vows before they are received as monks – of stability, conversion of life, and obedience. The vow of stability binds them for life to a single monastic community.

morning, and ensconces herself for some weeks at the manse with the elderly bachelor minister, the Revd Hector Drummond.

If she wasn't a niece, who could she be? She was too young to be his sister, surely. A shiver of excitement went through the island women. There was only one explanation – Mr Drummond's fiancée! They were engaged to be married. Soon there would be a lady at the Manse. 'And not before time. He'll be decently turned out. He'll get a bit of solid flesh on his bones. The dirty Manse windows'll be shining soon. The roses and lupins in the garden will bloom like they used to do in Mrs Abernethy's time . . .'

But a few of the younger women weren't all that pleased. Maybe one or two of them had had hopes of being the lady of the Manse.

But if she wasn't a niece, what was she doing staying unchaperoned up there with a bachelor minister? It wasn't right, surely . . .

Tina Lyde wondered whether somebody oughtn't to write to the General Assembly about it – or at least to the Presbytery in Kirkwall.

George felt bereft when Kenna departed. 'It's as if someone had broken a beautiful lamp and the house is all darkling and cold,' he wrote to her. 'Every time I open the door of that upstairs room, it seems to cry, "What about Kenna?" . . . "Where is she?" . . . "We miss her so very much".' A faint note of foreboding entered his letters: 'I think of you often, dear Kenna,' he writes on 17 January 1988, 'perhaps too much for my own good. All the same, nothing but good has come of it so far . . .'

Sometime later that year, Kenna met her future husband, Graham McGirk. In the spring of 1991, they were married. George liked Graham, and expressed his affection for him in a joint acrostic poem written for their wedding. Thereafter, the three of them stayed in touch by telephone. The letters, however, all but ceased. Some day, George had once told Kenna, he would add a verse chapter to his autobiography describing how she had arrived in Stromness and 'transfigured everything'. That chapter was never written. When, in 1993, he wrote an appendix to his autobiography, Kenna Crawford was not mentioned.

Yet Kenna's effect on George's life was profound and enduring. She had not only inspired him poetically, but had helped to shift the psychological block he had felt about seeing his work in print. After her arrival in George's life, he never once referred to this again, and during his last decade he published more work than in any other.

Norah Smallwood did not live to see George recover his nerve. She had died in 1984, leaving Carmen Callil as managing director of Chatto & Windus. Andrew Motion was appointed poetry editor the following year. Hugo Brunner, out of step with the new regime, had left to join the publishing firm of John Murray in 1985, and George was content to follow him there. George's value to Chatto & Windus had always been more literary than financial, and Callil was not inclined to stand in his way. 'Let him go if he wants to,' she scribbled in an internal note to Motion. 'I don't mind.'

The Golden Bird: Two Orkney Stories, dedicated to Kenna Crawford and published in the autumn of 1987, was George's first John Murray publication. The title story traces the slow decline of an island community living in a sea valley – unmistakably, though not explicitly, Rackwick – in the last quarter of the nineteenth century. The cohesion of the community is undermined not only by new values, and the introduction of compulsory education, but by stubborn private enmity. In the opening pages, the wives of two fishermen, Amos of Gorse and Rob of Feaquoy, fall out over the division of a haul of lobster. The lobsters in dispute scrabble about on the hot stones and are dead by sundown; but the squabble between the women of Gorse and Feaquoy grows into a feud that festers down three generations.

Despite the simplicity of the story, and its Orkney setting, Dennis O'Driscoll was not alone in recognizing *The Golden Bird* as the work of a master craftsman, touching on themes of universal significance. 'I know I could never produce fiction when I watch someone of your skills at work,' O'Driscoll wrote to George on 30 August 1987. 'It's like watching a thatcher! You are an enthralling story-teller but, after the story is told, one discovers that it is being retold in one's mind. For example, the lingering bitterness in the title story kept reminding me of Ulster and how impossible attempts at reconciliation have proved there.' Reviewers, too, applauded George's achievement; and in 1988 *The Golden Bird* was awarded the James Tait Black Memorial Prize.

The Golden Bird was followed, in the autumn of 1989, by the publication of *The Wreck of the Archangel*. George's first collection of poetry for six years gave Peter Levi, reviewing it in the *Catholic Herald*, 'hope for poetry and for the language'. Is poetry a fraud? George asks in the introduction. 'Or is it a quest for "real things" beyond the sea-glitters and shadows on the cave wall? I hope, very much, the latter.' The anxiety he had once expressed to Nora Kennedy that he was a charlatan dealing in a world of 'shadows and figments' had not completely left him, but it had greatly diminished. And it is 'real things' that George deals with in this collection, though in his hands they acquire a strange and fabulous edge.

The title poem is inspired by the true story of the wreck of a Russian ship off the island of Westray in the 1730s. George pictures the islanders safe in their crofts as a storm begins to brew:

> . . . In the dregs of sun
>   Westraymen had drawn high the yawls.
>   They fed their byred lantern-lit cows.
>
> Indoors, women tended the different flames
> Of lamp and hearth. The old ones chanted again
>   Mighty tempests of foretime.
>   The children tumbled gently into sleep.

The wind makes them deaf to the screams and sounds of splintering wood on the rocks below and, by the time they discover the wreck, they believe at first that all on board have been lost; but they are wrong:

> A man listens. This can't be! – One thin cry
> Between wavecrash and circling wolves of wind,
>   And there, in the lantern pool
>   A child's face, a dwindling, in seaweed tassels.

The infant lifted from the wreckage that night is said to have been lashed to the body of his mother. He was too young even to know his name. When the ship's sternpost was washed ashore some days later, however, it became clear that her port of registration had been Archangel, and the crofters who had given the boy a home christened him Archie Angel. He remained on Westray for the rest of his life:

> The seventy ploughtimes, creeltimes,
>   Harvests of fish and corn,
>   His feet in thrall always
>   To the bounteous terrible harp.

Archie married a local girl, Jean Drever, and there were Angels on the island until well into the nineteenth century.

The Wreck of the Archangel gave George an opportunity to bring to a wider public work that had previously appeared in privately printed limited editions. In 1985, he had begun work on *Stone*, a series of poems written in response to close-up photographs taken by Gunnie Moberg on walks along the Orkney shore:

> Who knows the stone music,
> One grain removed
> From silence? Hidden in that hardness
> A stone angel touches a string.

While working on these poems, George had received a letter from Charles Booth-Clibborn, a 22-year-old history student at Edinburgh University. Booth-Clibborn had an interest in fine printing, and had conceived the idea of producing a Scottish equivalent of the bestiaries printed in England and Wales in the Middle Ages. He wondered whether George might provide him with a text. To his amazement, within less than a month of his writing to George, Booth-Clibborn received through the post a bulging recycled envelope from Stromness containing nineteen poems about Scottish animals, both mythical and real, including two legendary Orcadian beasts, the Nucelavee and the Stoor-worm. Armed with these, he was able to persuade the artists John Bellany, Steven Campbell, Peter Howson, Jack Knox, Bruce McLean, June Redfern and Adrian Wiszniewski to provide illustrations for what became one of the biggest post-war private-printing projects undertaken in Scotland. *The Scottish Bestiary* was published by the Paragon Press in 1986.

George's response to his request, says Booth-Clibborn, was 'extraordinary – an almost unbelievable act of faith in a complete stranger'. But, on George's part, it had been entirely typical. More than ever, during his last decade, he welcomed all commissions, regardless of remuneration, or of whether the people requesting work were known to him. Writing had become like a drug, he told Jenny Robertson; without a daily 'shot' he felt miserable. He enjoyed the discipline of working to order, and to deadlines, and, as always, he was driven by a sense of guilt: 'I think of the marvels, beauties, and joys of the world that have passed me by and that now I can never celebrate, and the pen shrivels in my hand. So little has been achieved.'

Perhaps it was this sense of time running short, and of opportunities missed, that gave George a desire not only to celebrate the world but, finally, to see a little more of it. 'Old men ought to be explorers,' T. S. Eliot had believed, and George, in his last years, was more an explorer than ever before. In the spring of 1988, Gunnie Moberg began to make preparations to take him to Shetland for twelve days' holiday with Kulgin Duval and his partner Colin Hamilton. In his youth, working on the *Orkney Herald*, George had sailed once to Lerwick to report on a football match, and ever since he had longed to return. The Shetland islands were similar to Orkney in their lore and history, and to that extent familiar, but they were also wilder, and retained more of their Norse character. More than once, George had planned to revisit them, but always his nerve had failed him at the last moment, and when, on 28 May 1988, the eve of his departure with Gunnie, he was struck down by a cold, he acknowledged that this was almost certainly psychosomatic. Gunnie was having none of it. The following evening, as planned, they boarded the ferry *St Sunniva* at Stromness pier, and headed off on the eight-hour journey north through a thickening sea haar.

The Shetland holiday was an unalloyed success. George relished the company of Kulgin Duval, with his boundless energy, irreverent wit and insatiable curiosity about new people and places, more than that of any other male friend; and Colin Hamilton was a formidably good cook. Gunnie took complete practical command, leaving George free to rest, write and read in the rented house overlooking St Magnus Bay: 'The luxury,' he wrote, 'of stretching out in this comfortable bed, with *The Periodic Table*, in the long light of a summer evening'. By day, they travelled not only all over mainland Shetland, but to many of the smaller islands – islands with 'end-of-the-world' names like Vaila, Vementry, Yell and Unst – whose barbarous beauty took George's breath away. Orkney, he was forced to admit, had nothing to compare with this scenery and, a week after returning to Stromness, he remained dazzled. 'I am still brimming over with happiness on account of that most wonderful of holidays,' he wrote to Duval. 'Every day we were thrown a new jewel. I'll never never forget it.'

Gunnie Moberg had a gift for enabling George to overcome his fear of new experiences, and to throw caution to the winds. She had, George once wrote, 'the kind of temperament on which fortune smiles', and in her company he was prepared to trust that fortune would smile on him too. Emboldened by the success of their visits to Nairn and to Shetland, George raised no objections when Gunnie mooted the idea of a third and more daring adventure. Hugo Brunner had long urged George to come and stay with him in Oxford, and in mid-June 1989, having travelled from Stromness to Duval's home in Perthshire, George and Gunnie boarded a sleeper to Euston.

The journey south was interesting, and fraught. In a sense, Gunnie remembers, George assumed the role of guide, talking with authority as they passed through Newcastle, Durham, York. He had absorbed so much through his reading that he seemed to know these places better than she. At the same time, he was wary of every aspect of the Intercity train, and particularly alarmed by the folding, semi-automated lavatory doors. At bedtime, he took a sleeping pill, but a notice above the tap in his compartment advised that the water was not for drinking, and the pill remained lodged in his throat. He had no idea that there was a blind for his window, and throughout the night railway lights flashed across his face. By the time Hugo Brunner met the train, George was parched and weary. It was a beautiful Saturday morning and, with most of London still asleep, they drove to see the Cenotaph, Westminster Bridge, Big Ben, Hyde Park. Outside Buckingham Palace, Gunnie took George's photograph. He stood against the palace railings with a dazed expression, clinging to a carrier bag from Argo's Bakery in Stromness.

At Hugo Brunner's house in north Oxford George quickly recovered. On his first afternoon, elections were being held for the new Professor of Poetry, and he walked into the centre of the city to watch Brunner cast his vote.* Peter Levi, the retiring professor, spotted George

*Oxford poetry professors are, unusually, elected by graduate members of the university, and serve a five-year term. The poets running for election in 1989 were Seamus Heaney, Peter John King, Duncan William McCann, C. H. Sisson and Benjamin Zephaniah. To George's great delight, the winner, by a clear majority, was Seamus Heaney.

standing in the shadows of the Hall of Congregation. 'He was a formidably craggy elderly hairpin of a man,' Levi later wrote. 'Of everything I saw that day, his face is the only unforgettable experience.'

News of George's journey south had spread, and Sue MacGregor travelled to Oxford to interview him for BBC Radio 4's *Conversation Piece*. Ten years earlier, he mused, filing his weekly column for the *Orcadian* from Brunner's drawing room, an interview of this sort would have been as much of a torture to him as sitting in the electric chair; now, he found it not only acceptable but even stimulating. He also agreed, one evening, to talk to the sixth-formers at St Edward's School in Oxford – not about his own work, of course, but about the poetry of Edwin Muir. Again, he enjoyed himself. 'Hello, boys and girls' was the surprising greeting he offered his teenage audience, and from that moment on they were captivated. Something unique took place in the hour that George was in the school, David Christie, Warden of St Edward's, later reflected. None of those present, Christie believed, would ever forget the extraordinary atmosphere this shy Orkneyman had created, or the deep, respectful silence as he left the room.

Between these events, George wandered in and out of the colleges in the June sunshine. He went to evensong in New College, and travelled out one morning to Littlemore where John Henry Newman had stayed for a while with devoted friends, sifting for the last time through his religious feelings before becoming a Catholic. Two nuns took George to see Newman's austere room and the small chapel where he had been received in 1845 by Father Dominic Barberi the Passionist. He was deeply moved.

George had often imagined Oxford, the 'Cuckoo-echoing, bell-swarmèd, lark-charmèd, rook-racked, river-rounded' city so beloved of Gerard Manley Hopkins, and he had timed his visit to coincide with the centenary of Hopkins's death. In the Bodleian Library, he pored a long while over manuscripts of Hopkins's poems – 'unlike poems written in English before, or ever will be again, so daring and revolutionary they are in imagery and technique'. On the centenary itself, he visited St Aloysius's, the church where Hopkins had briefly served as curate in 1878–9. George had sensed Hopkins's spirit – 'sweet', 'eager', 'welcoming'– almost everywhere he turned in Oxford, but he felt it 'especially there in that little church . . . at evening Mass'.

The following day, George and Gunnie began their homeward journey. Gunnie had been aware, in arranging this trip south, that George minded more than he generally let on about being typecast as the writer who hardly left Orkney, and who had never been to London. As their train pulled out of King's Cross, she felt that his relief at heading north was coupled with a small sense of triumph.

18

Content with Silence

Death, critics say, is a theme that nags through my work: the end,
the darkness, the silence. So it must be with every serious artist,
but still I think art strikes out in the end for life, quickening, joy.
The good things that we enjoy under the sun have no meaning
unless they are surrounded by the mysterious fecund sleep.

GMB, 'A Writer in Orkney'

WHO KNOWS WHAT further adventures George might have
enjoyed, had his health not begun to fail him? Less than a
month after getting home from Oxford, in July 1989, he was diagnosed with bowel cancer, and was flown almost immediately to
Foresterhill, a hospital on the outskirts of Aberdeen. George received
the news that he had cancer calmly. Serious illness had accompanied
him for so much of his life that it had, perhaps, lost its terror. 'I have
no thought of dying as yet,' he wrote to his friend Roger Harris from
his hospital bed on 7 August, and he was optimistic that his illness
might even stimulate his imagination and 'pattern-making faculty'.
When the poet Tom Scott, also suffering from cancer, wrote from
Edinburgh to recommend a special diet to help combat the disease,
George's reply was grateful, but firm: 'I have a kind of thinking that
says, "Ignore illness, live as though you don't even want to fight it".'

Ignoring his illness became difficult. In April 1990, what was to
have been a routine check-up at Foresterhill resulted in two major
operations. Because of George's history of TB and chronic bronchitis, these were fraught with risk, and he was warned that he might not
survive them. Peter and Betty Grant, who visited George daily, were
with him as he was wheeled into the operating theatre. 'I just want

you to know, dear,' George told Betty, 'that my will is with the Bank of Scotland.' The operations were successful, but traumatic, and recovery was complicated by a cluster of infections. George told Paddy Hughes, who came to visit him, that, if any further surgery were thought necessary, he intended to refuse it. 'He was,' says Hughes, 'ready to turn his face to the wall.'

George remained in hospital until late June. To stave off depression, and to express his gratitude to the surgeons, doctors and nurses who were caring for him, he worked on a sequence of eighteen poems, *Foresterhill*. Forty years earlier, on his first prolonged stay out of Orkney, George had eased his homesickness by contemplating the Cistercian roots of Newbattle Abbey. Now, through his poetry, he imagined that Foresterhill, too, had monastic origins; that, where a vast modern hospital sprawled, there had once been nothing more than a clearing in a pine forest, a hut, a well, a hearthstone, and two monks,

> One with healing in his hands
> One with a psalter interleaved with herbs.

George portrays the sick and war-weary and footsore flocking to the little infirmary; and the monastic community growing. But the monks he conjures up can treat more than just physical ills. They understand anguish, and loneliness,

> And the bitter fruit of the selfhood of each man –
> Shame, regret, fear, sorrow, rage.

Foresterhill is not just a hospital, in fact, but

> A waiting room for the poor soul
> Before it whispers for entrance at the door of purification.

At midnight, a monk keeps watch on the road outside the monastery, holding a lantern, lest 'a soul go past bereft and weeping'.

Interviewed in the *Scotsman* shortly after coming out of hospital, George reflected on his feelings about death. It was something he had thought about a great deal, he said, but he was not afraid of it. The knowledge that the time left to him might now be very short heightened his appreciation of life, and particularly his pleasure in the company of friends. Home from Foresterhill, looking gaunt and grey, he slipped comfortably back into his old routine. His niece Allison Dixon had moved to a farm at Kirbuster, three miles from Stromness, and every Monday afternoon her husband Fraser collected George and drove him out there for tea. On Fridays, he had lunch with Archie and Elizabeth Bevan.

In 1987, Brian Murray, the retired Ayrshire headmaster who had persuaded George to publish *Letters from Hamnavoe* and *Under Brinkie's Brae*, had moved to Mayburn Court. Every morning, he called in on George and lit his fire. And at least once a week the redoubtable Renée Simm, now in her nineties, swept down into Stromness in her Citroën 2CV, and whisked George up to her cottage above the town for some French cuisine and an afternoon of dozing and chatting in front of her fire. Renée, who had finally moved to Stromness in 1983, shortly after her eighty-second birthday, had lived for some weeks in the youth hostel while overseeing the refurbishment of a derelict croft. She was a powerful character – too powerful for some. But George had always enjoyed the company of strong women, and there were elements of Renée that were reminiscent both of Willa Muir and of Norah Smallwood. 'She has the heart of a lion,' he wrote to a friend, Dr Jean Kay, and in a letter to Sister Margaret Tournour he marvelled at her 'seemingly bottomless well of hope'.*

Perhaps, also, as with Nora Kennedy, the fact that Renée was essentially foreign to Orkney appealed to George. His own rootedness made those from outside the islands particularly fascinating to him. In *Greenvoe*, one of the most sympathetic and intelligent characters George had created was the Indian, Johnny, an undergraduate studying English literature at Edinburgh University, who spends his summer holidays peddling exotic draperies to the people of Hellya. Twenty years later, in 1991, a man very like Johnny stepped into George's own life. Surinder Punjÿa was the son of Indian parents who had come to England from the Punjab in 1952. He had disappointed his father, who worked for Jaguar and Daimler in Coventry, by studying philosophy at Warwick University. Now, at the age of thirty, he wanted to try his hand at poetry. George took to him immediately. He was impressed by

---

* George always predicted that Renée would well outlive him. She died on Armistice Day 2005, aged 104.

Surinder's knowledge of languages, by his acute sense of humour, and by his discreet, natural goodness. 'I suppose,' he wrote to Jean Kay, 'he's as close to being a saint as anyone I'm likely to meet.' They began to spend a lot of time together. Surinder helped George with shopping, paying his bills, preparing his tax return. George, in return, looked over Surinder's poetry, and handed it back laced with corrections and tips. 'Write a little every day, for an hour or so: whether one feels like writing or not,' he suggests at the foot of one poem. 'It is like prayer, a discipline. The discipline becomes a joy.'

George had written much about the discipline of writing, but Surinder Punjÿa was unusual in witnessing his discipline in prayer. At the end of every morning's work, he remembers, George would wash, shave, brush his hair and move from the kitchen to his rocking chair by the fire. Here he prayed for half an hour or so before making lunch. On the feast-days of particular saints – Peter and Paul, Cecilia, Lucy, Magnus – he lit a candle.

In 'Song for St Magnus', written on 16 April 1993, George asks the Orkney saint to intercede not only for the islands' fishermen and shepherds, but for children all over the world, for the women of Bosnia and Somalia 'kneading dough smaller than fists', and for priests

> In this time of hate
> (Never such hate and anger over the earth)
>
> May they light candles at their altars
> This day and all days
> Till history is steeped in light.

Perhaps this gives some clue to the intentions uppermost in his mind as he settled in his rocking chair at the end of each morning. Certainly, when he spoke to Surinder, the breakdown of family life and the consequent suffering of children, the flight from faith, and war were the things that made George most apprehensive for the future of humanity.

None of these concerns is tackled explicitly in his work, yet for three hours every morning, George continued to write, and during these sessions he reflected more urgently than ever on death and the purpose of life. Just before his seventieth birthday, in the summer of 1991, he set to work on a new novel. If, in *Magnus*, George had written a sort of Orcadian New Testament, *Vinland* was his Old Testament, tracing the

life of a fictional character, Ranald Sigmundson, as the islands prepare
to exchange a blind belief in the workings of fate for faith in the inter-
action of free will and grace. Structured as a series of flashbacks, *Vinland*
is too episodic to work entirely satisfactorily as a novel; but it is written
with such a powerful combination of craft and utter conviction, that at
moments it can make the reader catch his breath. At the age of twelve,
Ranald Sigmundson stows away on Leif Ericson's ship on the journey
west to discover America, five hundred years before Columbus. He is
the only sailor awake as the ship, in the night, glides towards the undis-
covered country, and through the darkness he becomes aware of a boy
standing on the shore:

> The boy stood for a long time looking at the ship.
> It was likely that he saw Ranald outlined against the stars.
> The boy raised his hand, palm spread outwards: a greeting.
> Ranald put both hands out to greet the boy across the narrow fringe
>   of sea.
> Then the boy fluttered his hand like a bird, and turned, and was lost
>   among the rocks and dunes.

The trust between the two boys is not shared by their elders. One axe-
stroke, 'the thud of a body on the sand', and the pure possibilities of
that midnight greeting are lost for ever. For the rest of his life,
however, as soldier, farmer, husband and father, Ranald Sigmundson
is haunted by that moment of peace and unity, and by a yearning to
be 'in complete harmony with all nature – the plants and fish and
animals and stars'.

The voice of the sagas sounds throughout *Vinland*, but there are
near-contemporary influences at work too. For George, one of the
most moving allegories of the twentieth century was D. H.
Lawrence's 'Ship of Death' – 'O build your ship of death, for you will
need it . . .' With every good action and thought of his life, a man
helps to construct the ship that will carry him out on the death flood.
'It is such a moving image,' George writes, 'because it has always been
there, since men first arrived at the seashore, amazed.' In his last years,
Ranald Sigmundson retreats from his farm and family to live an
eremitical life in a hut above the Atlantic. He is, he tells his daughter, building a ship and preparing for a final voyage.

Vinland is so ambitious in scope that some reviewers assumed it to be a grand finale. In fact, by the time it was published in the summer of 1992, George had very nearly completed another novel, his fifth. In *Beside the Ocean of Time* he works again on an enormous canvas, covering, through the dreams of a twentieth-century Orkney schoolboy, Thorfinn Ragnarson, more than eight hundred years of Orkney history. It is a quieter novel than *Vinland*, but a braver one, because into the canvas George weaves a very personal thread. The arrival of Sophie, the mysterious guest at the manse, sends waves of excitement and delight through the whole island of Norday; the schoolboy Thorfinn, in particular, is enchanted by her, and heartbroken when she leaves. Years on, after Norday had been devastated by war, Sophie returns to the island. Thorfinn, by now an ex-prisoner of war and a writer, recognizes immediately the 'lost, loved, longed-for' voice, and they walk together in the evening, the waves throwing 'glories of light' about them as they tell each other how their lives have unfolded.

Hugh Mackay felt that in Sophie George had finally, and perfectly, caught the spirit of Stella Cartwright; but there is much of Kenna Crawford in her too. In the last pages of the novel, predicating a heaven, George appears to reconcile himself to the role that these two women had – and had not – played in his life. 'We never find what we set our hearts on,' Sophie says to Thorfinn as they wander along the shore. 'We ought to be glad of that.'

The company of women never lost its delight for George. In the summer of 1993, the poet Sheenagh Pugh visited him briefly in Mayburn Court. She found him not only friendly, unaffected and refreshingly modest, but 'also something I find hard to put into words but the nearest I can get is "flirtatious", in a curiously endearing way. It wasn't personal, the impression was more that he'd have been that way with any woman, and it wasn't quite gallantry either; it was as if he found the entire gender potentially attractive and went into automatic flirt mode.' Despite his warmth, however, she was aware of a certain distance: 'I had the feeling you could spend a lot of time with him and never get closer than he wanted you to, which would not be very close. He was a good man, and a very sweet one, but somewhere inside he seemed very much a loner.'

Solitude, and silence, had never been more important to George than in these last years. Writing was a greater joy to him than ever – 'The imagination is still working, and the tools of the workshop are bright with use' – and any disturbance to his morning stint left him feeling thwarted and irritable. Sometimes, the small square note pinned to his front door now read simply 'WORKING ALL DAY'. But it was not only his work for which George needed to left in peace. Like Ranald Sigmundson in *Vinland*, he was preparing for a voyage.

In the autumn of 1993, George wrote a short appendix to his auto-biography. He revealed little about what had happened to him in the years since Stella's death – 'there is nothing much to add' – but reflected instead on his religious beliefs. This was, felt Ian MacInnes's daughter Morag, a final attempt to explain to his fellow Orcadians the conversion to Catholicism that many of them had never understood. George writes of the beauty of the scriptural Passion and the Mass, and of the 'shaping divinity' which governs our lives. 'To lose one's own will in the will of God,' he concludes, 'should be the true occu-pation of every man's time on earth. Only a few of us – the saints – are capable of that simplicity.'

George would certainly not have numbered himself among the saints. 'Catholicism has meant a great deal to my writing,' he had once written. 'But, personally, I am as foolish and wayward and inconsiderate and inconsiderable as ever I was.' There was in these last years, however, a striving for personal purity of thought and word and deed that some-times bordered on neurosis. In 1991, John Murray published *Selected Poems 1954–1983*, a volume most striking not for what it includes, but for what George insisted must be left out. Poems with even the small-est sexual connotation have either been jettisoned or reworked, invari-ably for the worse. In 'Hamnavoe', for example,

> And lovers
>> Unblessed by steeples, lay under
>> The buttered bannock of the moon

becomes

> Ploughboy
>> and milklass tarried under
>> The buttered bannock of the moon.

A 'stallion' becomes a 'cart-horse'. In 'A Child's Calendar', the couplet for May:

> A russet stallion shoulders the hill apart.
> The mares tremble.

becomes

> Peatmen strike the bog with spades,
> Summoning black fire.

Poems like 'When You Are Old', in which George had imagined an elderly man and woman looking back on the spring, when 'whatever the parish talk, / We made one blessed rhyme / On a shaken branch of love', are omitted altogether.

George carried this censorship beyond his writing. In 1990, his old friend John Broom had suffered a stroke, with the effect that he lost all inhibition in his speech and became involuntarily foul-mouthed. George disowned him, and refused to attend the scattering of his ashes when he died in the early summer of 1992.* Three years later a young writer, Duncan McLean, who had lived in Orkney for some time and had always got on well with George, published his second novel, *Bunker Man*. George found some of the language in the novel unacceptable, and confided to Gunnie Moberg that he would have nothing more to do with McLean.

He had become similarly ascetic in his attitude to money. Appalled by Thatcher's Britain, and by 'the greed devouring the nation's spirit', George increasingly longed to live as simply as possible, unfettered by possessions. In 1993, when Judge Stephen Tumim offered to recommend him for a Civil List pension, he reacted almost with horror, insisting Tumim do no such thing: 'May the money go to some young genius with a black mortgage, and a wife who needs a change in June, and kids who need clothes and sweeties.' The following year, in a poem about an old man very like himself, he wrote:

> His house is crammed with books and manuscripts,
> Pictures, jars, music,

*Curiously, and perhaps reflecting a sense of guilt, George later wrote a poem, 'In Memoriam John L. Broom', in which he implies that he was, in fact, present at the scattering of Broom's ashes: 'Yesterday we gave the dust of a friend to the wind . . .'

One stone hollow heavy with coins.
Better a bare cell in Eynhallow
And a heart at peace.

All this helps to explain George's ambivalence and confusion when, in the middle of September 1994, John Murray called to tell him that *Beside the Ocean of Time* had been short-listed for the Booker Prize. George was no novice when it came to prizes, but nothing had prepared him for the frenzy surrounding the Booker. A succession of journalists flew into Kirkwall, and made their way to Mayburn Court. They rolled out all the old questions. Why had George not travelled more? Why had he become a Catholic? And then pressed him to address a new one: what might he do with £20,000? 'I could buy a little island and live the hermit's life there, and build a little cell like W. B. Yeats and live alone in the "bee-loud glade",' he told Valentine Low from the London *Evening Standard*. 'I wouldn't last the winter out, that's for sure.' For every interview, a new photograph was demanded. The telephone rang and rang.

Surinder Punjȳa had had to leave Orkney just before the Booker news broke, to look after his father who was dying. George desperately missed his support, both practical and moral. He spoke to Surinder almost daily on the telephone, and wrote to him regularly. The 'Booker business' was making him melancholy, he admitted in a letter on 17 September: 'They're not interested in good literature, really – only in competition and money like a greyhound race – Ugh!' Five days later, he wrote that he had had to abandon any attempt to work: ' "Booker" blocks the horizon.'

By early October, the prize was causing George such distress that he was taking antidepressants. On 5 October, he made the mistake of combining these with whisky in order to summon up the courage to deal with the television crew shooting the film to be broadcast on the evening of the Booker Prize presentation. He felt desiccated and disoriented as he faced the camera, and flinched painfully from the lens. Fortunately, he was spared seeing this film on the giant screen erected at Guildhall on the evening of 11 October. Out of loyalty to John Murray, George had not only entertained the media circus, but had also allowed speculation to continue up until the last moment as to whether he would travel south for the Booker dinner. In fact, he had known very well from the start that he would not.*

Instead, he watched the proceedings from his rocking chair in Mayburn Court, with Renée Simm and Nora Kennedy.† While the guests at Guildhall dined, television viewers were kept entertained with the reactions of a distinguished panel to the short-listed books. When it came to *Beside the Ocean of Time*, the discussion got off to an unpromising start. The novelist A. S. Byatt, while paying tribute to some of George's earlier work, felt that this time the 'imaginative effort' had not been 'fully realized'. Germaine Greer had felt unhappy about the book even before she opened it: what was 'the ocean of time', and how could one be beside it? Sarah Dunant, chairing the discussion, had found the novel instantly forgettable. The poet Tom Paulin, speaking last, silenced them all with praise and passion. This was a 'wonderful' novel, he said, displaying to the full George Mackay Brown's 'sacral, primitive, highly sophisticated and at the same time deeply naïve view of the world'. He quoted Hopkins – 'There lives the dearest freshness deep down things'; *Beside the Ocean of Time* had, Paulin said, left him 'joyous'.

Moments later, the cameras swung back to the diners, and John Bayley, chair of the judges, rose to make his speech. He was delighted to announce a Scottish winner, the first for twenty-six years – not George Mackay Brown, but James Kelman.

The following morning, George returned with relief to his normal routine. Four days later, on 16 October, Surinder Punjȳa 's father died in Coventry. George had just completed a letter to Surinder when the news came through. He wrote a small poem, 'Lux Perpetua', before sealing the envelope:

> A star for a cradle
>
> Sun for plough and net

---

*Of the many considerations conspiring against George's attending the dinner, one was his horror at the prospect of wearing that 'revolting' garment, a dinner jacket. He had worn one once before, when presented with an Hon. D.Litt. at Glasgow University in June 1985, and had not liked it.

†When Renée and Nora coincided in 3 Mayburn Court, the atmosphere tended to be strained. On the whole, George did his best to keep them apart. 'Renée came last night,' he wrote to Surinder on 17 September 1994. 'She came just after Nora left. I've got to stage-manage those comings and goings like an eighteenth-century play.'

A fire for old stories

A candle for the dead

*

Lux perpetua
By such glimmers we seek you.

'Strange how the mind at last grows like a child again,' George had once written to Renée Simm, 'taking out its toys and dolls over and over again.' In his own writing now there was, more than ever, a yearning back to boyhood. During the last months of 1994, George was compiling for John Murray a collection of short stories set in winter. More than half of the eighteen stories in *Winter Tales* centre in some way on the miracle of the Nativity. The approach of Christmas had always found George busier than ever with his writing, partly, as he explained to Sister Margaret Tournour, in an attempt to 'hide myself away from all the tinsel and commercialism, and be near the heart of the mystery', but partly also out of a longing to recapture something precious from his early years. As a child between the ages of five and eight, he had once reflected, Stromness had seemed to him a place very like Bethlehem, where a boy might not be surprised to meet angels, shepherds, kings on a winter night.*

He was working also on a new collection of poems, *Following a Lark*, and here again there is a powerful nostalgia for infancy – for the lure of the sweet shop, the thrill of snow, the wonderment of a small boy as winter gives way to spring:

And one day after school
The lamp stood gray on the dresser
That had lit all teatimes since October.

Willie dug his horn spoon in his egg.
Strange he thought it, the dead lamp
But he said nothing.

A leaf of light
Opened in the branches of his blood.

---

*Peter Maxwell Davies had a similar feeling in Hoy. 'I always imagine the nativity in a deserted Rackwick house,' he wrote to George on 16 July 1984.

George was still open to commissions. In the spring of 1995, Gunnie Moberg had asked him to compose captions for a new book of Orkney photographs. She brought her photographs one by one to Mayburn Court, and propped them up on a chair for George to contemplate. Unknown to her, he set to work not on captions but on full-length poems – forty-seven of them. The poems have an air-blown lightness, and a sense of George looking at places he loves – Maeshowe, Skara Brae, the ruins on Eynhallow – for the last time. He ends, in a poem to accompany a photograph of a farrier shoeing a horse, with a genuflexion to Edwin Muir.

The summer of 1995 was bright and warm in Orkney, but it was followed by a hard winter. The frosts were so severe, George wrote to a friend, that putting on his clothes in the morning felt like climbing into a suit of armour – 'the cold gnaws at my bones'. January brought blizzards, and news of the death of Norman MacCaig. George felt off-colour, though with nothing more serious than 'coughs and languor and old man's irritability'. He continued to write for three hours every morning, but his appetite for new projects had dried up. Instead, he looked back over work he had never completed.

Over the years George had learned that fragments of 'failed' writing were rarely lost beyond recall. In April 1992, on the back of an envelope, he had started to sketch out a poem about the hours between Good Friday and Easter Sunday, when Christ is said to have descended into hell to free the souls of the deceased from the bondage of death. The poem had been through seven drafts; now, in the cold early weeks of 1996, it finally came to birth. 'The Harrowing of Hell' is perhaps the most beautiful religious poem that George ever wrote. Clothed in the five wounds of his crucifixion, Christ makes a silent, spiral, luminous descent into the underworld, moving deeper and deeper into the past as he meets and frees first Solomon, and then David, Joseph, Jacob, Abel. Finally, on the seventh step of Christ's descent, Adam – 'tall primal dust' – turns to him from the shadows with a cry of joy. The way is now prepared for the resurrection:

> *Tomorrow the Son of Man will walk in a garden*
> *Through drifts of apple-blossom.*

For the first three months of 1996, George hardly left Mayburn Court. He had not the strength any longer to walk even as far as the Pierhead, but he travelled in his imagination. Renée Simm had given him a copy of William Dalrymple's book about Delhi, *City of Djinns*. He enjoyed it so much that he ordered *In Xanadu*, in which Dalrymple follows in the footsteps of Marco Polo through Iran, Pakistan and China to the site of Kubla Khan's pleasure dome. He wrote Dalrymple a postcard of praise: 'Pooh – I suffered and enjoyed and won through with you, sitting in my rocking-chair by a fire in Stromness.'

As the days began to lengthen and the light increased, however, George longed for a change of scene. Friends had suggested that he and Surinder spend ten days in early April looking after their house, Leagar, in Outertown, while they travelled south. He accepted. Leagar is less than two miles from Stromness, but it is surrounded by fields, and its garden looks out across the sea to the hills of Hoy. This was the view Stella had loved best when she visited Orkney in 1962.

On his first afternoon away from home, George wrote his weekly column for the *Orcadian*, delighting in the spring, and urging islanders 'to relish each one of the thirty days of April, the month that tastes of childhood'. In particular, he asked them to remember the feast of Saint Magnus on 16 April. He rejoiced in the fact that he had come through another winter, 'a little bruised maybe, but unbowed'.

In the days that followed, he gradually lost his energy. He had no appetite and, although he was exhausted, he could not sleep. On Friday 12 April, he felt unable to get up. Surinder sat at his bedside. 'The weaker George became,' he remembers, 'the more peaceful he seemed.' At teatime, George's GP, Dr Johnstone, decided to take him into hospital in Kirkwall. It was a beautiful evening and, as they drove out of Stromness, George seemed elated. The air, he remarked to Surinder, was like champagne.

The following day, in Rackwick, Peter Maxwell Davies completed his sixth symphony, dedicated to George. In Stromness, the postman delivered the first copies of *Following a Lark* to Mayburn Court. At Balfour Hospital in Kirkwall, George's condition was grave: his kidneys had failed and he was fading fast. After lunch, his family were telephoned and asked to come to his bedside. By the time they arrived, he was in a coma and, at 5.50 p.m., he died.

Just before he lost consciousness – before, in the language of the sagas, he passed 'out of the story' – George had spoken his last words to the doctor and nurses attending to him. Lying back against his pillows, he said: 'I see hundreds and hundreds of ships sailing out of the harbour.'

Three days after his death, on 16 April 1996, George Mackay Brown was buried with his parents in the kirkyard at Warbeth. On his head-stone were engraved his words

> Carve the runes
> Then be content with silence

The media, not so content, struggled for the last time to come to terms with a man who had doggedly avoided becoming a public figure – who had had, as Seamus Heaney put it, 'more interest in spiritual integrity than in any kind of literary success'. Nationally, both on radio and on television, George's death was reported on the evening news, and in Scotland the newspapers carried not only obituaries but leading articles appraising his exceptional gifts both as a writer and as a human being. For Iain Crichton Smith, George was a 'bard in the old tradition', who had 'done for the Orkneys what William Faulkner did for the south of America. He has created a kind of myth, a mythical area.' For Stewart Conn, he was 'a bonfire at which to warm the spirit'. In an obituary in the *Scotsman*, Douglas Gifford, Professor of Scottish Literature at Glasgow University, saluted George's refusal to be swayed by literary fashion, and his 'astonishing clarity and sureness of imagery'. 'His best works,' concluded Alan Bold's obituary in the *Herald*, 'establish him as one of the most dazzling stylists of the century.'

As an expression of the love felt for him by his fellow Orcadians, George's funeral was held in St Magnus Cathedral. It was the first time that a Catholic priest had celebrated a Requiem Mass in the cathedral since the Reformation. It happened, furthermore, to fall on the feast-day of Saint Magnus – 'And if you call that a coincidence,' declared Ron Ferguson, minister of St Magnus Cathedral, welcoming a con-gregation of six hundred, 'I wish you a very dull life.' Looking back, Ferguson had an uncanny feeling that the funeral had been scripted by George himself: clouds scudding across the sky, the great cathedral bell tolling over Kirkwall, and the Viking kirk packed with 'the great and the good and the humble and even the drink-filled'.

Among the mourners were Brigadier Malcolm Dennison, Lord Lieutenant of Orkney; George's publishers John Murray and Hugo Brunner from London; his last surviving sibling, Jackie;* friends like Ian MacInnes and Archie Bevan who had known George from boyhood; and others, like Kenna Crawford, Nora Kennedy, Gunnie Moberg, Brian Murray, Surinder Punjÿa and Renée Simm, whose friendship had enriched his later years. Mario Conti, Catholic Bishop of Aberdeen, preached a sermon based on George's poem 'The Harrowing of Hell'. Peter Maxwell Davies played 'Farewell to Stromness'.

Before the funeral, the coffin had lain uncovered in the Catholic church in Kirkwall, and here a number of friends gathered to pay their last respects. On George's face was an expression impossible either to describe or to forget. It looked as if, in his last moments, he had felt secure in the convictions in which he had invested so much:

> I have a deep-rooted belief that what has once existed can never die: not even the frailest things, spindrift or clover-scent or glitter of star on a wet stone. All is gathered into the web of creation, that is apparently established and yet perhaps only a dream in the eternal mind; and yet, too, we work at the making of it with every word and thought and action of our lives.

*Ruby had died on 3 March 1990. Jackie died on 1 May 2005.

Notes

Unless otherwise stated, texts and poems cited are by George Mackay Brown (GMB).

NLS: National Library of Scotland
EUL: Edinburgh University Library
OL: The Orkney Library
RUL: Reading University Library

Where no location is indicated, letters remain in private hands.
Where no reference is given, quotations are taken from conversations with the author.

PREFACE

ix **'decade met decade'**: Compton Mackenzie, 'Ave Atque Vale', in Ian Hamilton, *Jean: A Memoir*, Faber & Faber, 1942, p. 27.

x **'the buttered bannock of the moon'**: 'Hamnavoe', *Loaves and Fishes*, Hogarth Press, 1959, p. 24.

x **'a butcher blade in the day's throat'**: 'Haddock Fishermen', *Fishermen with Ploughs*, Hogarth Press, 1971, p. 58.

x **'galilees of sky'**: 'A Child's Calendar', Ibid., p. 62.

x **'turned a salt key'**: 'Thorfinn', *Loaves and Fishes*, p. 16.

x **'involved detachment'**: Stella Cartwright to GMB, 25 October 1965 (NLS).

x **'It has to be said, George'**: Ted Hughes to GMB, 18 January 1985.

x **'The encounter with that stuff'**: Seamus Heaney to the author, 25 August 2004.

x **'martyring himself to modernity'**: Seamus Heaney, *Benchmark*, BBC Radio Scotland, 21 April 1996.

xii **'I instinctively shrink from journalists'**: GMB to Ian Scott, 15 November 1986.

xii **'I hope you'll come back often'**: GMB to the author, 25 June 1992.

xiii **'In fact the lives of writers'**: *For the Islands I Sing*, John Murray, 1997, p. 38.

xiv **'One of the great experiences'**: Ibid., p. 79.

xiv **'I have never been in love'**: GMB to Kulgin Duval, 12 January 1975.

xiv **'We move from silence into silence'**: *For the Islands I Sing*, p. 181.

CHAPTER 1: A PLACE OF VISION

1 **'Orkney – "orcs"'**: From 'Haiku: for The Holy Places', *Travellers*, John Murray, 2001, p. 38.

1 **'a place of order'**: 'Writer's Shop', *Chapman*, No. 16, Summer 1976.

2 **'plotted and pieced'**: Gerard Manley Hopkins, 'Pied Beauty', *Poems and Prose of Gerard Manley Hopkins*, selected by W. H. Gardner, Penguin, 1981, p. 30.

7 **'country people, decent folks'**: T. S. Clouston, *Unsoundness of Mind*, Methuen, 1911, p. 298.

7 **'There is a trouble in the islands'**: 'The Drowned Rose', *Hawkfall*, Hogarth Press, 1974, p. 163.

CHAPTER 2: THE GREEN COAT

9 **'I dreamed I was a child'**: 'Magi', *Voyages*, Chatto & Windus, 1983, p. 20.

9 **'Early years are remembered in gleams'**: *For the Islands I Sing*, p. 25.

10 **'The kitchen was also the living-room'**: Ruby Ross (née Brown) to the Revd Andrew Burnet, 10 June 1986.

10 **'Of course I had no conception'**: *As I Remember: Ten Scottish Authors Recall How Writing Began for Them*, ed. Maurice Lindsay, Robert Hale, 1979, p. 13.

10 **'Down in yon garden'**: Quoted by GMB in 'Growing Up in Orkney', MS for BBC Radio Northern Ireland, November 1968 (EUL).

11 **'She sought him up'**: Ibid.

11 **'I was beginning to learn'**: Ibid.

11 **'He would never say more'**: 'Childhood in Orkney', *Scottish Field*, August 1968.

12 **'a drooping black column'**: *Weekend Scotsman*, 30 August 1986.

12 **'What could there be in our familiar surroundings'**: Draft of article for *Scottish Field*, 1986 (EUL).

12 **' "A simply lovely morning," '**: *Greenvoe*, Hogarth Press, 1972, p. 15.

14 **'Home we would go then'**: 'Mary Jane Mackay – 1891–1967 (A Memoir)', *Northern Lights: A Poet's Sources*, John Murray, 1999, p. 131.

15 **'the brass face beaten'**: 'New Year's Day: 1920s', Ibid., p. 76.

16 **'Thora found her way'**: 'The Pirate's Ghost', *The Sun's Net*, Hogarth Press, 1976, p. 158.

17 **'a serene black swan'**: *Orcadian*, 21 November 1974, reprinted in *Letters from Hamnavoe*, Gordon Wright, 1975, p. 124.

17 **'half blind with rain'**: 'Childhood in Orkney', *Scottish Field*, August 1968.

18 **'magical caves'**: *Orcadian*, 14 December 1972, reprinted in *Letters from Hamnavoe*, p. 64.

18 **'You pushed the door open'**: Ibid.

18 **' "Hurry on past the Jews" '**: 'John Brown – Tailor and Postman', *Northern Lights*, p. 147.

18 **'the rustling of the bag'**: *For the Islands I Sing*, p. 19.

19 **'with its wistful ghostly melancholy'**: *Orkney Herald*, 13 September 1955, reprinted in *Northern Lights*, p. 121.

19 **'A silent conquering army'**: 'Kirkyard', *Poems New and Selected*, Hogarth Press, 1971, p. 19.

20 **'Remote in the Scottish Highlands'**: *Orkney Herald*, 21 September 1948.

20 **'Our poverty never rankled'**: 'Childhood', *c.* 1955–56 (EUL).

21 **'turnings-away, seethings'**: 'Mary Jane Mackay', *Northern Lights*, p. 133.

21 **'He would say something scathing'**: 'John Brown', Ibid., p. 146.

21 **'standing behind his chair'**: 'Childhood in Orkney', *Scottish Field*, August 1968.

22 **'Much better to remain poor'**: 'John Brown', *Northern Lights*, p. 146.

22 **'Try and get on'**: Ruby Ross to the Revd Andrew Burnet, 10 June 1981.

22 **'loaded with pain'**: 'Childhood in Orkney', *Scottish Field*, August 1968.

22 **'a special sweetness'**: GMB to the Revd Andrew Burnet, quoted in Burnet, 'A Lamp Is Lit in Thule', M.Litt. dissertation, University of Cambridge, 1992.

22 **'She exhaled comfort'**: Ruby Ross to the Revd Andrew Burnet, 10 June 1981.

23 **'For she too was a stranger'**: 'John Brown', *Northern Lights*, p. 144.

23 **'This is true. Not wisdom or wealth'**: 'An Old Man in July', *Northern Lights*, p. 49.

CHAPTER 3: THE PRISON ON THE HILL

24 **'No more ballads in Eynhallow'**: 'Runes from a Holy Island', *Poems New and Selected*, p. 33.

24 **'with its wings folded'**: Edwin Muir, *An Autobiography*, Canongate Classics, 1993, p. 15.

24 **'In three weeks'**: *Orcadian*, 3 August 1995.

24 **'huge gray unimaginative machine'**: *As I Remember*, p. 19.

25 **'that enormous expense'**: *Orcadian*, 25 September 1930.

25 **'No endeavour is in vain'**: 'The Wind over the Chimney', *The Poetical Works of Longfellow*, Oxford University Press, 1913, p. 535.

25 **'was transparent to an intelligent child'**: Ruby Ross to the Revd Andrew Burnet, 10 June 1986.

26 **'commodious gymnasium'**: *Orcadian*, 11 March 1934.

26 **'Of all the dolorous noises'**: *Orcadian*, 19 September 1974, reprinted in *Letters from Hamnavoe*, p. 119.

26 **' "You will go home at once" '**: 'Five Green Waves', *A Calendar of Love*, Hogarth Press, 1967, pp. 41–2.

27 **'My zeal for education'**: GMB to Ernest Marwick, 8 December 1960 (OL).

28 **'as though children in our circumstances'**: *As I Remember*, p. 19.

28 **'that cutting up and examining'**: *For the Islands I Sing*, p. 29.

28 **'made the blood sing along my veins'**: Ibid., p. 31.

28 **'succession of grey schemers'**: *The Story of Scotland*, Scottish Daily Record and Sunday Mail, 1988, p. 310.

29 **'His mouth moulded the words'**: 'The Tarn and the Rosary', *Hawkfall*, pp. 181–2.

30 **'not unlike the Roman chariots of *Ben-Hur*'**: Jackie Brown, unpublished memoirs.

31 **'cloth-smelling cave'**: *As I Remember*, p. 13.

31 **'Because he had a flawless memory'**: 'Peter Esson', BBC Radio Scotland, 19 January 1967.

31 **'Peter at some immortal cloth'**: 'The Death of Peter Esson', *Loaves and Fishes*, p. 12.

32 **'Colm . . . discovered'**: 'The Tarn and the Rosary', *Hawkfall*, p. 184.

32 'like chewing hunks of stone': *Scotsman*, 11 August 1985.

33 'It may have been an early instinctive revolt': *Contemporary Authors: Autobiography Series*, Vol. 6, Gale Research Company, 1988, p. 66.

34 'as though Henry Hall was playing': 'The Last Ballad', *Listener*, 20 June 1968.

34 'He too died': 'January the Twenty-fifth', *Northern Lights*, p. 12.

34 'He could swerve and run': Jackie Brown, unpublished memoirs.

34 'Once again Stromness brought the ball': *Orkney Herald*, 23 May 1934.

35 'He was not a poetry-reading man': 'John Brown', *Northern Lights*, p. 150.

36 'iron-gray country of adulthood': *Contemporary Authors: Autobiography Series*, p. 66.

36 'That one should leave The Green Wood': 'In Memoriam I.K.', *The Wreck of the Archangel*, John Murray, 1989, p. 78.

37 'Suddenly, in mid-teens': *Contemporary Authors: Autobiography Series*, p. 66.

37 'intense loneliness and suffering': Ibid.

37 'I would shadow her': *For the Islands I Sing*, p. 46.

37 'The "black bird" has been with me all my life': GMB to Renée Simm, 15 November 1981.

37 'Sometimes such a mass of dark clouds': GMB to Stella Cartwright, 21 January 1983 (EUL).

37 'There *is* delight': GMB to Jenny Robertson, 2 March 1980.

37 'A lovely day, but depression': GMB to Renée Simm, 11 December 1982.

38 'and, on more than one occasion': John Gilmour quoted in Andrew Burnet, 'A Lamp is Lit in Thule'.

38 'like a youth shunned': *For the Islands I Sing*, p. 46.

39 'And I knew that the man reeling': Ibid., p. 50.

39 'That such an institution as the Church of Rome': Ibid., p. 51.

40 'Catholicism and its mysteries': Ibid., p. 49.

40 'As heroin addicts': *Contemporary Authors: Autobiography Series*, p. 66.

41 'The enormous pleasure we all got from those early "Penguins"!': *Orcadian*, 14 June 1973, reprinted in *Letters from Hamnavoe*, p. 81.

41 'I wondered how on earth he could read so many': John Gilmour quoted in Andrew Burnet, 'A Lamp is Lit in Thule'.

41 'a hobby, a pastime, a foible': *For the Islands I Sing*, p. 60.

41 **'I have cultivated this secret vice'**: GMB to Ernest Marwick, 5 May 1946 (OL).

41 **'The purple night is hushed and calm'**: 'The Island', September 1937 (OL).

41 **'those bad verses'**: *Contemporary Authors: Autobiography Series*, p. 66.

42 **'a tremble of joy'**: *For the Islands I Sing*, p. 60.

42 **'Blue swelling hills!'**: *Orkney Herald*, 14 June 1939.

CHAPTER 4: BLOODY ORKNEY

43 **'I thought it was absolute hell'**: Charles Causley, *Kaleidoscope*, BBC Radio 4, 23 April 1976.

43 **'It may be true that steel and fire'**: Harold Nicolson, *Diaries and Letters, 1930–39*, ed. Nigel Nicolson, Collins, 1966, p. 403.

45 **'This bloody town's a bloody cuss'**: Malcolm Brown and Patricia Meehan, *Scapa Flow*, Pan Books, 2002, p. 138.

45 **'Dear Mum, I cannot tell you'**: Ibid., p. 228.

45 **'Men with drawing-boards'**: *Greenvoe*, p. 242.

46 **'It soon became apparent'**: Ibid., p. 243.

47 **'We could not understand'**: *Orcadian*, 9 September 1971, reprinted in *Letters from Hamnavoe*, p. 19.

48 **'It is a very eerie sight'**: 'U-Boat Log Tells of Royal Oak Sinking', *Orkney Herald*, 25 November 1947.

48 **'It required little imagination'**: Archie Bevan to the author, 10 April 2005.

49 **'The islands shook'**: *For the Islands I Sing*, p. 59.

49 **'There was too much excitement'**: *Orcadian*, 22 March 1973, reprinted in *Letters from Hamnavoe*, p. 74.

49 **'The guns stabbed vividly'**: Ibid.

50 **'We felt then a first quickening'**: Ibid., p. 75.

50 **'Thank God the boys won't have to go'**: *For the Islands I Sing*, p. 58.

50 **'My next suit'**: 'John Brown', *Northern Lights*, p. 149.

50 **'more remote than a star'**: Ibid.

50 **'I have never felt a coldness so intense'**: Ibid.

50 **'a quintessence of dust'**: Ibid., p. 150.

51 **'I wish there was a Thomas Hardy'**: Ibid.

51 **'My father passed'**: 'Hamnavoe', *Loaves and Fishes*, pp. 23–4.

52 **'Sometimes I see my task'**: *Northern Lights*, p. 4.

53 **'like a leper'**: *For the Islands I Sing*, p. 62.

53 **'And what exactly do you feel?'**: *A Seat by My Bed*, BBC Scottish Home Service, 8 March 1957.

53 **'His first public performance'**: Archie Bevan to the author, 12 April 2005.

54 **'I resented his lethargic ways'**: Ruby Ross to the Revd Andrew Burnet, 9 March 1987.

CHAPTER 5: WHAT THE BLOOD DICTATES

55 **'Sometimes I think . . . recurrent illness'**: GMB interviewed by William Sharpton, *Chapman*, No. 84, 1996.

56 **'For months this increasingly dense fluid'**: *For the Islands I Sing*, pp. 57–8.

56 **'Tubercle attacks failures'**: Herbert de Carle Woodcock, *The Doctor and the People*, Methuen, 1912, quoted in Linda Bryder, *Below the Magic Mountain: A Social History of Tuberculosis in Twentieth-Century Britain*, Clarendon Press, Oxford, 1988, p. 20.

56 **'Two kinds of suffering'**: *Western Mail*, Cardiff, 5 November 1938, quoted in Linda Bryder, *Below the Magic Mountain*, p. 224.

57 **'The car takes me to the sanatorium'**: *A Seat by My Bed*.

57 **'I think there must be a secret wisdom'**: GMB to Jenny Robertson, 4 November 1982.

57 **'after a first qualm of dread'**: *Contemporary Authors: Autobiography Series*, p. 66.

57 **'coughing out a civilian soul'**: Rupert Brooke to John Drinkwater, 18–25 January 1915, in *The Letters of Rupert Brooke*, ed. Sir Geoffrey Keynes, Faber & Faber, 1968, p. 654.

58 **'How better to die'**: *Contemporary Authors: Autobiography Series*, p. 66.

58 **'At the door of the house called death'**: 'The House of Death', March 1945 (OL).

58 **'One could go dancing every night'**: Ruby Ross to the Revd Andrew Burnet, 30 May 1988.

58 **'Used to their laconic suitors'**: 'The Broken Heraldry', *Memoirs of a Modern Scotland*, ed. Karl Miller, Faber & Faber, 1970, p. 139.

60 **'He was, I think, a Congregational minister'**: *For the Islands I Sing*, p. 59.

60 **'First the seat by the bed'**: *A Seat by My Bed*.

61 **'and yet it is a very *native* church'**: Eric Linklater, *Orkney and Shetland*, 2nd edition, Robert Hale, 1971, p. 111.

62 **'There was an abundance of leisure'**: GMB to Jenny Robertson, 4 November 1982.

62 **'everyone knew the poem'**: 'Living in Orkney', *Saltire Review*, Winter 1955, p. 56.

62 **'men of evil dispositions'**: *The Orkneyinga Saga*, ed. Joseph Anderson, James Thin, 1981, p. 60.

63 **'as cheerful as if he were invited to a banquet'**: Ibid., p. 64.

63 **'like a precious stone'**: *For the Islands I Sing*, p. 52.

63 **'For me, Magnus was at once'**: Ibid.

63 **'still centre'**: Foreword to *A Calendar of Love*.

63 **'a small but agreeable surge of power'**: *For the Islands I Sing*, p. 62.

63 **'I had made something that I knew in my bones to be good'**: Ibid.

63 **'the mighty harvests had been reaped'**: Ibid., p. 44.

64 **'My ears brimmed with enchantment!'**: Ibid., pp. 61–2.

64 **'matter-of-factness and imagination'**: Francis Scarfe to GMB, 11 December 1981 (NLS).

64 **'George's writing was crosslit'**: Seamus Heaney to the author, 25 August 2004.

64 **'There are no forests in Orkney'**: 'Orkney', August 1944 (OL).

65 **'Suddenly we were back to pre-war quietness'**: Ruby Ross to the Revd Andrew Burnet, 30 May 1988.

65 **'often delivered more out of imagination'**: *Contemporary Authors: Autobiography Series*, p. 67.

66 **'thin and cadaverous'**: Unpublished pen portrait by Gerry Meyer.

CHAPTER 6: TIR-NAN-OG

67 **'But the fairest region of all Hoy'**: *Let's See the Orkney Islands*, William S. Thomson, 1948, p. 47.

67 **'not to be an Oliver Twist'**: GMB to Renée Simm, 26 October 1978.

67 **'years that the locusts ate'**: *For the Islands I Sing*, p. 78.

67 **'desert of time'**: Ibid., p. 60.

67 **'He wakens about 9 a.m.'**: *Orkney Herald*, 17 January 1950.

68 **'black, dishevelled Maxton-like mop'**: Profile of GMB by Gerry Meyer, *Orcadian*, 12 April 1951.

68 **'certain very intense experiences'**: *For the Islands I Sing*, p. 79.

69 **'The scenery through which we were now passing'**: *Orkney Herald*, 18 June 1946.

69 'The beauty of Rackwick struck me like a blow': *For the Islands I Sing*, p. 82.

69 'deep, indescribable peace and security': 'Living in Orkney', *Saltire Review*, Winter 1955, p. 57.

69 'Where falls not hail': *Orkney Herald*, 2 July 1946.

70 'a slow fire of rust': 'Dead Fires', *Fishermen with Ploughs*, p. 76.

70 'The whole nation seemed to burgeon': *An Orkney Tapestry*, Victor Gollancz, 1969, p. 46.

71 'aura of contentment': John Bremner, *Hoy: the Dark Enchanted Isle*, Bellavista, 1997, p. 106.

71 'Evil is universal': *An Orkney Tapestry*, pp. 46–7.

72 'Only two of the crew were left': Ibid., p. 47.

72 'The gravedigger consulted a map': 'Betty Corrigall', *Northern Lights*, p. 230.

73 'the gifts of progress': *An Orkney Tapestry*, p. 53.

73 'The notion of progress': Ibid.

74 'dung and fish-gut trades': Ibid.

74 'The novels that dribbled into the valley': Ibid.

74 'they began, with a sense of fatuous freedom': Ibid.

74 'The notion of progress is a cancer': Ibid.

75 'enriched by many thousands of pounds': *Orkney Herald*, 4 June 1946.

75 'Unique System of Cultivation by Tractor': *Orkney Herald*, 24 September 1946.

76 'The New Ferguson Tractor Is Now Here!': *Orkney Herald*, 29 October 1946.

76 'The time was 4.15 last Thursday afternoon': *Orkney Herald*, 6 May 1947.

76 'poor remnants of a once mighty race': *Orkney Herald*, 9 January 1945.

77 'ridiculous pampering of women': *Orkney Herald*, 28 January 1947.

77 'baking bere-bannocks': *Orkney Herald*, 11 December 1945.

77 'blue in the face': *Orkney Herald*, 30 October 1945.

78 'peculiar and perverse gift': *Orkney Herald*, 2 November 1948.

78 'like a young dog': *Orkney Herald*, 3 July 1951.

78 'one of life's great blessings': *Orkney Herald*, 18 October 1949.

78 'To think that we have to slave our guts out': *Greenvoe*, p. 37.

79 'I had no homosexual urges': *For the Islands I Sing*, p. 79.

79 'God, what an evening': 'Love Poem', July 1945 (OL).

79 **'The "Love Poem" you like best'**: GMB to Ernest Marwick, 5 May 1946 (OL).

80 **'but in their presence'**: *For the Islands I Sing*, p. 79.

80 **' "I am gall, I am heartburn" '**: *Orkney Herald*, 8 March 1949.

81 **'The black mould was aflame'**: *Orkney Herald*, 5 April 1949, reprinted in *Northern Lights*, p. 81.

81 **'no more a part of my life than the shadow'**: *Orkney Herald*, 8 March 1949.

81 **'None of them, fortunately, survives'**: *For the Islands I Sing*, p. 60.

81 **'I take this business of poetry'**: GMB to Ernest Marwick, 5 May 1946 (OL).

81 **'My own life strikes me'**: Notes for Ernest Marwick, 27 February 1969 (OL).

81 **'vast tracts of virgin soil'**: *Orkney Herald*, 14 January 1947.

81 **'Magnus Martyr . . . Pity us'**: 'Prayer to Magnus', October 1944 (OL).

82 **'At evening the dark sails returned'**: 'Summer Day', August 1947 (OL).

82 **'attempts to be pious'**: GMB to Ernest Marwick, 24 October 1946 (OL).

83 **'We . . . are very glad to see an improvement'**: *Orcadian*, 14 June 1945.

84 **'magnificent devastating logic'**: GMB to Ernest Marwick, 26 April 1947 (OL).

85 **'might be taken to represent the soul's flight'**: GMB to Ernest Marwick, undated [summer 1947] (OL).

85 **'Next morning in tranced sunshine'**: 'The Storm', *The Storm and Other Poems*, Orkney Press, 1954, p. 16.

85 **'Ideally I should be trying to communicate'**: GMB interviewed by Peter Orr of the British Council, 13 October 1964, National Sound Archive.

85 **'The modern poets'**: *Orkney Herald*, 14 January 1947.

85 **'Sir, Just who are they in Orkney'**: *Orkney Herald*, 4 November 1947.

86 **'May I very humbly suggest'**: *Orkney Herald*, 4 November 1947.

86 **'One feels sorry for this humourless bore'**: John B. J. Laurenson, Letter to the Editor, *Orkney Herald*, 16 July 1946.

86 **'a lanky, wild-haired'**: *Orkney Herald*, 3 December 1946.

86 **'almost traitorous'**: GMB to Ernest Marwick, 11 May 1947 (OL).

86 **'achieving anything spectacular'**: *Orkney Herald*, 3 February 1948.

CHAPTER 7: LATE BUT IN EARNEST

87 **'Some kind of ancient wisdom'**: *For the Islands I Sing*, p. 80.

88 **'I am one of those whom novelty depresses'**: 'From the Islands to the Old Quad', 7 February 1986 (EUL).

88 **'In Orkney every face'**: *Orkney Herald*, 5 October 1948.

88 **'A tree has grace'**: *Orkney Herald*, 12 October 1948.

88 **'The spell of the city'**: *Orkney Herald*, 26 October 1948.

88 **'long winter of darkness'**: Ibid.

88 **'old blind men and beautiful young women'**: Ibid.

89 **'to sing and tell extravagant stories'**: 'Hogmanay', *Northern Lights*, p. 75.

89 **'dreadful drink called whisky'**: Ibid.

89 **'for the benefit of the male population'**: *Orkney Herald*, 8 May 1945.

89 **'a revelation; they flushed my veins'**: *For the Islands I Sing*, p. 67.

90 **'Sober, waiting for the bar to open'**: Ibid., p. 68.

90 **'how under the drab surface complexities'**: Ibid., p. 69.

90 **'There is a state of drunkenness'**: Ibid., p. 70.

91 **'George Brown was taken home'**: Ibid., p. 68.

91 **'certain gray reputation'**: Ibid.

91 **'For a long time there was a divided allegiance'**: Ibid., p. 70.

91 **'but it contained the great English novelists'**: Ernest Marwick, 'A Sufficient Place', unpublished autobiography (OL).

92 **'through a galaxy'**: 'Ernest Marwick', *Northern Lights*, p. 156.

92 **'Your praise went to my head'**: GMB to Ernest Marwick, 5 May 1946 (OL).

92 **'a time when a writer'**: 'Ernest Marwick', *Northern Lights*, p. 154.

92 **'How priggish and stilted'**: GMB to Ernest Marwick, 15 February 1947 (OL).

93 **'No work ever left his hands'**: 'Ernest Marwick', *Northern Lights*, p. 155.

93 **'certainly one of the best'**: *Orkney Herald*, 11 March 1947.

93 **'from every angle, No'**: Letter of 24 April 1946, quoted in letter to GMB from Finlay J. Macdonald at BBC Scotland, 16 December 1969 (NLS).

94 **'Entering Westermill'**: 'Ernest Marwick', *Northern Lights*, p. 157.

94 **'History, folk-lore, literature'**: *For the Islands I Sing*, p. 77.

94 **'whose eyes seemed to glimmer'**: Ibid., p. 76.

95 **'behind the ludicrously austere mask'**: GMB to Ian MacInnes, 26 December 1960.

96 **'There is a man who lives in London'**: *Orkney Herald*, 15 March 1949.

96 **'and yet they had (it seemed) a secret and exact music'**: 'Edwin Muir at Newbattle', *Akros*, August 1981.

97 **'the slow stainings and renewings'**: Ibid.

97 **'every Orcadian who is proud'**: *Orkney Herald*, 6 February 1945.

97 **'rob Scotland of all the benefits'**: Edwin Muir, *John Knox: Portrait of a Calvinist*, Jonathan Cape, 1929, p. 309.

97 **'The Word made flesh'**: Edwin Muir, 'The Incarnate One', *One Foot in Eden*, Faber & Faber, 1956, p. 47.

97 **'as if a key had been turned'**: 'Edwin Muir at Newbattle', *Akros*, August 1981.

98 **'one mind working in isolation'**: *Orkney Herald*, 5 August 1952.

98 **' "The world is a pleasant place" '**: *Orkney Herald*, 20 August 1946.

98 **'gentle, clinging, sweet stench'**: Edwin Muir, *An Autobiography*, p. 123.

98 **'wall of glass'**: Ibid.

98 **'like a grimy deposit'**: Ibid., p. 125.

98 **'We printed his poems'**: Leonard Woolf, *Downhill All the Way*, Hogarth Press, 1967, p. 131.

99 **'a perfectly quiet place'**: Edwin Muir to GMB, 20 April 1951 (EUL).

99 **'out of boredom'**: *For the Islands I Sing*, p. 91.

99 **'from you and from Orkney'**: Edwin Muir to GMB, 20 April 1951 (EUL).

100 **'in a kind of slow glide'**: *Edwin Muir: A Brief Memoir*, Castlelaw Press, 1975, p. 7.

CHAPTER 8: ONE FOOT IN EDEN

101 **'Every life, like every civilization'**: 'Envoi', *Edwin Muir: Selected Prose*, ed. George Mackay Brown, John Murray, 1987, p. 211.

102 **'It was an aristocratic gesture'**: Bernard Bergonzi, unpublished memoirs.

102 **'And, declared she, the cure was *water*'**: 'Newbattle: Early Days', 5 March 1977 (EUL).

103 **'among the sea sounds'**: *Evening News*, Edinburgh, 18 August 1984.

103 **'cautious and suspicious'**: GMB to Ernest and Janette Marwick, 5 November 1951 (OL).

103 **'rain down leaves'**: Ibid.

103 **'a very fine show'**: Ibid.

103 **'fluent laterals'**: 'Newbattle: Early Days'.

103 **'If you are an Orkneyman'**: Edwin Muir, 'Revisiting Orkney', written for BBC, 1956, but never broadcast, quoted in P. H. Butter, *Edwin Muir: Man and Poet*, Oliver & Boyd, 1966, p. 7.

103 **'I think if I lived to be a hundred'**: GMB to Ernest and Janette Marwick, 5 November 1951 (OL).

103 **'drenched in Orkney sea spray'**: Ibid.

103 **'terror' 'majesty'**: *Orkney Herald*, 7 October 1952.

103 **'the stars are feebler'**: Ibid.

104 **'a shy young man'**: Willa Muir, *Belonging*, Hogarth Press, 1968, pp. 279–80.

104 **'When you walk through the streets'**: GMB to Ernest and Janette Marwick, 5 November 1951 (OL).

104 **'like coming to some fruitful place'**: GMB to Ernest Marwick, 19 October 1953 (OL).

104 **'not so very different from those old brothers'**: *Orkney Herald*, 7 October 1952.

105 **'arboreal cathedral'**: *Orkney Herald*, 8 July 1952.

105 **'incense of old gracious living'**: *Glasgow Herald*, 9 May 1987.

105 **'yet older sanctity'**: Ibid.

105 **'The vanished royalty'**: GMB to Ernest and Janette Marwick, 5 November 1951 (OL).

106 **'The blast of Scotland's east wind'**: Spike Mays, *No More Soldiering for Me*, Eyre & Spottiswoode, 1971, p. 171.

106 **'a deep smouldering passion'**: *For the Islands I Sing*, p. 92.

106 **'might-have-been'**: *Orcadian*, 16 July 1953.

106 **'Besides what they absorbed'**: Willa Muir, *Belonging*, p. 273.

107 **'more precious than pearls'**: 'Newbattle: Early Days'.

107 **'This is not merely a first impression'**: GMB to Ernest and Janette Marwick, 5 November 1951 (OL).

107 **'in the interests of truth'**: Ibid.

107 **'He sees little future for poets'**: GMB to Ernest Marwick, 30 April 1952 (OL).

107 **'Here a new poem came to birth'**: Spike Mays, *No More Soldiering for Me*, p. 170.

108 **'For the most part it is a vague aimless drift'**: GMB to Ernest and Janette Marwick, 5 November 1951 (OL).

108 **'as if these symbols were somehow sacred'**: *Edwin Muir: a Brief Memoir*, p. 9.

108 **'I am intellectually compelled'**: John MacMurray quoted in Spike Mays, *No More Soldiering for Me*, p. 175.

108 **'His name is Norman MacCaig'**: GMB to Ernest Marwick, 30 April 1952 (OL).

109 **'I try to encourage them'**: *Edwin Muir and the Labyrinth*, March 1987.

110 **'We were poor'**: *Evening News*, Edinburgh, 18 August 1984.

110 **'like a rugby forward'**: *For the Islands I Sing*, p. 96.

110 **'The full wonderment'**: 'Edwin Muir at Newbattle', *Akros*, August 1981.

110 **'some faint air of Eden'**: Edwin Muir to GMB, 20 December 1956 (EUL).

110 **'of himself only a legend'**: Willa Muir's diary, 15 January 1951, quoted in Patricia Rowland Mudge, 'A Quorum of Willas', *Chapman*, No. 71, Winter 1992–93.

111 **'I stress this unmistakable integrity'**: T. S. Eliot, Preface to Edwin Muir, *Selected Poems*, Faber & Faber, 1965.

111 **'they seemed stable'**: Kathleen Raine, *Listener*, 15 January 1959.

111 **'like a silent clock'**: George Barker, *London Magazine*, June 1956, pp. 51–2.

111 **'No, Edwin Muir was no more a saint'**: GMB to Kulgin Duval, 5 July 1966.

112 **'One foot in Eden still'**: Edwin Muir, 'One Foot in Eden', *One Foot in Eden*, p. 46.

112 **'It was something he could not help giving out'**: Willa Muir, *Belonging*, p. 269.

112 **'We have, almost literally, one heart'**: Edwin Muir to Alec Aitken, 12 June 1941, in *Selected Letters of Edwin Muir*, ed. P. H. Butter, Hogarth Press, 1974, p. 130.

112 **'one instinctively clothed her'**: Revd William Thompson to the author, 25 August 1999.

113 **'the most malicious woman'**: Bernard Bergonzi, unpublished memoirs.

113 **'a soft-centred creature'**: Willa Muir quoted in Catriona Soukup, 'Willa in Wartime', *Chapman*, No. 71, Winter 1992–93.

113 **'was a soft-shell crab'**: Ibid.

113 **'And the fact remains'**: Willa Muir's diary, 20 August 1953, quoted in Patricia Rowland Mudge, 'A Quorum of Willas', *Chapman*, No. 71, Winter 1992–93.

114 **'Where would you be now'**: *Edwin Muir and the Labyrinth*.

115 **'a hard and solid impact'**: Eric Linklater, 'The Great Gales of Orkney', quoted in Michael Parnell, *Eric Linklater*, John Murray, 1984, p. 12.

115 **'a chunk of iron'**: *Orkney Herald*, 8 July 1952.

115 **'like an Assyrian'**: *For the Islands I Sing*, p. 98.

115 **'seedy and worn ugly'**: Ibid., p. 101.

116 **' "Man, man," said an old man'**: *Orkney Herald*, 2 February 1954.

116 **'much warmer, much less temperamental'**: GMB to Ernest Marwick, 30 April 1952 (OL).

116 **'lyrical with lilac'**: 'Edwin Muir at Newbattle', *Akros*, August 1981.

116 **'like a song'**: GMB to Ernest Marwick, 30 April 1952 (OL).

116 **'the real natural grace'**: Edwin Muir to GMB, 16 July 1953 (EUL).

116 **'I only half believe in prose'**: Edwin Muir to GMB, 13 May 1953 (EUL).

116 **'rather Chinese in manner'**: GMB to Ernest Marwick, 30 April 1952 (OL).

117 **'the same end in view as Joyce's "Dubliners" '**: Ibid.

117 **'Purity? . . . / First the aborigines'**: 'Orcadians: Seven Impromptus', *The Storm*, p. 28.

118 **'desires falling across our bodies'**: *For the Islands I Sing*, p. 103.

118 **'I had a dream about Newbattle'**: GMB to Willa Muir, 3 May 1970 (NLS).

118 **'Springtime in the spirit'**: *For the Islands I Sing*, p. 103.

118 **'Like the bard'**: *Orkney Herald*, 1 July 1952.

CHAPTER 9: A POCKETFUL OF HOPE

119 **'tongue dry as an old rag'**: *Orkney Herald*, 12 August 1952.

120 **'The slow seepings and rottings'**: *For the Islands I Sing*, p. 166.

120 **'grey and forlorn'**: *Orkney Herald*, 9 September 1952.

120 **'Fish drying on wires'**: Ernest Marwick, *Orkney Herald*, 12 July 1955.

121 **'quite evaporated'**: GMB to Ernest Marwick, undated [summer 1952] (OL).

122 **'A medical examination is called for'**: GMB to Ernest Marwick, 23 February 1953 (OL).

122 **'book after book after book'**: GMB to Flora Jack, 8 March 1953.

122 **'It seems to me that if he cannot write'**: Ernest Marwick's diary, 11 February 1953 (OL).

122 '. . . some excitement in our little town': GMB to Flora Jack, 23 March 1953.

123 'the crocuses and daffodils': GMB to Flora Jack, 2 May 1953.

123 'I had to summon all my virile strength': GMB to Flora Jack, 2 May 1953.

123 'perpetually set upon': Ibid.

123 'as big as peppermint drops': GMB to Flora Jack, 7 August 1953.

124 'If I had known I must come home': GMB to Flora Jack, 19 April 1953.

124 'a kind of drowsy contentment': GMB to Flora Jack, 2 September 1953.

125 'candlewick, leatherwork, basketry': *Orkney Herald*, 29 September 1955.

125 'I murmur it to myself': GMB to Flora Jack, 2 September 1953.

125 'I must tell you about Robert Rendall': GMB to Ernest Marwick, 30 December 1953 (OL).

126 'here they found beauty': *For the Islands I Sing*, p. 53.

126 'I think that the work of some writers': 'Writer's Shop', *Chapman*, No. 16, Summer 1976.

126 'It included within itself everything': Ibid.

127 'The Magnustide long swords of rain': 'Elegy', *Loaves and Fishes*, p. 40.

128 'You must know that you have friends': Willa Muir to GMB, 1 December 1953 (NLS).

128 'Forgive me for preaching': Edwin Muir to GMB, 31 March 1953 (EUL).

128 'But O what love came then!': 'Saint Magnus on Egilshay', *The Storm*, p. 13.

129 'When Janet rails at Robbie': 'Orcadians: Seven Impromptus', Ibid., p. 31.

130 'greatly to be shunned': *Contemporary Authors: Autobiography Series*, p. 70.

130 'than to do something new': *Orkney Herald*, 29 June 1954.

130 'In a London office Eliot sits': GMB to Ernest Marwick, 19 January 1954 (OL).

131 'a great chasm': 'Living in Orkney', *Saltire Review*, Winter 1955.

131 'gray horde': GMB to Roger Harris, 7 November 1970.

131 'a meaningful pattern': 'The Literature of the Northern Islands', Autumn 1973.

131 'simple and forthright': GMB to Ernest Marwick, 12 January 1954 (OL).

131 'I get hideously tired': GMB to Ernest Marwick, 14 July 1954 (OL).

132 'that delightful condition': *Orkney Herald*, 24 January 1956.

132 'really ingenious ugliness': 'Living in Orkney', *Saltire Review*, Winter 1955.

132 'brittle, celluloid manners': Ibid.

132 'What brisk hard-headed': *Orkney Herald*, 27 September 1955.

132 'this startling box of tricks': *Orkney Herald*, 2 February 1954.

133 'shone like the hooves of a unicorn': *Orkney Herald*, 10 May 1955.

133 'I expect all nations': Edwin Muir to GMB, 20 December 1955 (EUL).

134 'luminous images': Alexander Scott, *Arts Review*, BBC Scottish Home Service, quoted in *Orkney Herald*, 27 July 1954.

134 'I admire these poems': Edwin Muir to GMB, 9 April 1956 (EUL).

134 'Heart sick of the land': 'Thorfinn', *Loaves and Fishes*, pp. 15–16.

135 'marvellous, fresh, new thing': Ted Hughes, 'The Weaver of Time', BBC Radio, October 1991.

135 'clustered in age': 'Tam', *A Calendar of Love*, p. 101.

135 'sweetness and power': *For the Islands I Sing*, p. 109.

136 'tide of the spirit': *Orkney Herald*, 15 May 1956.

136 'singing out to sea': Ibid.

136 'Here, I am perfectly happy': GMB to Ernest Marwick, 8 May 1956 (OL).

137 'All around was the blue and green': *Orkney View*, June–July 1987.

137 'sent word that for the poet': Ibid.

137 'It was Edwin Muir': Ibid.

CHAPTER 10: THE MUSE IN ROSE STREET

138 'The idea of the Muse': *For the Islands I Sing*, p. 136.

138 'a monkish disposition': GMB to Dr Jean Kay, 6 July 1995.

138 'like a pain': 'The Tarn and the Rosary', *Hawkfall*, p. 194.

139 'a stand-offish city': GMB to Ernest Marwick, 23 October 1956 (OL).

140 '"Why," he cried': *For the Islands I Sing*, Ibid., p. 119.

141 'They did not often wear shoes': Candia McWilliam, 'The Many Colours of Blood', in *The Granta Book of the Family*, ed. Bill Buford, 1995, pp. 200–1.

141 **'schizophrenia . . . that goes right through'**: GMB to Charles Senior, 17 March 1964 (EUL).

141 **'suddenly and lastingly'**: *Evening News*, Edinburgh, 23 April 1983.

141 **'a web of strength and laughter'**: *For the Islands I Sing*, p. 118.

142 **'I must lie down'**: 'The Circus Animals' Desertion', *The Collected Poems of W. B. Yeats*, Macmillan, 1933, p. 392.

142 **'My mind doesn't work logically'**: GMB to Sister Margaret Tournour, 5 January 1992.

143 **'In general, I do not *like* books'**: *For the Islands I Sing*, p. 133.

143 **'It's all a game, really'**: GMB to Ernest Marwick, undated [September 1956] (OL).

143 **'a factory for turning out M.A.s'**: GMB to Ernest Marwick, 23 October 1956 (OL).

143 **'a frightful waste of time'**: GMB to Ernest Marwick, 8 February 1959 (OL).

143 **'Withinne the cloistre'**: Chaucer, 'The Second Nonnes Tale', *The Canterbury Tales*.

143 **'alone and apart'**: GMB to Ernest Marwick, 15 November 1959 (OL).

143 **'He punctuated our stammering efforts'**: *For the Islands I Sing*, pp. 114–15.

145 **'the most powerful intellectually and emotionally'**: Compton Mackenzie, *Literature in My Time*, Rich & Cowan, 1933.

145 **'Ah, did you once see Shelley plain'**: 'Memorabilia', *The Poems of Robert Browning*, Oxford University Press, 1905, p. 49.

146 **'I think [they] should be heard'**: GMB to Kulgin Duval, 24 October 1970.

146 **'*the* great character'**: Alexander Moffat interviewed in *Seven Poets*, Third Eye Centre, Glasgow, 1981, p. 10.

147 **'most of the Scottish poets'**: GMB to Ernest Marwick, 8 August 1957 (OL).

147 **'to put at ease, despite his shyness'**: Stewart Conn, Introduction to *Beside the Ocean of Time*, dramatization in two parts, BBC Radio 4, 6 and 13 April 1997.

147 **'And Brown leads wi' his Viking chin'**: Sydney Goodsir Smith, *Kynd Kittock's Land*, M. Macdonald, 1965, p. 14.

148 **'the warmest and most approachable'**: Alexander Moffat to the author, 12 September 2003.

148 **'He often felt, in moods of depression'**: 'Sealskin', *Hawkfall*, p. 136.

150 **'I remember nothing of our dialogue'**: *For the Islands I Sing*, p. 137.

150 **'It was a joy to give her things'**: Ibid.

150 **'a delight I had not known before'**: Ibid.

152 **'A lassie frae the mune'**: Sydney Goodsir Smith, 'The Muse in Rose Street', *Honour'd Shade*, selected and edited by Norman MacCaig, W. & R. Chambers, 1959, p. 116.

152 **'it was on *poets*'**: *For the Islands I Sing*, p. 137.

152 **'In a world of deniers'**: GMB to Charles Senior, 13 February 1961 (EUL).

152 **'She laughed a great deal'**: *For the Islands I Sing*, p. 137.

153 **'Throu midlife's forests'**: Tom Scott, 'The Paschal Candill', *Honour'd Shade*, p. 96.

154 **'deep chasms and crags'**: GMB to Stella Cartwright, 18 June 1965 (EUL).

154 **'Dear George, it is so strange'**: Stella Cartwright to GMB, undated (NLS).

155 **'Do not think it phoney'**: Stella Cartwright to GMB, undated (NLS).

155 **'Cargoes of alien pain'**: 'Four Poems for Stella', *Gambit*, Autumn 1960.

155 **'Dearest Stel, How often I wish'**: GMB to Stella Cartwright, 14 July 1966 (EUL).

155 **'I confess that sometimes'**: Edwin Muir to T. S. Eliot, 17 October 1956, quoted in *Selected Letters of Edwin Muir*, p. 188.

156 **'a vivid sense of delight'**: Edwin Muir to GMB, 5 December 1957 (EUL).

156 **'Eliot is growing old'**: Edwin Muir to GMB, 31 March 1953 (EUL).

156 **'like a tigress'**: Willa Muir to GMB, 1 November 1967 (NLS).

156 **'I had never dreamed that such a thing'**: *For the Islands I Sing*, p. 164.

156 **'Great good news'**: Edwin Muir to GMB, 23 April 1958 (EUL).

156 **'a most deliberate and admirable artist'**: Frank Kermode, *Spectator*, 17 July 1959.

156 **'Out of the ruck'**: Sydney Goodsir Smith, *Weekly Scotsman*, 9 July 1959.

157 **'If any poet deserves'**: Stella Cartwright to GMB, 25 November 1960 (NLS).

157 **'or about 10 fish-&-chip suppers'**: GMB to Ernest Marwick, 15 November 1959 (OL).

157 **'You love the sea'**: Stella Cartwright to GMB, 10 April 1960 (NLS).

158 **'the long gowns and the Lucky Jims'**: GMB to Norah Smallwood, 5 October 1958 (RUL).

158 **'The only one who is genuinely interested'**: GMB to Willa Muir, 2 July 1959 (EUL).

158 **'It isn't a unilateral thing'**: GMB to Stewart Conn, 30 September 1964 (BBC Written Archives Centre, Caversham).

158 **'They say that Finn'**: 'The Story of Jorkel Hayforks', *A Calendar of Love*, p. 148.

159 **'You are a presence in my heart'**: Stella Cartwright to GMB, 17 March 1960 (NLS).

159 **'Dearest George, If only I could be beside you'**: Stella Cartwright to GMB, 23 March 1960 (NLS).

159 **'such sweet things'**: Stella Cartwright to GMB, 15 March 1960 (NLS).

159 **'None of the great religions'**: Stella Cartwright to GMB, 10 March 1960 (NLS).

160 **'As you said recently'**: Stella Cartwright to GMB, 21 March 1962 (NLS).

161 **'It seemed to me that gayness'**: Edwin Morgan to the author, 13 March 2003.

161 **'he was totally closeted'**: Edwin Morgan to the author, 1 March 2003.

161 **'unthreatened and unfazed'**: Edwin Morgan to the author, 13 March 2003.

161 **'a loner's lack'**: Edwin Morgan to the author, 1 March 2003.

162 **'first laughed with Stella'**: *For the Islands I Sing*, p. 143.

CHAPTER 11: GRIEF AT EVERY MILESTONE

163 **'It hurts me to think of you being unhappy'**: GMB to Stella Cartwright, 11 November 1965 (EUL).

163 **'I think in a few months'**: Edwin Muir to GMB, 15 October 1958 (EUL).

164 **'The thought of teaching'**: GMB to Kulgin Duval, 9 March 1961.

164 **'what it means to be a man'**: GMB to Ian MacInnes, 26 December 1960.

166 **'I fish too long at the rock'**: 'Master Halcrow, Priest', *A Calendar of Love*, p. 124.

166 **'an immense oncoming evil'**: Ibid., p. 126.

166 **'Yesterday began the cutting'**: Ibid., pp. 129–30.

166 **'MARIAN: It is the common thing'**: 'Witch', *A Calendar of Love*, pp. 110–11.

167 **'Because her toes'**: Ibid., p. 121.

167 **'For the imagination is not an escape'**: *Orkney Herald*, 15 March 1955.

167 **'in slow patience and power'**: GMB to Ian MacInnes, 26 December 1960.

167 **'The smiler with the knife'**: GMB to Stella Cartwright, 18 June 1965 (EUL).

167 **'a constant and tormenting worry'**: GMB to Hugh Mackay, 3 July 1961.

167 **'She is bound to suffer'**: GMB to Charles Senior, 13 February 1961 (EUL).

167 **'a man with a crusading zeal'**: GMB to Ernest Marwick, 8 December 1960 (OL).

168 **'He must find me curiously apathetic'**: Ibid.

168 **'a focus of stagnation'**: GMB to Charles Senior, 13 February 1961 (EUL).

168 **'Make a mess of it'**: Stella Cartwright to GMB, 2 February 1961 (NLS).

168 **'Employers shy away'**: GMB to Ian MacInnes, 24 June 1961.

169 **'a feeling of inevitability'**: Quoted in Andrew Burnet, 'A Lamp is Lit in Thule'.

169 **'Great fun there yesterday'**: GMB to Charles Senior, 20 September 1962 (EUL).

169 **'They came to Gallowsha'**: 'Witch', *A Calendar of Love*, p. 122.

170 **'Some Catholic you are!'**: 'Mary Jane Mackay', *Northern Lights*, p. 141.

170 **'When I think of drink'**: GMB to Charles Senior, 18 August 1962 (EUL).

170 **'History and ceremony'**: GMB to Ian Parsons, 24 March 1962 (RUL).

170 **'Your saga-esque and runic kinds of poem'**: Cecil Day-Lewis to GMB, 4 May 1962 (RUL).

171 **'rhythmic virtuosity'**: GMB to Cecil Day-Lewis, 21 April 1962 (RUL).

171 **'yet I seem to bring such sorrow'**: Stella Cartwright to GMB, 21 March 1962 (NLS).

171 **'joyful, free, useful'**: Stella Cartwright to GMB, 1 December 1961 (NLS).

171 **'For you and I (je crois)'**: Stella Cartwright to GMB, undated (NLS).

171 **'the sparkling and startling colours'**: Stella Cartwright to GMB, 1 May 1962 (NLS).

171 **'lovely temperament'**: Stella Cartwright to GMB, undated [March 1970] (NLS).

171 **'of confused happiness and pain'**: *For the Islands I Sing*, p. 138.

171 **'and they keep plaguing me'**: GMB to Charles Senior, 20 May 1962 (EUL).

172 **'a gifted child artist'**: *Orkney Herald*, 3 August 1948.

172 **'It's more than awful'**: GMB to Tom Scott, 13 May 1962.

173 **'This will qualify me'**: GMB to Flora MacArthur, 18 March 1962.

173 **'cold winds of the world'**: GMB to Ian MacArthur, 27 February 1964.

173 **'No English poet'**: *For the Islands I Sing*, p. 150.

174 **'O the mind, mind has mountains'**: Gerard Manley Hopkins, 'No Worst, There is None'.

174 **'The Yanks have done all the scholarly and pedantic stuff'**: GMB to Tom Scott, 27 May 1964.

174 **'I've a feeling it's best'**: GMB to Charles Senior, 20 September 1962 (EUL).

174 **'keep piling up'**: GMB to Stewart Conn, 30 September 1964 (BBC Written Archives Centre, Caversham).

175 **'the top layer of dirt'**: GMB to Charles Senior, 17 March 1964 (EUL).

175 **'Menu for Dinner'**: GMB to Stella Cartwright, 22 April 1964 (EUL).

175 **'There are different kinds of fighting'**: GMB to Stella Cartwright, 11 November 1965 (EUL).

175 **'We have given each other a lot of wounds'**: GMB to Stella Cartwright, 25 November 1963 (EUL).

176 **'Marks and Spencer's was a cave'**: 'Mary Jane Mackay', *Northern Lights*, p. 136.

176 **'a futureless future'**: GMB to Stella Cartwright, 14 September 1964 (EUL).

177 **'All these years he had carried Norday'**: 'Sealskin', *Hawkfall*, pp. 132–3.

177 **'Think of Beckett'**: *Scottish Life and Letters*, BBC Scottish Home Service, 18 June 1967.

177 **'They are all about Orkney'**: GMB to Norah Smallwood, 3 June 1964 (RUL).

178 **'Because of his long pilgrimage'**: 'The Funeral of Ally Flett', *The Year of the Whale*, Chatto & Windus with the Hogarth Press, 1965, pp. 9–10.

CHAPTER 12: HEAVEN AND HELL PLAY POKER

180 **'apparently so unprotected'**: Peter Orr to the author, 22 September 1997.

180 **'It depends who remembers it'**: GMB interviewed by Peter Orr of the British Council, 14 October 1964, National Sound Archive.

181 **'would not easily be deflected'**: Peter Orr to the author, 22 September 1997.

181 **'the most exciting new voice'**: Peter Davison to Norah Smallwood, 27 November 1964 (RUL).

181 **'a nuisance in the world'**: GMB to Charles Senior, 17 January 1965 (EUL).

181 **'Nobody I know of, anywhere'**: Norman MacCaig, *Arts Review*, BBC Scottish Home Service, 7 October 1965.

181 **'They are Bruegel-like'**: Giles Gordon, *Scottish Field*, 16 January 1966.

182 **'wedding the inner experience'**: Kathleen Raine to GMB, 4 September 1965 (NLS).

182 **'a feeling of being newly wakened'**: Seamus Heaney to the author, 25 August 2004.

182 **'with delight and (probably) envy'**: Seamus Heaney to GMB, 28 August 1967 (NLS).

182 **'From now on'**: GMB to Stella Cartwright, 11 November 1965 (EUL).

182 **'the mind full of bustle'**: GMB to Charles Senior, 29 March 1965 (EUL).

182 **'interrogation of silence'**: 'The Poet', *The Year of the Whale*, p. 22.

182 **'crammed with words'**: GMB to Charles Senior, 3 March 1967 (EUL).

182 **'snoring like a circular saw'**: GMB to Stella Cartwright, 21 July 1965 (EUL).

182 **'Pam has taken a craze'**: GMB to Charles Senior, 18 August 1965 (EUL).

183 **'talk of culture'**: GMB interviewed by Arthur Pottersman, *Sun*, 7 October 1965.

183 **'what talent I have'**: GMB to Charles Senior, 12 March 1965 (EUL).

183 **'stark perpetual drama'**: 'Writing in Orkney', *Scottish Life and Letters*, BBC Scottish Home Service, 9 December 1965.

183 **'You sounded to me'**: Iain Crichton Smith to GMB, 20 December 1965 (NLS).

183 **'The darkness of winter'**: GMB to Charles Senior, 18 December 1964 (EUL).

183 **'throb of early summer'**: GMB to Charles Senior, 10 May 1966 (EUL).

183 'The light now': GMB to Charles Senior, 18 May 1968 (EUL).

183 'like a leaf in the wind': GMB to Charles Senior, 5 March 1965 (EUL).

184 'enough to keep me in ease': GMB to Norah Smallwood, 30 November 1965 (RUL).

184 'Orkney is a small green world': Foreword to *A Calendar of Love*.

184 'the bitter ordinances of time': *Magnus*, Hogarth Press, 1973, p. 72.

184 'Has Walls been here tonight?': 'The Wheel', *A Calendar of Love*, p. 78.

184 'Robert carefully replaced': Ibid., p. 82.

185 'spare, beautiful accuracy': Hilary Corke, *Listener*, 27 June 1967.

185 'strange and fierce': Frederick Laws, *Daily Telegraph*, 8 June 1967.

185 'I find myself': Hilary Corke, *Listener*, 27 June 1967.

185 'I am a very ordinary reader': Alexander Kelly to GMB, 30 May 1967 (NLS).

185 'I used to think it would be heaven': GMB interviewed by James Aitchison, *Weekend Scotsman*, 4 November 1967.

185 'full of interior rejoicing': GMB to Charles Senior, 26 June 1967 (EUL).

185 'expired in a violent flare-up': GMB to Stella Cartwright, 31 August 1965 (EUL).

185 'So now . . . I see I'm cut out': Ibid.

185 'You should know': GMB to Stella Cartwright, 11 November 1965 (EUL).

186 'like the ebb tide': GMB to Charles Senior, 1 December 1964 (EUL).

186 'The thought of whisky': GMB to Stella Cartwright, 27 December 1964 (EUL).

186 'like shot birds': *For the Islands I Sing*, p. 70.

186 'At noon he went to the inn': 'A Writer's Day', *The Wreck of the Archangel*, p. 32.

186 'What perverse demon': GMB to Charles Senior, 27 June 1966 (EUL).

186 'one of the poor ones': GMB to Charles Senior, 2 November 1966 (EUL).

187 'George, my dear, dear friend': Stella Cartwright to GMB, undated [June 1965] (NLS).

187 'needles and pins': Ibid.

187 'George, pray for me': Ibid.

187 'Be good and patient': GMB to Stella Cartwright, 31 December 1964 (EUL).

187 **'A lot of white thoughts'**: GMB to Stella Cartwright, 23 January 1965 (EUL).

187 **'a little silent visible prayer'**: GMB to Stella Cartwright, 14 May 1965 (EUL).

187 **'Keep well. What would our world be'**: GMB to Stella Cartwright, 9 June 1965 (EUL).

187 **'Not a morning or an evening'**: GMB to Stella Cartwright, 11 November 1965 (EUL).

187 **'She was so good'**: GMB to Charles Senior, 25 October 1965 (EUL).

188 **'unhappy, sick, destitute'**: GMB to Charles Senior, 9 January 1965 (EUL).

188 **'You must not talk'**: GMB to Stella Cartwright, 24 February 1966 (EUL).

188 **'The horrible heresy'**: GMB to Charles Senior, 23 August 1967 (EUL).

189 **'tear up her old life'**: GMB to Charles Senior, 19 July 1965 (EUL).

189 **'Nothing but rain'**: GMB to Stella Cartwright, 30 September 1966 (EUL).

189 **'her old sweetness'**: GMB to Charles Senior, 10 May 1966 (EUL).

189 **'I drink because I'm frightened'**: 'Celia', *A Time to Keep*, Hogarth Press, 1969, pp. 15–16.

190 **'hideous spiral of drinking'**: GMB to Charles Senior, 15 July 1967 (EUL).

190 **'hopelessness and decay'**: GMB to Charles Senior, 15 October 1967 (EUL).

190 **'The air inside 27 Dundas Street'**: GMB to Charles Senior, 28 September 1967 (EUL).

CHAPTER 13: INVOLVED WITH MANKIND

191 **'No man is an island'**: *Weekend Scotsman*, 30 August 1986.

191 **'Somebody has been stealing my clothes'**: 'Mary Jane Mackay', *Northern Lights*, p. 137.

191 **'and a part totally unsuited'**: Ibid.

192 **'yellow beast'**: GMB to Willa Muir, 29 July 1967 (NLS).

192 **'not due to booze'**: Stella Cartwright to GMB, 25 August 1967 (NLS).

192 **'some land of Lear and Carroll'**: GMB to Charles Senior, 5 October 1967 (EUL).

192 **'twisted ... into confusion'**: GMB to Charles Senior, 28 September 1967 (EUL).

192 **'like bad weather in the offing'**: GMB to Charles Senior, 27 June 1966 (EUL).

192 **'urge and reason'**: GMB to Charles Senior, 28 September 1967 (EUL).

192 **'She was learning'**: 'Many Jane Mackay', *Nothern Lights*, p. 138.

193 **'It's very lonely here now'**: GMB to Willa Muir, 13 November 1967 (NLS).

193 **'Nothing in it but pubs'**: 'Mary Jane Mackay', *Northern Lights*, p. 141.

194 **'a world that's at the same time'**: Charles Causley to Cecil Day-Lewis, 10 November 1968 (RUL).

194 **'the most powerful story-teller'**: *Aberdeen Press and Journal*, 1 February 1969.

194 **'precise, poetic and dazzling'**: Janice Elliot, *Guardian*, 7 February 1969.

194 **'the magician's touch'**: Paul Bailey, *Observer*, 2 March 1969.

194 **'These stories are written'**: Alexander Scott, *Lines Review*, March 1969.

195 **'the best organiser'**: 'The Treading of Grapes', *A Time to Keep*, p. 66.

195 **'Magnus Learmonth'**: Ibid., p. 67.

195 **'So then, princes'**: Ibid., p. 74.

196 **'I took the sleeping baby'**: 'A Time to Keep', *A Time to Keep*, p. 60.

197 **'George Mackay Brown is a F—ing better'**: Stella Cartwright to GMB, undated (NLS).

197 **'the essential Stella'**: GMB to Stella Cartwright, 29 March 1969 (EUL).

197 **'*genuine religious sense*'**: GMB to Stella Cartwright, 17 September 1964 (EUL).

197 **'of that truly good woman'**: Ibid.

197 **'shot through with a new beauty'**: GMB to Stella Cartwright, 27 November 1964 (EUL).

198 **'I think I won't be in Edinburgh'**: GMB to George Bruce, 20 February 1969 (BBC Written Archives Centre, Caversham).

198 **'posh houses'**: GMB to Ernest Marwick, 25 April 1969 (OL).

198 **'But it should bring in'**: GMB to Charles Senior, 28 December 1967 (EUL).

199 **'wears the old Janus-mask'**: GMB to Ian MacInnes, 26 December 1960.

199 **'gray wash of uniformity'**: GMB to Stella Cartwright, 9 January 1979 (EUL).

199 **'like a sailor's rope'**: *Per Mare: The Stromness Pageant*, 1967.

199 **'Time is not in love with concrete'**: *Orcadian*, 1 July 1971, reprinted in *Letters from Hamnavoe*, p. 12.

200 **'His mind had been ranging'**: *An Orkney Tapestry*, pp. 170–1.

200 **'That's the way poets are tried'**: GMB to Roger Harris, 16 February 1968.

200 **'a great sense of achievement'**: GMB to Roger Harris, 5 October 1968.

201 **'I rather hope'**: GMB to Kulgin Duval, 26 December 1967.

201 **'But in a sense I think that [his] confidence'**: Seamus Heaney, *Benchmark*, BBC Radio Scotland, 21 April 1996.

202 **'Connemara is the weirdest wildest sweetest place'**: GMB to Charles Senior, 19 May 1968 (EUL).

202 **'Yestreen the Queen had four Maries'**: *The Oxford Book of Ballads*, chosen and edited by Arthur Quiller-Couch, 1927, p. 372.

202 **'It was a chanting'**: Seamus Heaney to the author, 25 August 2004.

202 **'elevated at being across the water'**: Seamus Heaney, *Benchmark*, BBC Radio Scotland, 21 April 1996.

203 **'The midsummer sunsets'**: GMB to Willa Muir, 13 July 1968 (EUL).

203 **'This is my last territorial claim'**: Ian MacInnes, 'A Man of Great Humour', *Orcadian*, 18 April 1996.

203 **'My new house'**: GMB to Stella Cartwright, 23 November 1968 (EUL).

204 **'full of children, music'**: GMB to Ian MacArthur, 4 January 1970.

204 **'agonised maturity'**: Ernest Marwick, *North*, March 1970.

204 **'One of the characters'**: GMB to Willa Muir, 23 November 1968 (EUL).

205 **'the thought of such responsibilities'**: Ibid.

205 **'swifter than a weaver's shuttle'**: GMB to Stella Cartwright, 17 October 1969 (EUL).

205 **'by fizzes and leaps'**: GMB to Stella Cartwright, 26 October 1968 (EUL).

205 **'tossed three times a day'**: GMB to David Morrison, 31 May 1969 (NLS).

205 **'like smashing your bare foot'**: GMB to Stella Cartwright, 3 October 1969 (EUL).

205 **'actual and dear'**: *Orcadian*, 28 September 1972, reprinted in *Letters from Hamnavoe*, p. 55.

205 **'I am now really dead'**: Willa Muir to J. Mary Bosdêt, 8 March 1959 (OL).

206 **'isolation in the heart of the biggest city'**: GMB to Willa Muir, 23 November 1968 (EUL).

206 **'lovely little Dutch interior pictures'**: Willa Muir to GMB, undated (NLS).

206 **'Take them dissolved in liquid'**: Willa Muir to GMB, 4 August 1968 (NLS).

206 **'the lovely stir and bustle'**: Willa Muir to GMB, 1 December 1968 (NLS).

206 **'Your stories and poetry, George'**: Willa Muir to GMB, 30 September 1968 (NLS).

207 **'i. No Milne's, No Howard's'**: GMB to Stella Cartwright, 7 January 1969 (EUL).

208 **'great electrical device'**: Stella Cartwright to GMB, 4 July 1969 (NLS).

208 **'Don't let anyone run away'**: Ibid.

208 **'thrown on the rubbish heap'**: Stella Cartwright to GMB, 19 January 1970 (NLS).

208 **'I feel suicidal'**: Stella Cartwright to GMB, 13 August [1969] (NLS).

209 **'Dearest Stel, You've got to have a rhinoceros hide'**: GMB to Stella Cartwright, 16 August 1969 (EUL).

209 **'Long since we were a family'**: Edwin Muir, 'The Ring', *Collected Poems*, Faber & Faber, 1960, p. 133.

209 **'but in a sense, *everyone* is the writer's concern'**: *American Who's Who of Literature*, 1983.

209 **'well considered, devastating'**: Ernest Marwick, *North*, March 1970.

210 **'through the eye of the needle of Orkney'**: Seamus Heaney, dust jacket of *Selected Poems 1954–1983*, John Murray, 1991.

210 **'Midnight. The shoal drifts'**: 'Fisherman's Bride', *Fishermen with Ploughs*, p. 75.

210 **'so bizarre in parts'**: GMB to Stella Cartwright, 27 September 1969 (EUL).

211 **'a regional pantheon'**: Peter Porter, *Guardian*, 12 August 1971.

211 **'if only a scream of horror'**: Maurice Wiggin, *Sunday Times*, 22 August 1971.

211 **'There are stories in the air'**: GMB interviewed by the author, *The Times*, 25 July 1992.

211 **'It's just that he's retreated'**: Ted Hughes, 'The Weaver of Time', BBC Radio, October 1991.

211 **'My hunch is'**: Seamus Heaney to the author, 25 August 2004.

212 **'Lately, I have hesitated'**: Naomi Mitchison to GMB, 5 September 1971 (NLS).

212 **'the fear of poetry in Scotland'**: Ernest Marwick, *North*, March 1970.

CHAPTER 14: WORDS OF RESURRECTION

213 **'Slowly the sun heaved itself'**: *Greenvoe*, p. 279.

213 **'extraordinary closing in'**: Peter Maxwell Davies, 'The Weaver of Time', BBC Radio, October 1991.

214 **'*Condemnation* / The winter jar of honey'**: *An Orkney Tapestry*, pp. 36–8.

215 **'a hyper state of tiredness'**: Peter Maxwell Davies, 'The Weaver of Time', BBC Radio, October 1991.

216 **'a slight small dark active man'**: Unpublished essay quoted in Mike Seabrook, *Max*, Victor Gollancz, 1994, p. 125.

216 **'in the tremulous hope'**: 'A Writer in Orkney', *Look Stranger*, BBC Television, 8 October 1970.

217 **'What did you do with a dead man?'**: *Greenvoe*, pp. 169–70.

218 **'Gino Manson placed a cut-out photograph'**: Ibid., p. 54.

218 **'*Pyjamas*, I say softly'**: Ibid., pp. 109–10.

218 **'the remnants of her life'**: Ibid., p. 97.

218 **'Afternoon was always the quietest time'**: Ibid., pp. 17–18.

219 **'over a glass of whisky'**: *For the Islands I Sing*, p. 177.

219 **'a glow under the northern horizon'**: 'Autumn in the Islands', October 1983 (EUL).

219 **'Autumn has come'**: GMB to Stella Cartwright, 23 August 1969 (EUL).

220 **'like a river in spate'**: GMB to Norah Smallwood, 30 March 1970 (RUL).

220 **'I wrote steadily for 3 hours'**: GMB to Roger Harris, 27 March 1970.

220 **'I just want to be at peace'**: GMB to Stella Cartwright, 29 December 1969 (EUL).

220 **'a certain condition'**: GMB to Norah Smallwood, 2 July 1971 (RUL).

221 **'The Glebe went down'**: *Greenvoe*, p. 269.

222 **'There's an awful breathless hush'**: GMB to Roger Harris, 12 April 1973.

223 **'The uranium is slumbering'**: GMB to Roger Harris, 16 March 1979.

CHAPTER 15: A PLACE OF BURNINGS AND ICE

224 **'So Magnus Erlendson'**: *Magnus*, p. 170.

225 **'To us writers'**: Iris Murdoch, *Bookseller*, 27 October 1984.

225 **'particular care'**: Norah Smallwood to I. P. M. Chambers, 26 February 1969 (RUL).

225 **'Perhaps we'll meet some day'**: GMB to Patricia Crowden, 23 August 1975 (NLS).

225 **'the thought . . . turns me on a gridiron'**: GMB to Norah Smallwood, 8 January 1972 (RUL).

226 **'it is good for none of us'**: GMB to Stella Cartwright, 4 January 1970 (EUL).

226 **'Dear Stella, *surely* there must be a job'**: GMB to Stella Cartwright, 31 January 1970 (EUL).

226 **'Selling cosmetics'**: GMB to Stella Cartwright, 17 February 1970 (EUL).

227 **'I am rather tight-fisted'**: GMB to Nora Kennedy, 28 July 1976.

227 **'Of course there is no need'**: Stella Cartwright to GMB, 11 March 1970 (NLS).

227 **'it is very curly'**: Norah Smallwood to Ronald Hjort, 11 February 1974 (RUL).

228 **'probed and peered into'**: GMB to Stella Cartwright, 22 September 1969 (EUL).

228 **'Writing is a trade'**: 'A Writer in Orkney', *Look Stranger*, BBC Television, 8 October 1970.

228 **'in no way like Larkin's "shit in the chateau" '**: Seamus Heaney to the author, 25 August 2004.

228 **'Then the routine'**: GMB to Roger Harris, 28 August 1971.

229 **'and also, I suspect, to have a good look'**: GMB to Norah Smallwood, 7 October 1972 (RUL).

229 **'some kind of summer peepshow'**: GMB to Norah Smallwood, 9 August 1973 (RUL).

229 **'slip in with folded hands'**: GMB to Roger Harris, 29 December 1971.

229 **'it's only that, when certain facets'**: GMB to Roger Harris, 16 February 1968.

229 **'like a gory battlefield'**: *Scotsman*, 19 December 1973.

229 **'And it sometimes happens'**: GMB to Roger Harris, 24 June 1972.

230 **'disgusted'**: *Orkney Herald*, 19 April 1949.

230 **'the marriage feast of Christ'**: *Magnus*, p. 70.

230 **'intermeshed with his diurnal existence'**: Ibid., p. 126.

230 **'Magnus looked at Ingerth'**: Ibid., p. 71.

230 **'Hold Ragnarson smiled'**: Ibid., p. 73.

231 **'dead foreign words'**: Ibid., p. 141.

231 **'as some old story'**: Ibid., p. 137.

231 **'His mind took the small infusion'**: Ibid., p. 145.

232 **'A weird tale, well told'**: Max Laidlaw, *Leader-Post*, Regina (Saskatchewan), 9 August 1974.

232 **'the most beautiful contemporary book'**: Jacky Gillott, *The Times*, 20 September 1973.

232 **'You and I must go there'**: Norah Smallwood to GMB, 9 January 1974 (RUL).

232 **'as no man alone'**: Stella Cartwright to GMB, 9 January 1974 (NLS).

233 **'gentle with my vast ignorance'**: Jay Parini to the author, 19 October 2004.

233 **'somehow willing conversation'**: Jay Parini to the author, 2 December 2004.

233 **'swing of the horny tail'**: GMB to Dr Michael Curtis, 26 May 1977.

233 **'a prison of the self'**: *Scotsman*, 15 November 1975.

233 **'All that winter of labour'**: *Scotsman*, 19 December 1973.

234 **'to entertain a small community'**: Introduction to *Letters from Hamnavoe*.

234 **'like raindrops off a farm gate'**: GMB to Roger Harris, 6 March 1975.

234 **'a machine that churns out poems'**: GMB to Roger Harris, 5 April 1975.

234 **'spin his web or die'**: GMB to Roger Harris, 14 November 1975.

235 **'lies'**: GMB to Stella Cartwright, 3 November 1974 (EUL).

235 **'drowsy and content'**: GMB to Kulgin Duval and Colin Hamilton, 30 October 1975.

235 **'I feel old and weary'**: GMB to Patricia Crowden, 18 June 1976 (NLS).

235 **'tired of years of writing'**: GMB to Roger Harris, 25 June 1976.

235 **'They will take it from your widowed hands'**: 'The Poet', *New Statesman*, 17 May 1974.

236 **'I have never been in love'**: GMB to Kulgin Duval, 12 January 1975.

236 **'If I remember her now'**: *Earth Gold, Sea Silver*, BBC Radio Scotland, 16 March 1976.

CHAPTER 16: A RACK OF FLOWERS

237 **'Do not expect a kind of love'**: GMB to Nora Kennedy, 4 May 1977.

238 **' "Can we come in, Margaret-Anne?" '**: *Orcadian*, 22 July 1976, reprinted in *Under Brinkie's Brae*, Gordon Wright, 1979, p. 29.

238 **'There is a deep sadness in you'**: GMB to Nora Kennedy, 13 August 1976.

239 **'a golden-gray crescent of sand'**: *Orcadian*, 19 August 1976, reprinted in *Under Brinkie's Brae*, p. 32.

239 **'dull life'**: GMB to Nora Kennedy, 18 August 1976.

239 **'enchantment'**: GMB to Nora Kennedy, 28 August 1976.

239 **'I hope you will understand'**: GMB to Nora Kennedy, 28 July 1976.

240 **'You have taken me into regions'**: GMB to Nora Kennedy, 13 August 1976.

240 **'Strange things have been happening'**: GMB to Roger Harris, 26 November 1976.

240 **'The verse fairly erupted'**: GMB to Roger Harris, 23 October 1976.

240 **'mining ore all winter'**: GMB to Patricia Crowden, 4 November 1976 (NLS).

240 **'I think now I am writing for you'**: GMB to Nora Kennedy, 18 August 1976.

240 **'I know I am very selfish'**: GMB to Nora Kennedy, 9 January 1977.

241 **'cold and unthinking'**: Nora Kennedy to GMB, 12 August 1977 (NLS).

241 **'busy coolness'**: Nora Kennedy to GMB, 4 October 1976 (NLS).

241 **'Do you really want me to say'**: GMB to Nora Kennedy, 22 February 1977.

242 **'All my friends like you'**: GMB to Nora Kennedy, 9 January 1977.

242 **'a low ebb of the mind'**: Ibid.

242 **'There are so many things I like'**: Ibid.

242 **'I know how the physical reality'**: Ibid.

242 **'It's as if the foundations'**: GMB to Nora Kennedy, 22 February 1977.

242 **'Poor Nora'**: GMB to Kenna Crawford, 4 February 1988.

243 **'I don't know what to do about Nora'**: GMB to Roger Harris, 3 February 1979.

243 **'The weather is bleak and cold'**: GMB to Roger Harris, 9 December 1977.

243 **'I am very upset'**: GMB to Roger Harris, 17 March 1978.

243 **'sterile carefree'**: GMB to Roger Harris, 3 August 1978.

243 **'making life "a tale told by an idiot"'**: GMB to Roger Harris, 21 August 1981.

243 **'a long tissue of boredom'**: GMB to Jenny Robertson, 2 March 1980.

243 **'suffused with anguish'**: GMB to Roger Harris, 11 September 1980.

243 **'True heroism'**: GMB to Stella Cartwright, 13 February 1972 (EUL).

244 **'all / Life death does end'**: Gerard Manley Hopkins, 'No Worst, There is None'.

244 **'shedding / Shadow from flesh'**: 'Spinster', *Island Wedding*, Celtic Cross Press, 2005.

245 **'lust unsanctified'**: *Magnus*, p. 70.

245 **'face the truth'**: GMB to Renée Simm, 10 April 1979.

245 **'so that I can learn to see things'**: GMB to Dr Michael Curtis, 28 July 1980.

246 **'Laziness is my constant companion'**: GMB to Jenny Robertson, 30 April 1981.

246 **'It becomes a burden'**: GMB to Renée Simm, 23 June 1981.

246 **'I had the time of my life'**: Seamus Heaney to the author, 25 August 2004.

246 **'There's something that Ted Hughes said'**: Seamus Heaney, *Benchmark*, BBC Radio Scotland, 21 April 1996.

247 **'The flute symbolises'**: *The Independent*, 3 August 1991.

247 **'more a sombre fable'**: Ibid.

247 **'gleams and fragments'**: GMB to Renée Simm, 1 February 1979.

248 **'I had an unpleasant experience'**: GMB to Jenny Robertson, 11 June 1982.

248 **'great shoots and ferns'**: GMB to Jenny Robertson, 13 February 1982.

248 **'snow over Orkney'**: GMB to Roger Harris, 12 January 1978.

248 **'Isn't it lovely being in April?'**: GMB to Jenny Robertson, 1 April 1982.

248 **'It has been bitterly cold'**: GMB to Jenny Robertson, 15 April 1982.

248 **'passionate, earthy, beautifully wrought'**: GMB to Renée Simm, 14 March 1979.

248 **'One flinches from the awful inevitable cruelty'**: GMB to Jenny Robertson, 24 March 1981.

249 **'If ever I feel suicidal'**: GMB to Roger Harris, 5 April 1968.

249 **'Such radiance, such goodness'**: GMB to Jenny Robertson, 6 June 1982.

250 **'the most glorious feeling'**: GMB to Renée Simm, 15 October 1978.

250 **'a taste of ashes'**: GMB to Patricia Crowden, 29 April 1978 (NLS).

250 **'a pure seeking'**: 'The Masque of Bread', *Loaves and Fishes*, p. 13.

250 **'unease and almost despair'**: GMB to Roger Harris, 14 April 1978.

250 **'a pollutant'**: GMB to Hugo Brunner, 10 March 1985 (RUL).

250 **'incriminating documents'**: GMB to Kulgin Duval, 22 January 1977.

250 **'thorns'**: GMB to Hugo Brunner, 24 March 1985 (RUL).

250 **'weird delusions'**: GMB to Jenny Robertson, 28 March 1985.

250 **'winding straight to the nut-house'**: GMB to Hugo Brunner, 10 March 1985 (RUL).

250 **'I am, most of the time, more a Sir Toby'**: GMB to Norah Smallwood, 15 December 1977 (RUL).

251 **'If ever anybody should not feel'**: Norah Smallwood to GMB, 7 March 1980 (RUL).

252 **'no great shakes at talking'**: GMB to Jenny Robertson, 2 March 1980.

253 **'especially the happy crazy carefree ones'**: Stella Cartwright to GMB, 7 December 1982 (NLS).

253 **'Home and *dry*'**: Stella Cartwright to GMB, 13 March 1983 (NLS).

255 **'The party was over'**: Stanley Roger Green to the author, 17 June 2004.

256 **'So, once in the 50s'**: GMB to Stella Cartwright, 15 March 1982 (EUL).

256 **'Two days now of sun'**: GMB to Stella Cartwright, 20 April 1982 (EUL).

256 **'The sun is weaving winter cloth-of-gold'**: GMB to Stella Cartwright, 6 November 1984 (EUL).

CHAPTER 17: A NEW STAR

258 **'All the sweet dear good things'**: GMB to Kenna Crawford, 3 May 1987.

259 **'Somewhere in the great music'**: *For the Islands I Sing*, pp. 139–40.

259 **'One knows that one is growing older'**: *Contemporary Authors: Autobiographical Series*, p. 74.

259 **'the brightening / Blizzard'**: 'That Night in Troy', *Loaves and Fishes*, p. 10.

259 **'Do you get wiser'**: BBC interview, 1991.

260 **'Where are the never-to-be-forgotten friends'**: *Contemporary Authors: Autobiographical Series*, p. 74.

260 **'To have got so far, alone'**: 'The Seventieth Mile Stone', *Scotsman*, 12 October 1991, published as 'One Star in the West' in *Following a Lark*, John Murray, 1996, p. 85.

261 **'I don't know what you did'**: GMB to Kenna Crawford, 17 February 1987.

261 **'confused at so much beauty'**: GMB to Kenna Crawford, 26 September 1987.

261 **'The latch lifted'**: 'A Writer's Day: 21 April 1986', GMB to Kenna Crawford, 29 November 1986, published in *The Wreck of the Archangel*, p. 33.

261 **'honey-coloured skin' 'sweep of bright hair'**: *For the Islands I Sing*, p. 137.

261 **'brought a radiance'**: GMB to Kenna Crawford, 11 July 1986.

261 **'left a rare sweetness'**: GMB to Kenna Crawford, 13 November 1986.

261 **'A new star'**: GMB to Kenna Crawford, 3 October 1987.

262 **'Please, please come back'**: GMB to Kenna Crawford, 7 November 1986.

262 **'Now she has found a way'**: 'Kenna's Return to Orkney', published as 'Kenna's Return to the Islands', *Aberdeen University Review*, Autumn 1993.

262 **'We and earth and sun and corn'**: 'Christmas Poem', *The Wreck of the Archangel*, p. 104.

262 **'. . . That dear one'**: 'Gossip in Hamnavoe', GMB to Kenna Crawford, 31 January 1987, published in *Travellers*, p. 63.

263 **'one flower in that garden'**: GMB to Kenna Crawford, 16 September 1986.

263 **'Many a day I feel lonely'**: GMB to Kenna Crawford, 17 September 1987.

263 **'What happiness yesterday'**: GMB to Kenna Crawford, 3 February 1987.

264 **'like a snake-charmer'**: GMB to Kenna Crawford, 25 December 1986.

264 **'pure inspiration'**: GMB to Kenna Crawford, 7 February 1987.

264 **'They come to me in sleep'**: 'A Dream of Fair Women', GMB to Kenna Crawford, 7 March 1987.

265 **'He thought, / Turning the last blank pages'**: 'The First of May: A Vanished Hamnavoe Merchant', *Northern Lights*, p. 37.

265 **'great ship of stone'**: 'Chorus of the Children', *A Celebration for Magnus*, Balnain Books, 1987, p. 69.

266 **'an event so unlikely'**: Father Giles Conacher to the author, 25 January 2005.

266 **'lovable, simple, open'**: Ibid.

266 **'a beautiful girl'**: *Beside the Ocean of Time*, John Murray, 1994, p. 110.

267 **'If she wasn't a niece'**: Ibid., pp. 113–14.

267 **'It's as if someone had broken a beautiful lamp'**: GMB to Kenna Crawford, 10 January 1988.

267 **'Every time I open the door'**: GMB to Kenna Crawford, 19 March 1988.

267 **'transfigured everything'**: GMB to Kenna Crawford, 7 February 1987.

268 **'Let him go if he wants to'**: Carmen Callil to Andrew Motion, undated (RUL).

269 **'hope for poetry'**: Peter Levi, *Catholic Herald*, 8 September 1989.

269 **'Or is it a quest for "real things"'**: Introduction to *The Wreck of the Archangel*.

269 **'In the dregs of sun'**: 'The Wreck of the Archangel', Ibid., pp. 1–2.

270 **'Who knows the stone music'**: 'Stone Music', *Stone*, Kulgin A. Duval and Colin H. Hamilton, 1987, p. 11.

270 **'I think of the marvels'**: *Contemporary Authors: Autobiographical Series*, p. 74.

271 **'Old men ought to be explorers'**: T. S. Eliot, 'East Coker'.

271 **'The luxury of stretching out'**: 'Shetland Diary', 30 May 1988, *Northern Lights*, p. 311.

271 **'I am still brimming over'**: GMB to Kulgin Duval, 17 June 1988.

272 **'the kind of temperament on which fortune smiles'**: GMB to Kulgin Duval, 21 November 1975.

273 **'He was a formidably craggy'**: Peter Levi, *Catholic Herald*, 8 September 1989.

273 **'Cuckoo-echoing, bell-swarmèd'**: Gerard Manley Hopkins, 'Duns Scotus's Oxford'.

273 **'unlike poems written in English before'**: *Orcadian*, 22 June 1989, reprinted in *Rockpools and Daffodils*, Gordon Wright, 1992, p. 213.

273 **'sweet' 'eager' 'welcoming'**: Ibid., pp. 213–14.

CHAPTER 18: CONTENT WITH SILENCE

275 **'Death, critics say'**: 'A Writer in Orkney', *Look Stranger*, BBC Television, 8 October 1970.

275 **'I have a kind of thinking'**: GMB to Tom Scott, 1 March 1990.

276 **'One with healing in his hands'**: 'Cutting Down Trees', *Foresterhill*, Babel, 1992.

276 **'And the bitter fruit'**: 'Homily', Ibid.

276 **'A waiting room for the poor soul'**: 'Lux Perpetua', Ibid.

276 **'a soul go past bereft'**: 'Homily', Ibid.

277 **'She has the heart of a lion'**: GMB to Dr Jean Kay, 29 May 1994.

277 **'seemingly bottomless well'**: GMB to Sister Margaret Tournour, 7 March 1996.

278 **'I suppose he's as close to being a saint'**: GMB to Dr Jean Kay, 26 March 1993.

278 **'Write a little every day'**: GMB to Surinder Punjÿa, 13 April 1993.

278 **'In this time of hate'**: 'Song for St Magnus', *Northern Lights*, p. 30.

279 **'The boy stood for a long time'**: *Vinland*, John Murray, 1992, p. 12.

279 **'the thud of a body'**: Ibid., p. 15.

279 **'in complete harmony'**: Ibid., p. 96.

279 **'It is such a moving image'**: *Contemporary Authors: Autobiographical Series*, p. 74.

280 **'lost, loved, longed-for'**: *Beside the Ocean of Time*, p. 212.

280 **'glories of light'**: Ibid., p. 217.

280 **' "We never find what we set our hearts on" '**: Ibid.

280 **'also something I find hard to put into words'**: Sheenagh Pugh to the author, 27 October 2004.

281 **'The imagination is still working'**: *For the Islands I Sing*, p. 184.

281 **'shaping divinity'**: Ibid., p. 186.

281 **'To lose one's own will'**: Ibid.

281 **'Catholicism has meant a great deal'**: Answers to a questionnaire from Alan Bold, 27 January 1977 (EUL).

281 **'And lovers'**: 'Hamnavoe', *Loaves and Fishes*, p. 23.

281 **'Ploughboy / and milklass'**: 'Hamnavoe', *Selected Poems 1954–1983*, p. 9.

282 **'A russet stallion'**: 'A Child's Calendar', *Fishermen with Ploughs*, p. 62.

282 **'Peatmen strike the bog'**: 'A Child's Calendar', *Selected Poems 1954–1983*, p. 65.

282 **'whatever the parish talk'**: 'When You Are Old', *Poems New and Selected*, 1971, p. 36.

282 **'the greed devouring the nation's spirit'**: GMB to Renée Simm, 8 February 1979.

282 **'May the money go'**: GMB to Stephen Tumim, 1 January 1993.

282 **'His house is crammed'**: 'An Old Man in July', *Northern Lights*, pp. 47–8.

283 **'I could buy a little island'**: GMB interviewed by Valentine Low, *Evening Standard*, 4 October 1994.

283 **'Booker business'**: GMB to Surinder Punjȳa, 17 September 1994.

283 **' "Booker" blocks the horizon'**: GMB to Surinder Punjȳa, 22 September 1994.

284 **'There lives the dearest freshness'**: Gerard Manley Hopkins, 'God's Grandeur'.

284 **'A star for a cradle'**: 'Lux Perpetua', published in *Following a Lark*, p. 34.

285 **'Strange how the mind'**: GMB to Renée Simm, 28 January 1981.

285 **'hide myself away'**: GMB to Sister Margaret Tournour, 21 December 1993.

285 **'And one day after school'**: 'Spring: The Kids of Feaquoy Farm', *Following a Lark*, p. 53.

286 **'the cold gnaws at my bones'**: GMB to Sister Margaret Tournour, 18 January 1996.

286 **'coughs and langour'**: Ibid.

286 **'tall primal dust'**: 'The Harrowing of Hell', *Northern Lights*, p. 25.

287 **'Pooh – I suffered and enjoyed'**: GMB to William Dalrymple, 1 April 1996.

287 **'to relish each one of the thirty days of April'**: *Orcadian*, 11 April 1996.

288 **'Carve the runes'**: 'A Work for Poets', *Following a Lark*, p. 86.

288 **'more interest in spiritual integrity'**: Seamus Heaney, *Benchmark*, BBC Radio Scotland, 21 April 1996.

288 **'bard in the old tradition'**: Iain Crichton Smith quoted in the *Herald* [Glasgow], 15 April 1996.

288 **'a bonfire'**: Stewart Conn quoted in the *Scotsman*, 15 April 1996.

288 **'astonishing clarity'**: Douglas Gifford, *Scotsman*, 15 April 1996.

288 **'His best works establish him'**: Alan Bold, *Herald* [Glasgow], 15 April 1996.

289 **'the great and the good'**: Ron Ferguson, *Herald* [Glasgow], 17 April 1996.

289 **'I have a deep-rooted belief'**: 'Mary Jane Mackay', *Northern Lights*, pp. 141–2.

Acknowledgements

'You'd get plenty of help from my old friends,' George wrote when this biography was first mooted, and to a number of his old friends I am particularly indebted. Without the unflagging cooperation of his literary executor, Archie Bevan, the book could never have been written, and I owe him, and his wife, Elizabeth, enormous thanks. I should also like to thank George's former editor Hugo Brunner, whose idea this project was, and who helped secure support for it both from George and from John Murray. I am deeply grateful to Hugh Mackay, who revisited old memories, not all of them happy, in order to help me tell the story of Stella Cartwright. I am grateful, too, both to Nora Kennedy and to Kenna Crawford for their generosity and trust in allowing me to read their letters from George, and thereby to understand the central role that each of them played in the latter years of his life.

I have been very fortunate in my editors, Grant McIntyre and Anya Serota, who have struck a cunning balance between encouragement and editorial rigour. Edward Faulkner at John Murray has been endlessly helpful, and Jane Birkett, a former editor of George's, was a sharp-eyed and sympathetic copy editor. My agent, Gillon Aitken, has been both patient and supportive.

Among my family and friends I am especially grateful to Jock Dalrymple, who first introduced me to George's work and who suggested many helpful amendments to the text. Anthony Gardner and Isabel Quigly also read the book in draft, and their comments and corrections were invaluable. I thank my parents, John and Christian Parham, for their support, practical and moral; my sister-in-law Madeline Fergusson for her painstaking and meticulous work in proofreading and assembling references; and my daughters, Flora and Isabella, who have never known life without George Mackay Brown.

My employers at the Royal Society of Literature could not have been kinder or more imaginative in enabling me to find time to write. In particular, I am grateful to Maggie Gee, Ronald Harwood and Michael Holroyd.

I am grateful to the staff of the BBC Written Archives Centre; the British Library; the Corrigall Farm Museum; Edinburgh University Library; Leeds University Library; the London Library; the National Library of Scotland; Reading University Library; St Andrews University Library; the Scottish Poetry Library; the Stromness Museum; and Sussex University Library. Above all, I am grateful to the Orkney Library – the oldest public library in Scotland – and in particular to its principal archivist, Alison Fraser.

Among the many others to whom I owe thanks are Richard Adams; the late Janet Adam Smith; Belinda Allan; Stephanie Allen; Alan Anderson; Verity Andrews; Judy Arnold; Marian Ashburn; Phil Astley; the Revd Peter Barry; Pamela Beasant; Professor Bernard Bergonzi; Anne Bevan; Ronald Blythe; the late Alan Bold; Charles Booth-Clibborn; the late Neville Braybrooke; Erlend Brown; Hazel Brown; the late Jackie Brown; the late George Bruce; Mary Rose Brunner; David Buckman; the Revd Andrew Burnet; David Burnett; Euan Cameron; David Campbell; William Cartwright; Anne Chisholm; David Christie; the Revd Giles Conacher OSB; Stewart Conn; the Most Revd Mario Conti; Liz Cooke; Harriet Craigie; Julia and Robby Crenian; Dr Jim Cromarty; Bill Crichton; Kevin Crossley-Holland; William Dalrymple; Tam Dalyell; Emma de Ath; Allison Dixon; David Dixon; Fraser Dixon; Michael Drever; Katherine Duncan-Jones; John Durkin; Kulgin Duval; Tabitha Elwes; Roger Fenby; R. P. Fereday; the Revd Ronald Ferguson; the late Dr Patrick Fergusson; Dr Debra Fitzherbert; Barbara and Donald Fraser; Simon Fraser; Marigold Freeman-Attwood; George Garson; Professor Douglas Gifford; the Revd Hugh Gilbert OSB; Susie Gilbertson; Debbie Gill; Peter and Betty Grant; Stanley Roger Green; Miriam Griffin; Johnny and Kate Grimond; John Halsey; Colin Hamilton; David Hammond; Roger Harris; Lady Selina Hastings; Seamus Heaney; Bevis Hillier; the late Professor Philip Hobsbaum; Rosemary Hobsbaum; the late David Hughes; Elizabeth Hughes; Paddy Hughes; Alan Jenkins; Paula Johnson; Margaret Johnston; Dr Derrick Johnstone; P. J. Kavanagh;

Dr Jean Kay; Professor Brendan Kennelly; Joanna Kitchin; Margaret Laurenson; Anne Leith; Robert Leslie; Jeremy Lewis; Flora and Ian MacArthur; Dr Marjory Palmer McCulloch; the late Sister Flora MacDonald RSCJ; the Very Revd Canon Robert McDonald; Morag McGill; Catrina McGillivray; Graham McGirk; the late Ian MacInnes; Jean MacInnes; David Mackie; Christopher MacLehose; Marjory McNeill; Tam McPhail; Gimma MacPherson; Candia McWilliam; Edward Maggs; the late Dr James Maitland; Pamela Mason; Allan Massie; Winifred Maynard; Sir Peter Maxwell Davies; Professor Edward Mendelson; Michael Meredith; Gerry and Nora Meyer; Professor Karl Miller; Gunnie Moberg; Alexander Moffat; Professor Edwin Morgan; Ingrid Morrison; William Mostyn-Owen; Barbara and Gregor Murray; Professor Isobel Murray; John and Virginia Murray; the Revd Kenneth Nugent SJ; Robert Nye; Dennis O'Driscoll; Angus O'Neill; Iona Opie; the late Peter Orr; Professor Jay Parini; Janette Park; Jim Parker; Christopher Prendergast; Sheenagh Pugh; Surinder Punjȳa; the late Kathleen Raine; Nick Rankin; Sally Ratcliffe; Dorothy and Jack Rendall; Rosemary Roberts; Jenny Robertson; John Robertson, Heather Scott; Ian Scott; the late Renée Simm; David Sinclair; the late Iain Crichton Smith; Dr Hilda Spear; Lachlan Stewart; Margaret Stewart; the late Professor Anthony Storr; Countess Temple of Stowe; Captain Robbie Sutherland; Ros Taylor; the Revd William Thompson; Sue Tordoff; the late Sister Margaret Tournour RSCJ; Kitty and Kevin Turley; Matilda Tumim; the late Sir Stephen Tumim; Doreen Wake; Lindsey Waddell; Brother Roland Walls; Caroline Westmore; and Helen Wylie.

Two generous grants have helped towards the costs of research. The first was from the K. Blundell Trust and the Authors' Foundation, both administered by the Society of Authors, the second from Somerville College, Oxford.

I am grateful to Archie Bevan for permission to quote from the work, published and unpublished, of George Mackay Brown; to Faber & Faber for permission to quote from 'The Incarnate One', 'For Ann Scott-Moncrieff', 'One Foot in Eden' and 'The Ring' by Edwin Muir; to Kenneth Ross for permission to quote from the letters, diaries and poems of Willa Muir; to Candia McWilliam for permission to quote from 'The Many Colours of Blood'; and to Steve Savage

Publishers for permission to quote from *Letters from Hamnavoe, Under Brinkie's Brae* and *Rockpools and Daffodils*. Every effort has been made to clear permissions. If permission has not been granted please contact the publisher who will include a credit in subsequent printings and editions.

Last, and most of all, I thank my husband, James Fergusson, whose gifts as researcher, editor, indexer and cook this book has exercised to the full.

Index

Index

Abbotsford (bar), Edinburgh, 138, 149, 152, 154, 162, 256

Aberdeen, 30, 65; GMB visits, 87–9; 102, 124, 136, 165, 167, 172, 191, 228, 237, 275, 289; Union Bridge, 87

Aberuchill (Perthshire), 150

Ackerley, J. R., 116

Adventure (comic), 33

Airdrie (Lanarkshire), 106

Alain-Fournier, Henri: *Le Grand Meaulnes*, 128

Albion (ship), 72

Allen, Walter, 201n.

America: emigrants to, 4, 71; 75; Lord Lothian ambassador to, 101; people's generosity and optimism, 133; sales figures of *Loaves and Fishes* gratifying in, 157; generosity of editors, 181; discovered by Leif Ericson before Columbus, 279; William Faulkner and, 288

Anderson, Willa *see* Muir, Willa

Andrew Duncan Clinic, Edinburgh, 253

Angel, Archie, 269–70

Angel, Jean (*née* Drever), 270

Aquinas, St Thomas, 104

Arbroath (Angus), 102

Archangel, 269

Arthur, King, 69

Astley Ainslie Hospital, Edinburgh, 257

Atlantic Monthly (periodical), 181

Attenborough, Sir David, 249

Auden, W. H., 63, 96, 135, 145, 211

Austen, Jane, 32

Australia, 245

Austria, 98

Bach, Johann Sebastian, 59

Bacon, Francis, 177

Bailey, Paul, 194

Bain, Miss (hospital visitor), 125

Baker, Bob, 48

Baker, Willie, 48

Balfour Hospital, Kirkwall, 245, 287

Ballantyne, R. M., 92

Balnain Books (publishers), 239n.

Bamber, Fr Herbert, 245

Bank of Scotland, Edinburgh, 141

Banks, Stewart, 76

Barabina, Nicolo, 84

Barberi, Fr Dominic, 273

Barclay, Jean *see* MacInnes, Jean

Barker, George, 96, 111

Barnes, William, xi

Barrett, Father, 142

Barrie, J. M. (Sir James), ix

Bathgate (West Lothian), 164, 173

Bayley, John, 284

BBC: 84n.; GMB sends work to, 93, extracts from 'Islandman' on Scottish Home Service, 93, in programme about Rackwick, 119, refuses to talk on 'Trends in Orkney Agriculture', 122, talks on Edwin Muir, 136, asks for job at, 168, work broadcast, 181, talk by, 183, invited to judge verse competition, 198, interviewed, 216, 259, 273, two dialogues broadcast on Radio Scotland, 236, recording for Radio Orkney, 263; *Arts Review*, 134, 197; *Conversation Piece*, 273; *Dr Who*, 182; *Horizon*, 249; *Housewives' Choice*, 68; *Life on Earth*, 249; *The Monkees*, 182; *New Poetry*, 134; *Omnibus*, 235; *Scottish Life and Letters*, 181; *Softly Softly*, 199; *Top of the Pops*, 199; *The Virginian*, 199; *Z Cars*, 182

Beatles, 164, 187

Beaton, Marie, 202 & n.

Beckett, Samuel, ix, 177, 191

Bede, Venerable: *Ecclesiastical History of England*, 138, 203

Beerbohm, Sir Max, ix

Beethoven, Ludwig van, 64, 105

Beldowski, Leszek, 189n.

Belfast, 182, 201–2, 246

Belgrade, 105

Bell, Titty, 12, 120

Bellany, John, 270

Belsen, 83

Bergen, 158

Bergonzi, Bernard, 102, 113

Bethlehem, 285

Betjeman, Sir John, x, 232

Bevan, Archie: at Stromness Academy with GMB, 26; 'Trafalg*ah*!', 36; on sinking of the *Royal Oak*, 48; on death of James Isbister, 50; on GMB in the Home Guard, 53; within five minutes' walk of Mayburn Court, 204; on Peter Maxwell Davies's first visit to Hoy, 215; meets Nora Kennedy, 241, Seamus Heaney, 256; St Magnus Festival and, 246 & n.; Friday lunches with, 277; at GMB's funeral, 289

Bevan, Elizabeth, 241, 246, 277

Biggar (Lanarkshire), 145

Birsay (Orkney), 20, 63; Brough of, 3

Black Craig (Orkney), 11

Blickling Hall (Norfolk), 101

Blunden, Edmund, ix

Blyth (Northumberland), 72

Bodleian Library, Oxford, 273

Bogarde, Sir Dirk, 225

Boghall School, Bathgate, 164

Bold, Alan, 146, 288

Booker Prize, 231, 283–4

Booth-Clibborn, Charles, 270

Boots (chemists), Glasgow, 118

Bosdêt, J. Mary, 206n.

Bosnia, 278

Botticelli, Sandro, 102, 149

Braal (Sutherland), 4–5

Braebister (Hoy), 70

Braes Hotel, Stromness, 233

Bremner, John, 71
Brian Boru, King of Ireland, 201
Brig o'Waithe (Orkney), 49
Brinkie's Brae (Orkney), 13, 24, 29, 34, 137
Bristol University, 36
British Council, 85, 99, 180
British Honduras, 141
Brodie, Dr (TB specialist), 123–4
Brodie, Deacon William, 140
Brontë, Emily, 58
Brooke, Rupert, ix, 57
Broom, John: jealous of Stella Cartwright, 154, makes advances, 172, suggests she holiday in Orkney, 192, buys flat for in Edinburgh, 255, at funeral, 258; GMB lodges with, 173, falls out with, 174; librarian in Stromness, 255; stroke, 282; dies, 282 & n.
Brown, Allison (GMB's niece) see Dixon, Allison
Brown, George Douglas, 151
Brown, George Mackay: Fellow of the Royal Society of Literature, ix; the perfect Poet Laureate, x; lantern-jawed, xi, long, tapering hands, xii, shock of black hair, bright blue eyes, hollow cheeks, 138; author interviews, xi-xii; Mary Queen of Scots a heroine, xii; prospect of a biography, xiii; 'never fell in love', xiv, 10, 79, 236; Highland ancestry, 1; *Morbus orcadensis*, 7, 136, 165, 219, 'black bird' of depression, 37–8, 81, 135–6, 233–5, 243–4, 246, 247–8, 251; born, x, 8; early memories, 9; interest in tinkers, 9, 90;
'a true Celt', 10; on tourists, 12–13; family visits to Stromness Museum, 14–15; John Gow the pirate, 16; sweets, 17–18, 54; childhood church-going, 18; walks to Warbeth, 18–19; visits Mackay grandparents, 19, 86; Strathy lonely and desolate, 20; holiday in 'Hell', 20; parents a worry, 20–1; living in a rut, 22; move to Melvin Place, 23; Stromness Academy a shock, 24; resistance to authority, 25–8; on education, 27; kings and queens of Scotland, 28; Ruby describes as boisterous, extrovert, 30, decidedly introvert, 40; 'a peacemaker', 30; milk rounds, 30; Peter Esson's tailor's shop, 30–2; gifts first recognized, 32; authors read at school, 32, *Grimms' Fairy Tales* and twopenny dreadfuls, 33; writes own magazine, 33; passion for football, 33–4; reads poetry to father, 35; affected by death of Jimmy, 36; poem on suicide of Bristol student, 36–7; measles, 37, 53; addicted to Woodbines, 38; hacking cough, 38; preoccupied with religion, 38; stirrings of interest in Catholicism, 39–40; reads Romantic poetry, 40; buys Penguins, 40–1; 'secret vice of poetry', 41; *Orkney Herald* accepts a sonnet, 42; fails Highers, 47; fills sandbags, 47; smoking when war breaks out,

Brown, George Mackay (*cont.*)
49; inspects bomb damage, 50;
poem on father's death, 51–2;
leaves Stromness Academy, 53;
job sorting mail, 53; Home
Guard, 53; disgusts Ruby, 54;
called up, 54; medical
examination, 54; bottom teeth
extracted, 54; diagnosed with
TB, 54; confined to Eastbank,
55–8, 60, discharged, 61; believes
himself unattractive, 57, 161,
225; TB his 'ally', 57, 123; visits
St Magnus Cathedral, 61; returns
to Well Park, 61; reads
Orkneyinga Saga, 62–3; inspired
by martyrdom of St Magnus, 63;
encouraged by Eric Linklater, 63,
by Francis Scarfe, 64–5; acquires
radiogram, 64; offered job by
Orkney Herald, 65, 'Islandman',
74, 86, 93; 'the stuff that failures
and geniuses are made of', 66;
'years the locusts ate', 67;
Rackwick a 'Tir-nan-Og',
69–74; deplores 'progress', 73–7,
120, 132, 199; contemplates
children, 77, no longer, 204–5;
women and their bad habits,
77–8; love poems, 79–81; TB
pushes towards Catholic Church,
82–3; the Holocaust and, 83;
reads Newman's *Apologia*, 84;
poetry for the common people,
85; visits Ian MacInnes in
Aberdeen, 87–9, attends Mass,
88–9; Jean MacInnes's first
impressions of, 87; drinking,
89–91, drinkers 90, 'beautiful in
drink', 142; meets Ernest
Marwick, 91–2, stays with, 94;
first book published, *Let's See the
Orkney Islands*, 93; meets Robert
Rendall, 94, sends him poems
95; T. S. Eliot a hero, 96, a
suspect figure, 130; reads Edwin
Muir's autobiography, 96, poems,
97–8; offered place at Newbattle
Abbey, 100, travels with
apprehension, 102–3, growing
sense of familiarity 104, 'the
wonderment of the winter
term', 103–10, spring term 1952,
114–15, summer term, 115–18,
winter term, 121–2, health
suffers, 122, returns to Orkney in
spring term 1953, 122, comes
back for summer term 1956, gets
drunk and is ordered to leave,
137, is reprieved, 137; first sees
television, 116, rails against it,
132, 199, recreation in *Who's
Who*, 249; crush on Dorothy
McCrory, 118, kisses in a dream,
118; BBC programme on
Rackwick, 119; disillusioned
with Orkney, 120–1; death wish,
122; health deteriorates, 123;
back in Eastbank, 123–31, starts
hospital magazine, 125; religious
development, 126; first book of
poems published, *The Storm*,
128–9; experiments with short
stories, 135; devastated by
Hughie's death, 136; in love with
student from Aberdeen, 136;
offered place at Edinburgh
University, 137, undergraduate

life, 138–43, degree ceremony, 162; Margaret Sinclair a heroine, 140; hesitating on brink of conversion, 142; drinking in Rose Street, 145–8; meets Stella Cartwright, 149, closeness to, 154–5; Hogarth Press accepts *Loaves and Fishes*, 156; physical breakdown, 158–9; proposes to Stella, 160, marriage called off, 160; sexuality, 160–1; death of Edwin Muir, 163; trains as a teacher, 164–5; perfect uncle, 164; teaches in Bathgate, 164–5; collapses with bronchitis, 165; admitted to Tor-na-Dee, 165; loses control of classroom, 168; seeks BBC job, 168; received into Catholic Church, 168–9; Hogarth Press turns collection down, 170–1; Stella visits in Orkney, 171; acute money worries, 172; considers training as librarian, 173; awarded grant to do postgraduate work on Hopkins, 173, grant discontinued, 174; applies to work in university library, 174; lodges with John Broom, 173–4; sublets from Edward Gaitens, 175; distress over Norrie's death, 176; Hogarth Press accepts *The Year of the Whale*, 179, published, 181; interviewed by British Council, 180; growing reputation, 181, 197; *A Calendar of Love* published, 185; breaks ribs after drinking, 186; mother dies, 192–3; *A Time to Keep* published,

194, wins Scottish Arts Council prize, 198; *An Orkney Tapestry* commissioned, 198; housework and, 200–1; offered Society of Authors travel scholarship, 201, goes to Ireland, 201–3; moves to Mayburn Court, 203, rent, 198n., buys from council, 243n.; letter-writing, 205, 252; *Fishermen with Ploughs* published, 210; meets Peter Maxwell Davies, 216; *Greenvoe* published, 221–2, launch party, 225–7, communes with Mrs McKee, 219; besieged by strangers, 228–9, 240–1, 241n., 246; *Magnus* published, 231–2; OBE, 232, contemplates peerage, 232n.; agoraphobia, 232–3, 235–6, 245; *Hawkfall* published, 234; *The Two Fiddlers* published, 234; weekly column in *Orcadian*, 234; meets Nora Kennedy, 238, breaks work routine for, 239, physical attraction, 239, 'half-enchanted, half-afraid', 240, affair consummated, 240, continuing affection, 242, reproach and remorse, 243; resumes work with enthusiasm, 240; most productive winter of his life, 240; 'harder than diamonds', 240, 'cold and unthinking', 241; mental state deteriorates, 242; *Voyages* and *Andrina* published, 250; writing a torment, 250; visits Stella in Edinburgh, 253; persuaded to install telephone at Mayburn Court, 256n.; reaction to Stella's

Brown, George Mackay (*cont.*)
death, 258; starts autobiography,
'not for publication', 258 & n.;
gout, 259; rheumatism, 259;
seventieth birthday poem, 260;
meets Kenna Crawford, 261, love
a kind of 'madness', 265; Colin
McPhail's wedding, 265–6; visits
Pluscarden Abbey, 266; moves to
John Murray, 268; *The Golden
Bird* published, 268, wins James
Tait Black Memorial Prize, 268;
The Wreck of the Archangel
published, 268; *The Scottish
Bestiary*, 270; visits Shetland, 271;
visits Oxford (via London),
271–4; diagnosed with bowel
cancer, 275; at Foresterhill,
275–6; discipline in prayer, 278;
Vinland published, 280;
'WORKING ALL DAY', 281;
Selected Poems 1954–1983
published, 281; self-censorship,
281–2; *Beside the Ocean of Time*
short-listed for Booker Prize,
283; holiday in Outertown, 287;
admitted to hospital, 287; dies,
287; last words, 288; obituaries,
288; funeral at St Magnus
Cathedral, 288–9; buried at
Warbeth, 288
WORKS: *Andrina*, 250; *Beside the
Ocean of Time*, 266–7, 280,
283–4; 'Betty Corrigall', 72;
'Bird in the Lighted Hall', 244;
A Calendar of Love, 185, 193, 194;
A Celebration for Magnus, 265;
'Celia', 189–90, 194; *The Celt*,
33; 'A Child's Calendar', 282;
'Country Girl', 236n.;
'Countryman', 244; 'The
Drowned Rose', 7; *Earth Gold,
Sea Silver*, 236; 'Easter Song', 95;
Edwin Muir and the Labyrinth,
109, 114; 'Edwin Muir at
Newbattle', 101; 'The Exile',
116; 'Fiddler's Song', 236n.;
Fishermen with Ploughs, 210–12,
217; 'Five Green Waves', 26;
Following a Lark, 285, 287;
Foresterhill, 276; *For the Islands I
Sing*, xiii, 9, 27, 79, 81, 87, 90,
138, 143, 150, 171, 173, 258 &
n., 261, 267, 281; 'Four Poems
for Stella', 160; 'From Stone to
Thorn', 214–15, 215n.; 'The
Funeral of Ally Flett', 178, 250;
*The Golden Bird: Two Orkney
stories*, 268; *Greenvoe*, 12–13, 28,
30, 45, 46–7, 78, 141, 151, 213,
217–25, 228–9, 231, 262, 277;
'Haiku: for The Holy Places', 1;
'Hamnavoe', 51, 82, 281–2; 'The
Harrowing of Hell', 286, 289;
Hawkfall, 234; 'The Hills of Hoy
at Sunset', 42–3; 'In Memoriam
John L. Broom', 282; 'Kenna's
Return to Orkney', 262; 'The
Laird's Story', 28; *Let's See the
Orkney Islands*, 67, 93; *Letters from
Hamnavoe*, 244 & n., 277; *Letters
to Gypsy*, 239n.; *Loaves and
Fishes*, 156–7, 163, 171, 193; *The
Loom of Light*, 229; 'Lord of the
Mirrors', 236n.; 'Love Poem',
79–80; 'Lux Perpetua', 284–5;
'Magi', 9; *Magnus*, 224, 229–33,
240, 245, 278; *Northern Lights*,

264; 'The Old Women', 134; *An Orkney Tapestry*, xii, 70, 72, 73, 198–200, 198n., 205, 212–14, 216–17, 229, 248; *Pictures in the Cave*, 234; 'The Pirate's Ghost', 16; 'The Poet', 235; *Portrait of Orkney*, 248; 'A Prayer to Two Angels', 121; 'Rackwick', 128; 'The Road Home', 128; *Rockpools and Daffodils*, 244n.; 'Runes from a Holy Island', 24; 'Saint Magnus on Egilshay', 128–9; *The Scottish Bestiary*, 270; 'Sealskin', 148, 177; *A Seat by My Bed*, 53, 57, 126; *Selected Poems 1954–1983*, 281; 'Song for St Magnus', 278; 'Song: Rognvald to Ermengarde', 79n.; *A Spell for Green Corn*, 166, 238; *Stone*, 270; 'The Storm', 85; *The Storm*, 79n., 119, 128–30, 130n., 133–4, 195; 'The Story of Jorkel Hayforks', 158; *The Sun's Net*, 234; 'Swan's Way', 93; 'Tam', 135; 'The Tarn and the Rosary', 28; 'Them at Isbister', 129; 'Thorfinn', 134–5; *Time in a Red Coat*, 247–8; 'A Time to Keep', 196; *A Time to Keep*, 194–5, 197–8; 'The Tramp', 128; *Travellers*, 264; 'A Treading of Grapes', 195; *The Two Fiddlers*, 234; *Under Brinkie's Brae*, 244n., 277; *Vinland*, xi, 278–81; *Voyages*, 244n., 250; 'Wedding', 236n.; 'The Wheel', 184; 'When You Are Old', 282; 'The Winds Embrace You My Lover', 79n.; *Winterfold*, 234, 252; 'A Winter's Tale', 234; *Winter Tales*, 285; 'Witch', 169; 'The Wreck of the Archangel', 269; *The Wreck of the Archangel*, 264, 268–70; 'A Writer's Day: 21 April 1986', 261; *The Year of the Whale*, x, 179, 181–2, 184–5, 193

Brown, Harold (GMB's brother): born, 8; dies, 8; ghost, 132–3

Brown, Hazel (GMB's sister-in-law): Norrie's future wife, 57; first visits Orkney, 57; impressions of GMB, 57, 66, 87, 157; daughters, 157, 164, 175; GMB visits, 157; Mhairi visits, 175; Norrie organizes papers for, 176; no suspicion of GMB's depressions, 244; GMB convalesces with, 246

Brown, Hugh ('Hughie'; GMB's brother): born, 8; apprenticed to a baker, 35; works in NAAFI, 46; heart attack, 132; dies, 135–6

Brown, Jackie (GMB's brother) *see* Brown, John

Brown, Jimmy (GMB's uncle): unstable, 6; believes in fairies, 6; depressive, 22; leaves wife, 36; doom-ridden, 36; presumed suicide, 36

Brown, John (GMB's father): stoutish, handsome, with waxed moustache, 5; meets Mhairi Mackay, 5, wins her over, 7; marries, 8; ancestry, 5–6; apprenticed as tailor, 7; postman's rounds, 7, 17, 51; gift for mimicry, sense of humour, 7; amateur dramatics, 7, 21; move

Brown, John (GMB's father) (*cont.*)
to Victoria Street, 10; visits to
Stromness Museum, 14–15;
church-going, 18, 38; ivory
crucifix, 18; Sunday walks, 18;
constant struggle, 20; singing, 21;
troubled, 21; 'better to remain
poor', 22; depressive, 22; happy
marriage, 22; move to Melvin
Place, 23; health failing, 35;
move to Well Park, 35; retires,
35; has teeth out, 35; relieved
boys won't go to France, 50;
takes job at Lyness, 50; dies,
50; buried at Warbeth, 50
Brown, John ('Jackie'; GMB's
brother): born, 8; memories of
church, 18; home a place of
harmony, 22; GMB on milk-cart,
30; amazed at GMB's football
skills, 34; joins bank, 35–6, GMB
attempts to follow, 53; delivers
uncle's alimony, 36; Ruby's
marriages, 65n.; no suspicion of
GMB's depressions, 244; at
GMB's funeral, 289; death, 289n.
Brown, Kitty (GMB's aunt):
depressive, 6, 22; certified, 6
Brown, Mhairi (*née* Mackay;
GMB's mother): born, 1, 5;
childhood in Strathy, 1; leaves
Sutherland, 1; arrives in
Stromness, 4; sings in Gaelic, 4,
21, Gaelic hospitality, 5, 228;
cheerfulness, 5; waitress–
chambermaid at Mackay's
Stromness Hotel, 5; attractive,
tall, blue-eyed, black-haired, 5;
meets John Brown, 5, won over,
7, marries, 8; children born, 8;
move to Victoria Street, 10;
weekly routine, 17; sweets in
church, 18; takes GMB to see
parents, 19; tendency to
extravagance, 20–1; asthma, 21;
'Try and get on', 22; happy
marriage, 22; popular in
Stromness, 22; tearful at leaving
Victoria Street, 23; delighted
with Well Park, 35; GMB
worried when she goes
shopping, 37; carries gas mask,
46; war breaks out, 49; takes
GMB back from Eastbank, 61–2;
The Waste Land and, 64; 'Puir
Georgie', 66; all-providing, 80,
91, 122–3, 132–3, 182; buries
Hughie, 136; travels to
Edinburgh for GMB's degree
ceremony, 162; upset by GMB's
drinking, 170; fond of Stella
Cartwright, 171; longs to see
GMB settled, 172; visits Norrie
in Edinburgh, 175–6, shocked by
his death, 191; GMB presents
with washing machine and spin-
drier, 184n.; has fall on train,
191; rapid decline, 191–2;
admitted to Eastbank, 192; dies,
192–3, 198, 204; leaves less than
£5, 193; appears in GMB's
dreams, 193; part model for Mrs
McKee, 219
Brown, Norrie (GMB's brother) *see*
Brown, Richard
Brown, Pam (GMB's niece),
157, 164, 168, 175–6, 182 & n.,
191

Brown, Richard ('Norrie'; GMB's brother): born, 8; visits grandparents with GMB, 19; Ruby writes about, 30; measles, 37; suddenly gregarious, 40; RAF, 54; wife, Hazel, 57, 66, 157; teaching English in Edinburgh, 157; daughters, 157, 164, 168, 175–6; GMB visits, 157; angry with GMB, 168; heart trouble, 168; mother visits, 175; dies, 176–7

Brown, Ros (GMB's niece), 157, 164, 168, 175–6, 191

Brown, Ruby (GMB's sister): born, 8; takes care of GMB, 10; gift for story-telling, 10; 'Willie Drowned in Yarrow', 10–11, 'The Queen's Maries', 202; chided by father, 22; twinges of jealousy, 22; teachers' snobbery, 25; GMB and kings and queens of Scotland, 28; trains as teacher, 30; 'My Brothers: Norrie and George', 30, 40; watches GMB play football, 34; teaches English at Stromness Academy, 36; watches German fleet sink, 44; disgusted by GMB, 54; dances every night, 58; *The Waste Land* and, 64; 'back to pre-war quietness', 65; marries Ted Ogilvie, 65; husband killed, 65 & n.; marries John Ross, 65n.; misses servicemen, 75; death, 289n.

Browning, Robert, 136, 145

Bruce, George, 136, 168, 181, 197

Bruegel, Pieter, 181

Brunner, Hugo, xiii; visits GMB, 224–5; GMB writes to, 250; leaves Chatto & Windus for John Murray, 268; GMB stays with in Oxford, 272–3; at GMB's funeral, 289

Budge, Isabella, 262

Bunyan, John: *The Pilgrim's Progress*, 21; 55

Burke, William, 140

Burns, Robert, 10, 59, 85, 89, 140, 145

Burray (island), 43

Burroughs, William, 177, 228

Byatt, A. S. (Dame Antonia), 284

Cairns, Fr Francis, 169

Callaghan, James, Lord Callaghan of Cardiff, 237

Callil, Carmen, 268

Calvin, John, 97

Calvino, Italo, 181

Cambridge, 155, 206–7

Cambridge University, 106, 122

Campbell, Attie, 169, 186; death, 260

Campbell, David, 160, 225

Campbell, Steven, 270

Campion, (St) Edmund, xi

Canada, 15

Canongate (publishers), 236

Cardiff, 228

Carmichael, Marie, 202 & n.

Carroll, Lewis, 192

Cartwright, Bill (SC's cousin), 150

Cartwright, Flora (SC's aunt), 208, 220

Cartwright, Jack (SC's father):
architectural draughtsman,
painter, pianist, 150; 'charming,
handsome, very foolish', 150–1;
drinking, 151–2; faithful, 157;
blesses GMB's marriage to Stella,
160; throws Stella out of
Baberton Crescent, 174; 254, 257
& n.

Cartwright, Stella: 'Rose Street
Muse', xiv, 138, 152; at school,
150–3, colourful and fearless,
150; reading, 150; nearly married
Polish refugee, 189n.; takes job
in photographic studio, 151,
sacked, 187; accompanies father
on drinking sprees, 152, 'good
working relationship with
alcohol', 153, 'the smiler with
the knife', 167, drinking
recklessly, 171, a slave to drink,
187; 'built for love', 152; and
Sydney Goodsir Smith, 152, 165,
190, 196–7, 207–8, 208n., 220,
226, 253; and Stanley Roger
Green, 152, 255; and Hugh
MacDiarmid, 152; and Norman
MacCaig, 153; and Tom Scott,
153–4; and John Broom, 154,
172, 192, 255, 258; and Hugh
Mackay, 172, 174 & n., 208,
253–5; meets GMB, 138, 149,
162, takes him for a fisherman,
149, closeness to, 154–5, 165,
171, writes to GMB, xiv, 159,
165, 168, 171, 187, 189, 192,
197, 208–9, 227, 232, 254, GMB
writes to, xiv, 154, 161, 163,
175–6, 182, 185–9, 196–7,
203–4, 207, 209, 210, 219–20,
226–7, 235–6, 243, 252–3,
256–7, early letters destroyed by
her mother, 154, 160, 175, GMB
birthday poems for, xiv, 238,
255–6, on GMB's work, 157,
prospects of marriage, 157, GMB
proposes, 160, marriage called
off, 160, parting poems, 160,
GMB's sexuality and, 160–1, 'a
constant and tormenting worry',
167, visits GMB in Orkney, 171,
cleans kitchen for GMB, 175,
GMB cooks for, 175, fighting,
175, consoles GMB after
Norrie's death, 176, GMB
models 'Celia' on, 189–90,
relations strained, 226, selling
GMB's correspondence, 235,
correspondence renewed, 252–3,
GMB visits in Edinburgh, 253,
'They Liked Each Other More
Than a Little', xiv, 256, in
GMB's autobiography, 259,
model for Sophie in *Beside the
Ocean of Time*, 280; poems, 160,
207, 254; bronchitis, 167, 170;
engagement to Hugh Mackay,
172, called off, 174 & n.; evicted
by parents, 174; admitted to
hospital, 187–8, 204, 208;
neuritis, 187, 192, 254; 'genuine
religious sense', 197; 'suicidal',
208; not asked to *Greenvoe*
launch party, 226; job with
Avon, 226; in debt, 226–7; and
Magnus, 230; in clinic, 253;
'home and *dry*', 253–4; gift for
painting, 254; in hospital, 255–7;

dies, 257; funeral, 258 & n.; 'part of the literature of Scotland', 259; and Kenna Crawford, 261, 264; 281; favourite Orkney view, 287

Cartwright, Winnie (SC's mother): nurse by training, fastidious housekeeper, 150–1; destroys GMB's letters to Stella, 154, 160; 157, 174; death, 257

Catherine I, Empress of Russia, 202n.

Catholic Herald (newspaper), 268

Causley, Charles, 43, 194

Cecilia, St, 278

Celtic FC, 33–4

Chabria, Rabindrath, 106, 111

Chalmers, Geordie, 12, 120

Chatto & Windus (publishers), 156, 224, 250–1, 268

Chaucer, Geoffrey, 143–4

China, 247, 287

Chiocchetti, Domenico, 83–4, 84n.

Chopin, Frédéric, 105

Christie, Dame Agatha, 40

Christie, David, 273

Churchill Barriers (Orkney), 49, 83, 239

Churchill, Sir Winston, 43, 48, 53

Clare, John, xi

Clark, Kenneth, Lord, 43

Clestrain (Orkney), 15

Clontarf (battle), 201

Clouston, Revd Charles, 15

Clouston, Ella, 76

Clouston, Tammack, 11, 46

Clouston, Sir Thomas, 6–7

Coats, James, 91–2

Coleg Harlech, 101n.

Coleridge, Samuel Taylor, 40

Coll (island), 261

Collins–Williams, Revd, 60

Columbus, Christopher, 279

Commercial College, Glasgow, 173

Commercial Hotel, Stromness, 46

Compiègne, 50

Conacher, Fr Giles, 265–6

Conn, Stewart: on GMB, 147; GMB writes to, 174; obituary of GMB, 288

Connolly, Cyril, 109

Conti, Most Revd Mario, 289

Cook, John, 41, 128

Coolags (Hoy), 68

Copenhagen University, 56

Corke, Hilary, 185

Corrigall, Betty, 72–3

Cory, William, 258

Costa Head (Orkney), 115

Costie, Christina, 94

Coventry, 277, 284

Craighouse (asylum), Edinburgh: 'Little Orkney', 6

Cranston, Maurice, 201

Crawford, Kenna, 258; GMB meets, 261; 'a woman from the sea', 261; similarities to Stella Cartwright, 261; Orkney ancestry, 262; GMB writes to, 262–4, 267, poems to, 261–4, 267; writes to GMB, 263; GMB's guest at a birthday dinner in Edinburgh, 263; goes to New Zealand, 263–5, returns 266, 'pure inspiration', 264; stays at Mayburn Court, 266–7; marries Graham McGirk, 267; not mentioned in GMB's

Crawford, Kenna (*cont.*)
autobiography, 267; dedicatee of
The Golden Bird, 268; model for
Sophie in *Beside the Ocean of
Time*, 280; at GMB's funeral, 289
Crichton Royal Hospital,
Dumfries, 208
Crossley-Holland, Kevin, 182, 228
Crowden, Patricia: GMB writes to,
235, 241n.
Curtis, Dr Michael: GMB writes
to, 233, 245–7, 252
Czechoslovakia, 43, 98

Daily Express (newspaper), 170
Dalkeith (Midlothian), 101, 103–4,
115, 126
Dalrymple, William: *City of Djinns*,
287; *In Xanadu*, 287; GMB
writes to, 187
Davies, Sir Peter Maxwell: buys *An
Orkney Tapestry*, 212, reads
213–15; meets GMB, 216; moves
to Rackwick, 216–17, 216n.; sets
to music 'From Stone to
Thorn', 215n.; Strathclyde
Concerto No. 2, 216 & n.; *Black
Pentecost* based on *Greenvoe*, 223;
Yellow Cake Revue, 223; *The
Martyrdom of St Magnus* based on
Magnus, 232, GMB's 'greatest
achievement', 232; St Magnus
Festival, 232; 'I always imagine
the Nativity in Rackwick',
285n.; completes sixth
symphony, dedicated to GMB,
287; plays 'Farewell to
Stromness' at GMB's funeral, 289
Davison, Peter, 181

Day-Lewis, Cecil, 156, 170–1, 177,
179, 194
Defoe, Daniel: *An Account of the
Conduct and Proceedings of the late
John Gow*, 16
Delhi, 287
Dennison, Brigadier Malcolm,
289
Dickens, Charles, 32
D'Israeli, Isaac: *Curiosities of
Literature*, 92
Dixon, Allison (*née* Brown), 157;
GMB a perfect uncle, 164; 168,
175–6, 191; marries, 204; 241;
GMB for Monday teas, 277
Dixon, Fraser, 204, 241, 249, 277
Dolomites, 84n.
Doloughan, Alex, 99
Donne, John, 209n.
Dounby (Orkney), 179
Drever, James, 71
Drever, Jean *see* Angel, Jean
Drinkwater, John, 57
Drysdale, Bill, 106, 108, 110, 115
Dublin, 201n.
Dumfries, 208
Dunant, Sarah, 284
Dundee, 33, 102, 105
Dunne, Ellen, 19
Dunoon (Argyll), 207
Duns Scotus, John, 173 & n.
Durham, 61, 169, 272
Durkin, John, 142, 152
Durrell, Lawrence: *Alexandria
Quartet*, 159; *Justine*, 159
Duval, Kulgin: on Stella
Cartwright, 153; on GMB's
sexuality, 160–1; GMB writes to,
164, 201, 232n., 236, 240, 246n.,

258n., 271; meets Peter Maxwell Davies crossing to Hoy, 215, introduces to GMB, 215–16; 251; accompanies GMB to Shetland, 271; boundless energy, irreverent wit, 271; GMB stays with in Perthshire, 272

Earl of Zetland (troopship), 44, 58
Eastbank (sanatorium), Kirkwall, 54, 55–6, 60, 105; part torture chamber, part charnel house, 123; 'Arcadia', 124; 124–7, 130–2, 192, 200
Edinburgh, xi, xiv, 6, 37, 98, 99, 102–3, 136, 138–62; 'a stand-offish city', 139; 164, 165, 171, 173, 177, 180, 183, 187, 188, 191, 197–8, 202n., 208, 218, 225–6, 228, 236, 238–9, 244, 249, 253–5, 257, 262–3, 275; Cramond, 154, 176; Fountainbridge, 142; Juniper Green, 150, 160, 171, 208n.; Marchmont, 139, 141, 156; Morningside, 6, 253; Murrayfield, 249; Oxgangs, 157, 175–6; Warriston Crematorium, 258; Waverley Station, 103, 118
Edinburgh Castle, 140
Edinburgh Festival, 225
Edinburgh University, x, 106, 137, 138–44, 158, 160, 162, 173, 270, 277
Edinburgh University Library, xiv, 174
Edward VII, King, 55 & n.
Egilsay (island), 62, 115, 128, 231

Egypt, 3, 65
Einstein, Alfred, 27
El Alamein (battle), 65
Eliot, T. S.: Anne Ridler assistant to, 59; GMB reads at school 63, acquires record of, 64, admiration for, 93, 'this side of idolatry', 96, lecture on, 93, suspect figure, 130–1; *The Waste Land*, 64; *Murder in the Cathedral*, 64; income tax, 109; on Edwin Muir's 'integrity', 111; at Milne's, 145; Muir writes to, 155–6; 'growing old', 156; enlisted to support Muir, 163; GMB quotes, 170; could be enlisted to support GMB, 172; 271
Elizabeth II, Queen: coronation, 125; 'pallace', 232
Empson, William, 135
Encounter (periodical), 134, 172
Enright, D. J., 250
ENSA, 59 & n.
Erebus, HMS, 15n.
Ericson, Leif, 279
Erlendson, Earl Magnus *see* Magnus, St
Esson, Peter: tailor's shop, 30–2; death, 31; 'heraldic on his bench', 31; 35
Eton College, 33
Evans, Billy, 169, 186
Evening Standard (newspaper), 283
Evie (Orkney), 91
Eynhallow (island), xiii, 24, 85; Eynhallow Sound, 95; 198, 229, 286
Exeter, 84
Eysteinson, Earl Sigurd, 201

Faber & Faber (publishers), 59n., 96, 118, 156
Fair Isle (island), 68, 158
Farrar, Dean F. W.: *St Winifred's*, 33
Faulkner, William, 288
Ferguson, Revd Ron, 288
Ferniehirst Castle (Roxburghshire), 101
Fields, Gracie, 59
Findlater, Richard, 201n.
Finstown (Orkney), 14
Firth, Tommy, 30
Fletcher, Bob, 106, 108
Flodden (battle), 34
Flotta (island), 44, 222
Foresterhill (hospital), Aberdeen, 275–6; 'a waiting room for the poor soul', 276
Forman, Werner, 248
Formby, George, 59
Forster, E. M.: *A Passage to India*, 41; 133, 249
Fort William (Inverness-shire), 93
Fotheringhay (Northamptonshire), 34
Fox, Davie, 124
Fox, Helen *see* Wylie, Helen
Fox, Roy, 58
France, xii, 16, 50, 98
Franklin, Sir John, 15 & n., 16
Fraser, Lady Antonia, 236
Fraser, G. S., 133, 156
Fraser, Simon, 265
Frost, Robert, 133
Fugaccia, Giulio, 40

Gaitens, Edward, 175
Gambit (university magazine), 160
Gandhi, Mahatma, 96

Garden, Mrs (hospital visitor), 125
Garioch, Robert, 145–6
Garson, Miss (teacher), 32
Gem (comic), 33
George (pirate ship), 16
Germany, 44 & n., 98, 231
Gibbon, Lewis Grassic, 151, 194
Gielgud, Sir John, 59
Gifford, Douglas, 288
Gilbertson, Susie, 90–1
Gillott, Jacky, 232
Gilmour, John, 38, 41
Gladstone, W. E., 74
Glasgow, 21, 98, 103, 108, 118, 145, 173, 198; Hampden Park, 34
Glasgow Herald see Herald
Glasgow University: GMB D. Litt. at, 284n.; 288
Gleaner (floating shop), 73
Glenfiddich (whisky): calming, 180
Gollancz, Victor (publishers), 198
Goodsir, Andy, 178
Gordon, General Charles, 14
Gordon, Giles: reviews *The Year of the Whale*, 181; commissions *An Orkney Tapestry*, 198–9, 201
Gordon, James, 16
Gordon, Robert, 73
Gorki, Maxim, 151
Gow, John, 16–17, 32
Graemsay (ferry), 68
Graham, Winston, 201n.
Grant, Alan, 237
Grant, Betty, 190, 237, 275–6
Grant, Peter, 237, 275
Gray's School of Art, Aberdeen, 87, 172
Green, Stanley Roger, 147–8, 152, 254

Green, Henry, 225
Greene, Graham: *The End of the Affair*, 197
Greer, Germaine, 284
Greyfriars Bobby (pub), Edinburgh, 138
Grierson, Sir Herbert, 143
Grieve, C. M. *see* MacDiarmid, Hugh
Grimm, Brothers (Jacob and Wilhelm), 33
Grimond, Jo, Lord, 217 & n., 222
Grimond, Laura, Lady, 222
Grimsby, 122n.
Guardian (newspaper), 211
Gullane (East Lothian), 118
Gunn, Neil: *Morning Tide*, 41; 108
Gurness (Orkney), Broch of, 95; Knowe of, 94

Hall, Henry, 34, 58
Hamilton, Colin, 160–1, 251; formidably good cook, 271
Hamilton, General Sir Ian, ix
Hamilton, Mary, 202 & n.
Hammer, Armand, 222
Hammond, David, 202
Hamnavoe *see* Stromness
Hancox, Nora *see* Meyer, Nora
Hardie, Keir, 107
Hardy, Thomas, 51
Hare, William, 140
Harper's Bazaar (magazine), 134
Harray (Orkney), 7; Loch of, 16, 63, 86
Harris, Roger: GMB writes to, 220, 222–3, 228–9, 235, 240, 243, 245, 249, 275
Harrow School, 33

Harvard University, 133–4, 155, 180
Hawick (Roxburghshire), 254, 257
Heaney, Seamus: reads *The Year of the Whale*, x, 182; on GMB's poetry, 64, 210–11, on GMB, 202–3, 228, 246, 288; writes to GMB, 182; GMB meets in Belfast, 201–3; GMB reads *North*, 235; visits GMB in Orkney, 246; elected Oxford Professor of Poetry, 272n.
Heath-Stubbs, John, x
Hemingway, Ernest, 40
Henry III, King of France, xii
Henryson, Robert, 174
Henty, G. A., 92
Herald (newspaper; formerly *Glasgow Herald*), 181, 288
Herbert, George, xi, 169
Herrick, Robert, xi
Hewlett, Donald, 59
Heywood, Mrs (hotelier), 137
Highland Park (whisky): 'marvellous stuff', 224
Hitler, Adolf, 43, 50, 53, 60
Hodgson, Ralph, 35
Hogarth Press (publishers), 98, 156–7, 163, 170–2, 177, 179, 184, 194, 198, 210, 224, 231, 234, 248, 250
Holms (islands), xiii, 13, 15
Hopkins, Christine, xii
Hopkins, Gerard Manley, 2, 80n.; GMB's postgraduate research on, 173–4, 177; 183, 244; in GMB's autobiography, 259; exhibition in Bodleian Library, 273; 284
Hotspur (comic), 33
Houton (Orkney), Bay of, 222

Howard's (bar), Edinburgh, 207
Howson, Peter, 270
Hoy (island), xiii; the 'high island',
2, 69; Old Man of, 11, 72; Hoy
Sound, 13, 35, 82, 166, 186, 242;
GMB sonnet, 42; 44; air-raid,
49; GMB's father dies in, 50;
garrison cinema, 59; 67; GMB
visits, 68–9, with Sylvia Wishart,
172, with Peter and Betty Grant,
237; 71–3; swimming pool, 75n.;
80, 82; shipwreck, 122; 137; 210,
233, 262, 265; Peter Maxwell
Davies visits, 215–16, moves to,
216–17; church, 216; 285n.; 287
Hrossey *see* Orkney
Hudson's Bay Company, 7, 15
Hughes, Paddy: on GMB, 147;
visits GMB in Orkney, 176, in
Foresterhill, 276; accompanies
GMB to Ireland, 201–3
Hughes, Ted: GMB a 'marvellous'
Poet Laureate, x; reads
'Thorfinn', 135; 181; on GMB's
work, 211; 212; GMB reads
Crow, 235; Seamus Heaney on
GMB and, 246
Hume, David, 140

Iceland, 60, 62
Independent (newspaper), 247
India, 210
Inglis, F. C. (photographic studio),
151, 187
Innes, George, 105
Iran, 287
Ireland, 3, 201–2, 217; Antrim, 201;
Connemara, 201–2; Donegal,
201; Galway, 201, 228

Iron Duke, HMS, 48
Isbister, James, 49–50
Isbister, Jimmy, 204, 220
Israel, 210
Italian Chapel (Lamb Holm), 83–4,
84n.
Italy, 84, 94, 98

Jack, Flora *see* MacArthur, Flora
Jackson, Mr (organist), 59
James Tait Black Memorial Prize,
268
Jenners (department store),
Edinburgh, 140
John Paul II, Pope, 249
Johnson, Mr (landlord), 59
Johnston, Margaret, 60
Johnstone, Dr Derrick, 287
Joyce, James: *Dubliners*, 117; 151
Julian of Norwich, Dame, 196n.
Justinlees (pub), Dalkeith, 110, 136
Jutland (battle), 44

Kafka, Franz, 99, 113, 128, 228
Kant, Immanuel, 106
Kashmir, 106
Kay, Dr Jean: GMB writes to, 277,
278
Keats, John, 27, 40, 58
Kelly, Alexander, 185
Kelman, James, 284
Kennedy, President John F., 170
Kennedy, Joseph, 43
Kennedy, Nora: 237; buys cottage
on South Ronaldsay, 238; meets
GMB, 238, dinner at Tormiston
Mill, 238, kindred spirit, cradle
Catholic, 238, letters exchanged,
238–42, physical attraction, 239,

consummated affair, 240, strains, 240–1, 252–3, 'physical difficulties', 241–2, Christmas at Mayburn Court, 241, 'miserable' together, 242, GMB's guilt, 244, GMB ceases to receive communion, 245; kitten Gypsy, 239 & n.; 'kindness, intelligence, sweetness', 242; moves to Stromness, 242; left life interest in 3 Mayburn Court, 243n.; dedicatee of *Voyages*, 250n.; not mentioned in GMB's autobiography, 259; Kenna Crawford a friend, 261–2; 269; foreignness, 277; watches Booker prizegiving with GMB, 284 & n.; at GMB's funeral, 289

Kermode, Sir Frank, 156

Khrushchev, Nikita, 170

King, Peter John, 272n.

King's College, Cambridge, 106

Kirbuster (Orkney), 277

Kirkwall (Orkney capital), 3, 7, 48, 60, 61, 62, 78, 87, 92, 94, 95, 110, 124, 125, 213, 222, 239, 245, 263, 283, 289; arts club, 93; bookshops, 91, 94; churches, 97, 126, 168–9, 245, 289; centralization of trade, 120; football match, 34; hospital, 54, 255, 287; jail, 12; sanatorium, 54; schools, 25, 97; temperance hall, 59; uranium protests, 223; wartime, 59–60; witches, 166–7; Glaitness Laundry Company, 7; Leonard's bookshop, 91; *Orkney Herald* office, 65, 91; Union Bank, 36, 53

Kitchin, George, 143–4, 173, 176

Kitt, Eartha, 172

Knox, Jack, 270

Knox, John, 97, 140

Kolson, Earl Rognvald *see* Rognvald, St

Kubla Khan, Emperor of China, 287

Lamb Holm (island), 43, 83–4

Lane, Sir Allen, 40–1

Larbert (Stirlingshire), 106

Largs (battle), 170

Larkin, Philip, 228

Larne (Co. Antrim), 201

Lawrence, D. H., 64, 152, 279

Lear, Edward, 192

Learmonth, John R., 26

Learmonth, Revd Peter, 6n.

Lee, Laurie: *Cider with Rosie*, 156

Leicester City (fishing vessel), 122n.

Leith, Anne, 150–1

Leo IX, Pope, 3

Leonard, Allison *see* Tait, Allison

Lepanto (battle), 201

Lerwick (Shetland capital), 271

Levi, Peter, 268, 272–3

Levi, Primo: *The Periodic Table*, 271

Lifolf (cook), 63

Lindsay, Maurice, 108–9

Lines Review (periodical), 180, 194

Linklater, Eric: author of one of first Penguins, 40; on St Magnus Cathedral, 61; encourages GMB, 63; on hills of Hoy, 68; leaves Orkney, 86; on January 1952 storm, 115; *Saltire Review*, 134

Linklater, Geordie, 14

Listener (periodical), 96, 107, 116, 180, 185, 198

Littlemore (Oxfordshire), 273

Lloyd's List and Shipping Gazette (newspaper), 14

London: ix, 15, 21, 43, 44, 85, 98, 116, 125, 130, 200, 201, 206, 228, 233, 245; GMB visits, 272, 274; Admiralty Dock, 16; Barnes, 185; Battersea, xii; Big Ben, 272; Buckingham Palace, 232, 272; Cenotaph, 272; Chelsea, 206; Euston Station, 272; Globe Theatre, 85; Guildhall, 283–4; House of Commons, 223; Hyde Park, ix, 272; Kensington, 108; Kensington Gardens, 115; King's Cross Station, 274; Lord's, 237; Marble Arch, xi; Notting Hill Carnival, 237; St Paul's Cathedral, 232; Shepherd's Bush, 211; Southwark, 85; Tyburn Convent, xi; Wapping, 16; Wembley, 34; Westminster Bridge, 272

London, Jack: *The People of the Abyss*, 21

Londonderry, 210

Longfellow, Henry Wadsworth, 25

Lothian, Philip Kerr, 11th Marquess of: 101–2, 101n., 109; family, 99–100, 104, 109, 110

Low, Valentine, 283

Lyness (Hoy), 50

MacArthur, Flora (*née* Jack): on GMB at Newbattle, 105; 108; on Edwin Muir, 109–10; on Willa Muir, 113; on GMB's flirting, 118; GMB writes to, 122–5, 173; marries Ian MacArthur, 173n.

MacArthur, Ian: at Newbattle with GMB, 106; on Edwin Muir, 109; GMB stays with in Paisley, 115; GMB writes to, 165, 172, 174; marries Flora Jack, 173n.

Macbeth, King of Scotland, 3

MacCaig, Isobel, 150

MacCaig, Norman, xi; lectures at Newbattle, 108, 'masterly sarcasm', 109, 149; *Saltire Review*, 134; at Milne's, 145–6; drinking continues with, 148–9; GMB's dislike of mutual, 149; Stella Cartwright develops a passion for the poetry of, 151, at parties of, 153, infatuation with, 153; gets things done, 158; reviews *The Year of the Whale*, 181; dies, 286

McCann, Duncan William, 272n.

McCormack, John, 140

McCrory, Dorothy, 118

MacDiarmid, Hugh, xi; GMB reads at school, 63; George Kitchin a champion of, 144; at Milne's, 145–6; *A Drunk Man Looks at the Thistle*, 145; 'lustful' towards Stella Cartwright, 152

McGill, Morag (*née* MacInnes), 281

McGill, Patrick: *The Rat-Pit*, 21; *Children of the Dead End*, 21

McGirk, Graham, 267

MacGregor, Sue, 273

MacInnes, Ian: at Stromness Academy with GMB, 25–7, tongue scrubbed with soap, 27, later headmaster, 26n.; recollections of GMB and headmaster, 30; at Peter Esson's tailor's shop, 30; 'George a very unhappy lad indeed', 66; GMB and threat of early death, 82; GMB visits in Aberdeen, 87; paintings, 89; and GMB's drinking, 91, 186, 193; illustrates *The Storm*, 128, *The Two Fiddlers*, 234; GMB's bedtime stories to children of, 164; GMB writes to, 164, 167–8, 199; takes Robert Rendall out from Eastbank, 200; within five minutes' walk of Mayburn Court, 204; meets Nora Kennedy, 241; GMB convalesces with, 246; and Seamus Heaney, 246; 281; at GMB's funeral, 289

MacInnes, Jean, 87, 241, 246

MacInnes, Morag *see* McGill, Morag

Mackay, clan, 4

Mackay, Angus (GMB's great-grandfather), 4–5

Mackay, Georgina (GMB's grandmother), 1, 5, 8, 19

Mackay, Hugh (crofter; GMB's grandfather), 1, 5, 19–20

Mackay, Hugh (librarian): on GMB, 147; on Stella Cartwright, 153, 157, engagement, 172, called off, 174 & n., offers lodgings, 208, helps, 253, meets at weekends, 254, pays bills, 255, spends Christmas with, 257, shock at death of, 258; GMB writes to, 167; moves to Hawick, 254; 257n.; on *Beside the Ocean of Time*, 280

Mackay, John (headmaster), 94

Mackay, John (hotelier), 1, 5

Mackay, Mhairi Sheena *see* Brown, Mhairi

Mackay's Stromness Hotel *see* Stromness Hotel

Mackenzie, Sir Compton, ix, 145, 225, 227

McLaughlan, Edward, 136

McLean, Bruce, 270

McLean, Duncan: *Bunker Man*, 282

MacLean, Sorley, xi, 146

McLeod, Mrs (neighbour), 182

MacMurray, John, 108

McNaught, Mr (teacher trainer), 167–8

MacNeice, Louis, 96

McPhail, Colin, 265–6

McPhail, Tam, 242

McWilliam, Candia, 139, 141

Maeshowe (Orkney), 3, 238, 286

Magnet (comic), 33

Magnus, St (Earl Magnus Erlendson): cloven skull, 61; character intrigues GMB, 62–3, an ally, 81; central role in spiritual life of north, 93; GMB poem, 128; 183; in *An Orkney Tapestry*, 199, 229, Peter Maxwell Davies moved by story of, 215; GMB and *Magnus*, 224, 229–31; celibacy, 230; 249; GMB *son et lumière*, 265; 278; feast day, 287, 288

Manchester, 169

Mann, Thomas, 62, 241; *The Magic Mountain*, 249

Manning, Cardinal Henry, 39

Manzoni, Alessandro, 151

Marks and Spencer's (department store), Edinburgh, 176

Marryat, Captain Frederick, 92

Marvell, Andrew, 169

Marwick, Ernest: GMB meets, 91, 127; kindred spirit, 92; impressed by GMB's poems, 92, encourages to send work to BBC, 93, to *New Shetlander*, 93; GMB holidays with, 94; house a meeting-place for Kirkwall intellectuals, 94; GMB writes to from Newbattle, 104–5, 107–8, 116–17, 136, from Eastbank, 123–5, 130–1, from Edinburgh, 139, 143, 147, 155, from Tor-na-Dee, 168; article in *Orkney Herald*, 120; GMB tells of disillusion with Orkney, 121, of impossibility of going to Cambridge, 122; writes of GMB in diary, 122; goes to Newbattle, 125; GMB publishes *The Storm* against the advice of, 130; 133; advice on reading, 165; writes of GMB to Willa Muir, 182, 204; GMB's look of 'agonised maturity', 204, conversation, 209; 212; reads *Greenvoe*, 220; on *Magnus*, 232; dies, 259

Marwick, Janette, 94, 125

Marwick, Rena, 83

Mary Celeste (brigantine), 3

Mary Erskine School for Girls, Edinburgh, 151–3

Mary Queen of Scots, xii, 140, 202 & n.

Masefield, John, 164

Mathieson, Bill, 14

Maugham, W. Somerset, 151

Maxfield, Thomas (martyr), xi

Maxton, James, 68 & n.

Maynard, Winifred, 144, 173–4

Mays, Cedric ('Spike'), 105; *No More Soldiering for Me*, 105; 106, 108

Mays, Vera, 105

Mee, Arthur: *The Children's Encyclopaedia*, 94

Mee, Paddy, 40

Melbourne University, 245

Meldrum (Aberdeenshire), 132

Mendelssohn, Felix: Violin Concerto, 64

Menuhin, Yehudi, Lord, 59

Meyer, Gerry: editor of *Orkney Blast*, 66; impressions of GMB, 66, *Orcadian* profile of GMB, 68; on GMB's drinking, 91, bedtime stories to children, 164, glimpse of depressiveness of, 244

Meyer, Nora, 66

Midland Hill (Orkney), 222

Miles, Bernard, Lord, 59

Miller, Karl, 198, 201n.

Millie, Bessie, 32

Mills, Sir John, 59

Milne's (bar), Edinburgh, 145–8, 152, 154, 196, 201, 207–8

Milton, John, 106

Mitchison, Naomi: writes to GMB, 212; *The Cleansing of the Knife*, 248

Moberg, Gunnie: meets Nora Kennedy, 241, and Seamus Heaney, 246; son's wedding, 265; photographs for *A Celebration for Magnus*, 265; dances with GMB,

266; collaborations with GMB, 270, 286; takes GMB to Shetland, 271; 'the kind of temperament on which fortune smiles', 272; takes GMB to London and Oxford, 272–4; 282; at GMB's funeral, 289

Moffat, Alexander: *Poets' Pub*, xi, 146, 148

Monteviot (Roxburghshire), 101

Montrose (Angus), 102, 113

Mooney, John, 94

Moose Factory (Ontario), 15

Moray Firth, 76

Moray House College of Further Education, Edinburgh, 164–5, 167–8

More, (St) Thomas, 252

Morgan, Edwin, 134, 146, 160–1

Morrocco, Alberto, 89

Motion, Andrew, 268

Mowat, Hugh, 121

Mowat, John, 121

Mozart, Wolfgang Amadeus: *Eine Kleine Nachtmusik*, 64

Muir, Edwin, 24; *The Story and the Fable*, 96–7; *The Voyage*, 97; marriage, 98; *First Poems*, 98, 99n.; appointed Warden of Newbattle, 99; encourages GMB to enrol, 99; *Chorus of the Newly Dead*, 99n.; meets GMB, 99–100; at Newbattle, 101, 103–18; collects GMB from station, 103; lectures, 108, 116; 'father and friend', 109; chest pains, 110; GMB on, 111; encourages GMB's poetry, 116; *Collected Poems*, 118; 'grace' in GMB's

work, 119, 130, 195; urges GMB to try for Cambridge, 122, sends book parcels, 128, assures of his gift, 128; introduction to *The Storm*, 129–30, sends book to friends, 133; writes to GMB, 131, 133–4, 163; harried by Newbattle Executive Committee, 131, resigns as Warden, 133; takes post at Harvard, 133; sends GMB poems to *Harper's Bazaar*, 134; advises GMB to stick to poetry, 135; Newbattle without, 136; GMB talks on, 136–7, 273; visits GMB in Orkney, 137; GMB writes to, 141; 142; on the Rose Street poets, 145; GMB sends work to, 155–6; buys own home, 155; 158; water on the lungs, 163; dies, 163; 170; GMB suggests research on, 174; Robert Rendall and, 200; 203; Willa without, 205–6; ghost, 206 & n.; 209, 224, 286

Muir, Gavin, 105, 205–6

Muir, Willa (*née* Anderson): marriage, 98; meets GMB, 99–100; 103–6; laughs head off, 109; on Edwin, 110, 112, 113; Kathleen Raine on Edwin and, 111; Edwin on, 112; crude jokes, 113; 'malicious', 113; background, 113; sacrifices, 113–14; generous, 114; GMB writes to, 118, about his mother, 193, about midsummer sunsets, 203, about life at Mayburn Court, 204–5; installs GMB in

Muir, Willa (*née* Anderson) (*cont.*)
spare bedroom, 122; writes to
GMB, 128, 206; 133; visits GMB
in Orkney, 137; 138, 141, 155,
158; distraught, 163; sends GMB
£50, 172; 182; wretched life,
205–6; moves into Kathleen
Raine's house, 206; presses GMB
to stay, 206; on GMB's work,
206; moves to Dunoon, 207;
dies, 207; Renée Simm and, 277
Murdoch, Dame Iris, 225
Murray, Brian, 244n., 277, 289
Murray, John (publishers), xiii, 268,
281, 283, 285
Murray, John R., 289
Mussolini, Benito, 43, 84

Naipaul, V. S. (Sir Vidia), 181
Nairn, 265, 272
National Association for the
Prevention of Tuberculosis,
55–6
National Gallery, 43
National Gallery of Scotland, 139
National Library of Scotland, xiv,
198
National Trust, 101 & n.
National Trust for Scotland, 101n.
Nelson, Horatio, 1st Viscount, 36
Newbattle Abbey, Dalkeith: Edwin
Muir appointed Warden, 99;
GMB enrols, 100, attends
102–16, 118, returns to, 121,
leaves sick, 122, returns to again,
136, threatened with expulsion,
137; history, 101–2; crocuses and
daffodils, 123; 124; Ernest
Marwick goes to, 125; 126, 128,

129, 130, 131–3, 140, 142, 149,
153, 245, 276
Newcastle upon Tyne, 102, 272
New College, Oxford, 273
Newman, Cardinal John Henry:
Apologia, 84; 273
New Shetlander (periodical), 93, 99
New Statesman (periodical), 116,
134, 156, 180, 235
New Zealand, 263–6
Nimbus (periodical), 135
Nottingham, 105
Noup Head (Westray), 117, 178
Nye, Robert, 194

Oban (Argyll), 183
Observer (newspaper), 108, 156
O'Casey, Sean, 145
Occidental Petroleum, 222
O'Connor, Flannery, 248
O'Driscoll, Dennis, 242, 268
Ogilvie, Ted, 65 & n.
Oliver, David, 152
Orcadian (newspaper): GMB
columns, 6n., 24, 29, 41, 233n.,
234, 237–8, 239, 244n., 273, 287;
25, 26; GMB profile, 68; and the
Holocaust, 83
Orkney (islands/county/Mainland
Orkney): x, xi, xii; 'a place of
order, a place of remembrance, a
place of vision', 1; 'Hrossey', 2;
landscape and agriculture, 2, 75,
85, 120–1; fishing, 121;
prehistory, 2–3; history, 3–4;
passes to Scottish rule, 4; Norn
language, 4; 9; links with
Canada, 15–16; First World War,
44; Second World War, 43–59;

'bloody', 45; MP, 217n.; and
Margaret Thatcher, 223
Orkney Blast (services newspaper),
58, 66
Orkney County Council, 100, 118,
121
Orkney Herald (newspaper), 25;
'Brown sent a rasping shot into
the rigging', 34; accepts sonnet
by GMB, 42; offers GMB job as
Stromness correspondent, 65;
GMB columns, 67–8, 69, 74–8,
80, 83, 84, 85–6, 87–9, 91, 92,
93, 96, 97, 98, 120, 132, 136,
172, 199, 230; 76, 93; reviews
The Storm, 129; closes down,
234; 271
Orkneyinga Saga, 62–3, 79n., 230–1
Orkney Press (publishers), 128
Orlof, Ivan, 202n.
Orphir (Orkney), 15, 137, 222
Orr, Peter, 180
O'Sullivan, Maurice: *Twenty Years
A-Growing*, 41
Our Lady and St Joseph, Church
of, Kirkwall, 168, 289
Outertown (Orkney), 287
Oxford, 242, 272–3, 275
Oxford University, 101n., 146;
Professorship of Poetry election,
272

Paisley (Renfrewshire), 115
Pakistan, 287
Palumbo (blacksmith), 84
Papa Westray (island), xii
Paragon Press (publishers), 270
Parini, Jay, 233
Paris, 177
Paris Review (periodical), 181
Parsons, Ian, 156, 210
Passchendaele (battle), 47
Paterson, Ian, 63
Paul, St, 278
Paul VI, Pope, 140n.
Paulin, Tom, 284
Paulson, Earl Hakon, 62–3, 230–1
Payne, Jack, 58
Pentland Firth, 2, 12n., 70, 71, 213,
254
Pentland Hills, xiv, 150, 154
Peter, St, 278
Peter I, Emperor of Russia, 202n.
Petropaulovsk, 202n.
Pius IX, Pope, 39
Plath, Sylvia, 135
Plato, 27
Plimpton, George, 181
Pluscarden Abbey (Morayshire),
245, 265–6
Poetry Society, 228
Pole Star (Northern Lighthouse
Board ship), 26, 169
Polo, Marco, 287
Pope, Alexander, 144
Porter, Peter, 210–11
Portobello High School,
Edinburgh, 157
Portugal, 16
Pound, Ezra, 63
Powel, Philip (martyr), xi
Prague, 99
Prien, Lt Gunther, 47–8
Pritchett, V. S. (Sir Victor), 151,
225
'Puffer' (one-eyed town crier), 12,
120
Pugh, Sheenagh, 280

Punjȳa, Surinder: meets GMB, 277; poetry, 277–8; helps GMB, 278; 'close to being a saint', 278; goes to care for dying father, 283; father dies, 284; 284n.; spends last days with GMB, 287; at GMB's funeral, 289

Queen's University, Belfast, 182, 203

Rackwick (Hoy): 'the fairest region of all Hoy', 67, 69; a 'Tir-nan-Og', 69, miniature Eden, 71; air of tragedy, 70, tragedy, 121; tough life, 71; 'bay of wreckage', 72; progress and, 73–4; 92, 210; spellbinding, 93; GMB contributes to BBC programme about, 119; 128, 150; Sylvia Wishart and, 172; GMB spends weekends at, 183; 196; in *An Orkney Tapestry*, 199, 214; GMB's poems about, 205, 210; Peter Maxwell Davies first visits, 215–16; GMB contemplates peerage, 232n.; GMB with Peter and Betty Grant in, 237; 262, 268; 285n., 287
Rae, John, 15–17
Raine, Kathleen: on the Muirs, 111; 172; writes to GMB, 181; 206
Rangers FC, 34
Reay (Caithness), 5
Redfern, June, 270
Reed, Talbot Baines: *The Fifth Form at St Dominic's*, 33
Rendall (Orkney), 130, 259

Rendall, Catherine, 121
Rendall, Jack, 216
Rendall, Robert: GMB meets, 94; Broch of Gurness and, 94–5; *Country Sonnets*, 95; 'mischief-loving troll', 95; encourages GMB, 95, visits at Eastbank, 125–6; writes a perfect sonnet, 125; in *An Orkney Tapestry*, 199–200; dies, 200
Reuter, Vice-Admiral Ludwig von, 44
Revenge (pirate ship), 16
Ridler, Anne, 59; *A Little Book of Modern Verse*, 59 & n.
Ridler, Vivian, 59
Ring of Brodgar (Orkney), 3, 246
Ritchie, Mr (teacher), 38
Robert the Bruce, King of Scotland, 28, 102
Robertson, Provost, 76
Robertson, Aileen, 252
Robertson, Jenny: GMB writes to, 252, 270
Robeson, Paul, 119
Rognvald, St (Earl Rognvald Kolson), 61, 249, 265
Rome, 3
Roper, Margaret, 252
Rora Head (Hoy), 117
Ross, John, 65n.
Roth, Philip, 181
Rover (comic), 33
Roxburgh, 32
Royal Athenaeum (pub), Aberdeen, 89
Royal Edinburgh Hospital, 188–9
Royal Hotel, Stromness, 238
Royal Literary Fund, 172

Royal Oak, HMS, 48 & n.
Royal Society of Literature, ix–xi
Rubens, Peter Paul, 149
Rundall, Jeremy: GMB scatters ashes of, 242
Ruskin College (formerly Ruskin Hall), Oxford, 101n.
Russia, 60

Saga (hospital magazine), 125
St Aloysius's Church, Oxford, 273
St Andrews University, 113, 233
St Edward's School, Oxford, 273
St Magnus Bay (Shetland), 271
St Magnus Cathedral, Kirkwall, 59; 'a very *native* church', 61; 62, 124, 232, 246, 249; 850th anniversary, 265; GMB's funeral, 288
St Magnus Festival, xii, 232, 246 & n.
St Ola (mail-boat/ferry), 8, 11; 'a serene black swan', 17; 19, 33, 46, 59, 171, 233
St Peter's Church, Stromness, 6
Saintsbury, George, 143
St Sunniva (ferry), 271
Salisbury, Robert Cecil, 3rd Marquess of, 55
Salonika, 26
Saltire Review (periodical), 134
Sanday (island), 75n., 94, 216n.
Savile, Sir Jimmy, 140n.
Sayers, Dorothy, 40
Scapa Flow, xiii, 13, 43–50, 59, 125, 137
Scarfe, Francis, 64–5, 128, 194
Schubert, Franz: Fifth Symphony, 64

Scotsman (newspaper), 191, 260; GMB interview, 276, obituary, 288
Scott, Alexander, 108, 134, 145, 194
Scott, Francis, 108
Scott, Tom, 145, 153–4, 172; GMB writes to, 174, 275
Scott, Sir Walter: on school syllabus, 32; *The Pirate*, 32, 92; in Edinburgh, 140
Scottish Arts Council, 184, 198, 263
Scottish National Portrait Gallery, xi
Scottish Royal Academy, 139
Scott-Moncrieff, Ann, 98
Seaton, Marie, 202 & n.
Senior, Charles: at Milne's, 145; on Stella Cartwright, 152; confidant of GMB, 158; GMB writes to, 167–8, 169, 171, 174, 182–3, 186–90, 198, 202; visits GMB in Orkney, 176; bookshop in Stromness, 204, 212, 228; dies, 260
Service, Robert, 169
Shakespeare, William, 59; *Hamlet*, 85; 92, 108, 136, 217
Shaw, Charlotte, 12
Shaw, George Bernard, 12 & n., 108
Shearer, Mrs (hospital visitor), 125
Shearer, John, 28
Shearer, Willie Duncan, 14
Shelley, Percy Bysshe, 27, 40, 107, 145
Shetland (islands), 98, 113, 124, 158, 217, 230, 265; GMB visits, 271–2

Sigtrygg Silkbeard, King of Dublin, 201

Sigurd, Earl of Orkney *see* Eysteinson, Earl Sigurd

Sigurdson, Earl Thorfinn ('the Mighty'), 3

Simm, Renée: visits GMB, 244; GMB writes to, 244–6, 250, 285; GMB visits in Edinburgh, 253; moves to Stromness, 277; 'heart of a lion', 277 & n.; watches Booker prizegiving with GMB, 284 & n.; 287; at GMB's funeral, 289; death, 277n.

Sinclair, Bill, 11, 46

Sinclair, Jimmy, 124, 130

Sinclair, Margaret, 140 & n.

Sisson, C. H., 272n.

Sitwell, Dame Edith, 146

Sitwell, Sir Osbert, 128

Skaill (Orkney), Bay of, 3

Skara Brae (Orkney), 3, 117, 286

Skeabrae (Orkney), 222

Skipper (comic), 33

Smallwood, Norah: Edwin Muir sends GMB's work to, 156; 'like a tigress for her cubs', 156; raising fund for the Muirs, 163; 181; *A Calendar of Love*, 184–5; *A Time to Keep*, 194; *Fishermen with Ploughs*, 210; *Greenvoe*, 217, launch party, 225–7; personal history, 224–5; Highland Park 'marvellous stuff', 224n.; 'comrade, leader, mother, business partner, muse', 225; on GMB's hairstyle, 227; 229; *Magnus*, 231; OBE, 232; *Voyages*, 250; GMB's loyalty to, 251; suggests GMB write an autobiography, 251, 258; correspondence with GMB, 251; death, 268; Renée Simm and, 277

Smallwood, Peter, 224–5

Smith, Fr Alex, 126

Smith, Hazel Goodsir (*née* Williamson), 190, 208

Smith, Iain Crichton, xi; at Milne's, 145–6; writes to GMB, 183; GMB obituary, 288

Smith, Janet Adam, 116, 134, 201n.

Smith, Stevie, 134, 145, 201

Smith, Sydney Goodsir, xi; at Milne's, 145–7; '*the* great character of all the poets, 146; *Kynd Kittock's Land*, 147; 'Brown leads wi' his Viking chin', 147; on first meeting Stella Cartwright, 152; reviews *Loaves and Fishes*, 156; GMB asks to keep eye on Stella, 165; visits GMB in Orkney, 176; affair with Stella, 190, 196–7, 207–8, 208n., 226, 253, love poetry, 190, 208; secretly married, 208, 220

Society of Authors, 201

Soldier John (retired bellman), 14

Somalia, 278

Somme (battle), 47, 222

South Africa, 210

South Ronaldsay (island), 43–4, 238–9

Spain, 16

Spark, Dame Muriel, 108 & n., 177

Spectator (periodical), 156

Spence, Tom, 94

Spender, Sir Stephen, 96, 111;
writes to GMB, 181
Stafford, Marquess of *see*
Sutherland, Duke of
Stalin, Joseph, 107
Stalingrad (battle), 201
Standing Stones Hotel, Stenness,
137
Starcevic, Vjera, 105–6
Stenness (Orkney), Loch of, 16
Stevenson, Robert Louis, 32, 140;
Dr Jekyll and Mr Hyde, 140
Stewart, Earl Patrick, 166
Stonehaven (Kincardineshire), 102
Stornoway (Lewis), 106
Strachey, Lytton: *Eminent Victorians*,
39; *Queen Victoria*, 249
Strangeways (jail), 169
Stranraer (Wigtownshire), 201
Strathalladale (Sutherland), 4
Strathnaver (Sutherland), 4–5
Strathy (Sutherland), 1, 5, 8, 20;
Strathy Point, 1
Stromness (Orkney): xi–xiv, 1, 2, 8,
11; and Hudson's Bay Company,
15; 17, 20, 21, 22, 26–7; GMB's
first poem a ballad in praise of,
29, 82; 30–1, 32, 38–9, 46, 49,
51, 53, 61, 63; GMB appointed
Orkney Herald correspondent for,
65; 68; electricity arrives, 76; 78,
81, 83, 87, 95, 110; after January
1952 storm, 115; trade going to
Kirkwall, 120; 122, 134, 135, 137,
165, 171–2, 187, 189, 204, 220,
222; Peter Maxwell Davies revue
performed in, 223; 227–9, 232–3,
238, 239, 242–3, 248, 252, 256,
266, 270, 271–2; like Bethlehem,
285; 287; amateur dramatics, 7;
cars, 11; chandler's, 14; churches,
38–40, 83; drapers, 14, 59;
drinking, 6 & n., 14, 89;
fishermen, 11–12; football
match, 34; golf course, 49;
grocer, 14; harbour, 6, 13, 17, 29,
36, 46, 120, 122, 134, 169, 203,
211; housing schemes, 75;
lamplighter, 17, 76; laundry, 7,
13; library, 21, 96, 255; main
street, 'like a sailor's rope', 199;
pier, 8, 11, 12n., 271; pierhead,
14, 68, 199, 287; pirates, 16;
police, 12; post office, 53–4;
pubs, 13–14, 89, 169, 199;
saddler, 14; state assistance, 78;
stationers, 41; sweetshops, 18;
swimming pool, 75 & n.; tailors,
7, 30–1; telephones, 13; tinkers,
9; tourists, 12; town hall, 14, 58;
uranium, 222; wartime, 13–14,
44–50, 58–9, 65; wireless sets, 13,
34; Alfred Café, 76; Argo's
Bakery, 272; Auld Kirk, 61;
British Legion Club, 135;
Brownsquoy, 6; Brownstown, 6;
Clouston's pier, 11, 17, 46; Free
Kirk, 31; 'Ginger Beerie Babbie',
18; 'Hamnavoe', 13, 34, 51–2,
82, 178, 190, 232n., 264, 281;
Humphrey's Bequest, 20; Kirk
Road, 14; John D. Johnston, 14;
Login's Inn, 6n.; Ma Cooper's,
18; Mayburn Court, 198n.,
203–4, 228, 233, 238–9, 241,
243n., 244, 246, 249, 256n., 258,
260, 277, 280, 283–4, 286, 287;
Melvin Place, 23, 28, 35; Pier

Stromness (Orkney) (*cont.*)
Arts Centre, 246; Rae's, 41;
Tulloch's, 59; United
Presbyterian Church, 18;
Victoria Street, 10, 17, 20, 22–3;
Well Park, 35, 41, 49, 50, 61, 64,
91, 115, 119, 122, 133, 136,
170–2, 176, 182, 192–3, 199, 203
Stromness Academy, 24–8, 26n.;
'parsing, analysis, vulgar
fractions', 27; 30, 32; Ruby
teaching at, 36; 39; party watches
German fleet sink, 44; 47, 49, 53,
63, 220
Stromness Hotel (Mackay's
Stromness Hotel): Mhairi
Mackay waitress–chambermaid
at, 1, 5; 12 & n., 46; bar reopens,
89; 99, 169, 186
Stromness Museum, 14–16, 203
Stronsay, 75n.
Sule Skerry (island), 38 & n.
Sun (newspaper), 182
Sunday Times (newspaper), 211, 242
Sutherland, Elizabeth, Countess-
Duchess of, 4
Sutherland, George Leveson-
Gower, 1st Duke of (and 2nd
Marquess of Stafford), 4 & n.
Swinburne, Algernon Charles, 40

Tait, Allison (*née* Leonard), 86, 127
Tait, Margaret, 85; *Rose Street*, 144
Tait, Teddy, 35
Telford College of Further
Education, 142
Tennyson, Alfred, 1st Lord, 29, 40,
41, 66, 69
Terror, HMS, 15n.

Thatcher, Margaret, Baroness, 223,
282
Thomas, Dylan: Francis Scarfe
introduces GMB to work of, 64;
personal hygiene, 109; Edwin
Muir on, 116; GMB poem
mourns, 127; at Milne's, 145;
GMB like, 147; *Greenvoe* and
Under Milk Wood, 220
Thompson, Andrew, 71
Thompson, Francis, 39, 58, 95,
107
Thomson, Mrs (landlady), 141
Thomson, Ali, 17, 76
Thomson, D. C. (newspaper
publishers), 33
Thomson, John, 34
Thomson, William S., 93
Thorfinn the Mighty *see* Sigurdson,
Earl Thorfinn
Thorndike, Dame Sybil, 59
Times (newspaper): GMB interview,
xi; 232
Tinch, Mrs (hospital visitor), 125
Tito, Josip Broz, Marshal, 106
Tomalin, Claire, 235
Tonge, John, 145
Tor-na-Dee Hospital, Milltimber,
165, 172, 199
Tormiston Mill (restaurant),
Maeshowe, 238
Tournour, Sr Margaret: GMB
writes to, 252, 277, 285
Trafalgar (battle), 36
Traherne, Thomas, 116, 169
Tudor, J. R., 72
Tulloch, Mrs (neighbour), 182
Tumim, Sir Stephen, 282
Twatt, James, 65

UK Atomic Energy Authority, 222
Ulster Arts Club, Belfast, 202
Unst (island), 271

Vaila (island), 271
Van Dyck, Sir Anthony, 102
Vaughan Williams, Ralph, 213
Vementry (island), 271
Vestrafiold (Orkney), 3
Victoria, Queen, 70, 105; Queen
    Victoria reel, xii
Vietnam, 187, 199, 210
Voes (Hoy), 72

Wain, John, 156
Wales, Prince of see Edward VII
Wallace, William, 28
Warbeth (Orkney), xii, 12, 18–19,
    24, 47, 50, 120, 136, 205, 235,
    242, 288
Warwick University, 277
Watchful (ferry), 215
Waterloo (battle), 201
Watkins, Vernon, 96
Watt, Bob, 145, 148, 208
Waugh, Evelyn: Brideshead Revisited,
    249
Webster, Mr (teacher), 150
Weekend Scotsman (newspaper), 185
Weekly Scotsman (newspaper), 156
Western Mail (newspaper), 56
Westray (island), 75n., 269
Who's Who, 249
Wick (Caithness), 224
Wiggin, Maurice, 211
Wilde, Oscar: The Ballad of Reading
    Gaol, 35

Wilhelm II, Emperor of Germany,
    44, 47
Williamson, Hazel see Smith, Hazel
    Goodsir
Wilson, J. Dover, 108, 143
Wilson, Tom, 106–7
Wishart, Mrs (neighbour), 182
Wishart, Sylvia: GMB on art and
    character of, 172; accompanies
    GMB to Hoy, 172, friendship
    'expires', 185; dedicatee of The
    Year of the Whale, 185; 187
Wizard (comic), 33
Wizniewski, Adrian, 270
Wood, Kenneth, 107
Woodland Hospital, Aberdeen, 124
Woolf, Leonard, 98–9, 99n., 156,
    170, 194
Woolf, Virginia, 98, 99n., 156
Wordsworth, William, 29, 41, 203
Workers' Educational Association,
    101n.
Wright, Gordon (publisher), 244n.
Wright, Tom, 145
Wylie, Archie, 55
Wylie, Helen (née Fox), 55
Wyre (island), 97

Yeats, W. B., 142, 202, 211, 217,
    228, 283
Yell (island), 271
Yesnaby (Orkney), 81, 222
York, 272
Young, Douglas, 108

Zephaniah, Benjamin, 272n.
Zola, Emile, 151

1	2	3	4	5	6	7	8	9	10
11	12	13	14	15	16	17	18	19	20
21	22	23	24	25	26	27	28	29	30
31	32	33	34	35	36	37	38	39	40
41	42	43	44	45	46	47	48	49	50
51	52	53	54	55	56	57	58	59	60
61	62	63	64	65	66	67	68	69	70
71	72	73	74	75	76	77	78	79	80
81	82	83	84	85	86	87	88	89	90
91	92	93	94	95	96	97	98	99	100
101	102	103	104	105	106	107	108	109	110
111	112	113	114	115	116	117	118	119	120
121	122	123	124	125	126	127	128	129	130
131	132	133	134	135	136	137	138	139	140
141	142	143	144	145	146	147	148	149	150
151	152	153	154	155	156	157	158	159	160
161	162	163	164	165	166	167	168	169	170
171	172	173	174	175	176	177	178	179	180
181	182	183	184	185	186	187	188	189	190
191	192	193	194	195	196	197	198	199	200
201	202	203	204	205	206	207	208	209	210
211	212	213	214	215	216	217	218	219	220
221	222	223	224	225	226	227	228	229	230
231	232	233	234	235	236	237	238	239	240
241	242	243	244	245	246	247	248	249	250
251	252	253	254	255	256	257	258	259	260
261	262	263	264	265	266	267	268	269	270
271	272	273	274	275	276	277	278	279	280
281	282	283	284	285	286	287	288	289	290
291	292	293	294	295	296	297	298	299	300
301	302	303	304	305	306	307	308	309	310
311	312	313	314	315	316	317	318	319	320
321	322	323	324	325	326	327	328	329	330
331	332	333	334	335	336	337	338	339	340
341	342	343	344	345	346	347	348	349	350
351	352	353	354	355	356	357	358	359	360
361	362	363	364	365	366	367	368	369	370
371	372	373	374	375	376	377	378	379	380
381	382	383	384	385	386	387	388	389	390
391	392	393	394	395	396	397	398	399	400